Y0-CLC-102

Mary Margaret McBride
ENCYCLOPEDIA OF COOKING

Mary Margaret McBride

Encyclopedia of

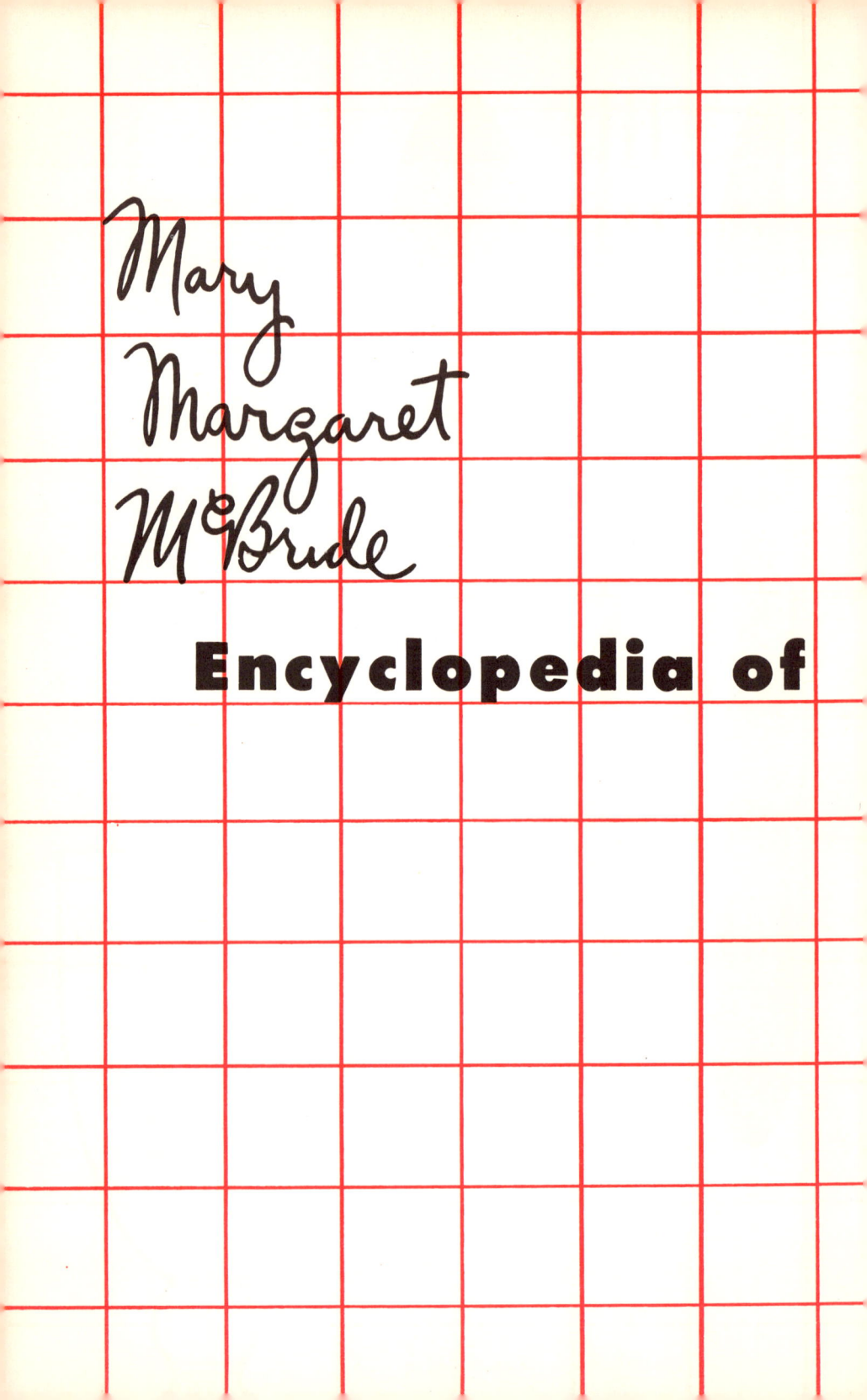

America's Most Complete Cookbook Edited by
HOMEMAKERS RESEARCH INSTITUTE

COOKING

Volume 10

Published by Homemakers Research Institute
Evanston, Illinois

ANNE LONDON, *Director*

Editor-In-Chief
ANNE LONDON
Director, Homemakers Research Institute

Test Kitchen Director
ESTHER BURNS
Assistant Director, Homemakers Research Institute

Associate Editors

BERTHA K. BISHOV
VIVIAN J. MALONE

FREDA C. DeKNIGHT
EUGENIA J. WHITE

Assistant Editors

LEONA SHAPIRO
DOROTHY KAHN

ETHEL I. UGELOW
RUTH SHEFER

Testing and Research Assistants

ESTHER B. GALLER
DEBORAH WINER
CAROLE OLDERSHAW
JACQUELINE KUCERA
RHODA SLITT
SYBIL B. GRUCCI
ROSE AXELROD
ANITA SHERMAN
SYLVIA POPUCH
STEVE LEE

HARRIET MILLER
CAROLE P. ROSENBERG
MARSHA LISITZA
LESLIE ANN WINER
ESTELLE FISHER
MARGARET MASI
ROSLYN BAKER
JEAN HIRSH
OLGA SHERMAN
JEFFREY ALAN

Art Director
BEN BURNS

Associate Art Director
BEN ROSEN

Illustrators

HENRY R. MARTIN
PAUL PINSON
PASCHA PHILLIPS

Copyright, ©, 1958, By Homemakers Research Institute
Box 342
Evanston, Illinois

MADE IN THE UNITED STATES OF AMERICA

What the Complete Encyclopedia of Cooking Contains

Volume 1
    ABC's for Cooks
    Appetizers and Snacks for Parties and Meals
    Bean Bakes for Parties and Meals

Volume 2
    Beverage Book
    Breads, Biscuits and Rolls Cookbook
    Buffet Meals

Volume 3
    Cake and Torte Book
    Candy Book
    Carving Guide
    Casserole Cookery

Volume 4
    Cheese Cookbook
    Chinese Cookbook
    Cookie Book
    Dessert Book
    Dessert Sauce Book
    Egg Cookery
    Electric Blender Cookery

Volume 5
    Fish and Shellfish Cookbook
    Freezing Guide and Frozen Food Cookery
    Frostings and Fillings Book
    Frozen Dessert Book
    Fruit and Fruit Dessert Cookbook
    Game Cookbook

Volume 6
    Hamburger Cookbook
    High Altitude Cookery
    Home Bartender's Guide
    Infant and Child Feeding
    Jiffy Cooking
    Leftover Cookbook
    Lunch Boxes

Volume 7
    Macaroni, Spaghetti and Noodle Cookbook
    Meal Planning and Nutrition
    Meals for Two Cookbook
    Meat Cookbook
    Older Folk's Food Guide

Volume 8
    Outdoor Cookery
    Pastry and Pie Book
    Pickling, Preserving and Canning Book
    Potato and Sweet Potato Cookbook

Volume 9
    Poultry Cookbook
    Pressure Cookery
    Quantity Cooking
    Refrigerator Dessert Book
    Rice and Other Cereal Cookery

Volume 10
    Salad Book
    Salad Dressings
    Sandwich Book
    Sauce and Gravy Cookbook
    Soufflé Manual
    Soups and Chowders
    Special Diet Book

Volume 11
    Stuffings and Dumplings
    Table Setting and Decoration Manual
    Vegetable Cookery
    Weight Control Through Proper Diet
    Wine Cookery for the Gourmet
    Wines, How to Buy, Store, and Serve
    Young People's Cookbook

Volume 12
    The Cook's Handbook:
    Dictionary of Culinary Terms
    Food Saver's Guide
    Spices and Herbs
    Kitchen Utensils and Equipment
    Oven Meals
    Rotisserie Cookery
    Chafing Dish Cookery
    Spots and Stains
    Personal Recipe File

Complete Index of Entire Encyclopedia

CONTENTS OF VOLUME 10

Salad Book	2257
Salad Tricks and Garnishes	2258
Tossed Salads, Salad Bowls	2261
Fruit Salads	2268
Fruit Salads with Cheese	2274
Apple Salads	2279
Avocado Salads	2281
Vegetable Salads	2282
Cole Slaws, Cabbage Salads	2288
Meat and Poultry Salads	2291
Fish and Shellfish Salads	2295
Egg and Cheese Salads	2300
Potato, Macaroni, Rice Salads	2302
Stuffed Tomatoes, Cucumbers	2305
Gelatin Salads, Hints	2306
Fruit Gelatin Salads	2307
Cheese Gelatin Salads	2316
Egg, Macaroni Gelatin Salads	2320
Fish, Shellfish Gelatin Salads	2322
Meat, Poultry Gelatin Salads	2330
Vegetable Gelatin Salads	2335
Frozen Salads	2340
Salad Dressings	2345
Hints for Choosing Salad Dressings	2345
Salad Vinegars	2345
French Dressings	2346
Italian Dressings	2349
Low Calorie Dressings	2350
Mayonnaise Dressings	2350
Cooked Dressings	2352
Whipped Cream Dressings	2354
Sandwich Book	2355
Sandwich Making Hints	2355
Fancy Party Sandwiches	2357
Sandwich Loaves	2360
Cheese Sandwiches	2364
Fish, Shellfish Sandwiches	2366
Egg Sandwiches	2369
Fruit, Vegetable Sandwiches	2370
Meat, Poultry Sandwiches	2372
Peanut Butter Sandwiches	2377
Hot Sandwiches	2378
Hot Cheese Sandwiches	2381
Hot Fish, Shellfish Sandwiches	2386
Hot Meat, Poultry Sandwiches	2389
Hamburger Sandwiches	2394
Sauce and Gravy Cookbook	2397
Master White Sauce	2397
Hollandaise Sauce	2402
Master Brown Sauce	2403
Meat and Poultry Sauces	2405
Gravies	2407
Fish and Shellfish Sauces	2409
Vegetable Sauces	2411
Tomato Sauces	2412
Quick Sauces with Canned Soups	2414
Cold Sauces	2415
Soufflé Manual	2417
Soufflé Hints	2417
Savory Soufflés	2419
Dessert Soufflés	2429
Soups and Chowders	2433
Soup-Making Hints	2433
Stocks and Soups Made with Meat and Poultry	2434
How to Clarify Stock	2434
What to Do if Soup is Too Salty	2436
How to Remove Excess Fat from Soup	2438
Creamed Soups, Miscellaneous	2447
Creamed Vegetable Soups	2449
Fish and Shellfish, Soups, Chowders, Bisques	2452
Meatless Soups	2458
Jellied Soups	2460
Fruit Soups	2461
Chilled Soups	2462
Quick Changes with Canned Soups	2463
Soup Garnishes and Accompaniments	2465
Special Diets	2469
Facts about Food-Charts	2492

Complete Index of Entire Encyclopedia in Volume 12

SALAD BOOK

Salads bring fruits and vegetables to the table crisp, cool, and color-bright. They are full of health-giving minerals and vitamins and add color, flavor, and texture to meals. With greens, fresh vegetables, or gay fruit, they add a light touch. Or they may be the sturdy kind that feature such items as meat, potatoes, cheese, or beans.

The salad-wise homemaker will choose salads to fit the meal. If they accompany the main course of the dinner, she will choose a light salad. If served as a first course, the salad will be made up of tart fruits or seafood. A frozen salad or a fruit salad will be chosen for the dessert course.

If a salad is chosen as the main course of the meal, it should have some protein-rich food such as meat, poultry, fish, eggs, or cheese as the main ingredient.

SALAD POINTERS

- Buy the freshest salad greens possible, wash them, dry thoroughly, and store in refrigerator in the vegetable compartment or bag or in a damp towel until ready to serve. Fresh, clean, crisp, tender greens are the basis of a good green salad.
- All ingredients should be well drained before they are combined with the dressing, to avoid giving the dressing a watery consistency. Dry greens thoroughly by patting with a towel.
- Use a variety of greens. Try shredded cabbage, endive, watercress, and romaine as a change from head or leaf lettuce. Tear lettuce into bite-size pieces instead of cutting. Outer leaves of lettuce should be discarded only when they are bruised.
- When mixing salads, toss ingredients gently until mixed. Don't stir vigorously.
- Add the dressing to salads at serving time to avoid wilting the greens, or, better still, serve the dressing from a separate bowl. People differ in the amount of dressing they prefer.
- Use leftover vegetables in salad bowls.
- The flavor of some salads, especially those containing cooked vegetables or meats, is improved by marinating the ingredients in French dressing. To do this, let foods stand in the dressing in a cool place until they are well seasoned. Drain before serving.
- Wooden salad bowls should not be washed. Wipe clean with a cold damp cloth. Before using, season with warm salad oil, followed by rubbing the bowl with a cut clove of garlic.
- Use a variety of dressings. It is not necessary to make a dressing for each salad. Most dressings keep well in the refrigerator.
- Avoid too much garnish. Depend upon the natural color and flavor of foods for an attractive appetizing salad. Arrange salads lightly and attractively.

Salad Tricks and Garnishes

Suitable garnishings for meat and vegetable salads are: sliced cucumbers, quartered and sliced tomatoes, canned beets cut into cubes, sticks, or slices, sliced or quartered hard-cooked eggs, green and red pepper, pimiento, stuffed olives, carrot sticks, sliced or diced pickles, cheese strips, cubes, or slices, and other suggested garnishes.

Fruit salads may be garnished with maraschino cherries, melon balls, mint leaves, herbs, strawberries, dark fruits, ripe olives, nuts, coconut, shredded dates, figs, and pitted prunes.

ASPARAGUS TIPS

Marinate small cooked or canned tips in French dressing. Sprinkle ends with paprika.

TO MAKE CARROT FLOWERS

Scrape tender carrots. Make lengthwise cuts $1/8$ inch deep into carrots. Cut crosswise into paperthin slices. Keep slices in ice water an hour or so to curl petals.

SALAD HINTS

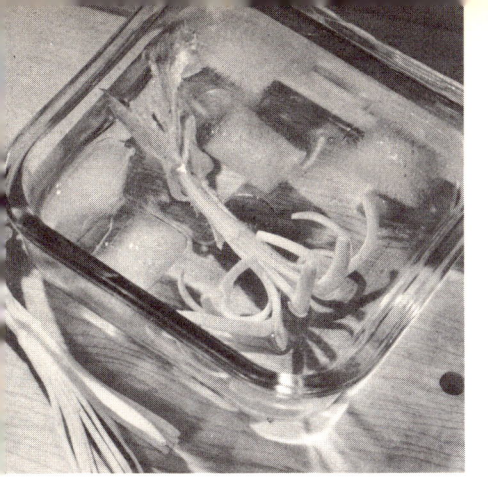

TO MAKE CELERY CURLS
Cut small stalks or short pieces of celery lengthwise into thin shreds, cutting to within 1/2 inch of the leaves or end of piece. Place in ice water to curl.

CALLA LILIES
Pare a white turnip. Cut into thin lengthwise slices. Chill in ice water until they curl and resemble calla lilies. Form stems from carrot strips.

CARROT CURLS
Slice carrot paper-thin lengthwise. Roll up each slice and fasten with wooden pick. Crisp in ice water. Remove pick.

CARROT STICK BUNDLES
Slice carrot lengthwise into small strips.
Cut pits from large olives. Push 3 or 4 strips through openings in olives.

CARROT STRIPS
Wash and scrape young, tender carrots. Cut into thin strips lengthwise. Chill in ice water.

CHEESE BALLS
Shape cream cheese into tiny balls. Sprinkle with paprika or roll in finely chopped nuts or olives.

CUCUMBER AND ONION SLICES
Peel and slice cucumbers and small white onions. Cover with equal amounts of vinegar and water. Let stand about 1 hour.
Drain. Sprinkle with salt and water.

CUCUMBER BALLS
With a French vegetable cutter, cut large cucumbers into balls.
Marinate in dressing. Sprinkle with paprika.

CUCUMBER STRIPS
Peel cucumber and cut in half. Remove seeds and cut solid part into narrow strips about 3 inches long.
Cover with damp cloth. Chill well before serving. Sprinkle with paprika.

CUCUMBER RADISH FANS
Cut ends of 2 unpeeled cucumbers. Quarter lengthwise. Slash each quarter in 1/8-inch slices. Do not cut all the way through.
Cut 8 large radishes crosswise into thin slices. Insert radishes between cucumber slices.

CUCUMBER BOATS
Remove seeds and pulp from a cucumber. Fill with cream cheese.
Chill well and slice again, if desired.
Beets and carrots may be cooked until just done and then filled with cottage cheese.

STUFFED PICKLES
Core large pickles. Fill with cream cheese. Chill thoroughly and slice.

TO MAKE GHERKIN FANS
Cut gherkins into thin parallel slices almost the length of each gherkin.
Carefully spread then press uncut end of pickle between thumb and forefinger so fan will hold its shape.

TO SECTION GRAPEFRUIT OR ORANGE

Pare grapefruit or orange with sharp knife. Slide knife blade down along each section wall of grapefruit or orange to center, then turn out with a twist of the knife.

FLUTED CUCUMBERS

Cucumbers may be left unpeeled or peeled. Run a fork down the length of cucumber, repeating completely around the cucumber. Slice.

GREEN OR RED PEPPER RINGS

Cut off tops. Remove seeds and centers. Cut crosswise into thin slices.
Crisp in ice water. Dry before using.

LETTUCE CUPS

For lettuce cups to lie flat on the plate, cut each leaf up from the stem end about 2 or 3 inches.
Fit 2 leaves together on each plate, interlocking the slits.

ONION JUICE

Peel and cut an onion in half. Holding one of the halves over a small bowl or cup, scrape downward with a knife until the desired amount of juice is obtained.

ONION RINGS

Cut large Bermuda or Spanish onion into thin slices. Crisp in ice water, then loosen rings and drain well.

RADISH FANS

Select firm and rather long radishes. With a thin, very sharp knife, cut thin slices crosswise almost through radish.
Chill in ice water. The slices spread fan-shaped as they chill.

RADISH ROSES

Cut down thin strips of red peel of radishes almost through to stems to form petals.
Place radishes in ice water and, as they chill, the peel will curl back like petals.

SCALLIONS
(Green Onions)

Trim washed green stalks, leaving about 3 inches. Trim onion if skin is loose or shriveled. Chill in ice water.

A festive assortment of well chilled relishes should accompany buffet salads.

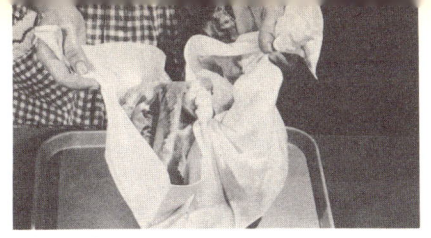

Tie washed "greens" in a dry towel and shake well before storing.

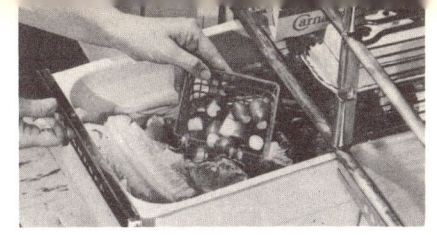

Store cleaned salad vegetables in refrigerator to chill them.

Tossed Salads

BASIC TOSSED GREENS AND VEGETABLE SALAD

This is the simplest of all bowl salads. Any number of fresh or cooked vegetables may be used. Choose one or several kinds of following greens: lettuce, chicory, romaine, endive, escarole, watercress, green dandelions, or raw spinach.

Add any of following: sliced or chopped radishes, onions, celery, green pepper, cucumber, tomato, carrot, bits of leftover snap beans, beets, carrots, peas, sliced cauliflower, etc.

Be sure greens are crisp, clean, and dry. Wash them thoroughly in cold water, then dry by shaking in a towel. No salad should ever be watery.

Break greens into desired pieces. Add chopped or sliced vegetables. Mix in salad dressing, using two forks, being sure not to break the vegetables. Serve on lettuce leaves or in individual salad bowls.

For a suggestion of garlic or onion, rub bowl, before adding ingredients, with a freshly cut surface of either.

For tossed salads, tear salad greens to bite-size pieces.

Add dressing to salad greens just before serving.

COMBINATION SALAD

1 cup cooked snap beans
½ cup shredded raw carrots
½ cup celery strips
2 cups shredded lettuce
1 hard-cooked egg
French dressing

Combine snap beans, raw carrots, celery strips, and lettuce. Mix lightly. Arrange sliced egg on vegetables. Serve with French dressing. Serves 5.

Vegetable and Egg Combination Salad: Increase eggs to 3 and add ½ cup chopped green peppers to Combination Salad recipe.

BEAN SPROUTS SALAD BOWL

Use 1 cup bean sprouts, ½ cup chopped celery, 1 sliced cucumber, ¼ cup sliced radishes, and 4 or 5 rings of green pepper. Toss with French dressing seasoned with a little soy sauce.

ITALIAN APPETIZER SALAD

¼ cup salad oil
2 tablespoons olive oil
1 clove garlic
3 tablespoons lemon juice
¼ teaspoon salt
1 teaspoon paprika
½ teaspoon prepared mustard
1 teaspoon sugar
1 teaspoon finely chopped onion
¼ teaspoon coarsely ground black pepper
2 quarts salad greens, torn
½ cup chopped celery
2 tablespoons grated Parmesan cheese
⅓ cup slivered salami

Put salad and olive oil in pint jar. Add garlic clove which has been peeled and cut in half. Shake jar and let stand 15 minutes.

Combine lemon juice, salt, paprika, mustard, sugar, and onion. Add to oil mixture. Shake thoroughly until the dressing is completely blended.

Remove garlic at serving time and pour dressing over greens and celery. Add cheese. Toss together lightly with two forks. Serve topped with slivered salami. Serves 8.

KIDNEY BEAN SALAD—FRENCH STYLE

1 No. 2 can red kidney beans, chilled
1 cup chopped celery
2 hard-cooked eggs, chopped
2 tablespoons chopped sweet pickle
1 teaspoon minced onion
4 tablespoons French dressing

Empty kidney beans into strainer and wash thoroughly with cold water. Add to remaining ingredients; toss together with two forks until well mixed.

Serve on lettuce leaf or in salad bowl lined with lettuce. Garnish with parsley or watercress. Serves 6.

LIMA BEAN SALAD

Use 1½ cups cooked lima beans, ½ cup diced pickled beets, 2 tablespoons minced onion, and 2 tablespoons chopped parsley. Toss with chopped lettuce and French dressing seasoned with Worcestershire sauce.

Salads are the sunshine in your meals. Fresh, clean, crisp, tender greens are the basis of a good green salad.

Spices and herbs add the character touches to salads and dressings—but use them lightly.

Luncheon Salad Bowl

TOSSED GREENS SALAD BOWL WITH DRESSING

1 small clove garlic, if desired
½ cup salad oil
3 tablespoons vinegar
¾ teaspoon salt
⅛ teaspoon pepper
½ teaspoon sugar
½ teaspoon dry mustard
½ teaspoon paprika
1 medium head lettuce, broken into 1½-inch chunks
4 large romaine leaves, cut into 1½-inch lengths
¼ bunch watercress, stems removed

Have all salad ingredients except seasonings chilled. Rub inside of salad bowl with cut surface of garlic clove and then discard garlic.

Add next 7 ingredients and beat with fork until well blended. Break lettuce and romaine into salad bowl in alternate layers. Add watercress.

Toss ingredients lightly until each piece of salad green is coated with dressing. Serve immediately. Serves 6.

LUNCHEON SALAD BOWL

2 pounds fresh asparagus
2 hard-cooked eggs
1 cucumber
3 green onions
2 tomatoes
1 small head lettuce
½ cup sliced ripe olives
Wine vinegar French dressing

Wash asparagus, break off tough ends and cook in small amount of boiling salted water until tender. Drain and cool.

Slice eggs. Peel and slice cucumber. Slice onions very thin. Cut tomatoes into wedges. Break lettuce into bite-sized pieces in salad bowl.

Arrange asparagus stalks, tomato, and cucumber in groups over lettuce as shown in picture. Sprinkle onions over all. Center with egg slices and sliced olives. Serve with wine vinegar French dressing. Serves 5.

Cauliflower Salad Bowl

CAULIFLOWER SALAD BOWL

1 medium head cauliflower
¾ cup French dressing
Lettuce
1 green onion, chopped
2 teaspoons lemon juice
1 tablespoon milk
½ cup mayonnaise
Slices of cucumber
Tomato wedges

Remove leaves and all of woody base and wash head of cauliflower. Cook whole in small amount of salted water in covered kettle about 15 minutes or until just tender.

Chill. Marinate in French dressing ½ hour.

Place head of cauliflower in salad bowl lined with lettuce. Combine green onion, lemon juice, milk, and mayonnaise and pour over cauliflower.

Garnish with cucumber slices and tomato wedges. Serves 6.

BEANS AND PEAS SALAD BOWL

Use 1 cup cooked string beans, ½ cup cooked peas, ½ cup sliced celery, ½ cup chopped apple, and about 1 cup salad greens. Toss with French dressing.

NAVY BEAN AND RADISH SALAD

Use 1½ cups well seasoned boiled navy beans, ½ cup sliced radishes, about 1 cup of shredded lettuce or other greens, and a few pitted olives. Toss with French dressing seasoned with onion juice.

WESTERN TOSSED SALAD

2   peeled cloves garlic, sliced
2   teaspoons salt
¼   cup lemon juice
½   teaspoon granulated sugar
½   teaspoon pepper
¼   teaspoon celery seeds
1   teaspoon paprika
1½ teaspoons dry mustard
10 tablespoons salad oil
2   medium heads lettuce
2   bunches watercress, or 1 small bunch romaine
1   cup toasted blanched almonds, sliced
1½ cups very tiny raw cauliflowerets
1   peeled clove garlic
1   very ripe avocado, cut in pieces
2   peeled tomatoes, sliced

Mash 2 sliced cloves garlic with salt; add lemon juice, sugar, pepper, celery seeds, paprika and mustard; blend well. Add oil; pour into jar and shake well. Chill.

Wash lettuce and watercress; dry well; tear. Prepare almonds and cauliflowerets for tossing. Chill greens and all vegetables.

Rub salad bowl well with 1 peeled clove garlic. In bowl, place prepared greens, cauliflowerets, almonds, avocado, and tomatoes. Add dressing and toss well. Serves 8.

Variations: Add bits of Cheddar or Roquefort cheese, grated raw carrot, or chopped hard-cooked egg.

BEET AND CAULIFLOWER SALAD BOWL

Use 1½ cups cooked cauliflower (chilled and broken into flowerets), ¼ cup chopped celery, ¾ cup diced beets, and a little grated onion, with thin dressing and lettuce.

BROCCOLI AND EGG SALAD

Use 1½ cups cooked broccoli (chilled), 4 chopped hard-cooked eggs, 4 tablespoons crumbled Roquefort cheese, and thinned salad dressing.

CAESAR SALAD

- 1 clove garlic
- ½ cup salad oil
- ½ head lettuce
- ½ bunch curly endive
- 1 cup croutons
- 1 2-ounce can anchovy fillets
- 3 or 4 tomatoes, diced
- 1 beaten egg
- 1 tablespoon Worcestershire sauce
- ¼ cup lemon juice
- ½ teaspoon pepper
- ½ teaspoon salt
- ½ cup grated Parmesan cheese

Mash garlic and add to salad oil. Break lettuce into large wooden salad bowl. Tear endive.

Add croutons, anchovies, and tomatoes. Strain oil to remove garlic and pour over vegetables.

Combine remaining ingredients and beat well. Pour over salad and toss lightly. Serves 4 to 6.

Croutons: Work 1 teaspoon thick bottled meat sauce or Worcestershire sauce into ½ cup butter and spread on slices of stale bread.

Cut into cubes and brown in the oven or in a frying pan. Sprinkle lightly with salt and use as a garnish for Caesar salad.

GREEK SALAD

Cut 1 head lettuce and the following vegetables very fine: 3 peeled tomatoes, 4 spring onions, 1 large cucumber, 2 green peppers, 1 bunch roka (Greek watercress) or substitute our watercress.

Toss mixture with 3 tablespoons vinegar, 1 teaspoon salt, and 12 black ripe olives.

Pour ⅓ cup olive oil over all; let stand ¼ hour to ripen and serve. Serves 6.

KIDNEY BEAN SALAD

Use 1½ cups cooked or canned kidney beans, ½ cup chopped celery, and ¼ cup chopped pickles. Toss with lettuce and salad dressing thinned with sour cream.

Caesar Salad

SHREDDED RAW VEGETABLE SALAD

1/3 cup shredded cucumbers
1/4 cup shredded raw beets
2 teaspoons wine vinegar
1/4 teaspoon sugar
1/3 cup shredded raw carrots
1/3 cup shredded or chopped celery or apple
1/2 cup sour cream or yogurt
1/4 teaspoon salt
Pepper
1/4 teaspoon dry mustard or curry powder
1 tablespoon lemon juice

Sprinkle cucumbers and beets with vinegar and sugar. Let stand while preparing other ingredients.
Add carrots and celery or apple and chill.
Mix sour cream, salt, pepper, mustard or curry powder, and lemon juice. Blend with vegetables just before serving. Serve on any salad greens. Serves 4 to 5 as a dinner salad.

Luncheon Salad: Serve Shredded Raw Vegetable Salad with cottage cheese as a luncheon main dish, in which case portions would be reduced to 3.

Appetizer Salad: Prepare Shredded Raw Vegetable Salad and garnish servings with anchovies to use as appetizer salad. Serves 8.

RAW BEET SALAD

Use 2 cups ground raw beets and 1/2 cup piccalilli. Toss with French dressing or thin mayonnaise and a few salad greens.

STRING BEAN AND RADISH SALAD

Use 2 cups cooked slivered string beans, 1 teaspoon chopped chives, and 1/2 cup thinly sliced crisp radishes tossed with a few greens and French dressing. If desired, add a few tablespoons crumbled Roquefort cheese.

GREEN SALAD WITH OLIVE MAYONNAISE

Lettuce, romaine, escarole
3 tomatoes, cut in wedges
15 to 20 cauliflower flowerettes
1 cucumber, scored and sliced
1 bunch green onions, chopped
1/2 cup mayonnaise
1 tablespoon wine vinegar
2 tablespoons heavy cream
1/4 cup chopped, stuffed olives

Wash, dry, and chill greens. Break up greens into bowl and add vegetables.
Blend mayonnaise, vinegar, and cream and add chopped olives. Toss gently but thoroughly to coat the greens. Serves 6.

CARROT, EGG, AND CELERY SALAD

Use 1 1/2 cups cooked diced carrots, 3/4 cup diced celery, 1 chopped hard-cooked egg, greens, and 1/2 teaspoon minced onion. Toss with thinned cooked dressing.

CORN SALAD BOWL

Use 2 cups drained whole kernel corn, 2 tablespoons chopped green pepper, 1 tablespoon minced onion, 1/2 chopped pimiento, and 1 chopped hard-cooked egg. Toss with thinned cooked dressing and lettuce.

CORN AND TOMATO SALAD

Use 2 tomatoes (cut in chunks), 1/2 cup whole kernel corn, 2 tablespoons chopped green pepper, and about 1 cup salad greens. Toss with French dressing.

CUCUMBER AND CARROT SALAD

Use 1 cucumber (unpeeled and sliced), 1 green pepper (cut in strips), 3 grated carrots, 1/2 cup chopped celery, and 1/2 small head of lettuce or other greens. Toss with thinned mayonnaise.

SALAD BOWLS

GARDEN SALAD BOWL

½ pound raw spinach (tender young leaves)
1 small head lettuce
1 large cucumber
1 bunch radishes
½ green pepper
2 or 3 tender stalks celery
½ cup salad oil
2 tablespoons lemon juice
2 tablespoons mayonnaise
2 tablespoons chili sauce
1 tablespoon confectioners' sugar
½ teaspoon paprika
½ teaspoon Worcestershire sauce
¼ teaspoon dry mustard
Dash of Tabasco sauce
¾ teaspoon salt
½ teaspoon Ac'cent
1 clove garlic, peeled
1 hard-cooked egg, chopped

Prepare vegetables and salad dressing several hours in advance of serving time.

Remove stems and any imperfect leaves from spinach; wash thoroughly and dry well; chill.

Remove any wilted outer leaves of lettuce; wash head quickly under cold running water; dry well; chill.

Wash and chill cucumber, radishes, green pepper, and celery.

Combine all remaining ingredients for dressing; chill.

Shortly before serving salad, peel and slice cucumber. Slice radishes. Cut green pepper in tiny slivers. Cut celery in match-like strips.

Place these vegetables in a good-sized salad bowl. Tear spinach and lettuce into bite-sized pieces; place in bowl. Toss salad lightly.

Remove garlic from dressing; stir dressing well; pour over salad. Toss lightly again. Serve at once.

Serves 6 to 8.

Garden Salad Bowl

Fruit Salads

A basic fruit salad as good to look at as it is to eat, and you can vary it with seasonal fruits.

Start with curly leaved lettuce and big cartwheel slices of oranges. Add other fruits in season in an attractive arrangement.

FRUIT SALAD DELIGHT

- 8 peach halves
- 1 cup blueberries
- Leaf lettuce
- 1 cup watermelon balls
- 1 cup honeydew melon balls
- 12 peeled cantaloupe slices
- Mayonnaise or salad dressing

For each serving, place 2 peach halves filled with blueberries opposite each other on lettuce arranged on a salad plate.

Between the peaches on one side of the plate place a mound of melon balls, and opposite it place 3 cantaloupe slices, petal fashion.

Garnish the center of the plate with mayonnaise or salad dressing. Serves 4.

HONEYDEW RING FRUIT SALAD

- 6 slices honeydew melon, peeled
- Lettuce
- 2 cups cantaloupe balls
- 2 cups fresh raspberries
- 2 cups seedless grapes
- Fresh mint
- $\frac{1}{4}$ cup salad oil
- $\frac{1}{4}$ cup lime juice

Place melon slices on lettuce, and fill centers with other fruits, combined.

Garnish with mint; serve with mixed oil and juice. Serves 6.

CRANBERRY-PEACH SALAD

Place a slice of canned jellied cranberry sauce on curly endive. Around it make a ring of overlapping canned peach slices.

Top cranberry sauce with a spoonful of cottage cheese. Pass mayonnaise.

PEACH BOWL SALAD

Mix drained canned sliced peaches, sliced celery, sliced stuffed olives, and shredded lettuce—to the cook's taste. Toss with French dressing or mayonnaise.

WINTER PEAR WALDORF SALAD

2 cups diced, pared pear, or 1 cup each diced pear and unpared red apple
2 tablespoons lemon juice
1 teaspoon sugar
½ cup mayonnaise
1 cup thinly sliced celery
½ cup coarsely chopped walnuts

Toss fruit with lemon juice, sugar, and 1 tablespoon mayonnaise.

Just before serving, add celery, walnuts, and remaining mayonnaise. Toss and serve on crisp lettuce. Sprinkle with French dressing. Serves 6.

Variations: Substitute, for pears, cubes of fresh or canned pineapple or banana or 1 cup orange sections and 1 cup grapes, or 2 cups apple, plus ½ cup raisins or fresh dates.

Coconut Waldorf: Substitute shredded coconut for nuts.

Salads in Party Fashion

Here are eight lovely fruit salads made from a variety of canned fruits. Back row: ready-to-serve fruits for salad; fruit cocktail molded in lemon gelatin with pecans; orange and grapefruit sections with cheese topped with a walnut; apricot halves put together with cream cheese.

Front row: a pear half filled with grated cheese; pineapple slices topped with coconut and maraschino cherries; a peach half filled with cream cheese and raisins; cottage cheese topped with pineapple chunks. These are all ideal dinner salads.

Easy-to-make picture salads include: Peach 'N' Cottage Cheese, Pineapple Chunks 'N' Cherries, Apricot 'N' Cream Cheese, Pineapple-Banana-Nuts, Molded Fruit Cocktail, Blushing Pear.

EASY FRUIT WALDORF

1 No. 2½ can fruit cocktail
½ cup sliced celery
½ cup chopped walnuts
Salad greens
Mayonnaise or cream dressing

Drain fruit cocktail well and mix lightly with celery and walnuts.

Serve on salad greens and top with mayonnaise. Serves 6.

Variation: Instead of mayonnaise, serve lemon-honey dressing in a separate bowl, to be spooned over the fruit at the table. Make the dressing by combining equal parts lemon juice and honey.

SPICED PEACH SALAD

½ cup vinegar
1 teaspoon cloves
1 stick cinnamon
½ cup sugar
6 canned peach halves
1 package (3 ounces) cream cheese
1 teaspoon lemon juice
¼ cup chopped pecans

Put vinegar in saucepan; add spices and sugar and cook 3 minutes. Pour over drained peaches. Chill 3 hours.

Drain and fill peach cavities with cream cheese seasoned with lemon juice and mixed with chopped pecans.

Arrange on lettuce and garnish with mayonnaise. Serves 6.

EGG AND GRAPEFRUIT SALAD

2 tablespoons lemon juice
1½ cups diced celery
2 large firm grapefruit
6 hard-cooked eggs
½ teaspoon salt
¼ cup mayonnaise
Paprika
2 olives (optional)

Pour lemon juice over celery placed in chilled bowl. Refrigerate while preparing other ingredients.

Peel and separate grapefruit sections, keeping as whole as possible and free from membrane.

Slice 1 hard-cooked egg, and set aside for garnish.

Add the 5 eggs coarsely cut, salt, half the mayonnaise, and the grapefruit to celery. Mix gently with 2 forks. Add more seasoning if desired. Heap into prepared grapefruit shells or lettuce cups.

Garnish top with egg slices. Finish with a dash of paprika. Place on chilled plates and serve promptly. Serve salad dressing on side if desired. Serves 4.

Note: Green celery makes an especially colorful salad. If used, add chopped olives to salad mixture. Pink grapefruit is especially nice.

Egg and Grapefruit Salad

FRESH GRAPEFRUIT SUMMER SALADS

Arrange on lettuce-covered salad plate.

Fruit-Cheese Luncheon Plate: Fill a peach or pear half with cream or cottage cheese, moistened with fruit mayonnaise. Circle with 5 or 6 grapefruit segments. Garnish with cube of red jelly. Pass fruit mayonnaise. Serves 1.

Grapefruit, Pear and Grape: Combine ¼ cup each of grapefruit pieces, diced pear, and seeded grapes. Serve with fruit mayonnaise. Serves 1.

Grapefruit-Egg: Cut a deviled egg in 6 lengthwise slices. Alternate these with grapefruit segments. Garnish with sliced stuffed olives. Serve with mayonnaise. Serves 1.

Grapefruit-Melon: Arrange 6 grapefruit segments in flower-petal pattern, alternately with long fingers of cantaloupe or honeydew melon. Marinate melon slices first in sweetened grapefruit juice. Serve with sweet grapefruit French dressing. Serves 1.

FRESH GRAPEFRUIT WINTER SALADS

Arrange on lettuce-covered salad plate.

Poinsettia: On 5 or 6 grapefruit segments arranged flower-petal fashion, place thin strips of pimiento. Center with 4 or 5 small pimiento cheese balls, sprinkle with paprika. Pass mayonnaise. Serves 1.

Grapefruit-Banana: Alternate 6 grapefruit segments with 6 banana fingers, rolled in chopped nuts, coconut, or vanilla wafer crumbs. Serve with any desired dressing. Serves 1.

Grapefruit-Apple: Alternate 6 grapefruit segments with 6 wedges of unpeeled, red-skinned apple. Serve with grapefruit French dressing. Serves 1.

Holiday: Fill center of an individual ring mold of cranberry jelly with 4 or 5 avocado or banana balls. Around base arrange 6 or 7 grapefruit segments. Garnish with chicory. Pass grapefruit French dressing.

If canned cranberry jelly is used, cut in inch-thick slices and cut out center with cooky cutter to simulate ring molds. Serves 1.

GOLDEN SALAD

4 pineapple slices
Leaf lettuce
2 oranges, peeled and sectioned
1 grapefruit, peeled and sectioned
6 maraschino cherries, sliced
Watercress
Mayonnaise or salad dressing

For each serving, place a slice of pineapple on lettuce on a salad plate.

Arrange alternate orange and grapefruit sections on the pineapple, with thin slices of maraschino cherry between the sections.

Garnish each salad with watercress. Serve with mayonnaise or salad dressing. Serves 4.

Fruit Salad 'N' Sherbet

For party luncheon, serve fresh fruit salad garnished with orange mint sherbet.

Assorted Pineapple Salads

ASSORTED PINEAPPLE SALADS

Pineapple-Apricot: Arrange pineapple slices on salad greens. Top each slice with an apricot half.

Pineapple-Apple: Alternate half slices of pineapple with lengthwise slices of unpeeled red apples on salad greens.

Pineapple-Cream Cheese: Arrange pineapple slices on salad greens. Garnish with watercress and cream cheese that has been formed into balls and rolled in chopped nuts.

Pineapple-Cottage Cheese: Arrange mounds of cottage cheese on salad greens. Surround each mound with pineapple slices, cut in quarters.

Pineapple-Banana: Arrange pineapple chunks and thick slices of banana (dip in pineapple syrup and roll in finely chopped nuts) on salad greens. Garnish with maraschino cherries.

Pineapple Chunks 'n' Cherries: Arrange drained canned pineapple chunks and dark sweet cherries on salad greens.

Pineapple - Banana - Nut: Arrange drained canned pineapple slices on salad greens. Place banana slices (which have been dipped in pineapple syrup) atop the pineapple and sprinkle with salted peanuts.

FRESH FRUIT SALAD

1 large honeydew melon
Lettuce
1/4 cup lemon juice
4 medium peaches, peeled and halved
4 bananas, sliced diagonally
1/2 pound fresh Bing cherries, pitted
Mayonnaise

Have all ingredients chilled. Cut honeydew melon into halves lengthwise. Remove seeds and cut halves into 4 lengthwise boat-shaped pieces. Peel and place on lettuce cups.

Drizzle lemon juice over peach halves and banana slices. Place a peach half in each slice of melon. Add several banana slices. Top with a few Bing cherries. Serve with mayonnaise. Serves 8.

Fig and Peach Salad

FIG AND PEACH SALAD

Arrange a peach half in a crisp cup-shaped lettuce leaf on each plate, using shredded lettuce underneath to hold cup in place.

Cut a fig in half and place, bowtie-fashion, beside the peach.

Cut remaining figs coarsely with scissors, and mix with about 1/2 cup mayonnaise, 1/4 cup sliced celery, and 1 tablespoon lemon juice. Heap a spoonful of this in each peach half and put a dot of it on figs. Decorate with walnut pieces, and serve.

Variation: For a luncheon salad, put a big spoonful of cottage cheese under peach, serve with cinnamon toast or hot muffins, and you have a complete meal.

FESTIVE SALAD

- 3 well beaten egg yolks
- 1/2 cup cream
- 1/4 cup lemon juice
- 1/8 teaspoon salt
- 1 No. 2 1/2 can Royal Anne cherries, pitted
- 1 No. 2 can pineapple, cut in small pieces
- 1 1/2 cups almonds, blanched and slivered
- 1/2 pound marshmallows, cut in pieces
- 1 cup heavy cream, whipped

Combine egg yolks, 1/2 cup cream, lemon juice, and salt. Place in top of double boiler and cook over boiling water, stirring constantly until thick.

Cool mixture. Fold fruit, nuts, and marshmallows into cooled sauce. Then fold in whipped cream.

Pour into large shallow pan or bowl and chill for several hours or overnight.

Serve on lettuce with cherry garnish. This salad may be served for dessert, if desired. Serves 12.

Fruit Salads with Cheese

Sunshine Cottage Cheese Salad

SUNSHINE COTTAGE CHEESE SALAD

2 cups creamed cottage cheese
$\frac{1}{2}$ teaspoon salt
1 teaspoon grated lemon rind
2 tablespoons lemon juice
3 tablespoons shredded orange rind
3 large oranges, peeled, sliced
1 head lettuce or other salad greens
Fresh strawberries

Add salt, lemon rind, lemon juice, and 2 tablespoons orange rind to cottage cheese; stir lightly to blend. Turn into oiled bowl and chill.

Wash and drain crisp lettuce and arrange on plate. Turn out cottage cheese in center of plate, sprinkling remaining orange rind on top.

Surround cottage cheese mound with overlapping sliced oranges and whole fresh strawberries. Serves 6.

ROSE PETAL SALAD

4 pineapple slices
Lettuce
1 3-ounce package cream cheese
Milk
4 radishes, thinly sliced
French dressing

For each serving, place a slice of pineapple in a lettuce cup.

Soften the cream cheese slightly with a small amount of milk and place a rounded scoop in the center of each pineapple slice.

Press thin radish slices into the cheese to resemble rose petals. Serve with French dressing. Serves 4.

PEAR-CHEESE SALAD

Arrange pear halves on lettuce leaves. Top with mayonnaise, then a sprinkle of grated American cheese.

FRUIT SALADS WITH CHEESE

PARTY FRUIT SALAD

1 3-ounce package cream cheese
1 tablespoon mayonnaise
1 No. 2½ can sliced pineapple
½ cup finely chopped parsley
2 cups watermelon wedges
2 cups cantaloupe wedges
2 bananas
Leaf lettuce or escarole
½ pound Tokay grapes

Mix cheese and mayonnaise; spread on edges of chilled pineapple slices. Roll edges in parsley.

Combine chilled watermelon and cantaloupe wedges.

Cut peeled bananas in half and into strips.

Outline platter with lettuce, and group fruit attractively. Garnish with French dressing. Serves 8.

Note: When melons are not available, use such fruits as apples, pears, or plums.

FRUIT SALAD BOATS

2 pineapples
2 cups grape halves
2 large bananas, sliced
8 ounces cottage cheese
Watercress

Cut pineapples in half and scoop out center. Remove core and cut in bite-sized pieces.

Mix pineapple with grape halves and banana. Pile back into pineapple shell.

Divide cottage cheese in four balls; place one on each salad. Garnish with watercress. Serve with crisp crackers. Serves 4.

Fruit Salad Boats

Flower Garden Salads

FLOWER GARDEN SALADS

Flower garden salads make an attractive luncheon dish—or, in a smaller size, a dinner salad.

First, arrange a bed of lettuce or greens. Next, place cottage cheese on top of this. Then arrange sliced cling peaches or peach halves in flower formation on or around cottage cheese.

A slice of green pepper can be the stem, and bits of cut green pepper the leaves. Maraschino cherry adds a colorful center.

PEAR DESSERT SALAD

- 2 large fresh pears
- 1 tablespoon lemon juice
- 1 pound cottage cheese
- 2 to 4 tablespoons sour cream
- 2 to 4 tablespoons chopped preserved ginger
- 1/8 teaspoon salt
- Lettuce or other salad green
- Mayonnaise

Cut pears into quarters, core, and slice. Brush cut surfaces with lemon juice.

Mix cheese, sour cream (enough to soften), ginger, and salt.

Place salad green on individual plates and top with a mound of cheese. Insert pear slices.

Serve with mayonnaise and a garnish of any other fresh fruits, if desired. Serves 4.

STUFFED PEACH SALAD

- 1/4 cup milk
- 1 3-ounce package cream cheese
- 1/2 cup chopped walnuts
- 1/2 cup chopped white seedless raisins
- 8 peach halves
- 8 large cooked prunes, pitted
- Leaf lettuce
- French dressing

Gradually add milk to cream cheese, blending until smooth. Add nuts and raisins and mix well.

Fill centers of peaches with mixture.

For each salad, arrange 2 stuffed peach halves and 2 pitted prunes on lettuce. Serve with French dressing. Serves 4.

FRUIT SALADS WITH CHEESE

COTTAGE CHEESE WITH FRESH FRUIT

- 2 cups cottage cheese
- 1 teaspoon salt
- 1 teaspoon lemon juice
- 1/4 cup chopped pecans
- Salad greens
- 1 melon, cut in round slices
- 2 oranges
- 2 bananas
- 1 pint fresh sweet cherries, or 1 pint strawberries
- 3 pineapple slices

Add salt and lemon juice to cottage cheese. Fold in part of chopped pecans. Turn into bowl that has been rinsed in cold water and place in refrigerator to chill.

Just before serving, unmold on large salad plate; surround with crisp salad greens or lettuce cups filled with fresh fruits—melon rounds, orange sections, banana slices (soaked in lemon or pineapple juice), pineapple sections, and red cherries or strawberries. Serves 6.

Cottage Cheese with Fresh Fruit

BLUSHING PEAR

Drain canned pear halves and put 2 halves together with softened cream cheese. If desired, sprinkle paprika on one side to make a blush.

Top with cream cheese and a short strip of green pepper or a leaf of watercress for a stem. Stand upright on salad greens.

Blushing Pear

FRUIT SALADS WITH CHEESE

COTTAGE CHEESE CORONATION SALAD

This easy-to-make salad combines a serving of cottage cheese with a delicious canned cling peach half, cut as a crown, with red and green maraschino cherries as crown jewels.

Nest the salad in endive or leaf lettuce to make a very attractive setting and add a sprig of watercress.

PINEAPPLE AND CHEESE SALAD

4 pineapple slices
Lettuce
1/2 cup shredded Cheddar cheese
French dressing

For each serving, place a slice of pineapple on lettuce on a salad plate, with a mound of shredded cheese in the center of the pineapple. Serve with French dressing. Serves 4.

Cottage Cheese Coronation Salad

PEACH 'N' COTTAGE CHEESE

Place drained halves of canned peaches cut-side-up on salad greens. Top with cottage cheese to which chives have been added.

APRICOT 'N' CREAM CHEESE

Place drained halves of canned apricots cut-side-up on salad greens. Top with softened cream cheese and chopped dates.

GRAPEFRUIT COTTAGE CHEESE SALAD

In a crisp lettuce cup placed at back of salad plate, pile 1/2 cup cottage cheese. Garnish with sprinkling of paprika and stuffed olive slices.

At front of plate, arrange a semicircle of 8 grapefruit segments, alternated with slices of avocado. Serve with any desired dressing. Serves 1.

ORANGE COTTAGE CHEESE SALAD

Combine 1 pound (2 cups) cottage cheese with sections from 2 oranges. Heap in salad bowl on bed of salad greens.

Sprinkle liberally with coconut, preferably fresh, and top with slices from 4 oranges. Serves 6.

CLUB FRUIT PLATE

6 oranges, peeled and sliced
3 bananas, cut in sixths
3 cups melon or avocado balls
1 pound (2 cups) cottage cheese
1 3-ounce package cream cheese
Walnuts
Salad greens

Arrange fruits, cottage cheese, and walnut bonbons (below) on salad greens for individual servings. Serve with lemon French dressing. Serves 6.

Walnut Bonbons: Place balls of cream cheese between walnut halves.

Harvest Salad

Apple Salads

APPLE LUNCHEON SALAD

Arrange wedges of unpeeled red apple on greens. Top with chicken, ham, tuna, or shrimp salad.

HARVEST SALAD

  8 large prunes
  1 3-ounce package cream cheese
Pistachio nuts, halved lengthwise
  2 red apples, cored and sliced
  1 Bermuda onion, sliced
  2 large oranges, sliced
Lettuce
Mayonnaise

Cut prunes in half lengthwise; remove pits, fill with softened cream cheese and top with half a pistachio nut.

Arrange apple, onion, and orange slices on lettuce on chop plate. Garnish with stuffed prunes. Serve with mayonnaise. Serves 4.

APPLE CUBES

Combine cubes of unpeeled red apples with orange and grapefruit sections. Moisten with French dressing. Serve on bed of shredded raw spinach.

APPLE-CHEESE RING SALAD

Core and slice large red apple. Put cottage cheese between and on top of 2 apple slices. Top with crumbled blue cheese.

APPLE AND ORANGE SALAD

Alternate slices of unpeeled red apple and orange on watercress. Serve with sweetened French dressing.

WALDORF SALAD

Combine 2 cups cubed apples, $\frac{1}{4}$ cup chopped nuts, and 1 cup cubed celery.

Moisten with $\frac{1}{2}$ cup mayonniase. Mix lightly with 2 forks. Serve on lettuce. Serves 5.

Cotton Blossom Salad

COTTON BLOSSOM SALAD

- 4 red apples
- 4 large oranges
- 1 pound cottage cheese
- 1 teaspoon grated orange rind
- ½ cup chopped maraschino cherries
- ½ cup sour cream
- ½ teaspoon salt
- Watercress
- Mayonnaise or salad dressing

Wash apples, quarter, core, and slice thin. Peel oranges and remove sections.

Combine cottage cheese, orange rind, cherries, sour cream, and salt; mix well.

Place ring of crisp watercress around edge of large round plate. Place alternate slices of apple and orange sections in a ring on watercress. Mound cottage cheese mixture in center.

Serve with mayonnaise or salad dressing. Serves 6.

APPLE AND PINEAPPLE SALAD

- 1½ cups diced unpeeled red apples
- French dressing
- 6 slices pineapple
- Lettuce

Toss apples with enough French dressing to moisten. For each serving, place a slice of pineapple on lettuce, with a mound of the apple salad in the center. Serves 6.

CURRIED APPLE-ONION-PEPPER SALAD

Combine strips of apple with thin onion rings and crisp slivers of red and green peppers. Serve with mayonnaise seasoned with curry powder.

WALDORF SALAD SPECIAL

- 6 apples
- 2 tablespoons lemon juice
- 1½ cups chopped celery
- ½ cup chopped walnuts or pecans
- ¾ cup mayonnaise or cooked salad dressing
- ½ cup heavy cream, whipped
- Apple slices and whole nuts for garnish

Wash, core, and dice apples coarsely without peeling. Sprinkle apples with lemon juice and toss quickly to prevent discoloration.

Add chopped celery and nuts and blend well. Fold mayonnaise or cooked salad dressing into whipped cream. Gently mix dressing with fruit.

Place in large bowl. Garnish with apple slices and nuts. Serves 8.

APPLE-CARROT-RAISIN SALAD

Combine bite-sized pieces of unpeeled red apple with shredded carrot and seeded raisins. Serve with mayonnaise.

APPLE CUPS

Use red-skinned unpeeled apples. Wash apples. Cut off a thin slice from stem end. Core without cutting through bottom of apple. With spoon, scoop out apple to form cup.

Fill with any of the following. Serve on crisp greens.

1. Combine equal amounts of chopped celery, peas, and chopped nuts. Moisten with mayonnaise.
2. Mix fruit salad with French dressing.
3. Add chopped celery and nutmeats to any fruit-flavored packaged gelatin. Fill apple cups; chill until set. Serve topped with a sour cream dressing.
4. Combine minced chicken with halved red grapes, chopped celery, and pecans; moisten with mayonnaise. Top with dressing.

Avocado Salads

AVOCADO WITH CHIVED COTTAGE CHEESE

Peel avocados; cut each in half lengthwise and remove the pits.

For each serving place half an avocado on curly endive. Fill the center with creamed chive cottage cheese. Serve with French dressing.

GUACAMOLE (AVOCADO) SALAD

2 small avocados
$1/2$ to 1 tablespoon onion juice
$1/4$ to $1/3$ cup chopped pimiento
Juice of 1 lemon
$1/2$ teaspoon salt
$1/8$ teaspoon pepper
Lettuce
2 tomatoes, quartered
Paprika

Pare and mash avocados. Add onion juice, pimiento, lemon juice, and salt and pepper to taste. Blend well.

Arrange lettuce in nests on 4 salad plates. Mound avocado mixture in each lettuce nest.

Garnish with tomatoes. Sprinkle paprika on top of each salad. Serves 4.

AVOCADO-CREAM CHEESE SALAD

2 medium-sized avocados
3 3-ounce packages cream cheese
1 teaspoon minced onion
$1/2$ teaspoon celery salt

Peel avocados halved lengthwise and hollow out stem ends slightly. Sprinkle inside and out with lemon or lime juice and salt.

Combine cheese, onion, and celery salt, and blend thoroughly. Fill halves with cheese mixture and press two filled

Avocado with Chived Cottage Cheese

halves together. Wrap in waxed paper and chill thoroughly. Cut into thick lengthwise slices and lay on lettuce garnished salad plates.

Allow one filled oval to each serving. Top with mayonnaise if desired. Serves 8.

Variations: Filling may be varied in flavor with minced capers; chopped celery; green pepper or sweet pickles; chopped green or ripe olives; chopped chives; chopped salted nuts; minced pimiento; finely shredded pineapple.

STUFFED AVOCADO HALVES

$3/4$ cup sliced celery
$1/3$ cup chopped ripe olives
3 tablespoons mayonnaise
3 tablespoons ketchup
1 teaspoon Worcestershire sauce
Dash of Tabasco sauce
$1/2$ teaspoon salt
$1/8$ teaspoon pepper
Dash of cayenne
2 soft ripe avocados, unpeeled
Lemon juice

Mix all ingredients except avocados and lemon juice; chill.

Just before serving, cut avocados in half, remove pits; sprinkle with lemon juice, and fill with the mixture. Serves 4.

HOLLYWOOD SALAD

On a bed of watercress, arrange a large mold of fresh pineapple, pears, and avocado cut in cubes.

Garnish with small cream cheese balls rolled in finely shredded carrots.

For the dressing, use fresh pineapple and orange juice thickened with raw egg yolk and olive oil.

Dutch Asparagus Salad

Vegetable Salads

DUTCH ASPARAGUS SALAD

- 2 pounds fresh asparagus
- ½ pound bacon, cut into tiny squares
- 3 to 4 tablespoons wine vinegar
- 1 teaspoon sugar
- Salt
- Pepper, freshly ground
- 2 hard-cooked eggs, sliced
- 2 green onions
- Iceberg head lettuce

Prepare and cook whole asparagus spears until tender. Chill.

Fry tiny bacon squares until crisp and brown. Remove browned bacon and stir vinegar, sugar, and seasonings into hot bacon fat.

Arrange chilled asparagus on lettuce-lined chop plate. Cover with sliced eggs. Sprinkle with bacon and finely cut green onions. Pour hot dressing over salad. Serve immediately. Serves 6.

ARTICHOKE SALAD

Cook artichokes and chill thoroughly. Cut in halves and remove chokes or leave whole.

Serve 1 whole or 2 halves on individual salad plates with mayonnaise and wedges of lemon or tiny cups of French dressing.

Or fill centers with a hearty salad such as a chicken or seafood salad.

SIMPLE ASPARAGUS SALAD

Drain and chill cooked or canned asparagus tips. Marinate ½ to 1 hour in French or other desired dressing.

Arrange 4 to 6 tips on tomato slices over crisp salad greens on individual plates. Serve with French dressing.

VEGETABLE SALADS

FRUIT AND VEGETABLE CHEESE SALAD

- 2 red apples, cut in wedges
- 1 cup cubed pineapple or orange slices
- 1 small bunch red grapes, cut in halves, or berries in season
- 2 or 3 tomatoes, cut in slices
- 2 medium-sized cucumbers, cut in strips
- 1 small bunch green onions or sliced sweet onion
- Salad greens (chicory, watercress, or lettuce)
- 3 cups shredded American cheese

Arrange wedges of apple in a semicircle on one side of large chop plate or tray. In center of the half-circle, pile pineapple cubes. At each, place grapes.

On opposite side, arrange vegetables on bed of salad greens. Fill center of plate with shredded American cheese.

Garnish with salad greens. Serve with sour cream salad dressing. Serves 6.

GRAPEFRUIT ASPARAGUS SALAD

On bed of endive, chicory, or lettuce, center 5 cooked or canned asparagus stalks. Arrange 5 grapefruit segments on each side of asparagus and garnish with strips of pimiento.

Serve with mayonnaise made with lemon juice. Serves 1.

FRENCH ENDIVE SALAD WITH LORENZO DRESSING

Wash about $1/2$ pound or 4 heads French endive thoroughly. Cut into quarters. Drain and place 4 quarters on individual salad plates.

Garnish plates with sprigs of watercress. Serve salad with Lorenzo dressing. Serves 4.

Lorenzo Dressing: Blend the following ingredients thoroughly: $1/2$ cup French dressing, 2 tablespoons chili sauce, 1 teaspoon minced pimiento, 2 tablespoons chopped watercress leaves, and 1 teaspoon minced chives or onion.

Fruit and Vegetable Cheese Salad

Cucumber-Cauliflower Salad

CUCUMBER-CAULIFLOWER SALAD

For an unusual salad to serve during the cucumber season, try this cucumber-cauliflower combination.

In each large crisp lettuce cup, arrange a small head of cauliflower or several cauliflower flowerets. Surround cauliflower in each cup with many thin slices of crisp cucumber. This gives the effect of petals around a center flower or bud.

Serve this in a large salad bowl or on individual salad plates with your favorite tangy French dressing.

MARINATED TOMATOES

- 4 to 6 tomatoes
- 1 clove garlic
- 1 tablespoon chopped chives
- 1/4 cup highly seasoned French dressing
- 2 sprigs parsley, chopped
- 1 teaspoon mixed dried herbs (mint, tarragon, and basil)

Wash tomatoes and cut in large chunks. Drain if necessary. Put in bowl.

Add remaining ingredients and toss lightly. Cover and marinate in refrigerator several hours. Remove garlic before serving. Serves 4.

GREEN BEANS PARMESAN

Cook 1 box French-style green beans as package label directs. Drain and cool.

Mix 1 small, minced onion, 1/4 cup olive oil, 3 tablespoons wine vinegar, 1 tablespoon chopped parsley, and 1/4 cup grated Parmesan cheese. Pour over beans. Chill.

Serve on salad greens. Serves 4.

Variations: Cut green or wax beans, broccoli, or asparagus are also good in this salad.

WILTED LETTUCE SALAD

- 2 bunches leaf lettuce
- 1 teaspoon sugar
- 1/2 teaspoon salt
- 1/8 teaspoon pepper
- 6 slices bacon
- 1/4 cup vinegar
- 2 tablespoons sweet or sour cream (optional)
- 2 hard-cooked eggs, sliced

Wash, drain, and shred lettuce into warm serving bowl. Sprinkle with sugar, salt, and pepper. Mix with fork and let stand about 10 minutes to wilt slightly.

Cut bacon in small pieces and fry until crisp. Add vinegar and cream and bring to boil. Pour over lettuce, mixing lightly with fork.

Serve immediately, garnished with sliced hard-cooked eggs. Serves 6.

MARINATED CUCUMBERS

Wash and slice 2 large chilled, unpeeled cucumbers in very thin slices. Sprinkle with 2 teaspoons salt and 6 tablespoons sugar.

Add 2/3 cup vinegar. Then press slices with the back of spoon until salad is quite juicy.

VEGETABLE SALADS **2285**

CARROT AND RAISIN SALAD

Combine 3 cups shredded carrots, 1/4 teaspoon salt, and 1 cup seedless raisins.

Add 1/2 cup mayonnaise and mix lightly. Serve on crisp lettuce. Serves 6.

CELERY VICTOR

4 hearts of celery (1 1/2 pounds)
1 cup chicken broth
1/4 teaspoon Ac'cent
1/2 cup French dressing
Anchovies
Tomato wedges
Lettuce or watercress

Wash celery thoroughly without separating stalks. Cut lengthwise into 2 or 4 pieces, depending on size. Cut off most of leafy tops.

Place celery in pressure saucepan with broth and Ac'cent. Cook at 15-pound pressure for 6 to 8 minutes. Remove and drain.

Place celery in shallow dish; pour French dressing over and marinate 1 hour or more as it cools. Turn occasionally. Chill thoroughly.

Arrange celery with two strips of anchovies over each heart, with tomato wedges, on watercress or lettuce.

Serves 6 to 8.

Vegetable Salad Platter

VEGETABLE SALAD PLATTER

Place a bed of salad greens on a large serving plate. Unmold a mixed garden vegetable aspic and place it in the center.

Chill and marinate canned peas and whole green beans in French dressing and circle the mound with mounds of them.

Garnish peas with tiny celery slices and separate the vegetables with rows of cucumber slices.

Celery Victor

2286 SALADS

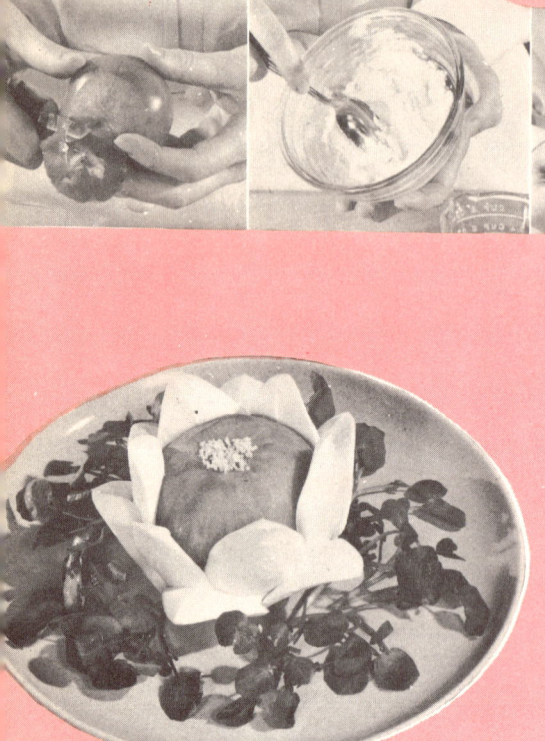

TOMATO ROSE SALAD

Peel one firm tomato for each tomato rose salad.

Slightly soften a 3-ounce package of cream cheese with milk.

Form a row of petals on the upper side of each tomato by pressing level teaspoons of the softened cheese against the side of the tomato, then drawing the teaspoon down with a curving motion.

Make a second row of petals on the lower side of the tomato, placing each of these petals between the two petals above it on the top row.

Place each tomato on watercress on a salad plate. Press hard-cooked egg yolk through a sieve onto the center of the tomato. Serve with French dressing.

TURKISH EGGPLANT SALAD

- 3 medium eggplants
- 6 tablespoons olive oil
- Salt
- Juice of 1 lemon
- 1 tablespoon vinegar
- 2 medium tomatoes, sliced
- 2 green peppers, sliced and seeded
- 1 medium onion, chopped
- 10 black olives

Put eggplants on spit or hold with tongs and cook, preferably over charcoal fire, but gas flame will do. Skin must be allowed to burn black as this gives a delicious smoked flavor to salad.

Skin eggplants while still hot (the skin will come off like that of a scalded tomato).

Place eggplants in bowl containing olive oil and sprinkle with salt and lemon juice. Mash with potato masher.

Add vinegar and beat smooth. Shape into a form and place on platter. Decorate with tomatoes, peppers, onion, and black olives. Serves about 6.

Variation: Mayonnaise can be used in place of olive oil, vinegar, and lemon juice.

WATERCRESS SALAD

Wash 2 bunches watercress thoroughly. Remove yellow leaves. Mix with $\frac{1}{2}$ cup French dressing and serve at once.

Onion rings may be mixed with the watercress. Serves 4.

VEGETABLE SALADS

CHINESE CELERY CABBAGE SALAD

Place 2 cups shredded Chinese celery cabbage on crisp outer leaves.

Serve with Thousand Island dressing or nippy mayonnaise. Serves 4.

CALIFORNIA VEGETABLE SALAD

Slice $\frac{1}{2}$ cup ripe olives from pits and combine with 2 cups finely shredded cabbage or coarsely grated carrot, 2 tablespoons diced green sweet pepper, and $\frac{1}{4}$ cup thinly sliced green onion.

Toss together lightly with $\frac{1}{4}$ cup mayonnaise seasoned with 1 teaspoon Worcestershire sauce, $\frac{1}{2}$ teaspoon salt, $\frac{1}{4}$ teaspoon dill seed, and pepper to taste. Serves 4.

MARINATED BROCCOLI SALAD

Cook 1 package frozen broccoli as label directs. Drain and cool.

Rub a small bowl with cut clove of garlic. Put 2 tablespoons oil in bowl. Add juice of 1 lemon and small pinch each of tarragon and oregano. Season and pour over broccoli.

Chill. Serve on salad greens. Serves 3.

Variations: Also try marinated asparagus, cauliflower, green or wax beans, peas, or peas and carrots.

MARINATED GREEN BEANS AND ONIONS

Wash 1 pound green beans and remove stem ends. Cut beans in half or in thirds. Simmer, covered, in boiling water to barely cover until just tender, 5 to 8 minutes. Drain and cool.

Put in bowl and add 1 medium onion sliced thin. Drizzle with 2 tablespoons highly seasoned French dressing and toss lightly.

Cover and marinate in refrigerator several hours before serving. Add more salt and pepper, if necessary. Serves 4.

CARROT AND APPLE SALAD

Coarsely dice 3 unpeeled apples. Combine with 2 cups grated carrots and 1 tablespoon finely minced onion.

Add $\frac{1}{2}$ cup sweet or freshly soured cream blended with 2 tablespoons lemon juice, $\frac{3}{4}$ teaspoon salt, and $\frac{1}{8}$ teaspoon pepper. Mix well. Serve on lettuce. Serves 6.

CARROT AND GREEN PEPPER SALAD

Combine 3 cups shredded carrots with 1 cup chopped green pepper, and 3 mint leaves, chopped.

Moisten with mayonnaise. Serve in lettuce cups. Serves 6.

EGGPLANT AND PEPPER SALAD

1 medium eggplant (about $1\frac{1}{2}$ pounds)
3 sweet red peppers
1 small onion, chopped
$\frac{1}{4}$ cup garlic French dressing
Salt and pepper

Wash eggplant and peppers. Bake in hot oven (400°F.) until tender when pierced with a fork, about 30 minutes for eggplant and 20 minutes for peppers. Cool.

Cut eggplant in halves. Scoop out pulp and break up with spoon. Remove seeds from peppers and cut into $\frac{1}{4}$-inch slices.

Add remaining ingredients and mix well. Chill and serve on lettuce. Serves 4.

BEET 'N' ONION RING

Sliced canned beets marinated in French dressing and garnished with onion rings.

GRATED CARROT SALAD

Wash young, tender carrots. Grate on fine grater. Using a fork, gently combine with French dressing.

Place on lettuce leaves. Serve at once. A bit of cheese may be grated with carrots.

Party Cole Slaw Platter

Cole Slaws and Other Cabbage Salads

BASIC COLE SLAW

Use fresh, tender cabbage. Mix 4 cups of finely shredded cabbage with 1 cup of cooked evaporated milk, sour cream, or vinegar dressing.

Cabbage and Pepper Slaw: Add ½ cup chopped green pepper to cabbage.

Red and White Slaw: Use equal amounts of red and white cabbage.

CABBAGE AND CARROT SLAW
(Master Recipe)

1½ cups shredded carrots
3 cups shredded cabbage
½ teaspoon salt
2 teaspoons sugar
1 tablespoon vinegar
3 tablespoons mayonnaise

Combine carrots, cabbage, salt, sugar, and vinegar. Moisten with mayonnaise. Mix lightly.

Arrange on crisp lettuce. Sprinkle with minced parsley or paprika. May be garnished with orange slices. Serves 6.

Cabbage and Apple Salad: In master recipe, substitute 1½ cups thinly sliced unpeeled tart red apples for carrots.

Cabbage, Carrot and Celery Salad: In master recipe, decrease shredded cabbage to 2 cups. Add 1 cup thinly sliced celery.

DUTCH SLAW

½ head crisp cabbage
¼ cup vinegar
1 teaspoon salt
1 egg
1 tablespoon brown sugar
1 tablespoon celery seeds

Shred the cabbage, place in deep pan. Add vinegar, sprinkle with salt.

Cover and steam over low heat until tender (about 15 minutes). Drain.

Beat the egg, add other ingredients and pour over the cabbage. Replace cover and let stand for 5 minutes before serving. Serves 4 to 6.

COLE SLAWS, CABBAGE SALADS **2289**

BULL'S EYE SALAD

- 2 large tomatoes
- 1/4 head cabbage
- 3 large carrots
- 2 tablespoons chopped chives
- 1 cucumber
- 1 head escarole, curly endive, or romaine
- Mayonnaise

Double an 18-inch strip of waxed paper lengthwise and then double again. Lap ends to form circle about 5 inches in diameter and fasten with wooden pick.

Cut slice from stem end of tomatoes so they will set flat. Cut in eighths and stand up inside paper. Fill center with mayonnaise and garnish with chopped chives.

Radiate greens from tomatoes to edge of plate. Place ring of crisp shredded cabbage around tomatoes, half slices of unpeeled cucumber, and shredded carrots.

Garnish with cucumber twists, made by cutting from center through each. Turn one cut edge to right, the other to left and fasten with pick. Let stand in ice water 1/2 hour and remove pick. Remove waxed paper. Serves 6.

ITALIAN PEPPER SLAW

- 1 clove garlic
- 2 cups finely shredded cabbage
- 1/4 cup chopped green pepper
- 1/4 cup chopped pimiento
- 1/2 teaspoon salt
- 1/2 teaspoon celery seed
- Dash of red pepper
- Dash of paprika
- 1 tablespoon soft breadcrumbs
- 2 tablespoons tomato paste
- 2 1/2 teaspoons water
- 1/4 teaspoon salt
- 1/8 teaspoon sugar
- 2 1/2 teaspoons salad oil
- 2 teaspoons cider vinegar

Rub salad bowl with cut garlic clove. Put vegetables, 1/2 teaspoon salt, celery seed, red pepper, and dash paprika in bowl.

Mix remaining ingredients thoroughly. Pour over contents of salad bowl. Toss. Serves 6.

Bull's Eye Salad

Pineapple Slaw

PENNSYLVANIA PEPPER CABBAGE

- 2 cups shredded cabbage
- 1 green pepper, cut fine
- 1 teaspoon salt

Mix shredded cabbage, pepper, and salt and let stand about 1 hour.

Drain off all liquid. Pour hot salad dressing (below) over the cabbage and mix well. Serve at once. Serves 4 to 5.

Hot Salad Dressing:

- 3 slices bacon
- 1 tablespoon flour
- ½ cup vinegar
- 1 tablespoon sugar
- ½ teaspoon dry mustard
- ½ teaspoon salt
- ⅛ teaspoon pepper
- 1 egg yolk, beaten

Cut bacon in small cubes and fry crisp. Remove cubes of bacon from grease and put aside.

Blend flour into grease and brown. Add vinegar and stir until it thickens.

Mix together sugar, mustard, salt, and pepper and add to the mixture. Pour over the beaten egg yolk and mix well.

Put on heat again and cook 1 minute longer. Add bacon cubes when ready to use.

CABBAGE AND ONION SALAD

Shred cabbage. Cut onions into very thin rings. Season with salt, celery salt, pepper, and paprika.

Mix with mayonnaise or French dressing. Serve on cabbage leaf.

PINEAPPLE SLAW

- 3 cups shredded cabbage
- 2 tablespoons chopped green pepper
- ½ cup diced unpeeled apple
- 4 slices pineapple
- 1 teaspoon salt
- 1 tablespoon sugar
- ½ cup vinegar
- Salad greens
- 1 cup shredded carrots

Combine cabbage, green pepper, apple, and 2 slices pineapple, cut into sections.

Mix salt, sugar, and vinegar, and add. Place in bowl lined with salad greens.

Top with shredded carrots and remaining drained pineapple slices cut into halves. Serves 4.

MEXICAN SLAW

Crisp a small head of cabbage by removing a few of the outer leaves, then cutting in half, and let stand in ice water ½ hour. Shake out water well, and shred.

Dice cold cooked ham or tongue, celery, green pepper, and pimiento. Sprinkle with salt.

Mix salad with mayonnaise which has been thinned with sweet or sour cream.

Line a serving dish with outside leaves of cabbage and fill center with slaw. Squeeze ½ lemon over all.

HONEY COLE SLAW

Beat 1 cup cold sour cream until thick. Add ¼ cup honey, 1 teaspoon salt, and 2 teaspoons celery salt. Pour over 4 cups finely shredded cabbage.

HOT SLAW

Combine in saucepan 2 slightly beaten egg yolks, ¼ cup cold water, ¼ cup vinegar, 1 tablespoon butter or margarine, 1 tablespoon sugar, and ½ teaspoon salt.

Cook on low heat, stirring constantly until mixture thickens.

Add 3 cups shredded cabbage and reheat. Serves 5.

Meat and Poultry Salads

MEAT SALAD BOWL
(Master Recipe)

- 1/4 cup sliced onions
- 1 small head lettuce
- 2 tomatoes, cut in wedges
- 2 cups cooked or canned peas
- 1/4 cup sliced, stuffed olives
- 1 cup cooked meat, cut in strips
- 1 teaspoon salt
- 1 cup French dressing

Separate onion rings. Break lettuce in bite-sized pieces. Arrange vegetables and meat on lettuce. Sprinkle with salt. Add dressing. Toss lightly. Serves 6.

Variations: Tongue, beef, veal, lamb, duck, turkey, liver, or chicken may be used for the meat. Cabbage may be used in place of celery.

Tuna or Salmon Salad Bowl: Use tuna or salmon in place of the meat. Omit onion. Add 1 cup chopped celery.

WHOLE-MEAL SALAD BOWL

- 1 clove garlic, if desired
- 1/2 cup salad oil
- 2 tablespoons vinegar
- 3/4 teaspoon salt

A salad for the main course of the meal should have some protein-rich food as the main ingredient. This salad bowl features chunks of turkey.

- 1/8 teaspoon pepper
- 1/2 teaspoon dry mustard
- 1/4 teaspoon paprika
- 1/2 head lettuce, broken into 1 1/2-inch chunks
- 2 tablespoons chopped green pepper
- 1/2 cup sliced celery
- 1/2 cup thinly sliced raw cauliflowerets
- 1 cup cooked asparagus tips
- 1 hard-cooked egg, cut in eighths
- 1/2 pound baked ham or salami, cut julienne style

Have all salad ingredients chilled. Rub inside of salad bowl with cut surface of garlic clove and then discard garlic.

Stir in salad oil and vinegar. Add seasonings and beat with fork until well mixed.

Combine remaining ingredients in order given. Toss lightly until each piece of salad is coated with dressing. Serve immediately. Serves 6 to 8.

For a summer luncheon serve chicken salad in a tomato.

CHICKEN SALAD
(Master Recipe)

    2   cups diced cooked chicken
    1   cup chopped celery
    Salt and pepper to taste
    Mayonnaise
    2   hard-cooked eggs, sliced

Remove all gristle, skin, and hard, dry parts of chicken before dicing. Combine with celery. Season to taste. Moisten with mayonnaise. To serve, garnish with mayonnaise, sliced hard-cooked eggs, and capers.

If desired, pimiento strips, sliced olives, or sliced cucumbers, toasted almonds, or marinated asparagus tips may be used for a garnish. Serves 4.

With French Dressing: Marinate chicken in French dressing. Chill. Drain and combine with other ingredients. Blend with mayonnaise, if desired. Season to taste.

CALIFORNIA CHICKEN SALAD

Combine 1½ cups cubed cooked chicken with 1½ cups sliced celery and ¾ cup ripe olives cut from pits. Sprinkle with juice from 1 lemon.

Blend together 3 tablespoons mayonnaise, 3 tablespoons cream, and ½ teaspoon prepared horseradish. Toss with chicken mixture. Season to taste with salt and pepper. Serves 4 to 6.

CHICKEN AND SWEETBREADS SALAD

Use 2 cups diced cooked chicken, 1 cup diced cooked sweetbreads, and ½ cup chopped cucumber. Moisten with mayonnaise.

CHICKEN AND AVOCADO SALAD

Use 2 cups diced cooked chicken, 1 cup diced avocado. Moisten with Russian dressing.

CHICKEN AND MUSHROOM SALAD

Use 2 cups diced cooked chicken, ½ cup sautéed button or sliced mushrooms, and ½ cup diced celery. Moisten with desired dressing.

CHICKEN WITH NUTS AND OLIVES SALAD

Use 2 cups diced cooked chicken, ½ cup diced celery, ½ cup sliced ripe olives, and ½ cup sliced toasted almonds. Moisten with mayonnaise.

CHICKEN-TOMATO SALAD

Use 1 cup diced cooked chicken, ½ cup diced crisp cracklings, and 1 cup diced tomato. Moisten with desired dressing.

CHICKEN-TONGUE SALAD

Use 1 cup diced cooked chicken, 1 cup diced cooked tongue, ½ cup chopped celery, and ½ cup chopped stuffed olives. Moisten with desired dressing.

CHICKEN-FRUIT-NUT SALAD

Use 2 cups diced cooked chicken, ½ cup chopped celery, ½ cup diced pineapple (or whole grapes or cherries), and ½ cup sliced toasted almonds. Moisten with mayonnaise.

MEAT SALAD

In master recipe for Chicken Salad, substitute any kind of diced cooked meat for chicken. For large groups, veal may be economically combined with chicken. For 25 servings, use 3 quarts meat and/or chicken or turkey and 2 quarts diced celery.

CHEF'S SALAD BOWL

Line a salad bowl with romaine; fill in center with bite-sized pieces of chicory or any combination of greens.

Arrange strips of ham, turkey, and Cheddar cheese in groups on top of chicory, with tomato wedges and thin sliced unpeeled cucumber between. Top with wedges of hard-cooked eggs.

Carry to the table for all to see, then toss with your stoutest French dressing and serve.

TONGUE AND VEGETABLE SALAD

- 1 cup cooked tongue
- 2½ cups canned or cooked vegetables
- 1 cup thinly sliced celery
- 1 tablespoon chopped onion
- 2 tablespoons chopped sweet pickle
- ½ cup sharp mayonnaise
- 1 head lettuce
- 1 hard-cooked egg, sliced

Cut tongue in strips. Drain chilled vegetables.

Combine tongue, vegetables, onion, and pickles with mayonnaise. Chill 1 hour to blend flavors.

Serve in lettuce cups. Garnish each serving with a slice of egg. Serves 6.

Variations: Use cooked or canned chicken, canned tuna, salmon, or other cooked meats or fish instead of tongue.

Snappy Sauerkraut Salad: Add 1 cup sauerkraut to tongue and vegetable salad with the mixed vegetables.

CHICKEN LIVER AND EGG SALAD

- 3 onions, minced
- 3 tablespoons chicken fat or salad oil
- ½ pound chicken livers
- 4 hard-cooked eggs
- 2 ribs of celery, minced
- Salt and pepper

Sauté onions in melted fat until lightly browned. Remove onions. Sauté livers until tender.

Chop livers with eggs and celery. Mix with browned onions. Season with salt and pepper.

Moisten with fat in which onions were fried. Serve on salad greens. Serves 6.

Chef's Salad Bowl

Florida Chicken Salad

FLORIDA CHICKEN SALAD

- 1 No. 2 can orange and grapefruit sections
- 2 cups diced cooked chicken
- 1 cup diced celery
- 2 tablespoons lime juice
- 1/4 cup mayonnaise
- 1/4 teaspoon salt
- 1/8 teaspoon pepper
- Salad greens

Drain citrus sections thoroughly. Add drained sections to chicken and celery in mixing bowl.

Mix together lime juice, mayonnaise, and seasonings. Add to salad and toss lightly.

Serve with salad greens and garnish with additional fruit sections.

Serves 5 to 6.

HAM SALAD

- 3 cups cubed, cooked ham (about 1 pound cut into 1/2-inch cubes)
- 15 radishes, sliced thin
- 8 sweet pickles, sliced thin
- 2 hard-cooked eggs, chopped
- 1/2 cup cooked salad dressing
- 1/2 cup mayonnaise
- 1 teaspoon prepared mustard
- 1/2 teaspoon salt
- 1/8 teaspoon pepper
- Hard-cooked egg slices

Combine ham, radishes, pickles, and chopped hard-cooked eggs.

Blend salad dressing and mayonnaise; season with mustard, salt, and pepper. Stir salad ingredients into dressing.

Pile salad into lettuce cups placed in individual bowls or on large serving platter.

Garnish each serving with hard-cooked egg slices. Serves 6.

CHICKEN SALAD—GUEST STYLE

- 2 cups diced, cooked or canned chicken
- 1 cup chopped celery
- 1 cup seedless green grapes, or seeded Tokay grape halves
- 1/2 cup toasted almonds
- 1/2 cup mayonnaise
- Crisp lettuce

Combine chicken, celery, grapes, and nuts. Chill.

Add mayonnaise and toss lightly. Serve in lettuce cups. Serves 4 to 6.

PORK SALAD

- 2 cups cubed cooked pork
- 1 cup diced pared apples
- 1 1/2 cups chopped celery
- 1 teaspoon minced onion
- 1/4 cup minced parsley
- 1/4 cup chopped green pepper
- 1 teaspoon salt
- 1/4 cup cooked salad dressing
- 1/4 cup mayonnaise
- 1/4 cup sour cream
- 1 tablespoon lemon juice
- 1 can jellied cranberry sauce
- Crisp salad greens

Combine pork, apples, celery, onion, parsley, and green pepper.

Blend together salt, salad dressing, mayonnaise, sour cream, and lemon juice. Mix dressing lightly with meat and vegetables.

Serve salad on crisp salad greens. Garnish with slices of jellied cranberry sauce. Serves 4.

Fish and Shellfish Salads

Salmon Hollandaise Mold

SALMON HOLLANDAISE MOLD
Hollandaise Sauce:

    2 egg yolks
    Dash of cayenne pepper
    1/2 cup butter or margarine, melted
    3 tablespoons lemon juice

Beat egg yolks until thick and lemon colored; stir in pepper. Blend in 3 tablespoons butter, a little at a time, beating constantly.

Slowly beat in remaining butter with lemon juice.

Mold:

    34 saltine crackers, finely crushed
    1 1-pound can salmon, well drained
    2 cups chopped celery
    1/2 medium onion, chopped
    1/4 teaspoon pepper
    Hollandaise sauce (above)

Combine all ingredients; blend well. Pack into 1-quart mold; chill.

When ready to serve, unmold on bed of chicory and garnish with olives and lemon wedges. Serves 6 to 8.

CRAB LOUIS

    Whole lettuce leaves
    Shredded lettuce leaves
    2 cups cooked or canned crabmeat
    2 hard-cooked eggs, sliced
    Chopped chives
    1/2 cup French dressing
    1/2 cup chili sauce
    2 tablespoons mayonnaise
    1/2 teaspoon Worcestershire sauce (optional)
    Salt and pepper to taste

Arrange lettuce leaves around the inside of a salad bowl. Place some shredded lettuce leaves on bottom.

Heap crabmeat on top of shredded lettuce. Garnish with slices of hard-cooked egg. Sprinkle with chopped chives.

Mix remaining ingredients in another bowl and pour over salad. Serves 4.

Salmon Salad Tropical

SALMON SALAD TROPICAL

1 cup sliced or diced, ripe firm bananas
½ cup drained, diced, canned pineapple
1 to 1½ cups cooked, flaked salmon (1 7-ounce or 1 16-ounce can)
½ to 1 cup diced celery
2 tablespoons chopped, sweet pickle
1 teaspoon salt
1 tablespoon mayonnaise or salad dressing
1 tablespoon prepared mustard
Lettuce
Salad greens for garnish

Combine bananas and pineapple. Add salmon, celery, pickle, and salt.

Mix together mayonnaise or salad dressing and mustard and add to salad mixture. Mix lightly.

Combine 2 or 3 crisp lettuce leaves to form a cup and arrange on each salad plate. Fill each lettuce cup with salad mixture.

Garnish salad with crisp salad greens. Serves 4 to 6.

Variations of Salmon Salad Tropical

Tuna and Banana Salad: In place of salmon, use 1 to 1½ cups (1 7-ounce or 1 12-ounce can) flaked tuna.

Chicken Salad Tropical: In place of salmon, use 1 to 1½ cups diced cooked chicken.

Note: When canned salmon or tuna is used, drain and mix liquid with mayonnaise or salad dressing. One tablespoon lemon juice may be added to mayonnaise or salad dressing, if desired.

For additional color and texture contrast, cold cooked peas, crisp carrot strips or radishes may be arranged on each salad.

MASTER FISH SALAD

Use cooked or canned fish. Cut into ¼- to ½-inch cubes or flake. Toss lightly with mayonnaise or cooked salad dressing. Add salt, if necessary.

Chill and serve in salad bowl or individual plates. Garnish with dressing, crisp greens, cooked or raw vegetables.

Apple and Fish Salad: Use 2 cups flaked fish and 2 cups diced tart apple.

Cucumber and Fish Salad: Use 2 cups flaked fish, ½ cup each of diced cucumber and celery, ½ shredded head lettuce, 1 finely chopped small onion, and a few diced radishes.

Seafood Salad: Use 1 cup cooked or canned shrimp, 1 cup flaked canned crabmeat, and ½ cup diced tart apple. Marinate in French dressing.

Lobster Salad: Use 2 cups cooked or canned lobster meat and 1 cup chopped celery. Marinate in French dressing for 20 minutes. Mix with mayonnaise.

SHRIMP SALAD—GUEST STYLE

1 pound shrimp
½ cup diced celery
¼ cup sliced black olives
1 hard-cooked egg, coarsely cut
½ cup sour cream
¼ cup mayonnaise
1 tablespoon lemon juice
Salt and pepper to taste
Dash of cayenne

Shell, cook, and chill shrimp. Combine chilled shrimp with remaining ingredients.

Serve on mixed greens, preferably with thin-sliced pumpernickel or salty rye. Serves 5 to 6.

ANTARCTIC SALAD

- 2 cups (16 ounces) diced, boiled rock lobster tail meat
- 1/4 cup French dressing
- 2 tablespoons minced, sweet onion
- 1 1/2 cups diced celery
- 1/2 cup mayonnaise
- 1/2 teaspoon salt
- 1/8 teaspoon paprika
- Lettuce leaves
- Pimiento strips
- Green olives
- Lemon wedges

Antarctic Salad

Stir together lobster meat and French dressing. Chill thoroughly.

Add onion and celery. Stir in mayonnaise until all ingredients are well mixed, with salt and paprika. Correct seasoning if necessary.

Line salad bowl with crisp lettuce leaves. Pile salad in center.

Garnish with pimiento strips, green olives, and additional mayonnaise if desired. Serve with lemon wedges. Serves 4.

CURRIED TUNA-RICE SALAD

- 2/3 cup packaged pre-cooked rice
- 1 cup water
- 1/4 teaspoon salt
- 1 cup mayonnaise
- 2 teaspoons curry powder
- 2 tablespoons diced pimiento
- 1 teaspoon salt
- 1/2 teaspoon Ac'cent
- 1 cup cooked peas
- 1 6 1/2-ounce can chunk style tuna

Combine rice, water, and the 1/4 teaspoon salt in saucepan. Mix just until all rice is moistened. Bring quickly to boil over high heat, fluffing rice gently once or twice with fork (do not stir). Cover; remove from heat; let cool to room temperature.

Blend mayonnaise and curry powder; add pimiento, the 1 teaspoon salt, and Ac'cent; add remaining ingredients and rice; toss well to mix. Chill.

Serve on salad greens with additional mayonnaise. Serves 6.

Note: If the brand of tuna fish already contains monosodium glutamate, slightly less Ac'cent will be needed.

Curried Tuna-Rice Salad

Salmon and Cucumber Salad

SALMON AND CUCUMBER SALAD

- 2 cups diced cucumber
- 1 cup sliced celery
- 1 teaspoon Ac'cent
- 1 1-pound can salmon
- 1 tablespoon capers (optional)
- ½ cup mayonnaise
- Melon balls
- Celery seed dressing (below)

Combine cucumber and celery; sprinkle with Ac'cent; toss well to mix. Let stand while preparing remaining ingredients and dressing.

Flake salmon, removing skin and bones; add capers. Combine with cucumber mixture and mayonnaise.

Serve on salad greens; garnish with melon balls. Serve dressing separately. Serves 4 to 6.

Celery Seed Dressing:

- ½ cup mayonnaise
- ½ cup sour cream
- 1 teaspoon celery seed
- ¼ teaspoon Ac'cent
- 2 tablespoons ketchup

Combine all ingredients; mix well.

LOBSTER SPRING SALAD

- 2 rock lobster tails
- 1½ cups diced celery
- 1 tablespoon minced onion
- ½ cup mayonnaise
- ½ cup sour cream
- 1 teaspoon paprika
- 1 tablespoon lemon juice

Boil lobster tails according to directions on package or see index. Remove meat from shell, chill and dice.

Combine with celery and onion. Blend mayonnaise, sour cream, and seasonings and toss with lobster. Serves 6.

OYSTER SALAD

- 1 pint oysters
- ¼ teaspoon celery salt
- 1 tablespoon butter or margarine
- ¼ cup chopped lettuce
- 2 hard-cooked eggs, diced
- ½ cup diced celery
- 1 pimiento, chopped
- 1 teaspoon grated onion
- 1 teaspoon lemon juice
- ½ cup mayonnaise or salad dressing
- ½ teaspoon salt
- ⅛ teaspoon pepper
- Lettuce

Drain oysters. Add celery salt and cook in butter until edges begin to curl. Chill and dice oysters.

Combine all ingredients and serve on lettuce cups. Garnish with paprika. Serves 6.

SHRIMP SALAD

- ½ cup sharp mayonnaise
- 1 tablespoon lemon juice
- 2 cups canned or cooked shrimp
- 2½ cups canned peas
- 3 sliced hard-cooked eggs
- ⅔ cup thinly sliced celery
- Salad greens
- 3 stuffed olives
- Lemon wedges

Thin mayonnaise with lemon juice and 2 tablespoons liquid from shrimp. Add drained shrimp, peas, eggs, and celery. Mix gently.

Place on salad greens. Garnish with sliced stuffed olives and lemon wedges. Serves 6.

Variations: Crabmeat, lobster, salmon, tuna, or flaked fish may be used instead of shrimp.

FISH AND SHELLFISH SALADS

SWEDISH HERRING SALAD

- 2 No. 2 cans ocean herring or 3 salt herrings, cooked
- 4 cups diced cooked beets
- 3 medium apples, diced small
- 1/2 cup chopped onion
- 1/2 cup minced dill pickle
- 3 hard-cooked eggs, minced
- French dressing
- Hard-cooked egg, sliced
- Watercress

Drain canned herring. (Soak salt herring in cold water 1 hour; drain; cook until tender in boiling water.)

Remove skin and bones; cut into small pieces.

Combine all ingredients, mixing lightly with French dressing.

Decorate with slices of hard-cooked egg and sprigs of watercress. Serves 12.

AVOCADO AND SHRIMP APPETIZER SALAD

- 2 avocados
- 1/2 pound cooked, cleaned shrimp

Sauce:

- 1/2 cup mayonnaise
- 1/4 cup chili sauce
- 1/4 teaspoon grated onion
- 1 tablespoon finely chopped green pepper
- 1 1/2 teaspoons Worcestershire sauce
- 1 tablespoon lemon juice
- 1/4 teaspoon salt
- Dash of Tabasco sauce

Prepare sauce by combining all sauce ingredients. Chill until ready to serve.

Cut avocados into halves, lengthwise, and peel if desired. Place each avocado half on lettuce leaf. Place shrimp over cut side of fruit. Serve with sauce. Serves 4.

GRAPEFRUIT SALMON SALAD

- 2 grapefruit
- 1 1-pound can salmon
- 1/2 cup mayonnaise
- 1/4 cup chili sauce
- 1/2 teaspoon Ac'cent

Halve grapefruit, making scalloped edge if desired. Spoon out pulp; remove all membrane with scissors.

Drain salmon; flake, removing skin. Combine salmon and grapefruit pulp.

Combine mayonnaise, chili sauce, and Ac'cent; add to salmon mixture; toss to mix. Fill grapefruit shells.

Serve on watercress or other salad greens. Serves 4.

Grapefruit Salmon Salad

Cottage Cheese and Vegetable Salad

Egg and Cheese Salads

COTTAGE CHEESE AND VEGETABLE SALAD

- 1 garlic clove (optional)
- 2 cups cottage cheese
- 1 teaspoon salt
- Paprika
- 2 tablespoons chopped chives or green onion
- 2 tablespoons chopped pimiento
- ¼ cup chopped celery
- 2 cucumbers
- 1 medium-sized onion
- 2 large tomatoes
- 2 carrots
- French dressing
- Salad greens

Rub mixing bowl with cut clove of garlic. Add cottage cheese, salt, and paprika. Fold in chopped chives, pimiento, and chopped celery. Turn into bowl that has been rinsed in cold water; chill in refrigerator.

Unmold on center of large salad plate; surround with watercress, thin cucumber slices, onion rings, carrot flowers, and tomato wedges. Serve with French dressing. Serves 6.

Variation: The cottage cheese mixture can be served in whole tomatoes in lettuce cups, topped with toasted almonds or peanuts. French dressing is served with it.

DEVILED EGG APPETIZER SALAD

- 4 deviled eggs
- 4 small tomatoes or 4 thick slices of tomato
- 8 ripe olives
- 4 3-inch pieces of celery stuffed with sharp cheese

Arrange ingredients on salad plates with olives and tomatoes. Dribble French dressing over all, if desired. Serves 4.

EGG AND CHEESE SALADS

CHEESE AND ANCHOVY APPETIZER SALAD

1/2 pound Roquefort or blue cheese
1 3-ounce package cream cheese
1/2 teaspoon minced onion
1 1/2 teaspoons prepared mustard
Dash of Tabasco sauce
4 thick slices tomato
4 leaves lettuce
8 rolled anchovies

Blend the 2 cheeses with onion, mustard, and Tabasco. When smooth, pack into pastry tube.

Place slice of tomato on lettuce leaf on small salad plate. Pipe cheese spread into mound on tomato slice. Top each with 2 rolled anchovies.

Serve with crisp crackers or Melba toast. Serves 4.

MOLDED EGG SALAD

8 hard-cooked eggs
1 cup finely diced celery
1/4 cup salad dressing
1 teaspoon Worcestershire sauce
1 tablespoon lemon juice
1 teaspoon scraped onion
Salt and pepper
6 thick slices of tomato
Salad greens
Paprika
Celery curls

Chop eggs coarsely. Add celery, dressing, and seasoning. Season to taste with salt and pepper. Press into molds and chill.

Unmold on tomato slices placed in a bed of salad greens. Sprinkle with paprika. Garnish with celery curls and additional dressing if desired. Serves 6.

ANCHOVY CHEESE SALAD

1 2-ounce can anchovies, drained
1 teaspoon finely cut chives
1 pint creamed cottage cheese
Crisp lettuce leaves
6 small tomatoes, peeled and sliced

Chop 2/3 of the anchovies into small pieces. Cut 1/3 into long strips for garnish.

Add chives and anchovy pieces to cottage cheese, and mix lightly.

Cover and place in refrigerator for at least 1/2 hour to blend flavors.

Arrange lettuce cups on large chop plate.

Put mound of cottage cheese in center and overlap tomato slices on lettuce around edge.

Place strips of anchovies on top of cheese as a garnish.

Serve mayonnaise or French dressing on the side. Serves 6.

SIMPLE COTTAGE CHEESE SALADS

Season 2 cups cottage cheese with salt and pepper to taste. Add light cream to form desired consistency.

Serve on lettuce leaves topped with French dressing or vary as suggested below. Serves 6.

Cottage Cheese with Chives: Season and cream as above. Add 1/4 cup chopped chives. Serves 6.

Cottage Cheese with Olives: Add whole or sliced stuffed olives to seasoned, creamed cottage cheese.

Cottage Cheese with Orange Wedges: Combine 1 cup orange wedges with 1 1/2 cups seasoned, creamed cottage cheese. Flavor with a little chopped fresh mint. Serves 6.

Cottage Cheese with Raisins and Green Pepper: To 1 1/2 cups seasoned, creamed cottage cheese add 1/2 cup seedless raisins and 1/4 cup chopped green pepper.

If desired, use mayonnaise instead of cream with the cottage cheese. Serves 6.

Cottage Cheese with Fresh Strawberries: Fold 1 cup fresh strawberries into 1 1/2 cups seasoned, creamed cottage cheese. Flavor with a little chopped fresh mint. Serves 6.

Hot Potato Salad

Potato, Macaroni, Rice Salads

MASTER POTATO SALAD

- 3 cups diced cooked potatoes, cooked in jackets
- 1 tablespoon grated onion
- 3 tablespoons French dressing
- 1 tablespoon minced parsley
- 1 teaspoon salt
- 1/4 teaspoon paprika
- Mayonnaise

Combine ingredients, except mayonnaise, tossing lightly with a fork. Chill 3 to 4 hours.

Just before serving add mayonnaise, mixing carefully. Serve on lettuce or watercress. Serves 6.

Potato Salad Variations

Potato Salad with Celery: To master potato salad, add 1 cup diced celery.

Potato-Egg Salad: To master potato salad, add 1 cup diced celery and 3 chopped hard-cooked eggs.

Gourmet Potato Salad: To master potato salad, add 1/2 cup tartar sauce and 1/3 cup chow-chow and stuffed olives, minced.

Potato Salad with Carrots: To master potato salad, add 1 cup diced celery and 1 cup grated raw carrot.

Potato Salad with Cabbage: To master potato salad, add 1 cup finely cut cabbage.

Potato Salad with Nuts: To master potato salad, add 1 cup diced celery and 3/4 cup salted peanuts, chopped Brazil nuts, or toasted filberts.

Potato Salad with Cucumber: To master potato salad, add 1 cup diced celery and 1 diced cucumber.

Cornucopia Potato Salads: Roll thin slices of bologna to form cornucopias. Fill with potato salad.

Molded Potato Salad Ring: Pack potato salad into medium-sized ring mold. Chill.

Unmold on bed of greens. Garnish with assorted sliced cold meats, radish roses, and quartered tomatoes.

HOT POTATO SALAD

- 6 slices bacon, chopped
- 1 tablespoon flour
- 1 tablespoon sliced green onions, including tops
- 1/4 cup vinegar
- 1 1/2 teaspoons salt
- 1/2 teaspoon pepper
- 1 tablespoon sugar
- 1/2 cup water
- 4 cups hot sliced cooked new potatoes

Fry bacon until crisp and stir in flour and blend. Add onions, vinegar, salt, pepper, sugar, and water. Cook 5 minutes.

Pour over hot potatoes and mix lightly. Serve while still warm.

If potatoes are cooked ahead of time, they may be reheated gently with sauce in top of double boiler. Green onion tops may be reserved and tossed with salad just before serving to preserve their flavor and color.

Arrange hot potato salad on large platter. Surround with hot frankfurters. Serves 6.

LUNCHEON RICE SALAD

- 3 cups cooked rice, chilled
- ½ cup French dressing
- ½ cup minced onion (young green onions preferred)
- 1 head lettuce
- Grated sharp cheese (optional)
- 1 pint pickled beets
- Watercress or other greens to garnish
- 4 whole tomatoes, peeled and quartered
- 1 pimiento, cut in long thin strips
- Egg slices and radish roses to garnish

Pour French dressing over rice and toss lightly with fork. Let stand 1 hour, then drain thoroughly.

Add minced onion and mold in timbales (glass custard cups make a nice size mold).

Unmold timbales of rice in center of lettuce cups. Sprinkle with grated cheese if desired; garnish with pickled beets, watercress, peeled and quartered tomatoes, and top the rice with thin strips of pimiento. Egg slices and radish roses may be added. Mayonnaise may accompany this salad if desired. Serves 6.

WESTERN RICE SALAD BOWL

- 1 garlic clove, peeled
- 1 No. 2 can bean sprouts, drained and rinsed
- 1 cup thinly sliced unpeeled radishes
- 1 cup diced unpeeled cucumber
- 1 cup thinly sliced celery
- 1 cup chopped watercress
- 2 small sweet onions, chopped
- ¼ cup chopped green pepper
- 1 to 1½ cups cold cooked rice
- 1 to 1½ teaspoons Ac'cent
- 1 cup mayonnaise
- Soy sauce (optional)

Rub salad bowl with garlic. Have all vegetables and rice well chilled; layer them into bowl in order given.

Blend Ac'cent into mayonnaise; pour over top layer of salad (which should be rice). Lift and toss carefully to blend but not crush.

Taste and if salt is needed try adding soy sauce. Serves 6 to 8.

Luncheon Rice Salad

Macaroni and Chicken Salad

MASTER MACARONI SALAD

 3 cups cooked elbow macaroni, chilled
 ½ green pepper, minced
 1½ tablespoons minced onion
 ½ cup chopped celery
 ⅓ cup French dressing
 Lettuce
 Mayonnaise or cooked dressing

Combine macaroni, green pepper, onion, celery, and French dressing. Chill.

Arrange on lettuce and garnish with mayonnaise or cooked dressing. Serves 6.

Macaroni Salad Variations

Macaroni Salad with Hard-Cooked Eggs: Slice and add 3 hard-cooked eggs to master macaroni salad.

Macaroni Salad with Tuna Fish: In master macaroni salad, use a little less macaroni. Add a 7-ounce can flaked tuna fish. Use additional mayonnaise.

Macaroni Salad with Vegetables: To master macaroni salad, add 1 cup mixed cooked or canned carrots, peas, and diced string beans. If desired, marinate vegetables first.

Baked Bean Salad: Follow master macaroni salad recipe and substitute cold baked beans for macaroni.

Brown Bean Salad: Follow master macaroni salad recipe and substitute cold baked brown beans for macaroni.

HAWAIIAN POTATO SALAD

 4 hard-cooked eggs
 1 cup hot cooked rice
 1 large potato, hot mashed
 ¼ cup French dressing
 ½ teaspoon salt
 2 tablespoons chopped pimiento
 1 tablespoon chopped green pepper
 1 tablespoon finely chopped onion
 1 tablespoon chopped parsley

Press 2 of the hard-cooked eggs through a sieve and combine with rice and potatoes. Blend in French dressing. Chill.

Just before serving, add remaining ingredients. If desired, add more seasoning. Garnish with remaining eggs, sliced or sieved, and parsley. Serves 4.

MACARONI AND CHICKEN SALAD

 ½ cup diced cooked chicken
 2 cups cooked elbow macaroni
 1 tablespoon grated onion
 ¾ cup cooked mushrooms
 1 teaspoon salt
 ¼ teaspoon pepper
 ¾ cup cooked salad dressing or mayonnaise
 Curly endive
 2 tomatoes, quartered

Combine all ingredients except endive and tomatoes. Place in refrigerator about 2 hours to chill.

Wash endive thoroughly and arrange it in 9-inch crinkle-edge glass pie plate.

Place salad mixture on endive and garnish with quartered tomatoes.

Serves 6 to 8.

SOUR CREAM POTATO SALAD

 5 cups sliced cooked potato
 ½ cup minced celery
 1 onion, chopped
 4 radishes, sliced
 ¼ cup French dressing
 1 cup sour cream
 Salt, pepper, and cayenne
 Chopped fresh dill

Combine potato, celery, onion, and radishes. Pour French dressing over mixture, and let stand in refrigerator for several hours.

Just before serving, fold in sour cream. Season to taste. Sprinkle with chopped dill. Serves 4.

Stuffed Tomatoes

Stuffed Tomatoes and Cucumbers

STUFFED TOMATO SALADS

Select medium-sized smooth tomatoes. Scald and peel tomatoes. Cut a slice from top and remove some of the pulp.

Sprinkle inside with salt, invert, and let stand in refrigerator 30 minutes to chill. Fill with stuffing. Serve on salad greens.

Avocado Stuffing: Mix diced avocado with chopped celery hearts. Moisten with French dressing.

Cabbage Stuffing: Mix 1½ cups shredded cabbage, ¼ teaspoon celery seed, ¼ teaspoon salt, and 2 tablespoons French dressing.

Chicken Stuffing: Mix diced cooked chicken, diced cucumber, and chopped tomato pulp. Moisten with mayonnaise.

Cottage Cheese and Chives: Mix cottage cheese and chopped chives. Stuff tomatoes.

Top with a spoonful of desired dressing and stuffed olives.

Pineapple-Cheese Stuffing: Combine finely chopped fresh or canned pineapple, tomato pulp, cream cheese, and minced watercress. Moisten with mayonnaise.

Crabmeat Stuffing: Mix flaked crabmeat, diced celery, shredded carrot, tomato and cucumber pulp. Moisten with mayonnaise.

Other Suggested Stuffings: Waldorf salad, egg salad, tuna fish, or any meat salad.

CUCUMBER "BOATS"

- 3 medium-sized cucumbers
- 1 cup cooked elbow macaroni
- 1 12-ounce can luncheon meat, cubed
- ½ cup grated carrots
- ¼ cup chopped green pepper
- ½ cup mayonnaise
- 2 tablespoons vinegar
- 2 tablespoons horseradish
- Salt and pepper

Cut cucumbers in half lengthwise. Scoop out pulp from each half, leaving a shell ¼ inch thick.

Chop pulp and combine with macaroni, luncheon meat, carrot, and green pepper.

Blend together mayonnaise, vinegar, and horseradish. Add to meat mixture and toss lightly. Season to taste with salt and pepper. Pile salad into cucumber shells. Serves 6.

Molded dinner loaves are always a big attraction at a buffet.

Gelatin Molded Salads

HINTS FOR ATTRACTIVE MOLDED SALADS

Gelatin molded salads are especially suitable when you entertain a crowd and so much of the food preparation has to be done well in advance. They are not tricky to prepare, but a few "do's" and "don'ts" may be helpful.

● Use syrup from canned fruits as part of liquid in gelatin salads for added flavor.
● For large molds, cut liquid to 1¾ cups for 1 package fruit-flavored gelatin, or 1 tablespoon (1 envelope) unflavored gelatin.
● Chill gelatin until slightly thickened (unbeaten egg white consistency) before adding solid ingredients. Carefully fold well drained fruits and vegetables into thickened gelatin, distributing them evenly.
● A gelatin salad may be molded in several ways—in large ring or fancy mold, in individual molds, or in shallow pan.
● To mold fruits or vegetables in definite pattern, arrange in thin layer of slightly thickened gelatin. Chill until firm, then add balance of gelatin.
● To make molded layered salads, be sure each layer is firm before adding next layer.
● Prepare large gelatin molds a day ahead of serving, so they will be thoroughly set before unmolding.
● Fill molds as full as possible for easy unmolding.

Fruit Gelatin Molds

MASTER FRUIT SALAD MOLD

1 tablespoon (1 envelope) unflavored gelatin
¼ cup cold water
1 cup hot fruit juice or water
¼ cup lemon juice
¼ cup sugar
¼ teaspoon salt
1½ cups canned or fresh fruit (below)

Soften gelatin in cold water 5 minutes. Add hot fruit juice or water and stir until dissolved.

Add lemon juice, sugar and salt. Chill until syrupy.

Fold in diced fruits. Rinse mold in cold water. Line bottom with thinly sliced fruits. Pour in thickened mixture. Chill until firm.

Unmold on lettuce. Serve with desired dressing. Serves 6.

Master Fruit Salad Mold Variations

1. ½ cup diced apples, ½ cup cut up orange segments, ¼ cup chopped dates, and ¼ cup chopped nuts.

2. ½ cup each diced grapefruit, orange sections, and diced canned pineapple.

3. ½ cup each diced orange sections, diced pears, and peaches, fresh or canned.

4. ¾ cup diced apple, ½ cup chopped celery, and ¼ cup chopped nuts.

5. ½ cup each diced canned pineapple, diced apple, and sliced strawberries.

6. ½ cup each diced canned pineapple, shredded raw carrot, and shredded new cabbage.

7. ¾ cup each diced pears, fresh or canned, and diced cucumber.

8. ¾ cup each diced canned pineapple and diced raw cucumber.

9. ½ cup each sliced bananas, diced orange sections, and white grapes.

10. ½ cup each sliced red cherries, diced melon, and diced orange sections.

11. 1½ cups of cantaloupe and honeydew melon balls.

HOW TO UNMOLD GELATIN SALADS

Brush salad oil in mold so the "set" gelatin will unmold easily.

To unmold, loosen edge of mold with spatula or small knife which has been dipped in warm water. Then quickly immerse the mold just to top in lukewarm water—hot water will melt the mold. Shake mold to loosen gelatin. Place serving dish over top of mold, invert, and lift mold off carefully.

For large molds, moisten surface of gelatin and serving plate and unmold as directed above. When the 2 surfaces are wet, it is easy to center mold. Remove excess moisture with towel.

Surround large molds with salad greens after unmolding; they may break if unmolded on crisp greens. Individual molds may be turned out directly on greens.

Peach and Grape Emerald Salad

PEACH AND GRAPE EMERALD SALAD

- 2 packages lime-flavored gelatin
- 1 cup boiling water
- 1 cup liquid from canned cling peach slices
- 2 cups cold water
- 1 No. 303 (1 pound, 1 ounce) can sliced cling peaches
- 1 cup red or green grapes, seeded and halved
- 1 red maraschino cherry

Dissolve gelatin in boiling water. Add peach liquid and cold water and mix well. Pour a small amount of this mixture into bottom of a well-oiled 6-cup mold. Let chill until partially set.

When set, press peaches into gelatin in bottom of mold and place a cherry in center. Chill remaining gelatin until partially set also.

Dice any peach pieces that are not used in decoration. Then add sliced grapes and diced peach slices. Pour into the mold and chill until set.

Unmold on a serving plate and surround with lettuce leaves filled with cottage cheese. Serves 8 to 10.

SPICED PEACH SOUFFLÉ SALAD

- 1½ cups peach juice
- 4 whole cloves
- ¼ teaspoon cinnamon
- 2 tablespoons vinegar
- 2 tablespoons sugar
- 1 package orange-flavored gelatin
- Mayonnaise
- 2½ cups chopped canned peaches

Combine peach juice, cloves, cinnamon, vinegar, and sugar. Heat just to boiling.

Empty gelatin into small bowl. Pour hot liquid through fine strainer and over gelatin; stir until gelatin is dissolved.

Add mayonnaise and blend at a medium to high speed on mixer or with rotary beater.

Pour into ice tray. Chill in freezer compartment of refrigerator about ½ hour or until set but not icy.

Empty mixture into small mixer bowl and beat at a high speed until smooth and fluffy. Fold in chopped peaches.

Pour into 1-quart lightly oiled mold. Chill in fresh foods compartment of refrigerator until firm, about 1 hour. Serves 6 to 8.

GELATIN FRUIT SALADS

BANANA GELATIN SALAD

1 package fruit-flavored gelatin or 1 tablespoon (1 envelope) unflavored gelatin
2 ripe bananas
Salad greens
Salad dressing

Mix gelatin according to package directions. Chill only until slightly thickened.

Partly fill 1 pint-sized mold with gelatin. Peel bananas, slice and arrange on top of gelatin. Fill mold with remaining gelatin. Chill until firm.

Unmold. Garnish with additional slices of ripe banana or other fruit if desired. Garnish with crisp salad greens. Serve with sour cream, mayonnaise, or a tart French-style salad dressing.

Serves 4 to 6.

Note: Four to six individual molds may be used in place of 1 large mold.

CRANBERRY SALAD MOLD

1 cup sugar
1 cup water
2 cups fresh cranberries
1 tablespoon (1 envelope) unflavored gelatin
½ cup cold water
½ teaspoon salt
½ cup diced celery
½ cup chopped nuts

Make cranberry sauce by combining sugar and 1 cup water. Boil 5 minutes. Add cranberries. Cook without stirring until all skins pop open, about 5 minutes.

Soften gelatin in cold water. Add to hot cranberries with salt. Stir until gelatin is dissolved. Strain.

Chill until mixture is consistency of unbeaten egg whites.

Stir in celery and chopped nuts. Pour into individual molds. Chill until firm.

Unmold on salad greens. Garnish with whole nutmeats. Serve with mayonnaise. Serves 6.

Variation: Canned cranberry jelly, (1½ cups) may be used in place of fresh cranberry sauce. Either may also be used without straining.

Banana Gelatin Salad

GELATIN FRUIT SALADS

STRAWBERRY BAVARIAN SLIMMER

- 1 package strawberry-flavored gelatin
- ¼ cup sugar
- 1 package frozen strawberries, thawed and drained
- ⅓ cup ice water
- 1 tablespoon lemon juice
- ⅓ cup non-fat dry milk

Combine gelatin and sugar. Make gelatin according to label directions, using 1 cup hot water. Add ½ cup berry syrup. Cool.

Add berries and chill until slightly thickened.

Combine ice water and lemon juice, sprinkle non-fat dry milk over top. Beat until stiff, 8 to 10 minutes.

Fold into thickened gelatin mixture. Turn into 1-quart mold and chill until firm. Serves 8.

Strawberry Bavarian Slimmer

WALDORF SALAD MOLD

- 1 tablespoon (1 envelope) unflavored gelatin
- ½ cup cold water
- 1 cup hot water
- ⅓ cup sugar
- ½ teaspoon salt
- ¼ cup mild vinegar or lemon juice
- ½ cup diced celery
- 2 cups diced tart apples
- ¼ cup chopped pecans

Soften gelatin in cold water. Add hot water, sugar, and salt and stir until dissolved. Add vinegar. Chill until consistency of unbeaten egg whites.

Fold in celery, apples, and chopped nuts. Pour into molds. Chill until firm.

Unmold on salad greens. Serve with any preferred salad dressing. Serves 6.

GUACAMOLE RING MOLD

- 2 tablespoons (2 envelopes) unflavored gelatin
- ½ cup cold water
- 1¼ cups hot water
- 6 tablespoons lemon juice
- 2 tablespoons sugar
- ½ teaspoon salt
- 3 avocados, sieved
- ¾ cup mayonnaise

Soften gelatin in cold water and dissolve in hot water. Add lemon juice, sugar, and salt. Cool.

Add avocado and mayonnaise and stir only until blended. Turn into 5-cup ring mold and chill until firm.

Unmold and garnish with avocado slices and parsley. Fill center with marinated fruits. Serves 10.

Ginger Guacamole Ring Mold: Fold ⅓ cup minced preserved ginger or chutney in with mayonnaise. Fill center with poultry or fruit salad.

Zesty Guacamole Ring Mold: Omit sugar from recipe and add 1 teaspoon chili powder, juice of 1 clove garlic, 1 teaspoon minced onion, and 1 green or red pepper, minced. Serve with fish, meat, poultry, or vegetable salad.

Easter Bonnet Salad

EASTER BONNET SALAD

- 2 packages lime-flavored gelatin
- 4 cups boiling water
- Salad greens
- 1 cup mayonnaise
- 3 tablespoons orange juice
- Maraschino cherries

Dissolve gelatin in 4 cups boiling water. Pour 3 cups into a 7-inch round mold which has been rinsed in cold water. Place in refrigerator to set.

Allow remaining cup of liquid to chill until thick and syrupy. Whip with a rotary beater until light and fluffy. Pile into a 5-inch round mold and allow to set until firm.

Unmold plain gelatin on a bed of lettuce. Unmold whipped gelatin on top of larger one.

With a pastry tube, decorate "bonnet" with 1/4 cup mayonnaise. Garnish with maraschino cherries.

Serve with 3/4 cup mayonnaise combined with orange juice. Fresh fruit makes a delicious accompaniment. Serves 6 to 8.

APPLE AND CHEESE LAYERED MOLD

- 1 package lemon-flavored gelatin
- 2 cups boiling water
- 2 tablespoons lemon juice
- 1/2 teaspoon salt
- 1 diced red apple
- 1 teaspoon sugar
- 1 3-ounce package cream cheese
- 1/2 cup broken nutmeats

Dissolve gelatin in boiling water. Add 1 tablespoon lemon juice and salt. Chill.

Combine apple, sugar, and remaining lemon juice. When gelatin mixture is slightly thickened, fold apples into half the mixture. Turn into mold and chill until firm.

Place remaining gelatin mixture in a bowl of cracked ice and beat with a rotary beater until thick and fluffy like whipped cream. Fold in mashed cheese and nuts. Pour over gelatin-apple layer and chill until firm.

To serve, cut in slices and arrange on lettuce leaves. Top with mayonnaise or any desired dressing. Serves 6.

Tawny Salad Molds

TAWNY SALAD MOLDS

1 No. 2½ can fruit cocktail
1½ tablespoons (1½ envelopes) unflavored gelatin
3 tablespoons lemon juice
1 6-ounce can frozen orange juice
Salad greens

Drain syrup from fruit cocktail, measure, and add water to make 1½ cups liquid. Heat.

Soften gelatin in ⅓ cup cold water and dissolve in hot syrup. Stir in lemon juice and undiluted orange juice. Cool until slightly thickened.

Fold in fruit cocktail. Turn into molds and chill until firm.

Unmold on salad greens and garnish with additional fruit cocktail as desired. Makes 8 6-ounce molds.

AVOCADO SALAD RING MOLD

1½ tablespoons (1½ envelopes) unflavored gelatin
¼ cup cold water
2½ cup tomato juice or purée
2 bay leaves
5 whole cloves
¼ cup chopped onion
½ teaspoon salt
Pepper
Few drops of Tabasco sauce
2 avocados
½ cup diced celery
Lettuce hearts

Soften gelatin in cold water. Combine tomato juice or purée, bay leaves, cloves, onion, salt, pepper, and Tabasco sauce. Boil 5 minutes and strain. Add softened gelatin and stir until dissolved. Cool.

When gelatin begins to set, stir in 1 cubed avocado and celery. Mold in ring mold.

To serve, fill center of ring with lettuce hearts and remaining avocado sliced. Serve with desired dressing. Serves 6 to 8.

Variations:

Substitute any flavored gelatin mold, and vary form of avocado pieces as desired.

Emerald Mold: Lime gelatin, sliced stuffed olives and cocktail onions, and diced cucumbers.

Waldorf Mold: Lemon gelatin, diced apple, finely cut celery, and a few walnuts or almonds.

Seafood Mold: Lime or lemon gelatin flavored with lemon juice and condiments, and seafood.

Nectar Mold: Apricot, plum, nectarine, or berry gelatin base, bananas, and pineapple.

GREENGAGE-LIME MOLD

Dissolve 1 package lime-flavored gelatin in 1 cup hot water. Add 1 cup plum juice and water, and 2 cups canned greengage plums. Chill. Serves 4 to 6.

GINGER ALE-GRAPE MOLD

Dissolve 1 package lemon-flavored gelatin in 1 cup hot grape juice. Cool. Add 1 cup ginger ale. Turn into molds and chill. Serves 4 to 5.

MOLDED CRUSHED PINEAPPLE

Dissolve 1 package lemon-flavored gelatin in 2 cups hot water. Chill until slightly thickened.

Fold in ½ cup drained crushed canned pineapple, 1 cup diced unpeeled red apple, and ¼ cup chopped pecans.

Turn into individual molds. Chill until firm; unmold. Serves 4 to 6.

GELATIN FRUIT SALADS

PARTY FRUIT RING MOLD

2 packages lemon-flavored gelatin
1½ cups hot water
2 cups fruit syrup (drained from peaches and pineapple)
Peach halves, drained
Pineapple slices, canned, drained
Dark sweet cherries, drained
Salad greens

Dissolve gelatin in hot water. Add fruit syrup and chill mixture until slightly thickened.

Pour ½ cup gelatin into the bottom of an 8-inch ring mold (1½ quarts) and chill until almost firm.

Set pineapple slices in gelatin with a dark sweet cherry in the center and pour in gelatin just to cover. Chill until firm.

Stand peach halves upright against sides of mold and place cherries above pineapple slices.

Pour in gelatin to cover peaches about one-half and chill until firm.

Add remaining gelatin and chill thoroughly. Unmold and garnish with salad greens. Serve with a whipped cream dressing. Serves 6 to 8.

TOP-AND-BOTTOM FRUIT LOAF

2 packages fruit-flavored gelatin
1¾ cups boiling apricot juice and water
2 tablespoons lemon juice
2 cups cold water
1½ cups drained apricots, cut small
1 cup seeded Tokay grape halves
1½ cups sliced apples
2 firm bananas, sliced

Dissolve gelatin in hot apricot juice (measure juice drained from apricots and add water to measure 1¾ cups; heat to boiling). Add lemon juice and cold water. Cool completely but do not chill.

Lightly oil loaf pan (8 x 3½ x 2½-inches); place apricots and grapes in layer over bottom. Pour in cooled gelatin.

Place sliced apples and bananas in layer on top; pressing fruit just below surface of gelatin. Chill until firm. Fruits will stay in place with layer of clear gelatin between.

Cut in slices and serve on watercress with a fruit salad dressing. Serves 8.

Party Fruit Ring Mold

Cranberry-Orange Salad

CRANBERRY-ORANGE SALAD

- 1 tablespoon (1 envelope) unflavored gelatin
- 2 tablespoons cold water
- 1 cup orange juice, heated to boiling
- 2/3 cup evaporated milk, chilled icy cold
- 1 teaspoon lemon juice
- 1 12-ounce package frozen cranberry orange relish, thawed

Soak gelatin in cold water and dissolve in hot orange juice. Chill until mixture is of a jelly-like consistency.

Meanwhile, chill a bowl and beater and chill evaporated milk in refrigerator tray until ice crystals form around edge.

Beat evaporated milk in chilled bowl until it forms peaks; add lemon juice, and beat until stiff. Fold whipped evaporated milk and cranberry-orange relish into gelatin.

Pour into an oiled star-shaped mold and chill until set.

Unmold on greens and garnish with orange slices and cranberry sauce. Serves 6.

PINEAPPLE-COTTAGE CHEESE SALAD

Dissolve 1 package lemon- or lime-flavored gelatin in 1 cup hot water. Add 1 cup cold water. Cool.

Add 1 cup seasoned cottage cheese and 1/2 cup drained crushed canned pineapple. Pour into mold rinsed in cold water and chill until firm.

Unmold on crisp lettuce and garnish with mayonnaise. Serves 6.

GINGER ALE-LEMON MOLD

Dissolve 1 package lemon-flavored gelatin in 1/2 cup boiling water. When cool, add 1 1/2 cups ginger ale.

Chill until slightly thickened and fold in 1 cup diced mixed fruits (fresh or canned and drained), 1/4 cup chopped celery, and 1/4 cup chopped nuts. Pour into molds and chill. Serves 6.

CRANBERRY-LEMON MOLD

Dissolve 1 package lemon-flavored gelatin in 1 cup boiling water.

Put 1 cup raw cranberries through food chopper and add 1 cup orange juice and 1/2 cup sugar. Add to cooled gelatin.

Pour into mold and chill. Serves 6.

GOLDEN SALAD MOLD

- 1 tablespoon (1 envelope) unflavored gelatin
- 1/4 cup cold water
- 1/4 cup sugar
- 1/4 teaspoon salt
- 1 cup hot pineapple syrup or juice
- 1/4 cup cold orange juice
- 1/4 cup vinegar
- 3/4 cup coarsely grated raw carrots
- 3/4 cup orange sections, cut into small pieces
- 1 1/2 cups drained canned pineapple, cut into small pieces

Soften gelatin in cold water. Add sugar, salt, and hot pineapple syrup. If necessary add water to pineapple syrup to complete measurement. Stir until dissolved.

Add orange juice and vinegar. Chill until consistency of unbeaten egg whites. Stir in carrots, oranges, and pineapple.

Pour into mold. Or, if individual molds are used, place 1 teaspoon clear jelly in bottom of each. When nearly firm, place on it 1 tablespoon mayonnaise. When this is firm fill molds with salad mixture. Chill until firm.

Unmold on salad greens. Decorate with pineapple. Serve with mayonnaise or salad dressing, if desired. Serves 6.

salads

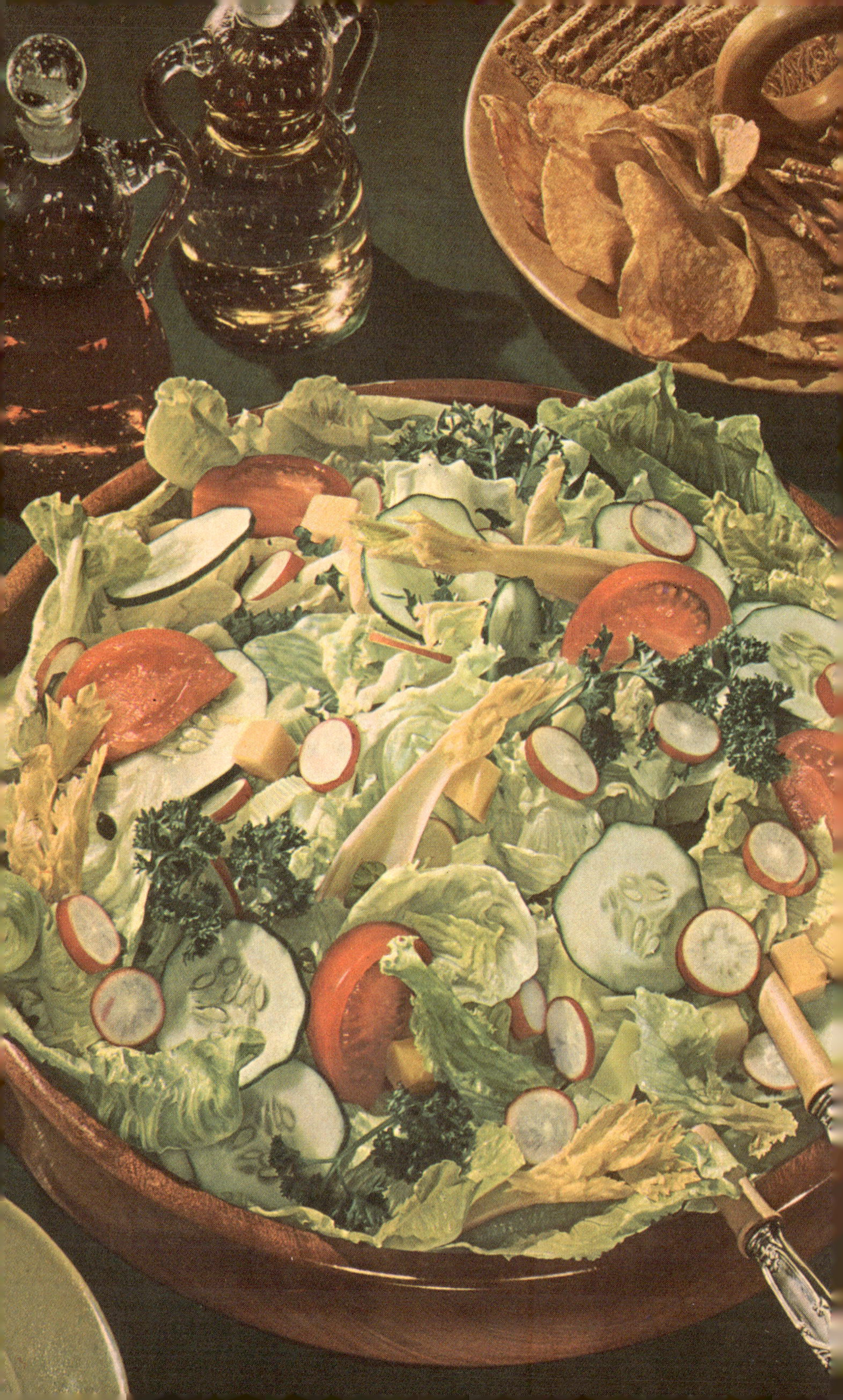

GELATIN FRUIT SALADS

SPICY FRUIT RING

- 1 No. 2½ can (3½ cups) fruit cocktail
- 1 3-inch stick cinnamon
- 1 teaspoon whole cloves
- 1 teaspoon whole allspice
- 2 envelopes (2 tablespoons) unflavored gelatin
- ⅓ cup lemon juice

Drain fruit cocktail. Simmer syrup with spices 10 minutes. Strain out spices, measure syrup and add water to make 3½ cups liquid. Heat.

Soften gelatin in lemon juice and dissolve in hot liquid. Cool until slightly thickened.

Fold in fruit cocktail. Turn into 8½-inch ring mold and chill until firm.

Unmold and garnish with watercress. Fill ring with chicken salad. Garnish with avocado balls and slivered almonds. Serves 8.

CHERRY-OLIVE MOLD

Dissolve 1 package cherry-flavored gelatin in 1 cup hot water. Add 1 cup cherry juice and cold water.

When slightly thickened, add 1½ cups pitted sour red cherries (slightly sweetened), ¼ cup chopped pickle, and ¼ cup sliced stuffed olives. Chill. Serves 6.

APPLE-LIME MOLD

Dissolve 1 package lime-flavored gelatin in 1 cup hot water. Add 1½ cups sweetened, unflavored applesauce. Pour into molds and chill. Serves 4 to 6.

LOGANBERRY AND BANANA MOLD

Dissolve 1 package raspberry-flavored gelatin in 1 cup hot water. Add 1 cup loganberry juice and cold water.

When slightly thickened fold in 1 sliced banana and 1 cup loganberries. Serves 4 to 6.

Spicy Fruit Ring

Cheese Gelatin Molds

Molded Plum and Cottage Cheese Salad

MOLDED PLUM AND COTTAGE CHEESE SALAD

- 1 No. 303 can blue plums
- 1 package orange-flavored gelatin
- Plum syrup plus water to make 1 cup
- 1 cup creamed cottage cheese
- ½ cup chopped celery
- ½ cup chopped pecans
- 2 tablespoons lemon juice
- ½ cup evaporated milk, chilled icy cold

Drain plums and save syrup. Cut plums in halves, remove and discard pits. Place plum halves fairly close together in the bottom of an 8-inch ring mold or in 8 individual molds. If any plum halves remain, save for use for some other purpose.

Empty gelatin into a medium-sized mixing bowl. Heat syrup and water to boiling. Add to gelatin and stir until gelatin is dissolved.

Chill gelatin until it begins to thicken, then add cottage cheese, celery, pecans, and lemon juice.

Whip milk until it will hold a stiff peak. Fold into chilled gelatin mixture. Spoon carefully over plums. Chill until firm, about 2 to 3 hours.

Unmold on chilled platter. Garnish with orange or grapefruit segments, if desired. Serves 6 to 8.

ROQUEFORT-CREAM CHEESE MOLD

- ½ pound Roquefort or blue cheese
- 2 3-ounce packages cream cheese
- 1 tablespoon (1 envelope) unflavored gelatin
- ½ cup heavy cream, whipped

Mash cheeses to a smooth paste.

Soften gelatin in ½ cup cold water and stir over hot water until dissolved.

Add cheese paste to whipped cream and stir in gelatin. Turn into mold rinsed in cold water. Chill until firm. Serve with mayonnaise or French dressing. Serves 6 to 8.

OLIVE SALAD LOAF

- 2 tablespoons (2 envelopes) unflavored gelatin
- 1/4 cup cold water
- 1 cup tomato sauce
- 2 tablespoons vinegar
- 1/2 teaspoon salt
- 2 cups cottage cheese
- 1 cup ripe olives
- 1/2 cup mayonnaise
- 1 cup finely chopped celery
- 1/3 cup finely chopped green sweet pepper
- 1/4 cup diced pimiento

Soften gelatin in cold water. Heat tomato sauce to boiling. Add gelatin and stir until it is dissolved.

Blend in vinegar and salt. Cool to room temperature.

Force cottage cheese through sieve. Cut olives into large pieces.

Blend cheese, olives, mayonnaise, celery, green pepper, and pimiento into gelatin mixture. Turn into loaf pan (about 8 1/2 x 4 1/2 x 2 1/2 inches), and chill until firm.

Unmold on salad greens to serve. Serves 8 to 10.

LIME GELATIN WITH COTTAGE CHEESE AND APPLE SALAD

- 1 package lime-flavored gelatin
- 1 cup hot water
- 1 cup water or fruit juice
- 1/2 cup chopped celery
- 1/2 cup chopped, unpeeled apple
- 1 cup dry cottage cheese
- 1/4 teaspoon salt
- Mayonnaise

Dissolve gelatin in hot water. Add the other cup of water or fruit juice. Chill until slightly thickened, then stir in the celery, apple and cottage cheese.

Pour into a ring mold or individual molds and chill until firm. Unmold on lettuce and serve with mayonnaise. Serves 6.

Olive Salad Loaf

GELATIN SALADS

SPRING BEAUTY SALAD

- 1½ tablespoons (1½ envelopes) unflavored gelatin
- 3 tablespoons cold water
- 1 cup cottage cheese, sieved
- 1 cup American cheese, grated
- 1 teaspoon salt
- ⅛ teaspoon white pepper
- 2 tablespoons chopped pimiento
- 2 tablespoons chopped green pepper
- ½ cup diced American cheese
- 1 pint heavy cream, whipped

Soften gelatin in cold water 5 minutes and dissolve over hot water.

Soften cottage cheese with a little plain cream and press through sieve. Add grated American cheese, gelatin, seasonings, pimiento, pepper, and diced American cheese. (Some of diced cheese may be sprinkled in bottom of mold.)

Fold in stiffly beaten cream. Turn mixture into wet mold and chill.

Serve on large chop plate with center filled with fresh fruit or vegetable salad. Garnish with crisp lettuce, endive, or watercress. Serves 6.

CRANBERRY COTTAGE SALADS

- 1 tablespoon (1 envelope) unflavored gelatin
- ¼ cup cold water
- 1 1-pound can cranberry sauce (jellied or whole)
- 2 teaspoons prepared horseradish
- ¾ teaspoon dry mustard
- ¼ cup lemon juice
- 1 teaspoon grated lemon rind
- ¼ teaspoon salt
- Pinch of cayenne
- ¼ cup cottage cheese

Place gelatin in custard cup. Add cold water. Let stand 2 minutes. Place custard cup in pan of boiling water until gelatin dissolves.

Combine cranberry sauce and gelatin. Stir in other ingredients, beating slightly to blend.

Spoon into molds which have been rinsed in cold water. Chill until firm.

Unmold and serve in lettuce cups. Serves 4 to 6. An excellent accompaniment for fish.

Spring Beauty Salad

PINEAPPLE-COTTAGE CHEESE MOLD

- 2 teaspoons (⅔ envelope) unflavored gelatin
- 3 tablespoons cold water
- 1 cup pineapple juice or pineapple juice plus water
- 2 tablespoons lemon juice
- 2 tablespoons sugar
- Pinch of salt
- ½ cup drained crushed pineapple (9-ounce can)
- ⅓ cup finely chopped celery
- ⅓ cup cottage cheese

Sprinkle gelatin on cold water and soak a few minutes.

Heat fruit juices; add sugar, salt, and gelatin. Stir until gelatin is dissolved.

Chill until thick enough to hold solid food in place. Stir in pineapple, celery, and cottage cheese. Chill until firm. Serves 4.

Cranberry Cottage Salads

GELATIN SALADS 2319

Creamy Cheese Salad Mold

COTTAGE CHEESE AND CANTALOUPE SOUFFLÉ SALAD

- 1 package lime-flavored gelatin
- 1 cup hot water
- ½ cup cold water
- 1 tablespoon lemon juice
- ½ cup mayonnaise
- 1 cup cottage cheese
- 1½ cups diced cantaloupe

Empty gelatin into small bowl; pour hot water over it and stir until dissolved.

Add cold water, lemon juice, and mayonnaise. Blend ingredients at a medium to high speed on mixer or with rotary beater.

Pour into ice tray. Chill in freezer compartment of refrigerator about ½ hour or until set but not icy. Empty mixture into small bowl and beat at high speed until smooth and fluffy.

Fold in cottage cheese and cantaloupe. Pour into 1-quart lightly oiled mold. Chill in fresh food compartment of refrigerator until firm, about 1 hour. Serves 6 to 8.

Red and White Salad

CREAMY CHEESE SALAD MOLD

- 1 tablespoon (1 envelope) unflavored gelatin
- ¼ cup cold water
- 3 eggs
- 2 cups milk
- ¼ teaspoon salt
- 1½ cups diced American cheese
- ¾ teaspoon onion juice
- ½ cup sliced stuffed olives
- ¼ cup chopped sweet pickles
- ½ cup finely diced celery
- 1 tablespoon vinegar or pickle juice

Lettuce, chicory, or watercress
Paprika

Soften gelatin in cold water.

Beat eggs, add milk and salt, and cook over boiling water, stirring constantly, until mixture thickens slightly.

Remove from heat and stir in softened gelatin until dissolved. Add remaining ingredients (except greens and paprika) until well mixed, not until cheese melts.

Decorate large or individual molds with additional olive and pickle slices. Pour in a little of gelatin mixture (not enough to float garnish) and chill until firm.

Then add remainder of mixture and chill until whole mold is firm.

Unmold on crisp salad greens, on one large or individual plates. Garnish with paprika. Serves 6 to 8.

RED AND WHITE SALAD

- 1 tablespoon (1 envelope) unflavored gelatin
- ½ cup water
- 1 can (1¼ cups) condensed tomato soup
- 1 teaspoon grated onion
- 1 cup creamy cottage cheese

Soften gelatin in cold water. Heat soup; mix in softened gelatin and grated onion.

Pour into 1 large or 4 individual molds that have been rinsed with cold water. Chill until firm.

Unmold on lettuce. Serve with top knot of cottage cheese. Serves 4.

Asparagus-Egg Mold

Egg and Macaroni Gelatin Molds

ASPARAGUS-EGG MOLD

- 1 tablespoon (1 envelope) unflavored gelatin
- 1/4 cup cold water
- 1 cup hot asparagus liquid
- 1/2 teaspoon salt
- 1/8 teaspoon pepper
- 1 tablespoon minced onion
- 2 tablespoons lemon juice
- 2 cups diced cooked or canned asparagus
- 4 hard-cooked eggs
- 1 cup chopped celery
- 1 cup sour cream

Soften gelatin in cold water and dissolve in hot asparagus liquid. Add salt, pepper, onion, and lemon juice. Cool.

When mixture begins to thicken, fold in asparagus, 3 chopped eggs, celery, and sour cream.

Slice remaining hard-cooked egg and place around side of rinsed mold. Pour asparagus mixture into mold. Chill until firm.

Unmold and garnish with sliced tomatoes. Serve with French dressing. Serves 4 to 6.

EGG SALAD MOLD

- 2 tablespoons (2 envelopes) unflavored gelatin
- 1 cup cold water
- 1 1/2 cups mayonnaise or salad dressing
- Juice of 1 lemon
- 1/2 teaspoon salt
- 2 drops Tabasco sauce
- 1 teaspoon grated onion
- 12 hard-cooked eggs
- 1/4 cup chopped parsley
- 1/2 cup finely chopped green pepper or celery

Soften gelatin in cold water. Dissolve over boiling water. Cool slightly.

Add mayonnaise, lemon juice, salt, Tabasco sauce, and grated onion.

Place center slices of hard-cooked egg around inside of oiled 1- to 1 1/2-quart ring mold.

Separate remaining yolks and whites of eggs. Sieve yolks. Chop whites.

Combine yolks and 1/2 the gelatin mixture; place as a layer in ring mold. Then add parsley and green pepper as a layer. Cover with egg whites mixed with remaining 1/2 of gelatin mixture. Chill until set.

Unmold on large platter. Fill center of ring with chicken or vegetable salad. Garnish with salad greens. Serve with French dressing. Serves 6 to 8.

MOLDED EGGS AND VEGETABLES

- 1 tablespoon (1 envelope) unflavored gelatin
- 1/2 cup cold water
- 1 teaspoon salt
- 2 tablespoons lemon juice
- 1/4 teaspoon Worcestershire sauce
- Dash of cayenne pepper
- 3/4 cup mayonnaise or salad dressing
- 1 1/2 teaspoons grated onion
- 1/2 cup finely diced celery
- 1/4 cup finely diced green pepper
- 1/4 cup chopped pimiento
- 4 hard-cooked eggs, chopped

Soften gelatin in cold water. Place over boiling water and stir until gelatin is dissolved. Add salt, lemon juice, Worcestershire sauce, and cayenne pepper. Cool.

Add mayonnaise; mix in remaining ingredients.

Turn into large or individual molds and chill until firm. Unmold and garnish with sliced hard-cooked eggs. Serves 6.

HAM AND MACARONI MOLD

- 4 ounces macaroni
- 1 tablespoon (1 envelope) unflavored gelatin
- ¼ cup cold water
- 2 tablespoons butter or margarine
- 2 tablespoons flour
- 2 cups milk
- ½ teaspoon salt
- ¼ cup pickle juice
- ½ teaspoon Worcestershire sauce
- ½ cup chopped or sliced stuffed olives
- ½ cup chopped sweet pickles
- 1¼ cups diced celery
- 3 cups ground cooked ham
- 3 hard-cooked eggs, sliced

Cook macaroni in salted boiling water until tender (about 20 minutes). Drain and rinse thoroughly with cold water; drain.

Soak gelatin in cold water.

Melt butter, blend in flour, add milk, and cook over direct heat, stirring constantly, until sauce boils and thickens; add salt. Remove from heat and stir in softened gelatin until dissolved.

Add pickle juice and Worcestershire sauce, and cool.

Combine cold macaroni with olives, pickles, celery, ham, and eggs, reserving a few center slices of egg and a few olive slices for garnishing. Add cold sauce and mix lightly with other ingredients.

Rinse a 6-cup mold with cold water and arrange reserved egg and olive slices in the bottom in any desired pattern. Pack the salad mixture into mold and chill until firm.

When ready to serve, unmold onto chilled serving plate and garnish with pickle fans and lettuce. Serves 6.

LEMON EGG-OLIVE MOLD

- 1 package lemon-flavored gelatin
- 2 cups hot water
- ¼ teaspoon salt
- 1 tablespoon vinegar
- Dash of cayenne
- 2 hard-cooked eggs, coarsely chopped

Ham and Macaroni Mold

- ⅓ cup chopped stuffed olives
- 1 cup chopped celery
- 1 teaspoon grated onion

Dissolve gelatin in hot water. Add salt, vinegar, and cayenne. Chill until slightly thickened.

Fold in eggs, olives, celery, and onion. Pour into 1-quart mold and chill until firm.

Unmold and surround with lettuce. Serve with mayonnaise or salad dressing. Serves 4 to 6.

MACARONI AND CHEESE MOLD

- 1 tablespoon (1 envelope) unflavored gelatin
- ½ cup cold water
- ¾ cup hot water
- 1 cup grated American cheese
- 1 tablespoon lemon juice
- 2 teaspoons grated onion
- 1 teaspoon salt
- 2 tablespoons chopped parsley
- 1 tablespoon chopped pimiento
- ½ cup diced celery
- 1½ cups cooked, broken macaroni
- ½ cup mayonnaise or salad dressing

Soften gelatin in cold water. Add hot water. Stir constantly until gelatin is dissolved.

Add grated cheese. Stir until cheese has softened.

Stir in lemon juice, grated onion, and salt. Chill until mixture is consistency of unbeaten egg whites.

Stir in remaining ingredients. Pour into 1 large or 6 individual molds. Chill until firm. Unmold on salad greens. Serves 6.

Salmon Mousse

Fish and Shellfish Gelatin Molds

SALMON AND CUCUMBER MOUSSE

- 1 tablespoon (1 envelope) unflavored gelatin
- 1/4 cup cold water
- 1 bouillon cube
- 1/2 cup boiling water
- 1/2 cup mayonnaise
- 1 teaspoon Worcestershire sauce
- 1 tablespoon onion, scraped
- 1 tablespoon vinegar
- 1 teaspoon salt
- 1/4 teaspoon pepper
- 2 cups flaked cooked or canned salmon
- 1 1/2 cups diced cucumber
- 1/2 cup heavy cream, whipped

Soften gelatin in cold water. Dissolve bouillon cube in boiling water and add to gelatin. Stir until gelatin dissolves.

Let cool. Add mayonnaise, Worcestershire, onion, vinegar, salt, and pepper. Blend well and chill until thick.

Beat with rotary egg beater until light and foamy. Fold in salmon, cucumber, and whipped cream.

Turn into 1-quart fish-shaped mold. Chill until firm. Serve on greens with slices of cucumber. Serve with mayonnaise. Serves 4.

SALMON MOUSSE

- 1 tablespoon (1 envelope) unflavored gelatin
- 1/4 cup cold water
- 1 cup mayonnaise
- 1/2 cup light cream or top milk
- 2 tablespoons lemon juice
- 1 teaspoon salt
- 1 cup finely chopped celery
- 1/4 cup finely chopped sweet pickles
- 1 tablespoon grated onion
- 2 teaspoons prepared horseradish
- 1 1-pound can salmon, drained and flaked

Soften gelatin in cold water; dissolve over hot water.

Combine remaining ingredients. Add gelatin and blend. Pour into a 1-quart mold. Chill until firm.

Unmold and garnish with salad greens, deviled eggs, and slices of lemon. Serves 6 to 8.

TUNA SOUFFLÉ SALAD

1 package lemon-flavored gelatin
1 cup hot water
½ cup cold water
½ cup mayonnaise
1 tablespoon lemon juice
¼ teaspoon salt
Dash of pepper
½ cup flaked tuna
½ medium cucumber, diced
1 hard-cooked egg, diced
1 tablespoon chopped onion

Dissolve gelatin in hot water. Mix in cold water, mayonnaise, lemon juice, salt, and pepper.

Pour into refrigerator tray. Quick-chill in freezing unit 15 to 20 minutes, or until firm about 1 inch from edge but soft in center.

Turn into bowl and whip with rotary egg beater. Fold in remaining ingredients; pour into 1-quart mold. Chill in refrigerator until firm (about 60 minutes). Unmold onto a bed of chicory; garnish with cucumber slices.

Serves 4 to 6.

LOBSTER IN ASPIC

2½ tablespoons (2½ envelopes) unflavored gelatin
½ cup cold water
2 cups boiling water
1½ teaspoons salt
4 tablespoons sugar
¼ cup lemon juice
½ cup lobster liquid or cold water
2 cups shredded, cooked lobster
1 cup blanched almonds

Soak gelatin in cold water 5 minutes. Add boiling water, salt, sugar, and lemon juice. Cool.

Add lobster liquid, shredded lobster and blanched almonds. Pour into a mold which has been dipped in cold water. Chill until firm. Unmold and serve on lettuce. Serves 6.

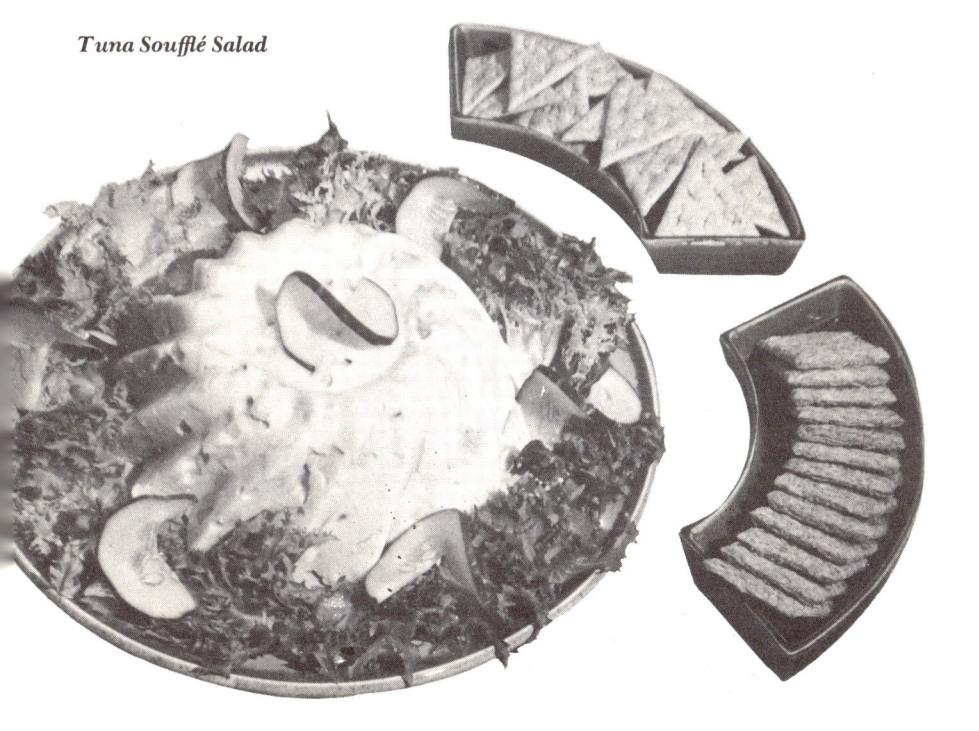

Tuna Soufflé Salad

SHRIMP PARTY RING SALAD

- 2 tablespoons (2 envelopes) unflavored gelatin
- ¾ cup cold water
- 1½ cups hot water
- ¼ cup honey
- ¾ teaspoon salt
- 6 tablespoons lemon juice
- 1 cup mayonnaise
- 1 cup cooked shrimp pieces
- 1 cup chopped celery
- 1 tablespoon minced onion
- 2 tablespoons chopped parsley
- 2 tablespoons chopped pimiento

Chicory
Spinach leaves
Cooked whole shrimp
Pimiento strips
- 1 cup mayonnaise
- ½ teaspoon grated lemon rind
- 2 teaspoons lemon juice

Thin lemon slices

Soften gelatin in cold water. Add hot water, honey, salt, and lemon juice. Chill.

Stir mixture into 1 cup mayonnaise. Pour ½ cup of mixture in an 8½-inch ring mold. Chill until firm.

To remaining mixture add shrimp pieces, celery, onion, parsley, and pimiento. Chill until beginning to thicken. Pour into ring mold and chill until firm.

Unmold on serving platter. Place chicory and spinach leaves in center of mold. Garnish with whole shrimp and additional chicory and spinach leaves. Place pimiento strips on top of mold in a pattern.

Combine 1 cup mayonnaise with lemon rind and juice thoroughly. Serve salad garnished with thin slices of lemon. Serves 6.

Shrimp Party Ring Salad

Avocado and Tuna Loaf

AVOCADO AND TUNA LOAF

Tuna Layer:

- 1 tablespoon (1 envelope) unflavored gelatin
- ½ cup cold water
- ¾ cup boiling water
- 3 tablespoons lemon juice
- 1 teaspoon salt
- 1 7-ounce can tuna, flaked
- 1 cup diced celery
- ⅓ cup diced pimiento

Sprinkle gelatin on cold water to soften. Add boiling water and stir until gelatin is dissolved.

Add lemon juice and salt. Chill until mixture is consistency of unbeaten egg white. Fold in flaked tuna, celery, and pimiento.

Turn into a 9 x 5 x 3-inch loaf pan; chill until almost firm.

Avocado Layer:

- 1 tablespoon (1 envelope) unflavored gelatin
- ¾ cup cold water
- 1 teaspoon sugar
- 2 tablespoons lemon juice
- 1 cup mashed avocado (1 large)
- ½ cup sour cream
- ½ cup mayonnaise
- 1 teaspoon salt
- ⅛ teaspoon Tabasco sauce

Sprinkle gelatin on cold water to soften. Place over boiling water and stir until gelatin is dissolved.

Add sugar and 1 tablespoon lemon juice.

Chill until mixture is consistency of unbeaten egg white.

Immediately after mashing avocado, add remaining tablespoon lemon juice, sour cream, mayonnaise, salt, and Tabasco. Fold in gelatin mixture.

Turn on top of almost firm first layer; chill until firm.

Unmold; if desired, garnish with additional avocado slices, ripe and stuffed olives. Serves 8.

GELATIN FISH AND SHELLFISH SALADS

CANADIAN SALMON MOLD

- 2 tablespoons (2 envelopes) unflavored gelatin
- ½ cup cold water
- 1 cup hot chicken broth or bouillon
- 1 cup salad dressing or mayonnaise
- 3 tablespoons chili sauce
- 2 tablespoons lemon juice
- 1 tablespoon grated onion
- ½ teaspoon Worcestershire sauce
- Dash of cayenne
- ½ teaspoon Ac'cent
- Salt to taste
- 1 8-ounce can salmon, or 1 cup cooked salmon
- 1 cup finely diced celery
- ½ cup sliced stuffed olives

Soften gelatin in cold water; dissolve in hot chicken broth.

Cool slightly. Add slowly to mayonnaise, blending well after each addition.

Add chili sauce, lemon juice, onion, Worcestershire sauce, cayenne, Ac'cent, and salt. Chill until consistency of unbeaten egg whites.

Flake salmon; fold in with celery and olives. Turn into an oiled 5-cup mold; chill until firm.

Unmold on crisp salad greens. Serve with any desired dressing. Serves 8.

Variations: Use 1 package lemon- or lime-flavored gelatin instead of unflavored gelatin. Substitute water for chicken broth.

Canadian Salmon Mold

TUNA MOUSSE

- 2 tablespoons (2 envelopes) unflavored gelatin
- ½ cup cold water
- 1 cup mayonnaise
- 2 6½- or 7-ounce cans tuna
- ½ cup chopped cucumber
- 3 tablespoons chopped stuffed olives
- ¼ cup lemon juice
- 1½ teaspoons prepared horseradish
- 2 teaspoons onion juice
- ¼ teaspoon salt
- ¼ teaspoon paprika
- 1 cup heavy cream, whipped

Soften gelatin in cold water. Dissolve over boiling water and stir into mayonnaise.

Flake tuna and add with remaining ingredients except cream. Mix well.

Fold in whipped cream. Pour into 1½-quart mold. Chill until firm. Unmold on crisp lettuce. Serves 8.

Shrimp Mousse: Substitute cooked or canned flaked shrimp for tuna.

SHRIMP-AVOCADO ASPIC

- 1 tablespoon (1 envelope) unflavored gelatin
- 2 tablespoons cold water
- 1 cup boiling water
- 1 cup sieved avocado
- 1½ tablespoons lemon juice
- ¾ teaspoon salt
- ½ teaspoon Worcestershire sauce
- Dash of Tabasco sauce
- 1 pimiento, minced
- 1½ cups cooked or canned shrimp, cleaned

Soften gelatin in cold water. Dissolve in boiling water. Add avocado, seasonings, and pimiento. Chill until mixture begins to thicken.

Add shrimp and turn into mold rinsed in cold water. Chill until firm. Unmold on lettuce. Serves 6.

Tuna Luncheon Mold

TUNA LUNCHEON MOLD

- 1 tablespoon (1 envelope) unflavored gelatin
- ½ cup cold water
- 1 cup mayonnaise
- ⅓ cup lemon juice
- ¾ cup diced celery
- ⅓ cup diced green pepper
- Salt and pepper
- 2 6½-ounce cans grated or flaked tuna

Soften gelatin in cold water and dissolve it over hot water. Combine mayonnaise and lemon juice and add to celery, green pepper, seasonings, and tuna which have been tossed together.

Add gelatin to mixture, and mix lightly. Pour into ring mold and chill until firm.

Unmold ring on curly endive arranged on chop plate. Fill center with radish roses. Serves 6 to 8.

SEA GARDEN SALAD

- 1 pound fillet of halibut or other white fish
- ½ teaspoon Ac'cent
- 2 packages lime-flavored gelatin
- 3 cups hot water
- 1 cup pineapple juice
- 2 tablespoons lime juice
- 1 cup diced canned pineapple
- ½ cup seedless white grapes (optional)
- 1 cup diced melon

"Poach" fish in water to cover to which Ac'cent has been added, about 10 minutes or until done. Drain; cool; break into small chunks.

Dissolve gelatin in hot water; add pineapple juice and lime juice. Chill until consistency of unbeaten egg white.

Fold in fruits and fish. Turn into lightly oiled mold. Chill until firm.

Unmold on salad greens. Serve with mayonnaise. Serves 6 to 8.

Sea Garden Salad

Shrimp Salad Mold

SHRIMP SALAD MOLD

- 2 tablespoons (2 envelopes) unflavored gelatin
- 2½ cups cold water
- 1 cup boiling water
- ½ cup lemon juice
- ½ teaspoon salt
- 1 teaspoon Worcestershire sauce
- 1 or 2 drops Tabasco sauce
- 1 teaspoon grated onion
- 1 pound shrimp, cooked and cleaned
- 1 cup diced celery
- ½ cup diced green pepper
- ½ cup sliced pimiento stuffed olives
- Deviled eggs
- Sliced olives

Soften gelatin in 1 cup cold water. Add 1 cup boiling water and stir until gelatin is dissolved.

Add remaining water and lemon juice. Stir in salt, Worcestershire, Tabasco, and onion.

Pour thin layer of gelatin mixture into 1-quart mold and arrange shrimp in it. Chill until set.

Chill remaining gelatin mixture until slightly thickened, then fold in celery, pepper, and olives. Carefully pour over shrimp. Chill until firm.

Unmold and garnish with additional sliced olives, deviled eggs, and salad greens. Serve with mayonnaise or sour cream dressing. Serves 6.

MOLDED KING CRAB SALAD

- 2 6-ounce packages frozen king crabmeat
- 1 cup chopped celery
- ¼ cup French dressing
- 1 package lemon-flavored gelatin
- 1½ cups hot water
- ½ cup lemon juice
- ½ teaspoon salt
- Salad greens
- ½ cup mayonnaise or salad dressing

Thaw crabmeat and remove any cartilage. Marinate crabmeat and celery in French dressing.

Dissolve gelatin in hot water. Add lemon juice and salt. Place about ⅓ of the gelatin in a ring mold; chill until almost congealed.

Arrange crabmeat and celery attractively over the gelatin base and cover with remaining gelatin. Chill until firm.

Unmold on round platter and garnish with salad greens. Fill center with mayonnaise. Serves 6.

LEMON-TUNA MOUSSE

- 1 package lemon-flavored gelatin
- 1¾ cups boiling water
- 2 tablespoons vinegar
- 1 tablespoon grated onion
- 1 can (7-ounces) tuna, drained and flaked
- ¼ cup chopped green pepper
- 1 pimiento, chopped
- ½ teaspoon salt
- 2 teaspoons prepared horseradish
- 1 cup heavy cream, whipped

Dissolve gelatin in boiling water; add vinegar and onion; chill until partially firm.

Combine remaining ingredients, except cream; fold into gelatin mixture. Fold in whipped cream.

Pour into oiled 1-quart mold; chill until firm. Unmold on salad greens. Serves 4 to 6.

MASTER SOUFFLÉ SALAD

Ingredients:
- 1 package lemon-flavored gelatin
- 1 cup hot water
- ½ cup cold water
- 3 tablespoons vinegar or canned lemon juice
- ½ cup mayonnaise
- ¼ teaspoon salt
- Dash of pepper
- 1 cup minced celery
- 4 tablespoons minced parsley
- 1½ tablespoons minced onion

Choose One:
- 1 1-pound can salmon, drained and flaked
- 2 7-ounce cans tuna, drained and flaked
- 1 12-ounce can luncheon meat, chopped
- 1 No. 303 can (1 pound) peas, peas and carrots, or mixed vegetables, drained (Use 1 cup hot tomato juice in place of hot water.)
- 1 12-ounce can boned chicken, diced
- 2 6-ounce cans boned turkey, diced
- 1 12-ounce can tongue or tongue loaf

Dissolve gelatin in hot water. Add cold water, vinegar or lemon juice, mayonnaise, salt, and pepper; blend well with rotary beater; pour into refrigerator tray.

Chill in freezing unit 15 to 20 minutes, or until firm around edges but soft in center.

Turn into bowl; whip with rotary beater until fluffy; fold in remaining ingredients. Pour into 1-quart mold or 6 individual molds.

Chill (not in freezing unit) 30 to 60 minutes, or until firm. Unmold; garnish with salad greens. Serves 6.

Note: For Fruit-Soufflé Salad, omit pepper, parsley, and onion; reduce salt to ⅛ teaspoon and vinegar to 1 tablespoon. Choose 1 No. 303 or No. 2 can fruit cocktail, peaches, apricots, grapefruit sections, or pears. Use syrup drained from fruit as part of liquid. Follow same directions.

Easy to prepare ahead of time and store in the refrigerator, soufflé salads make ideal entrées for summertime luncheons or supper parties.

Tomato-Ham Salad Mold

Meat and Poultry Gelatin Molds

CHICKEN MOUSSE

1 tablespoon (1 envelope) unflavored gelatin
¼ cup cold water
½ cup milk, scalded
1 can condensed cream of chicken soup
2 cups ground cooked chicken
¼ cup mayonnaise
1 tablespoon grated onion
½ teaspoon salt
¼ teaspoon pepper
1 cup heavy cream

Soak gelatin in cold water 5 minutes; dissolve in hot milk. Combine with undiluted soup, chicken, mayonnaise, onion, salt and pepper; blend well. Chill until almost set.

Whip cream stiff; fold into chicken mixture. Pour into 5- or 6-cup mold rinsed with cold water. Chill about 4 hours or until set.

Unmold just before serving and garnish with mayonnaise. Accompany with marinated asparagus, cranberry sauce, and crackers. Serves 8.

TOMATO-HAM SALAD MOLD

1½ tablespoons (1½ envelopes) unflavored gelatin
⅔ cup water
1 chicken bouillon cube
1⅓ cups condensed tomato soup
1 tablespoon finely chopped onion
2 cups ground cooked ham or luncheon meat
½ cup chopped celery
¼ cup chopped pimiento
½ cup chilled evaporated milk, whipped
2 tomatoes, thinly sliced
2 hard-cooked eggs
½ cup mayonnaise
1 teaspoon mustard-with-horseradish
Salad greens

Soften gelatin in ⅓ cup cold water. Mix bouillon cube with rest of water and dissolve in hot soup.

Add onion and ground meat and cool until slightly thickened.

Fold in celery, pimiento, and stiffly whipped evaporated milk. Turn into heart-shaped mold (1¼ quarts) rinsed in cold water and chill until firm.

Unmold and surround with salad greens. Form heart outline with sliced egg white on top of mold. Fill with mayonnaise mixed with mustard-with-horseradish and arrange thinly sliced tomatoes around edge. Serves 6.

Chicken Mousse

TWO-TONE JELLIED CHICKEN DINNER

Chicken Salad Layer:

- 1 tablespoon (1 envelope) unflavored gelatin
- 3/4 cup cold chicken broth
- 1/4 teaspoon salt
- 1/4 teaspoon Ac'cent
- 1 tablespoon lemon juice
- 3/4 cup mayonnaise
- 1 cup diced steamed chicken
- 3 tablespoons finely diced green pepper
- 3/4 cup thinly sliced celery

Pour gelatin into top of double boiler; add cold chicken broth; dissolve over hot water. Cool.

Add salt, Ac'cent, and lemon juice; add slowly to mayonnaise, blending well. Stir in chicken, green pepper, and celery.

Turn into 6-cup mold; chill until almost firm.

Vegetable Aspic Layer:

- 1 tablespoon (1 envelope) unflavored gelatin
- 1 3/4 cups cold canned mixed vegetable juice
- 1/4 teaspoon Ac'cent

Pour gelatin into top of double boiler. Add vegetable juice and Ac'cent; dissolve over hot water. Chill until consistency of unbeaten egg white.

Spoon on top of first layer; chill until firm. Garnish with salad greens, cucumber slices, and radish roses. Serves 8.

CHICKEN CRANBERRY LOAF

Cranberry Layer:

- 1 tablespoon (1 envelope) unflavored gelatin
- 1/4 cup cold water
- 2 cups hot cranberry sauce

Chicken Layer:

- 1 1/2 tablespoons (1 1/2 envelopes) unflavored gelatin
- 1/3 cup cold water

Two-Tone Jellied Chicken Dinner

- 4 chicken bouillon cubes
- 2 cups boiling water
- 1/4 teaspoon crumbled rosemary
- 1 teaspoon onion salt
- Few grains pepper
- 1 teaspoon Ac'cent
- 2 cups diced, cooked or canned chicken
- 1/2 cup finely sliced celery
- 2 tablespoons minced green pepper

For cranberry layer: Soften gelatin in cold water; dissolve in hot cranberry sauce. Pour into loaf pan (8 x 5 x 3 inches). Chill until set.

For chicken layer: Soften gelatin in cold water; dissolve with bouillon cubes in boiling water; add rosemary, onion salt, pepper, and Ac'cent. Chill until consistency of unbeaten egg white.

Combine remaining ingredients; fold in. Spoon on top of cranberry sauce. Chill until firm. Unmold on salad greens. Serves 8.

Chicken Cranberry Loaf

Deviled Ham Mousse

DEVILED HAM MOUSSE

1 tablespoon (1 envelope) unflavored gelatin
¼ cup cold water
¾ cup mayonnaise
2 3-ounce cans deviled ham
1½ teaspoons grated onion
½ cup chopped celery
¼ cup chopped green pepper
¼ cup chopped sweet pickles

Soften gelatin in cold water; dissolve over hot water.

Blend mayonnaise with deviled ham, onion, celery, green pepper, and pickles.

Stir in dissolved gelatin. Pour mixture into a pint mold; chill until firm.

Unmold and garnish with salad greens. Surround with chilled Vienna sausages and slices of corned beef. Serves 6 to 8.

HAM AND CABBAGE MOLDS

1 tablespoon (1 envelope) unflavored gelatin
¼ cup cold water
1¼ cups hot water
1 tablespoon vinegar
½ teaspoon salt
¾ cup mayonnaise or salad dressing
1 teaspoon prepared mustard
1½ cups cubed cooked ham
1 cup shredded cabbage
2 tablespoons minced onion

Soften gelatin in cold water. Add hot water and stir to dissolve. Add vinegar and salt. Cool to room temperature.

Stir in mayonnaise and mustard. Chill until partially set.

Fold in ham, cabbage, and onion. Pour into custard cups. Chill until firm. Serves 5.

HAM MOUSSE

1 tablespoon (1 envelope) unflavored gelatin
2 tablespoons cold water
½ cup boiling water
1 teaspoon dry mustard
½ teaspoon salt
1 tablespoon prepared horseradish
½ teaspoon brown sugar
Speck of cayenne
2 cups ground cooked ham
1 cup heavy cream, whipped

Soften gelatin in cold water. Dissolve in boiling water. Chill until partially thickened.

Mix remaining ingredients except cream together. Add gelatin and mix lightly. Fold in cream.

Turn into mold. Chill until firm. Unmold and garnish with crisp salad greens, pickles, and radishes. Serves 6.

JELLIED HAM MOLD

- 2 tablespoons (2 envelopes) unflavored gelatin
- 2 tablespoons cold water
- 3 cups consommé
- 1 tablespoon prepared horseradish
- 2 teaspoons prepared mustard
- 1 tablespoon minced onion
- Dash of pepper
- 3½ cups ground cooked ham (or ground luncheon meat)

Soak gelatin in cold water. Heat consommé and add gelatin, stirring until dissolved. Cool.

Add horseradish, mustard, onion, and pepper. Place in refrigerator.

When mixture begins to thicken, stir in ham. Pour into ring mold, loaf pan, or decorative mold, which has been well rubbed with salad oil or rinsed with cold water. Serves 6 to 8.

MEAT LOAF MOLD
(With Leftover Meats)

- 1 tablespoon (1 envelope) unflavored gelatin
- ¾ cup cold water
- 1 10½-ounce can condensed consommé
- 2 tablespoons lemon juice
- ¼ teaspoon salt
- 1 cup finely diced leftover meat (lamb, veal, beef, pork, chicken, etc.)
- ½ cup chopped celery
- 2 tablespoons chopped green pepper (optional)

Soften gelatin in ¼ cup cold water. Combine soup with remaining ½ cup water and bring to boil.

Add softened gelatin and stir until dissolved. Add lemon juice and salt. Cool.

When mixture begins to thicken, fold in meat and celery and green pepper if used.

Turn into 4-cup mold, loaf pan, or individual molds that have been rinsed in cold water. Chill.

Unmold on salad greens. Serve with mayonnaise. Serves 6.

Variations: 1½ cups boiling water and 2 bouillon cubes may be used instead of canned consommé. Homemade soup stock may also be used, in which case you would soften gelatin in ¼ cup cold water and dissolve it in 1½ cups hot soup.

Any desired combination of leftover vegetables such as corn, string beans, cabbage, carrots, peas, etc., may be used instead of celery.

Jellied Ham Mold

JELLIED CHICKEN LOAF

9 slices cooked white meat of chicken
2 tablespoons (2 envelopes) unflavored gelatin
1/4 cup cold water
4 cups chicken stock
2 1/2 cups diced cooked chicken
1/4 cup diced pimiento
2 cups diced celery
2 cups cooked peas
1/4 cup lemon juice
2 tablespoons Worcestershire sauce
Salt

Arrange white meat in well-oiled loaf pan (8 1/2 x 4 1/2 x 2 1/2 inches).
Soften gelatin in cold water; dissolve in hot chicken stock. Cool; pour 1/2 cup over white meat; chill until set.
Add diced chicken and rest of ingredients to remainder of gelatin mixture. Fill pan. Chill until firm, invert to unmold. Garnish as desired. Serves 8 to 10.

Molded Chicken Salad

CHICKEN ALMOND MOUSSE

1 1/2 tablespoons (1 1/2 envelopes) unflavored gelatin
3 cups chicken stock or broth
1 teaspoon salt
1/4 teaspoon pepper
1 teaspoon minced onion
1/8 teaspoon paprika
3 egg yolks
1/2 cup finely chopped almonds
2 cups diced cooked chicken
1 cup heavy cream, whipped

Soften gelatin in 1/2 cup cold chicken stock. Add salt, pepper, onion, and paprika to remaining stock and heat.
Stir a little of hot stock into egg yolks. Mix well and return to double boiler. Cook over hot water until smooth and thick. Strain if necessary.
Stir in and blend softened gelatin. Cool until partially thickened.
Fold in nuts, chicken, and whipped cream. Turn into ring mold. Chill until firm.
Unmold on serving platter. Fill center with crisp greens. Garnish with tomato wedges. Serves 6.

Variations: Vary seasonings by adding a little horseradish and dry mustard.

MOLDED CHICKEN SALAD

1 tablespoon (1 envelope) unflavored gelatin
2 tablespoons lemon juice
2 chicken bouillon cubes
1/2 teaspoon salt
1 3/4 cups hot water
1/3 cup mayonnaise
1 diced, peeled avocado
1 cup diced, cooked chicken
3/4 cup diced apples
Salad greens

Soften gelatin in lemon juice.
Dissolve bouillon cubes and salt in hot water; add gelatin. Cool until consistency of unbeaten egg white.
Fold in mayonnaise, avocado, chicken, and apples. Pour into 6 small molds; refrigerate until firm. Unmold on crisp salad greens. Serves 4.

Vegetable Gelatin Molds

MASTER VEGETABLE SALAD MOLD

- 1 tablespoon (1 envelope) unflavored gelatin
- 1/4 cup cold water
- 1 cup hot water
- 1/4 cup mild vinegar
- 1 tablespoon lemon juice
- 1/2 teaspoon salt
- 2 tablespoons sugar
- 1/8 teaspoon pepper
- 1 1/2 cups diced or shredded vegetables (below)
- 1 tablespoon minced onion

Use raw or cooked vegetables. Add more sugar if desired.

Soften gelatin in cold water 5 minutes. Dissolve in hot water. Add vinegar, lemon juice, salt, sugar, and pepper. Cool until syrupy.

Fold in vegetables. Turn into mold which has been rinsed in cold water. Chill until firm.

Unmold on lettuce. Serve with desired dressing. Serves 6.

Vegetable Salad Mold Variations

1. 1/2 cup diced celery, 1/2 cup diced cucumber, 1/4 cup sliced radishes, and 2 tablespoons chopped green pepper.

2. 1/2 cup shredded raw cabbage, 1/2 cup grated raw carrots, 1/4 cup diced apples, and 1/4 cup chopped nuts.

3. 1 cup shredded raw cabbage, 1/2 cup chopped celery, and 2 tablespoons chopped green pepper or pimiento.

4. 1/2 cup each chopped celery, shredded raw carrots, and cooked peas.

5. 1 cup shredded raw cabbage and 1/2 cup sliced green olives.

6. 3/4 cup each shredded raw cabbage and shredded raw carrots.

7. 1/2 cup each canned asparagus tips, canned green peas, shredded raw carrots, and 2 tablespoons chopped pimiento.

8. 3/4 cup each cubed pickled beets and chopped celery.

9. 1/2 cup each chopped celery, diced cooked beets, and shredded raw cabbage.

10. 3/4 cup each cooked peas and chopped roasted peanuts.

11. 1/2 cup each diced celery, canned lima beans, and diced or shredded carrots, raw or cooked.

12. 1/2 cup each canned red kidney beans and peas, 1/2 cup chopped celery, 1/4 cup chopped green pepper, and 1 tablespoon grated onion.

PERFECTION SALAD

- 1 tablespoon (1 envelope) unflavored gelatin
- ¼ cup cold water
- 1 cup hot water
- ¼ cup sugar
- ½ teaspoon salt
- 1 tablespoon lemon juice
- ¼ cup vinegar
- ½ cup finely shredded cabbage
- 1 cup finely diced celery
- 1 pimiento, finely chopped or 2 tablespoons chopped sweet red or green pepper

Soften gelatin in cold water in top of double boiler. Add hot water, sugar, and salt. Stir over boiling water until dissolved.

Add lemon juice and vinegar. Chill until mixture is consistency of unbeaten egg whites.

Stir in vegetables. Pour into mold. Chill until firm.

Unmold on salad greens. Garnish with mayonnaise. Or, cut salad in cubes and serve in green pepper cases. Serves 6.

BROCCOLI SALAD MOLD

- 1 tablespoon (1 envelope) unflavored gelatin
- ¼ cup cold water
- 1 cup hot consommé or bouillon
- ¾ cup mayonnaise
- ¼ teaspoon salt
- ⅛ teaspoon pepper
- 2 cups chopped cooked broccoli
- 2 hard-cooked eggs, chopped
- 2 hard-cooked eggs, sliced
- Greens

Soften gelatin in cold water 5 minutes. Dissolve in very hot consommé. Chill until slightly thickened.

Fold in mayonnaise and seasonings, mixing until well blended. Fold in broccoli and chopped eggs. Turn into 1-quart mold. Chill until firm.

Unmold on large platter. Garnish with crisp greens and sliced hard-cooked eggs. Serves 6.

JELLIED GREEN PEPPER RINGS

- 4 large green peppers
- 1 package lemon-flavored gelatin
- 2 cups boiling water
- 1 cup chopped celery
- 1 cup chopped raw carrots
- 1 cup shredded cabbage
- 1 cup drained chopped cucumbers

Cut the stem ends from green peppers; remove seeds.

Dissolve gelatin in boiling water. When gelatin is cool and somewhat thickened, add remaining ingredients.

Spoon gelatin-vegetable mixture into pepper shells and chill until firm.

Cut each pepper into 6 crosswise slices. For each portion of salad, place 2 slices on crisp lettuce.

Garnish with a radish rose and serve with mayonnaise. Serves 6.

TOMATO ASPIC
(Master Recipe)

- 2 tablespoons (2 envelopes) unflavored gelatin
- ½ cup cold water
- 2½ cups canned tomatoes
- 1 tablespoon minced onion
- 1 tablespoon sugar
- 1 teaspoon salt
- 4 whole black peppers
- ½ bay leaf
- 4 cloves
- 2 tablespoons lemon juice

Soften gelatin in cold water 5 minutes.

Cook tomatoes and seasonings (except lemon juice) 5 to 10 minutes. Strain.

Pour 2 cups hot tomato mixture over softened gelatin.

Add lemon juice and pour into molds rinsed with cold water. Chill.

Unmold on lettuce. Serve with mayonnaise or cooked dressing. Serves 6.

Tomato Aspic Ring: Prepare master tomato aspic. Pour into large ring mold or individual small molds. Chill until firm.

Unmold and fill center with chicken, tuna, or salmon salad.

Tomato Aspic with Celery and Peas: Prepare master tomato aspic; add 1 cup canned peas and 1 cup diced celery to thickened aspic.

Tomato Aspic with Cottage Cheese: Prepare master tomato aspic; fill molds only ⅔ full of tomato aspic.

When firm, complete filling molds with seasoned cottage cheese. Unmold with cottage cheese on the bottom.

Tomato Aspic with Cucumber: Prepare master tomato aspic and add 2 cups diced cucumber to thickened aspic.

Tomato Aspic with Salmon Salad

GELATIN VEGETABLE SALADS

CUCUMBER SALAD MOLD

1 package lime-flavored gelatin
2 cups hot water
1 tablespoon lemon juice or vinegar
1 teaspoon scraped onion
1/2 teaspoon salt
Dash of pepper
1 cup finely chopped cucumber

Dissolve gelatin in 2 cups hot water. Add lemon juice or vinegar and seasoning. Chill.

When slightly thickened, fold in cucumber. Turn into square pan and chill until firm.

Cut into squares and serve on lettuce. Serves 4 to 6.

Pineapple and Carrot: Use orange-flavored gelatin with shredded carrot and pineapple instead of cucumber.

Pineapple and Cucumber: Substitute 1/2 cup crushed canned pineapple for 1/2 cup cucumber.

EASY TOMATO ASPIC

1 package lemon-flavored gelatin
1 cup (8-ounce can) tomato sauce
1 cup hot water
1/2 teaspoon salt
1 tablespoon lemon juice

Dissolve gelatin in hot water. Stir until dissolved.

Add tomato sauce, salt, and lemon juice. Mix thoroughly. Chill until syrupy. Pour into molds and chill until firm. Unmold on crisp lettuce leaves.

Serves 4.

Layers of tomato aspic and well seasoned cottage cheese make up this two-tone mold.

ASPARAGUS AND TOMATO MOLD

Simmer 2 cups tomato juice, bit of bay leaf, 1 clove, 1/2 teaspoon salt, and 1/2 onion (sliced) 15 minutes.

Add 1 tablespoon (1 envelope) unflavored gelatin soaked in 4 tablespoons cold water. Dissolve. Strain and cool mixture.

When slightly thickened, add 1 1/2 cups tender cooked or canned asparagus cut into 1/2-inch pieces. Turn into molds and chill. Serves 4 to 6.

CUCUMBER AND SOUR CREAM SALAD MOLD

1 tablespoon (1 envelope) unflavored gelatin
1/4 cup cold water
1/2 cup hot water
1/4 cup sugar
1 cup grated cucumber, well drained
1 cup thick sour cream
2 tablespoons lemon juice
1 tablespoon grated onion and juice
1/2 teaspoon salt
Cucumber slices, ripe olives, and watercress

Soften gelatin in cold water. Combine hot water and sugar and heat to boiling point. Add softened gelatin, stirring until dissolved. Chill until slightly thickened.

Fold in cucumber, sour cream, lemon juice, onion juice, and salt. Pour into mold and chill until firm.

Unmold and garnish with thin slices of cucumber, ripe olives, and parsley or watercress. Serves 4.

LEMON VEGETABLE MOLD

Dissolve 1 package lemon-flavored gelatin in 1 cup hot water. Add 1 cup cold water and 1 tablespoon lemon juice. Cool.

Add 1 cup shredded raw cabbage, 1/2 cup cooked peas, 1/2 cup cooked diced carrots, and 1/4 teaspoon salt.

Mix well. Pour into molds and chill. Serves 4 to 6.

HOME GARDEN BARBECUE SALAD

1 package lemon-flavored gelatin
1¼ cups hot water
1 8-ounce can tomato sauce
1½ tablespoons vinegar
½ teaspoon salt
Few grains pepper
1 cup diced cucumber
1 cup sliced radishes
½ cup sliced green onions
1 teaspoon Ac'cent

Dissolve gelatin in hot water. Add tomato sauce, vinegar, salt, and pepper. Chill until consistency of mayonnaise.

Meanwhile combine vegetables; sprinkle with Ac'cent; toss well to mix.

Fold into gelatin mixture; fill into oiled ring mold. Chill until firm.

Unmold; fill center with salad greens. Serve with mayonnaise. Serves 4 to 6.

Home Garden Barbecue Salad

Pineapple Cucumber Mold

CARDINAL SALAD

1 package lemon-flavored gelatin
1 cup hot water
¾ cup beet juice
3 tablespoons vinegar
½ teaspoon salt
1 tablespoon prepared horseradish
2 teaspoons grated onion
¾ cup diced celery
1 cup cooked diced beets
Mayonnaise

Dissolve gelatin in hot water. Add beet juice, vinegar, salt, horseradish, and onion. Chill until partly set.

Fold in celery and beets. Pour into mold rinsed in cold water and chill.

Serve on watercress garnished with mayonnaise. Serves 6.

PINEAPPLE CUCUMBER MOLD

Pineapple Layer:

1 cup crushed canned pineapple (not drained)
1 package lemon-flavored gelatin
½ teaspoon salt
½ cup finely grated carrots

Cucumber Layer:

1 tablespoon (1 envelope) unflavored gelatin
¼ cup cold water
1 cup mayonnaise
½ cup light cream
½ teaspoon salt
1 tablespoon grated onion
½ cup finely chopped celery
½ cup grated cucumber, drained

Pineapple Layer: Drain pineapple. Add enough water to syrup to make 1¾ cups liquid. Heat to boiling; dissolve gelatin in it.

Chill until the consistency of unbeaten egg whites. Add salt, carrots, and crushed pineapple.

Turn into a 1½-quart ring or fancy mold. Chill until firm.

Cucumber Layer: Soften gelatin in cold water; dissolve over hot water.

Combine remaining ingredients. Add gelatin and blend. If desired, tint pale green. Pour over pineapple layer.

Chill until firm. Unmold and garnish with salad greens. Serves 8 to 10.

Frozen Salads

Frozen salads are especially suitable when the thermometer soars in summer or for entertaining menus when so much of the food preparation must be done well in advance. When the salad is frozen, you simply cut it in squares or slice, place a serving on a bed of salad greens and garnish with a little dressing.

TO FREEZE SALADS

(1) Turn the mixture into refrigerator trays or other molds and place in freezing compartment of refrigerator or in the freezer. Set refrigerator at coldest point. Freeze until firm.

(2) Pack mixture into oiled mold. Seal tightly with paraffin or adhesive tape. Cans with lids such as baking powder cans make good molds. Pack mold in 5 parts ice to 1 part salt and let stand about 4 hours or until firm.

Note: Do not freeze salad long enough for fruits to become frozen or icy.

FROZEN CRANBERRY LOAF

- ¾ cup finely ground toast crumbs
- ½ cup brown sugar
- 1 teaspoon cinnamon
- ½ teaspoon nutmeg
- ¼ teaspoon allspice
- ¼ teaspoon cloves
- ¼ teaspoon ginger
- 3 tablespoons melted butter or margarine
- 1 1-pound can jellied cranberry sauce
- ½ cup heavy cream
- 1 3-ounce package cream cheese
- Green food coloring

Frozen Cranberry Loaf

Mix first 7 ingredients together. Work in melted butter. Press mixture evenly against sides and bottom of an ice cube tray. Chill in freezing compartment for at least 1 hour.

Crush jellied cranberry sauce with a fork and spread over crumb crust.

Whip cream. Soften cream cheese and whip with cream. Tint green with green food coloring. Spread whipped cream-cheese mixture over cranberry sauce.

Place in freezing compartment and freeze until firm. Slice to serve. Serves 8.

FROZEN PEACH SALAD

1   No. 2½ can peach halves
1   tablespoon butter or margarine
1½ tablespoons flour
1   tablespoon sugar
¼   teaspoon salt
½   cup syrup from peach halves
¼   cup orange juice
1   stiffly beaten egg white
½   cup evaporated milk, whipped

Place 8 drained peach halves cut-side-down in refrigerator tray.

Melt butter; add flour and blend. Add sugar, salt, peach syrup, and orange juice. Cook, stirring constantly, until thick and smooth.

Fold in stiffly beaten egg white. Cool. Dice remaining peaches and add to mixture. Fold in whipped evaporated milk. Pour over peaches. Freeze until firm.

Cut in squares and place in lettuce cups, peach half up. Place a maraschino cherry in center of each peach. Serves 8.

FROZEN COTTAGE CHEESE AND FRUIT SALAD

¾   pound cottage cheese
1   tablespoon mayonnaise
1   tablespoon lemon juice
¼   teaspoon salt
2   oranges, cut in small pieces
2   bananas, diced
1   cup grated pineapple
2   sliced red cherries
2   sliced green cherries
1   cup heavy cream, whipped

Mix cottage cheese, mayonnaise, lemon juice, and salt until cheese is free from lumps.

Add fruit and fold in whipped cream. Freeze. Serves 6.

FROZEN SPICED APRICOT SALAD

1   pound dried apricots
2   cups water
1½ teaspoons whole cloves
Pinch of salt
4   tablespoons sugar
1   tablespoon grated lemon rind
2   tablespoons lemon juice

Cook apricots until tender in water to which cloves, salt, sugar, and lemon rind have been added.

Put through coarse sieve. Add lemon juice.

Turn into refrigerator tray. Freeze. Serve on crisp lettuce with mayonnaise. Serves 6.

FROZEN DELIGHT SALAD

1   cup heavy cream, whipped
¼   cup mayonnaise
1   teaspoon (⅓ envelope) unflavored gelatin
3   tablespoons syrup from pineapple
1   cup crushed canned pineapple
½   cup chopped ripe olives
½   cup chopped celery
½   teaspoon prepared horseradish
Salt
Salad greens

Fold mayonnaise into whipped cream. Soften gelatin in cold syrup and heat over hot water until dissolved. Cool slightly and fold into cream mixture.

Fold in pineapple, olives, celery, horseradish, and salt to taste.

Pour into refrigerator tray and freeze. Stir occasionally during freezing. When firm, cut into squares and serve on salad greens. Serves 8.

Frozen Peach Salad

Frosty Fruit Cream

FROZEN CREAM CHEESE AND FRUIT SALAD

- 1 3-ounce package cream cheese
- ½ cup mayonnaise
- ½ cup heavy cream, whipped
- ½ cup canned or fresh seedless grapes
- ¼ cup red maraschino cherries
- 1 cup (9-ounce can) canned crushed pineapple, drained
- 1½ cups diced marshmallows (about 14)

Blend cheese and mayonnaise until smooth. Fold in whipped cream, fruits, and marshmallows.

Turn into refrigerator tray. Freeze until firm. Serve on lettuce. Serves 6.

CALIFORNIA FROZEN SALAD

- 1 3-ounce package cream cheese
- 3 tablespoons mayonnaise
- ⅛ teaspoon salt
- 1 cup heavy cream, whipped
- ¼ cup chopped kumquats
- ¼ cup chopped dates
- ¼ cup chopped maraschino cherries
- ¼ cup crushed pineapple
- 1 tablespoon finely chopped preserved ginger
- ½ cup chopped blanched almonds

Blend cheese smoothly with mayonnaise; add salt. Fold in whipped cream and fruit and ginger mixture.

Pour into refrigerator tray; sprinkle almonds over top. Freeze. Serve on crisp lettuce. Serves 8.

EASY FROZEN FRUIT SALAD

Freeze overnight 1 17-ounce can fruit cocktail or other canned fruit.

Immerse can in hot water a few seconds. Open both ends. Push frozen fruit through and slice.

Or pour fruit into refrigerator tray and freeze. Turn out and cut into slices. Serve at once on lettuce with mayonnaise. Serves 6.

FROSTY FRUIT CREAM

- 1 3-ounce package cream cheese
- 1 tablespoon lemon juice
- ⅛ teaspoon salt
- ¼ cup sugar
- 1 cup diced canned peaches, well drained
- 1 cup fresh blueberries, washed and well drained
- 2 cups (1 pint) sour cream
- Chicory
- Blueberry cream dressing

Set refrigerator control at coldest point.

Let cream cheese soften at room temperature. Gradually stir in lemon juice, salt, and sugar. Add peaches and blueberries, stirring until well blended. Fold in sour cream.

Pour into freezing tray lined with waxed paper or aluminum foil. Fold ends of waxed paper or aluminum foil over top of fruit salad. Freeze until firm, about 1½ to 2 hours.

Unmold on chilled platter on bed of chicory. If desired, garnish with additional peaches and blueberries and serve with blueberry cream dressing. Serves 6.

Blueberry Cream Dressing:

- 1 tablespoon lemon juice
- 1 to 2 tablespoon sugar
- ⅛ teaspoon salt
- ¼ cup crushed blueberries
- 1 cup sour cream

Add lemon juice, sugar, and salt to blueberries, mixing well. Fold in sour cream. Chill. Makes 1¼ cups.

FROZEN BANANA SALAD

4 ripe bananas
2 tablespoons lemon juice
1 cup heavy cream, whipped
½ cup mayonnaise
½ pound marshmallows, cut in pieces
3 pimientos, puréed, and juice
¾ teaspoon salt

Slice bananas and mix with lemon juice. Fold in whipped cream, mayonnaise, marshmallows, and pimientos. Add salt.

Mix well and turn into refrigerator trays. Freeze until stiff, about 3 hours.

To serve, cut into squares. Serve on lettuce or watercress with French dressing. Serves 6.

FROZEN ROQUEFORT CHEESE SALAD

¼ pound Roquefort cheese
2 tablespoons cream cheese
1 teaspoon lemon juice
1 cup celery, chopped fine
Chopped onion or chives
Paprika
1 cup heavy cream, whipped

Blend Roquefort and cream cheese with lemon juice, using a silver fork. Add remaining ingredients, folding in whipped cream. Freeze. Serves 6.

FROSTED STRAWBERRY SALAD

1 pint strawberries
1 10-ounce package marshmallows, cut small
2 3-ounce packages cream cheese
⅔ cup mayonnaise
1 cup heavy cream, whipped
Chicory

Wash and hull berries; reserve some for garnish and slice remaining ones.

Combine sliced berries with marshmallows and let stand while preparing other ingredients.

Mash cream cheese with fork and blend in mayonnaise. Fold in whipped cream. Fold in berry mixture and pour into freezing tray or loaf pan and freeze until firm.

Unmold on serving tray; garnish with chicory and whole strawberries. Slice and serve with additional mayonnaise, if desired. Serves 6 to 8.

Frosted Strawberry Salad

FROZEN CHICKEN SALAD

1 teaspoon (⅓ envelope) unflavored gelatin
2 tablespoons cold water
⅔ cup mayonnaise
1½ cups cold minced cooked chicken
¼ cup chopped blanched almonds
½ cup halved Malaga grapes
⅛ teaspoon salt
⅔ cup heavy cream, whipped

Soften gelatin in cold water 5 minutes, then dissolve over boiling water.

Cool and combine well with mayonnaise. Add other ingredients, folding in whipped cream last.

Turn into refrigerator tray and freeze. Slice and serve on crisp greens. Serves 6.

FROZEN VEGETABLE MEDLEY

¾ cup mayonnaise
1 cup finely shredded cabbage
1 cup chopped celery
½ cup raw grated carrot
¼ cup shredded green pepper
1 teaspoon grated onion
Salt and pepper
½ cup heavy cream, whipped

Add mayonnaise to vegetables and mix well. Season with salt and pepper; fold in whipped cream.

Turn into refrigerator tray. Freeze until firm. Serves 8.

FROZEN TOMATO MOUSSE

1¾ cups canned tomatoes
2 teaspoons vinegar
½ teaspoon minced onion
½ teaspoon salt
½ teaspoon celery seed
½ teaspoon allspice
1 tablespoon (1 envelope) unflavored gelatin
1½ cups heavy cream, whipped stiff

Simmer tomatoes, vinegar, and seasoning 15 minutes and strain carefully.

Add gelatin, which has been softened 5 minutes in ¼ cup cold water, and stir until dissolved.

Cool and, when partially congealed, fold in cream. Turn into refrigerator tray and freeze. Serve on bed of watercress. Garnish with latticed cucumber slices. Serves 6.

FROZEN CHICKEN, PINEAPPLE AND PECAN SALAD

1½ cups cold diced cooked chicken
¾ cup crushed pineapple
½ cup chopped pecans
1 cup salad dressing
1 cup heavy cream, whipped

Toss together chicken, pineapple, and nuts.

Fold salad dressing into whipped cream. Combine with chicken mixture. Freeze until firm.

Serve on crisp greens with or without dressing. Serves 6.

FROZEN SHRIMP SALAD

1 tablespoon (1 envelope) unflavored gelatin
½ cup cold chicken stock
1 cup minced cooked or canned shrimp
½ cup medium white sauce
⅓ teaspoon salt
Dash of cayenne pepper
½ cup mayonnaise
¾ cup heavy cream, whipped

Soften gelatin in stock, then melt over hot water. Add shrimp, white sauce, salt, and pepper.

Let cool until partially set, then thoroughly fold in mayonnaise which has been mixed with whipped cream. Turn into refrigerator tray and freeze.

Cut in squares and serve in lettuce cups with additional whipped cream and mayonnaise. Garnish with sliced sweet pickle. Serves 6.

FROZEN FRUIT SALAD

Finely cut fruit from 1 No. 1 can mixed fruits.

Combine with ½ cup fruit salad dressing or honey dressing and ½ cup heavy cream, whipped. Freeze. Serves 6.

SALAD DRESSINGS

HINTS FOR CHOOSING THE CORRECT SALAD DRESSING

Add sparkle to salads with extra-good dressings and garnishes. Try for contrast in texture, flavor and color when choosing salad dressings and garnishes. Serve salad dressing with the salad or pass it at the table.

What type of dressing to choose—sweet or tart, thick or thin—may be determined by your family's taste. Main-dish salads made with meat, fish, poultry, eggs, beans, cheese or potatoes usually call for a mayonnaise-type or cooked salad dressing. But some of these more substantial salads are good with tart French dressing—salad oil combined with lemon juice or vinegar plus seasonings.

Tart French dressing is the most likely choice for vegetable salads and vegetable-fruit combinations. But some vegetable salads may well take a mayonnaise or cooked dressing.

Reserve the sweet, clear French dressings for fruit salads. Mayonnaise made milder with whipped cream or thinned and sweetened with fruit juice is good for fruit salads too.

SALAD VINEGARS

There are 3 basic types of vinegars: cider vinegar, white vinegar, and wine vinegar. Herb vinegars may be made from any of them.

Do not keep herb vinegars in the refrigerator. If they become too strong after standing, simply dilute with the same type of vinegar from which they were made, or lemon juice may be used. Do this when using the vinegar.

TARRAGON VINEGAR

Put several sprigs of fresh tarragon or 2 tablespoons dried tarragon in vinegar. Proceed as directed for garlic vinegar.

SALAD DRESSINGS

GARLIC VINEGAR

Mash 6 garlic cloves through a garlic press into just slightly less than a pint of cider vinegar in a scalded pint jar.

Put uncovered jar in shallow pan of water. Bring water to boil and remove from heat. Let stand 45 minutes.

Remove from water to cool. Cover tightly. Let stand a week, shaking jar occasionally. Strain, bottle, and label.

MIXED HERB VINEGAR

Add a pinch each of basil, chopped chives, dill, oregano, parsley, tarragon, and thyme to 1 pint cider vinegar.

Place uncovered jar in pan of water. Bring to boil. Remove from heat and let stand 45 minutes.

Remove from water to cool. When cool, add 1 small onion which has been pierced many times with a fork. Let stand 1 week, then strain, bottle, and label.

QUICK SPICED VINEGAR

1 bottle cider vinegar
½ teaspoon cloves
½ teaspoon cinnamon
½ teaspoon mace
2 teaspoons sugar

To cider vinegar add a small spice bag composed of cloves, cinnamon, and mace.

Add sugar and let bottle stand in a warm place for 1 hour. Rebottle or use at once.

QUICK HERB VINEGAR

1 cup wine or cider vinegar
1 teaspoon dried crushed herbs (basil, tarragon, etc.)
2 tablespoons chopped parsley
1 tablespoon chopped chives

Combine vinegar and herbs. You may use this at once with salad oil.

You may add ½ clove of garlic and remove it later. Shortly before you serve it, add parsley and chives.

French Dressing

FRENCH DRESSING
(Master Recipe)

¼ teaspoon dry mustard
⅛ teaspoon freshly ground pepper
¾ teaspoon salt
¼ cup vinegar
¼ to ½ teaspoon paprika
1 teaspoon sugar
¾ cup salad oil

Measure all ingredients into a mixing bowl or glass jar. Beat with a fork or rotary beater or cover jar tightly and shake to mix thoroughly.

French dressing may be made in larger quantities and stored in the refrigerator. Always beat again or shake well just before serving. Makes 1 cup.

Variations of French Dressing

Grapefruit French Dressing: Use grapefruit juice instead of vinegar in master recipe.

Chiffonade Dressing: To master recipe add following finely chopped: 2 tablespoons parsley, 2 hard-cooked eggs, 2 tablespoons chopped red pepper, 1 tablespoon each chopped olives and cucumber pickle, and ¼ teaspoon paprika.

Chutney French Dressing: In master recipe, use half lemon juice and half vinegar. Add ¼ cup finely chopped chutney.

Cottage Cheese French Dressing: To master recipe add ¼ to ½ cup cottage cheese and shake.

Caesar Salad is the traditional western appetizer. Chef Caesar is credited with originating the salad during the heyday of the famous resort, Aqua Caliente.

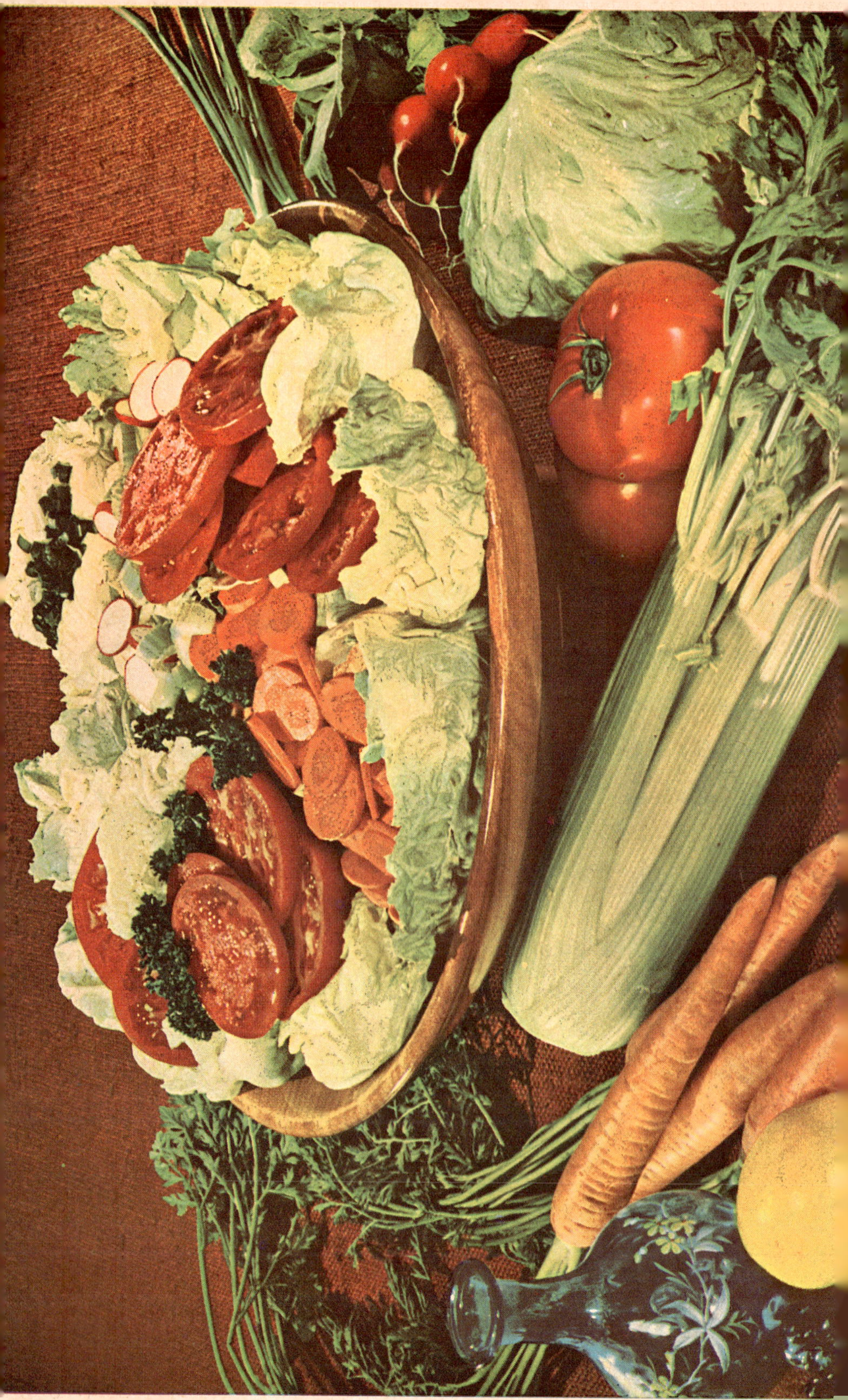

Cream Cheese French Dressing: Mash 1 3-ounce package cream cheese. Stir in French dressing to form a smooth paste. Add to remainder of French dressing and shake well.

Cream French Dressing: To master recipe add 2 tablespoons sweet or sour cream.

Cucumber French Dressing: To master recipe add 1 cup well drained, grated cucumber. Serve very cold with fish salads.

Curry French Dressing: To master recipe add ¾ teaspoon curry powder before beating.

Egg-Cheese French Dressing: To master recipe add 1 hard-cooked egg (chopped fine), 4 tablespoons grated American cheese, 1 tablespoon each chopped parsley and chives, and 1 tablespoon each chopped green pepper and pimiento.

Foamy French Dressing: Prepare cream French dressing and fold in 1 egg white, beaten until dry but not stiff.

Fruit French Dressing: In master recipe, substitute ¼ cup orange juice for ¼ cup vinegar. Add 1 tablespoon lemon juice. May be sweetened with additional sugar or corn syrup or honey.

Garlic French Dressing: Before preparing master recipe, pare and rub clove of garlic over bottom of bowl. If desired, clove of garlic may be left in dressing about 1 hour.

Ginger French Dressing: To master recipe add 1½ tablespoons finely chopped preserved ginger. Use on fruit salads.

Brandy French Dressing: To master recipe add 2 tablespoons brandy, 2 tablespoons tarragon vinegar, 6 tablespoons olive oil, and salt and pepper to taste.

Honey French Dressing: In master recipe, omit mustard and pepper. Add ½ cup strained honey and beat until frothy. Use on fruit salads.

Horseradish French Dressing: To master recipe add 2 tablespoons horseradish before serving.

Lemon French Dressing: In master recipe, substitute lemon juice for vinegar.

Lime French Dressing: In master recipe, use equal parts lime and lemon juice, or 3 tablespoons lime and 1 tablespoon lemon juice instead of vinegar.

Mint French Dressing: To master recipe add 1 tablespoon chopped mint.

Olive French Dressing: To master recipe add ¼ cup chopped olives before serving.

Roquefort French Dressing: Crumble ½ cup Roquefort cheese and add to French dressing before serving.

Spanish Dressing: To master recipe add ½ teaspoon chili powder.

Spicy French Dressing: To master recipe add 2 tablespoons prepared mustard and 2 teaspoons Worcestershire sauce.

Swiss Dressing: To master recipe add ¼ cup grated Swiss cheese and ¼ teaspoon Worcestershire sauce.

Tarragon French Dressing: In master recipe, use tarragon vinegar.

Tomato French Dressing: To master recipe add 2 teaspoons tomato juice and a few drops onion juice.

Vinaigrette French Dressing: Follow master recipe. Before beating, add 1 tablespoon chopped pickles, 1 tablespoon minced capers, 1 tablespoon chopped green olives, 1 tablespoon chopped pimiento, 1 teaspoon minced onion, and 1 teaspoon dry mustard.

"TRADITIONAL" FRENCH DRESSING

Many food experts insist this is the only "genuine" French dressing. To ½ cup vinegar (wine, cider, or malt vinegar) add ¾ teaspoon salt and ¼ teaspoon ground white pepper. Stir well with a fork and add 1½ cups olive oil. Beat the mixture with fork until it thickens.

For a garlic flavor, hang a garlic clove by a thread into the bottle containing the vinegar for at least 3 or 4 days before making the dressing.

LORENZO DRESSING

- ½ cup French dressing
- 2 tablespoons chopped watercress
- 2 tablespoons chili sauce
- 1 teaspoon minced pimiento
- 1 teaspoon minced chives or onion

Blend ingredients thoroughly and serve over salad greens. Makes ¾ cup.

HERB FRENCH DRESSING

- 1 teaspoon salt
- ½ teaspoon sugar
- ¼ teaspoon pepper
- ½ teaspoon dry mustard
- ½ teaspoon paprika
- ¼ cup vinegar
- ¾ cup salad oil
- 1 tablespoon mixed dried herbs
- ½ teaspoon Worcestershire sauce

Measure all ingredients into jar in order given. Cover and shake well. Chill.

Shake well again before serving. Makes 1 cup.

'FRISCO GREEN GODDESS DRESSING

- 1 cup mayonnaise
- 1 clove garlic, minced or grated
- 3 anchovies, chopped
- ¼ cup finely cut chives or green onions with tops
- ¼ cup chopped parsley
- 1 tablespoon tarragon vinegar
- 1 tablespoon fresh lemon juice
- ½ teaspoon salt
- Pepper, coarsely ground
- ½ cup sour cream, whipped

Combine ingredients, folding in the whipped sour cream after the other ingredients have been blended.

Tear iceberg lettuce into bite-sized pieces and toss with a generous amount of dressing. Makes 2 cups.

CREOLE FRENCH DRESSING

- 6 tablespoons salad oil
- ¼ cup ketchup
- ½ teaspoon Worcestershire sauce
- 1 tablespoon vinegar
- 1 tablespoon lemon juice
- 4 drops Tabasco sauce
- 1 teaspoon salt
- 1 teaspoon sugar
- ¼ teaspoon pepper
- ¼ teaspoon dry mustard

Measure ingredients into jar in order given. Cover and shake well. Chill.

Shake well again before serving. Makes about 1 cup.

SPECIAL FRENCH DRESSING

- 1 clove garlic, grated fine
- ½ cup sugar
- ⅓ cup mild vinegar
- 1 teaspoon Worcestershire sauce
- 1 small onion, grated
- ⅔ cup tomato ketchup
- 1 teaspoon salt
- 2 cups salad oil

Mix in order given and beat thoroughly. Pour into quart jar. Store in cool place.

LOUIS DRESSING

- ½ cup chili sauce
- ½ cup mayonnaise or salad dressing
- ½ cup creamy French dressing
- 1 teaspoon Worcestershire sauce

Slowly stir chili sauce into mayonnaise. Add French dressing and Worcestershire sauce. Mix well.

Serve with lettuce and tomato salads. Makes 1½ cups.

EVAPORATED MILK DRESSING

1/2 cup sugar
1/3 cup vinegar
1/2 cup evaporated milk
1/2 teaspoon salt

Add sugar to vinegar. Stir until sugar is dissolved. Beat in milk until mixture thickens. Add salt.

Pour over salad. Use fork to blend dressing through salad ingredients.

GRAPEFRUIT FRENCH DRESSING

4 tablespoons grapefruit juice
6 tablespoons salad oil
1/4 teaspoon salt
1/4 teaspoon paprika

Stir or shake well before serving. Serves 4 to 5.

Sweet Dressing: Add 1/4 cup red jelly.

GOLDEN DRESSING

2 tablespoons melted butter or margarine
2 tablespoons flour
1/3 cup sugar
1/8 teaspoon salt
1 cup pineapple juice
3/4 cup orange juice
2 tablespoons lemon juice
2 slightly beaten eggs
1 cup heavy cream, whipped

Blend butter and flour, mixing until smooth. Add sugar and salt. Stir in fruit juices and cook, stirring constantly, until smooth and thickened.

Add small amount of hot mixture to eggs; return to pan and cook 3 minutes longer. Cool.

Fold in whipped cream and serve with fruit salads.

This dressing will keep a week to 10 days in refrigerator if whipped cream is omitted. Add whipped cream just before serving. Makes 1 quart.

HONEY LIME DRESSING

Combine 2 parts honey and 1 part lime juice. Serve over chilled fruits.

Evaporated Milk Dressing

ITALIAN DRESSING
(Master Recipe)

1 clove garlic
1/2 teaspoon dry mustard
1/2 teaspoon salt
4 tablespoons wine vinegar
1/2 cup olive oil

Cut garlic clove in half. Mix mustard, salt, garlic, and vinegar thoroughly. Add oil and stir until all ingredients are blended.

Store in covered jar in cold place. Shake well just before using. Makes 3/4 cup.

Variations of Italian Dressing

Roquefort Cheese Italian Dressing: Crumble 2 ounces cheese. Add to dressing just before using.

Gorgonzola Cheese Dressing: Crumble 2 ounces cheese. Add to dressing just before using.

Other Variations: Most of the variations of French or cooked dressing may be used.

SALAD DRESSINGS

LOW CALORIE SALAD DRESSING

- 16 non-caloric sweetening tablets, crushed
- 2 beaten eggs
- 2 tablespoons cornstarch
- ½ teaspoon dry mustard
- 1 teaspoon celery seed
- Salt and pepper
- ¼ cup lemon juice
- 2 cups water

Add crushed non-caloric sweetening tablets to eggs and mix well. Add cornstarch, dry mustard, celery seed, salt, and pepper. Add lemon juice and mix well.

Add water. Cook over medium heat, stirring constantly, until mixture begins to thicken. Cool. Makes 40 tablespoons dressing, each containing 5 calories.

Tomato Salad Dressing: To 1 cup of low calorie salad dressing, add 1 cup tomato juice, 1 teaspoon grated onion, 8 non-caloric sweetening tablets, crushed, and 1 teaspoon cornstarch.

Mix well and cook over medium heat, stirring constantly, until mixture thickens. Cool. Makes 32 tablespoons dressing, each containing 5 calories.

Thousand Island Dressing: To 1 cup low calorie salad dressing, add ½ cup each chopped pimiento, chopped olives, chopped dill pickle, and chili sauce or ketchup.

Chop 1 hard-cooked egg fine and add to mixture. Makes 32 tablespoons, each containing 10 calories.

LOW CALORIE SALAD DRESSING #2

- 1 cup tomato juice
- 2 tablespoons salad oil
- 1 tablespoon Worcestershire sauce
- ¼ teaspoon salt
- 2 tablespoons vinegar
- ¼ cup grated onion
- 2 tablespoons chopped parsley
- ¼ teaspoon pepper

Combine all ingredients. Chill. Shake thoroughly for serving.

Salad Bowl with Mayonnaise

MAYONNAISE (Master Recipe)

- 1 whole egg or 2 egg yolks
- 1 teaspoon dry mustard
- 1 teaspoon salt
- 1 teaspoon syrup
- Pepper
- Cayenne pepper
- Dash of paprika
- 1½ cups cold salad oil
- 2 tablespoons vinegar or lemon juice

Combine the first 7 ingredients and beat thoroughly. Add oil 1 tablespoon at a time, beating thoroughly after each addition, until half the oil has been added.

Then add remaining oil in larger quantities, and lastly add vinegar or lemon juice. Makes 2 cups.

MAYONNAISE VARIATIONS

Use these variations with homemade or purchased mayonnaise.

Caper Mayonnaise: To 1 cup mayonnaise, add a scant ½ cup finely chopped well-washed capers.

Caviar Mayonnaise: To 1 cup mayonnaise add 1 tablespoon caviar.

SALAD DRESSINGS

Horseradish Caviar Mayonnaise: To 1 cup mayonnaise add 1 tablespoon each of drained horseradish and caviar.

Anchovy Caviar Mayonnaise: To 1 cup mayonnaise, add 4 washed, dried, and finely chopped anchovy fillets and 1 tablespoon caviar.

Chili Mayonnaise: To 1 cup mayonnaise add ¼ cup chili sauce, 1½ tablespoons vinegar, ¾ tablespoon Worcestershire sauce, and ¼ teaspoon chopped chives. Serve with fish salads.

Chutney Mayonnaise: To 1 cup mayonnaise add 1½ tablespoons chopped chutney.

Cranberry Mayonnaise: To 1 cup mayonnaise add 2 tablespoons well-beaten cranberry jelly and 1 teaspoon grated orange rind.

Whipped Cream Mayonnaise: Fold 1 cup mayonnaise into ⅓ cup heavy cream, whipped. Serve with fruit salads.

Whipped Cream Fruit Mayonnaise: Fold into 1 cup mayonnaise, ½ cup heavy cream, whipped, and ¼ cup each chopped almonds and currant jelly.

Green Mayonnaise: Color mayonnaise with green food coloring or spinach juice.

Honey Cream Dressing: Blend ¼ teaspoon dry mustard with 1 tablespoon honey and ½ teaspoon lemon juice. Add to mayonnaise. Serve with fruit salads.

Horseradish Mayonnaise: To 1 cup mayonnaise add 3 tablespoons prepared horseradish. Serve with cold beef.

Ideal Salad Dressing: To 1 cup mayonnaise add 2 tablespoons condensed tomato soup, ½ tablespoon lemon juice, 1 teaspoon Worcestershire sauce, and 1½ teaspoons powdered sugar.

Nippy Mayonnaise: To 1 cup mayonnaise add 3 teaspoons prepared horseradish, 3 teaspoons prepared mustard, and 1 small chopped sweet pickle. Serve with tomato salads, head lettuce, or salad bowl.

Piquante Mayonnaise: To 1 cup mayonnaise add 2 tablespoons each finely chopped olives and pickles and 1 teaspoon each chopped onion and chives.

Ravigotte Mayonnaise: Mix and chop ½ cup watercress, ½ cup parsley, 2 teaspoons chives, 1 tablespoon capers, and 4 anchovies.

Force mixture through fine sieve and add to 1 cup mayonnaise. Serve with fish and vegetable salads.

Red Beet Mayonnaise: To 1 cup mayonnaise add 1 tablespoon strained beet juice and 2 tablespoons finely chopped cooked beets.

Red Mayonnaise: Tint mayonnaise with red food coloring.

Roquefort Mayonnaise: To 1 cup mayonnaise add 2 tablespoons crumbled Roquefort cheese, a few drops Worcestershire sauce, 1 tablespoon French dressing, and 1 tablespoon minced chives.

Rum Cream Mayonnaise: To 1 cup mayonnaise add 1 teaspoon rum, mixed with ½ cup whipped cream, and add ¼ cup chopped toasted almonds. Serve with fruit salads.

Russian Dressing: To 1 cup mayonnaise add 1 chopped hard-cooked egg, ¼ cup chili sauce, and 2 tablespoons chopped green pepper.

Spicy Mayonnaise: To 1 cup mayonnaise add ¼ teaspoon each Worcestershire sauce, paprika, and dry mustard. Serve with fish, meat, or vegetable salads.

Thousand Island Dressing: To 1 cup mayonnaise add 2 tablespoons chili sauce, 2 tablespoons chopped green pepper, 2 tablespoons pimiento, and 2 tablespoons chopped sweet pickle. Serve with vegetable salads.

SALAD DRESSINGS

LEMON MAYONNAISE

1 egg or 2 egg yolks
¼ cup lemon juice
1 teaspoon mustard
1 teaspoon salt
1 tablespoon sugar
Dash of pepper or paprika
2 cups salad oil

Beat egg or egg yolks, 2 tablespoons lemon juice and seasonings thoroughly. Add salad oil very slowly until mixture begins to get very thick; then add remaining lemon juice. Gradually beat in the rest of the oil and continue beating until well combined. Makes about 2½ cups.

Orange "Marmalaise": To 1 cup lemon mayonnaise add ¼ cup orange marmalade and fold into ½ cup cream, whipped.

Palm Springs Dressing: Just before serving on a fruit salad add to lemon mayonnaise the following ingredients: grated orange rind, chopped toasted almonds, dates cut into slivers, and finely cut candied ginger.

FRUIT MAYONNAISE

⅓ cup grapefruit juice
½ cup mayonnaise
1½ teaspoons sugar

Blend thoroughly. Serves 8.

CUBAN AVOCADO MAYONNAISE

Put 1 average-sized peeled and pitted avocado through sieve, or in a blender for a few seconds until reduced to pulp. Put pulp in a bowl.

Stir in slowly 3 tablespoons olive oil, 1 tablespoon vinegar, 1 tablespoon lemon juice, salt and pepper to taste (increasing or decreasing these ingredients, in same proportion to taste and until proper consistency is obtained.)

Use as dressing on a salad of diced cold vegetables heaped on hollow of halved avocados. Serve cold on salad or fish, if desired.

Cooked Dressing

COOKED DRESSING
(Master Recipe)

¼ tablespoon salt
2 tablespoons sugar
1 tablespoon flour
¾ teaspoon dry mustard
Few grains cayenne
2 slightly beaten eggs
2 tablespoons butter or margarine
¾ cup milk
¼ cup vinegar or lemon juice

Sift dry ingredients; add eggs, butter, milk, and vinegar very slowly.

Stir and cook over boiling water until mixture begins to thicken. Strain and cool. Makes about 1 cup.

Note: For a thinner dressing use one egg yolk. Store covered until ready to use.

Cooked Dressing Variations

Almond and Cucumber Dressing: To cooled dressing add ½ cup diced cucumber and ¼ cup blanched and shredded almonds. Serve with fruit salad.

Banana Nut Dressing: To ¼ cup cooked dressing add 3 tablespoons peanut butter and 1 mashed banana. Thin with a little cream, if necessary. Serve with fruit salads.

Chutney Dressing: To ¾ cup cooked dressing add 2 tablespoons chopped chutney and ¼ cup whipped cream. Serve with fruit or vegetable salads.

Cream Dressing: In master recipe omit butter; use 1 cup light cream instead of milk.

Fruit Dressing: In master recipe increase flour to 2 tablespoons. Substitute 1 cup orange juice for milk.

Ham Salad Dressing: To 1 cup cooked dressing add ½ cup minced ham and 1 tablespoon minced green pepper. Serve with any vegetable or green salad.

Honey Dressing: In master recipe, substitute 2 to 4 tablespoons honey for sugar.

Peanut Butter Dressing: Prepare master recipe. Blend ¼ cup peanut butter with hot dressing after removing from heat.

Sardine Cooked Dressing: Skin, bone, and mash 6 sardines. Mix with 1 tablespoon lemon juice. Add to 1 cup cooked dressing. Serve with fish or vegetable salad.

Sour Cream Dressing: Prepare master recipe. Fold in 1 cup whipped sour cream when cool.

Toasted Nut Dressing: Prepare master recipe. Add ⅓ cup toasted chopped nuts when cool. Serve with potato, tomato, or plain fruit salads.

Whipped Cream Dressing: Prepare master recipe. Fold in ½ cup heavy cream, whipped, when cool.

BLUE CHEESE (OR ROQUEFORT) DRESSING

1 cup salad oil
½ cup cider vinegar
1½ teaspoons salt
Few grains cayenne
¼ teaspoon paprika
1½ teaspoons sugar
½ cup crumbled or chopped blue cheese (2 ounces)

Combine all ingredients but the cheese and beat with rotary beater.

Add cheese. Store in covered jar in refrigerator. Stir or shake well before using. Makes 1½ cups.

CONDENSED MILK SALAD DRESSING

2 teaspoons dry mustard
1½ teaspoons salt
½ teaspoon paprika
2 eggs
1 can condensed milk
⅓ cup melted butter or margarine
½ cup vinegar

Combine all ingredients in a large bowl. Beat thoroughly with rotary beater until thick. Pour into 2 pint jars. Cover.

If desired, whipped cream may be added before serving.

SOUR CREAM DRESSING FOR VEGETABLE OR FRUIT SALADS

1 cup thick sour cream
1 tablespoon lemon juice
1 tablespoon prepared horseradish
2 tablespoons sugar
½ teaspoon salt
⅛ teaspoon dry mustard

Whip sour cream; fold in remaining ingredients. Serve at once. Makes about 2 cups.

FRUIT SALAD DRESSING

½ cup orange juice
3 tablespoons lemon juice
¼ teaspoon salt
¼ teaspoon paprika
Few grains nutmeg

Shake well or stir just before serving. A delicious fresh fruit dressing, excellent for those who do not care for oil.

Cottage Cheese Salad Dressing

COTTAGE CHEESE SALAD DRESSING

2/3 cup sweetened condensed milk
1/2 cup creamed cottage cheese
6 tablespoons vinegar
1/2 teaspoon salt
3/4 teaspoon dry mustard
1/2 teaspoon paprika

Combine milk and cottage cheese. Add vinegar, salt, mustard, and paprika. Beat with rotary egg beater until mixture is well blended and thickened.

If thicker consistency is desired, chill before serving. Makes 1 1/2 cups.

WHIPPED CREAM DRESSING
(Master Recipe)

1/2 cup heavy cream
1/4 teaspoon salt
2 tablespoons lemon juice or vinegar
Few grains of pepper

Beat cream until stiff. Fold in other ingredients very slowly. Chill and add to salad just before serving.

Whipped cream dressing may be used as a sweet or savory dressing by the addition of flavorings and seasonings. It may be delicately tinted with a very small amount of liquid or paste food coloring.

Whipped Cream Dressing Variations

Anchovy Cream Dressing: Add 3 anchovy fillets, washed, dried, and minced fine, with 1 teaspoon grated lemon rind to 1 cup whipped cream dressing just before serving.

Caviar Cream Dressing: Add 1 tablespoon red or black caviar and a few drops onion juice to 1 cup whipped cream dressing just before serving.

Ginger Cream Dressing: Add 1 teaspoon chopped, candied ginger and 1 teaspoon grated lemon rind to 1 cup whipped cream dressing just before serving.

Savory Cream Dressing: Add 1/4 teaspoon anchovy paste and a little minced parsley and chives to 1 cup whipped cream dressing just before serving.

Horseradish Cream Dressing: Fold 2 tablespoons grated fresh horseradish into 1 cup whipped cream dressing just before serving. Omit vinegar in master recipe if bottled horseradish is used.

Jelly Cream Dressing: Add 1/2 cup tart red jelly, such as currant, cranberry, or raspberry, to 1 cup whipped cream dressing just before serving.

Mustard Cream Dressing: In master recipe, beat in 1 tablespoon prepared mustard as cream begins to thicken. Add salt to taste.

Nut Cream Dressing: Add 3 tablespoons chopped nuts to 1 cup whipped cream dressing just before serving.

California Cream Dressing: Add 1 tablespoon each chopped dates, figs, and raisins to 1 cup whipped cream dressing just before serving.

Pepper Cream Dressing: Add 1/3 cup finely chopped green pepper and 2 tablespoons finely chopped pimiento to 1 cup whipped cream dressing just before serving.

Gourmet Cream Dressing: Combine 1 tablespoon capers, well washed and finely minced, 1 tablespoon finely minced sweet-sour gherkins, and 1 teaspoon grated orange rind; add to 1 cup whipped cream dressing just before serving.

SANDWICH BOOK

SANDWICH-MAKING POINTERS

Bread for Sandwiches

● For more interesting sandwiches, use different kinds of bread—even in the same sandwich.

● To facilitate slicing and spreading of ordinary sandwiches, use day-old bread of firm texture.

● For rolled sandwiches, use very fresh bread.

SANDWICHES, HINTS

- For very thin, dainty sandwiches, buy unsliced bread and cut with a razor-sharp knife into slices not more than 1/4 inch thick. If many sandwiches are to be made, sharpen knife frequently.
- When a lot of sandwiches are to be made without crust, cut the crust from the loaf before slicing. Incidentally, sandwiches will stay moist longer if the crust is left on and there'll be no waste.
- For fancy sandwiches to be cut with cooky cutter, slice the bread lengthwise.

Butter for Sandwiches

- Cream butter or margarine until softened before spreading. Never melt butter. To facilitate creaming, keep butter at room temperature for about an hour.
- Butter prevents the sandwich from becoming soggy when a moist filling is used.
- For savory sandwiches, soften butter with mayonnaise; for sweet sandwiches, with a little cream or whipped cream.

Sandwich Fillings

- Sandwich fillings are often a blend of the cook's ingenuity and whatever there is on hand. The recipes and hints that follow should serve as suggestions—starting points for your imagination. An infinite variety of fillings will be developed from them.
- For additional fillings, refer to the spreads in the appetizer and salad sections. The canapé spreads should be used for dainty, attractive tea sandwiches.
- Use a variety of fillings for contrast in color, flavor, shape, and texture.
- Vegetables, such as cucumber, sliced tomato, and lettuce, should be prepared and added just before serving.
- Sliced fillings such as meat and cheese should be cut very thin and arranged to fit the sandwich.
- For color in fillings, add chopped pimiento, pepper, parsley, olives, or pickle.

To Keep Sandwiches

- If possible, avoid making sandwiches with moist fillings in advance, since the bread tends to become soggy.
- If sandwiches must be made in advance, wrap in waxed paper or slightly dampened cloth.
- To keep sandwiches for an hour or longer, wrap first in waxed paper, then in a damp cloth, and place in refrigerator.
- To prevent an interchange of flavors from various fillings, wrap each variety of sandwich separately in waxed paper.
- Ribbon, checkerboard, loaf, and other sandwiches, which have to be chilled or even frozen in the refrigerator, should always be well wrapped to preserve the flavor and prevent drying out.

Keep Frozen Sandwiches on Hand

- Sandwich fillings that freeze are those made of sliced cooked meat, meat loaf, chicken, or cheese.
- Sandwich spreads also lend themselves to freezing—especially those made of chopped or ground meat, chicken, canned fish (tuna, salmon, etc.), cheese, peanut butter.
- All sandwich fillings should be thoroughly chilled before being used.
- Butter both slices of bread before adding the filling. This will prevent the filling soaking into the bread.
- Work quickly and wrap each sandwich separately in moisture-vapor-proof freezer paper, excluding as much air as possible. Seal or tape and freeze.
- Sandwiches may be stored 2 to 3 months.
- When making sandwiches for the freezer, include a variety of breads such as white, cracked wheat, rye, raisin, or other family preferences.
- Pack sandwiches, right from freezer, in lunchbox.

Fancy Party Sandwiches

PARTY SANDWICH TRAYS

 Party glamor is added to the snack tray by a patterned arrangement of the sandwiches.

 Many of these tiny finger sandwiches can be prepared beforehand, chilled in the refrigerator and brought to the serving table freshly sliced and tempting.

2358 FANCY PARTY SANDWICHES

RIBBON SANDWICHES

Start with 2 slices white bread and 2 slices whole wheat.

Stack these alternately (light-dark-light-dark) with a filling of softened butter or margarine, cream cheese, meat or fish spread, jam or jelly between each slice.

Press stack firmly together and slice crusts from all sides.

Wrap tightly in waxed paper and chill in refrigerator for several hours.

Just before serving cut stack down into 1/4 inch thick ribbon slices.

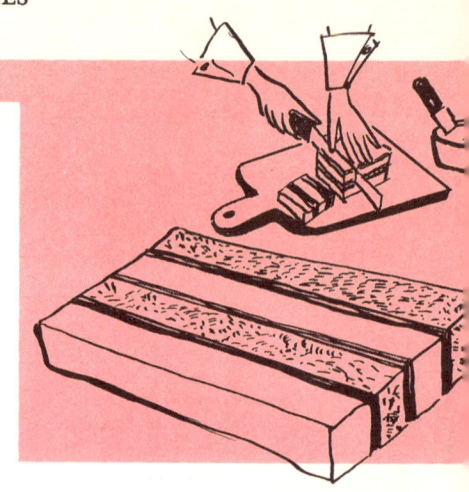

LITTLE LAYERS

Cut crusts from slices of sandwich bread. Spread with softened butter or margarine.

Cut into circles with a 2 1/2-inch biscuit cutter.

Use three rounds for each sandwich. Cover bottom round with pimiento cheese spread. Top with another circle of bread and spread with egg salad. Now place a buttered circle, plain side up, on top.

Frost sandwiches all over with cream cheese, moistened with a little cream.

CHECKERBOARD SANDWICHES

Prepare 2 stacks as directed for ribbon sandwiches.

Cut each stack into 1/2 inch slices. Then put 3 alternating slices together, with softened butter or a spread between, so that light and dark breads alternate to form a checkerboard design.

Wrap each block in waxed paper and chill for several hours.

To serve, remove from refrigerator and with a sharp knife, immediately cut each block crosswise into checkerboard slices, 1/2 inch thick.

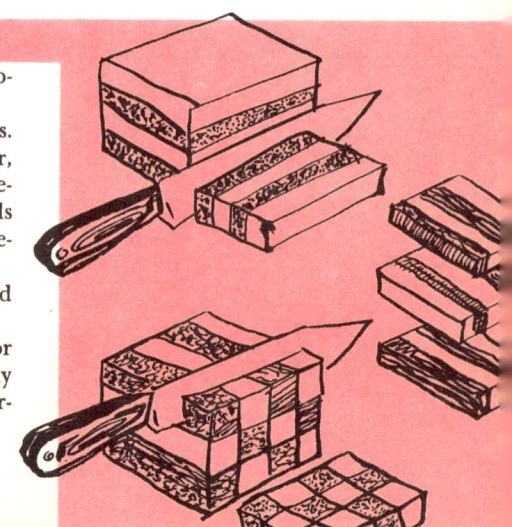

FANCY PARTY SANDWICHES **2359**

VALENTINE SANDWICHES

Trim crusts from slices of bread, then with a heart-shaped cooky cutter, cut out a heart design from the center of each slice.

Spread half of the "hearts" with sandwich filling and top with a matching heart.

Let the remaining portion of the bread, from which the heart was taken, serve as top or a second sandwich to eliminate waste of bread. Just trim the edges of the two slices to be sure they are the same size.

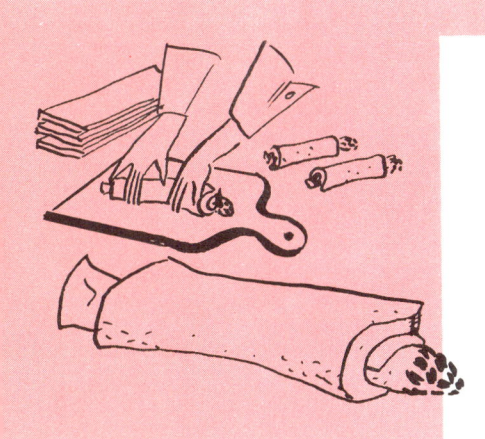

ROLL-UPS

Cut crusts from thin-sliced white or whole wheat bread. Lightly flatten out with rolling pin.

Spread with softened butter or margarine to keep bread from getting soggy.

Place asparagus tip, celery heart, or watercress sprig across one end of slice.

Roll up each slice jelly-roll fashion into a tight roll.

Cover with a damp cloth until serving time. Serve roll-ups whole or cut in half.

PINWHEELS

Using an unsliced loaf of bread, cut crusts off all sides.

Cut into lengthwise slices about 1/4 inch thick.

Run rolling pin lightly over the slices to make the bread easy to handle and less likely to crack.

Spread with softened butter or margarine, then if desired with a spread.

Arrange stuffed olives, pickles, or Vienna sausage across short end of bread.

Roll up tightly as you do a jelly roll. Wrap rolls individually in waxed paper or aluminum foil, twisting ends securely. Chill several hours or overnight.

To serve, cut each chilled roll down into 1/4 to 1/2 inch slices.

Ham 'n' Egg Salad Sandwich Loaf

Sandwich Loaves

HAM 'N' EGG SALAD SANDWICH LOAF

Remove crusts from small loaf of unsliced bread, leaving top rounded. Cut in 3 lengthwise slices.

Spread bottom slice with egg filling (below); cover with middle slice. Spread with ham filling (below). Cover with rounded top slice.

Wrap in waxed paper. Chill. Frost thinly with mayonnaise.

Garnish with "flowers" made of pimiento strips and capers and sprays of chicory. Cut in slices to serve. Serves 8.

Egg Filling:

4 hard-cooked eggs, chopped
2 tablespoons minced green pepper
Few grains pepper
1/4 teaspoon Ac'cent
2 tablespoons mayonnaise

Combine all ingredients; mix well.

Ham Filling:

1/4 pound cooked ham, ground
3 tablespoons minced celery
Few grains pepper
1/4 teaspoon Ac'cent
1 1/2 tablespoons mayonnaise

Combine all ingredients; mix well.

YULE LOG SANDWICH

Prepare the following fillings: Deviled ham-peanut butter; egg-bacon; avocado-pineapple; cheese-shrimp; cranberry-cheese.

Remove crusts from an unsliced loaf of enriched bread and cut lengthwise into 5 slices.

Butter slices and spread each with one of the first four fillings as named. Stack and top with 5th bread slice.

Press loaf firmly together. Wrap in waxed paper and chill for 1 hour.

Frost top and sides of loaf with cranberry-cheese mixture, making lengthwise ridges with a spatula.

Garnish platter with cinnamon pear halves set on lettuce leaves, with their cherry bell clappers. Cut into thick slices to serve.

Sandwich Fillings for Yule Log

Deviled Ham-Peanut Butter: Combine 1/3 cup peanut butter, a 3-ounce can deviled ham, 1/4 cup mayonnaise, 3 tablespoons chopped dill pickle.

Egg-Bacon: Combine 2 chopped hard-cooked eggs, 1/3 cup chopped cooked bacon, 3 tablespoons mayonnaise.

Avocado-Pineapple: Combine 1/3 cup mashed avocado, 2 tablespoons drained crushed pineapple, 1 teaspoon lemon juice, 1 tablespoon mayonnaise, and a dash of salt.

Cheese-Shrimp: Combine 1/2 cup pimiento cream cheese, 1/2 teaspoon chili sauce, 1/3 cup finely chopped cooked shrimp, and 1/2 teaspoon lemon juice.

Cranberry-Cheese: Combine two 3-ounce packages cream cheese with 2/3 cup strained cranberry sauce, mixing with a rotary beater until smooth.

POOR BOY SANDWICH

This hearty snack, native to New Orleans, is made in dozens of different ways, depending on the tastes of the maker and what is available.

A medium-long, thin loaf of French bread is slit in half lengthwise and generously buttered. Then the loaf is sliced in thirds or fourths, not quite through the bottom crust. A different kind of filling goes in each section.

Fried oysters almost invariably go in one part. The other sections can be filled with slices of well seasoned tomato with a slice of broiled bacon, another with sausage, chicken salad, fried egg with hot chili sauce, or chopped green pepper and onion, and so on, using any appetizing tidbit desired.

TURKEY 'N' CRANBERRY ROUNDS

- 18 slices bread
- 4 tablespoons softened butter or margarine
- 1 1-pound can jellied cranberry sauce
- 3/4 cup diced turkey
- 3 tablespoons sliced olives
- 3 tablespoons chopped pickle
- 1/4 cup diced celery
- 1 tablespoon minced onion
- 3 tablespoons mayonnaise
- 1/2 teaspoon salt
- 1 teaspoon poultry seasoning, optional
- 3 3-ounce packages cream cheese, softened

Cut bread slices into rounds the size of cranberry slices. Spread with softened butter or margarine.

Cut cranberry sauce into 6 plump slices. Place a slice on 6 rounds of bread.

Top each with 2nd round of bread. Spread 2nd round with turkey filling made by combining turkey, olives, pickles, celery, onion, mayonnaise, salt, and poultry seasoning.

Top with 3rd bread round. Frost with cheese. Serves 6.

BAKED TUNA OR SALMON SANDWICH LOAF

- 1 medium loaf white or whole wheat bread
- 1 6-ounce can tuna or salmon
- 3 hard-cooked eggs, chopped
- 1 can condensed mushroom soup
- 1/2 teaspoon celery salt
- 1/4 teaspoon onion salt
- Dash of pepper
- 1/4 cup melted shortening or salad oil
- 1/3 cup milk

Remove crusts from the loaf of bread and slice lengthwise in thirds.

Combine tuna and eggs and moisten with 1/3 cup of the mushroom soup. Season with celery and onion salt and pepper. Spread filling between bread slices.

Brush top and sides of loaf with melted shortening or oil. Bake in moderate oven (375°F.) 20 minutes or until lightly browned.

Add milk to remaining soup; heat and serve as a sauce. Serves 6.

Turkey 'n' Cranberry Rounds

Hot Chicken Salad Loaf

HOT CHICKEN SALAD LOAF

- 1 (1 pound) loaf day-old white bread, unsliced
- 1 tablespoon soft butter or margarine
- 1½ cups chopped, cooked chicken
- ¾ cup finely chopped celery
- 2 teaspoons chopped onion
- 1½ teaspoons chopped parsley
- ½ cup mayonnaise or salad dressing
- ¼ teaspoon salt
- Dash of pepper

With a sharp knife, remove crusts from loaf of bread to make an even, box-shaped loaf. Cut a lengthwise slice from the top.

Hollow out the center of loaf, leaving sides and bottom at least ½ inch thick. Spread butter on inside walls of the cavity. (Save center of loaf for breadcrumbs or stuffing.)

Combine chicken, celery, onion, parsley, mayonnaise, salt, and pepper. Fill center of the loaf with chicken salad.

Cover with top slice of bread. Wrap loaf with heavy waxed paper. Chill in refrigerator for 6 hours.

Loaf Topping: Beat 2 egg whites until stiff. Fold in ¼ cup mayonnaise and a dash of salt.

To Complete Loaf: Unwrap and spread top and sides of loaf with topping mixture. Place on cooky sheet and brown in very hot oven (450°F.) 10 minutes. Serve hot and cut crosswise into 6 sections. Serve with whole cranberry sauce. Serves 6.

GOURMET SANDWICH LOAF

- 4 hard-cooked eggs
- 1 cup finely chopped cooked turkey
- ¼ cup chopped sweet pickles or pickle relish
- 1 can cream of mushroom soup
- Salt and pepper
- 12 slices bread
- 2 tablespoons softened butter or margarine
- ¼ cup milk

Chop 2 of the eggs. Combine with turkey, pickles, and half of the soup. Season to taste with salt and pepper.

Trim crusts from bread and cut slices in half to make 24 pieces. Place 6 pieces of bread close together on baking sheet or heat-proof serving platter. Spread with turkey mixture. Top with layer of bread.

Repeat until there are 3 layers of turkey and 4 layers of bread. Brush top with softened butter.

Bake in moderate oven (375°F.) until lightly browned, 15 minutes.

Blend milk with remaining soup. Heat to boiling. Add remaining chopped eggs. Serve over 6 sandwiches.

SANDWICH LOAVES **2363**

FROSTED SALMON SANDWICH LOAF

1 large loaf bread
Butter or margarine
1 small can salmon
3 tablespoons chopped pickle
Mayonnaise
2 large tomatoes
Salt and pepper to taste
½ green pepper, chopped
1 cup grated raw carrots
½ cup chopped celery
¾ pound cream cheese
1½ cups cream

Remove crusts from bread. Cut into four slices lengthwise. Spread each slice with softened butter.

Drain and flake salmon. Combine with chopped pickle, moisten with mayonnaise, and spread on first slice.

Cover second slice of bread with sliced tomatoes. Season.

Combine green pepper with mayonnaise. Spread over sliced tomatoes.

Combine grated carrots and chopped celery. Season with salt and pepper, moisten with mayonnaise, and spread on third slice of bread.

Put the four slices together, press into loaf shape, wrap tightly in waxed paper. Chill.

Spread top and sides with cream cheese softened with cream. Keep in refrigerator until ready to serve.

Garnish with radish roses, parsley, carrot strips, stuffed olives, pimiento, etc. Cut into 1-inch-thick slices.

MEAT STUFFED RYE LOAF

1 large onion, sliced
2 tablespoons fat
½ pound ground beef
¼ cup chopped parsley
1 carrot, grated
2 teaspoons salt
1 tablespoon chili sauce
¼ teaspoon pepper
¼ teaspoon paprika
1 loaf rye bread, unsliced
1 medium onion, grated

Cook sliced onion in fat until lightly browned. Add beef, and cook until browned. Add parsley, carrot, and seasonings; cook 5 minutes.

Cut a slice from one end of bread, and put aside; take out soft center of bread, and mix with meat mixture. Add grated onion, ½ cup water; mix well; stuff into loaf. Put back cut slice, and fasten with toothpicks.

Bake in moderate oven (350°F.) 25 minutes. Slice to serve. Serves 4.

Frosted Salmon Sandwich Loaf

Vary not only the bread and fillings but also the way you cut the sandwiches.

Cheese Sandwiches

RELISH CHEESE FILLING

  2 3-ounce packages cream cheese
  3 tablespoons India or pickle relish
  1/8 teaspoon salt

Soften cream cheese at room temperature; blend with relish and salt. Makes spread for 6 to 8 sandwiches.

CREAM CHEESE AND CARROT FILLING

Mix cream cheese with 1/3 as much grated raw carrot. Cover with watercress.

CREAMY CHEESE FILLING

  1/4 cup mayonnaise
  3 3-ounce packages cream cheese
  1/4 cup chopped green pepper
  1 1/2 teaspoons minced onion

Blend all ingredients to spreading consistency. Makes 1 1/3 cups.

PINEAPPLE-CREAM CHEESE FILLING

  1 3-ounce package cream cheese
  1/4 cup crushed pineapple

Combine cream cheese and crushed pineapple. Makes 4 sandwiches.

BACON-CHEESE FILLING

1 3-ounce package cream cheese
1/4 cup chopped cooked bacon
1/2 teaspoon horseradish
1/2 teaspoon Worcestershire sauce
1 tablespoon milk

Blend all ingredients well. Store in refrigerator until used.

SAVORY GRATED CHEESE FILLING

Mix grated Parmesan or American cheese with onion juice, butter, and chopped parsley.

COTTAGE CHEESE-CUCUMBER FILLING

1 large cucumber
1 tablespoon grated onion
1/2 teaspoon salt
1 pint cottage cheese
Dash of pepper

Peel cucumber and remove seeds. Grate or grind and mix with onion and salt. Put in a strainer and let set over a bowl until just ready to make sandwiches.

Mix well with cottage cheese and dash of pepper. Additional salt to taste may be added. Makes 8 to 10 sandwiches.

COTTAGE CHEESE-GREEN PEPPER FILLING

1/2 pound dry cottage cheese
1/3 cup evaporated milk
1 teaspoon salt
1/8 teaspoon pepper
3 tablespoons chopped green pepper
1 tablespoon minced onion

Cream cottage cheese with evaporated milk until smooth. Add salt, pepper, green pepper, and minced onion. Mix well. Makes 5 sandwiches.

COTTAGE CHEESE-OLIVE-PIMIENTO FILLING

Mix creamed cottage cheese with chopped olives and chopped pimiento.

CREAM CHEESE, JELLY AND NUT SANDWICHES

For each sandwich, trim the crusts from three slices of whole wheat bread. Spread one of these slices with jelly, the second with margarine or butter and the third with softened cream cheese. Sprinkle the cream cheese with chopped nuts.

Put the three slices of bread together to make a sandwich and cut the sandwich in quarters diagonally. Arrange the quarter sandwiches on a chop plate, points upward.

CREAM CHEESE-DRIED BEEF FILLING

1 3-ounce package cream cheese
2 tablespoons milk
1/4 cup shredded dried beef
1 teaspoon grated onion

Cream the cream cheese with milk. Add shredded dried beef and grated onion. Blend well. Makes 1/2 cup.

CREAMY CHEESE-OLIVE FILLING

1 3-ounce package cream cheese
1 to 2 tablespoons milk or cream
1/3 cup chopped ripe olives
Dash of Tabasco sauce
Salt to taste

Soften cheese and gradually blend in milk to make spreading consistency. Blend in olives and seasonings to taste. Makes about 1 cup.

Cream Cheese, Jelly and Nut Sandwiches

Fish and Shellfish Sandwiches

Jumbo Sandwiches

AVOCADO-SHRIMP FILLING

1 cup minced avocado
½ cup chopped cooked shrimp
1 tablespoon lemon juice
¼ cup mayonnaise or salad dressing

Combine all ingredients well.

SHRIMP SPECIAL FILLING

1 cup chopped, cooked or canned shrimp
3 tablespoons chopped celery
¼ teaspoon salt
1 teaspoon lemon juice
Mayonnaise

Combine all ingredients well and moisten with mayonnaise.

ANCHOVY FILLING

½ cup mashed anchovies or anchovy paste
¼ cup chopped olives
¼ cup butter or margarine

Mix ingredients together to form a smooth paste. Store in refrigerator. Makes 1 cup.

JUMBO SANDWICHES

1 No. 1 can or 2 cups salmon, boned and flaked
1 tablespoon lemon juice
1 cup finely chopped celery
½ cup mayonnaise or salad dressing
¾ teaspoon salt
1 loaf Vienna bread
¼ cup soft butter or margarine
6 lettuce leaves
6 tomato slices

Combine salmon, lemon juice, celery, mayonnaise, and salt.

Cut bread in half lengthwise and spread butter on both cut sides. Place lettuce leaves on bottom half and spread salmon salad over lettuce.

Arrange tomato slices over salmon salad. Cover tomatoes with top half of bread loaf.

To serve: Cut into 6 portions, using tomato slices as a guide to the size of each sandwich. Makes 6 Jumbo Sandwiches.

FISH AND SHELLFISH SANDWICHES

FLAKED FISH FILLING #1

- 1 cup canned fish flakes
- 1 tablespoon chopped celery
- 1 tablespoon chopped pickle (sweet or sour)
- 3 tablespoons mayonnaise
- 1/2 tablespoon horseradish
- 1/4 teaspoon salt
- 1/8 teaspoon pepper

Combine all ingredients and mix well.

FLAKED FISH FILLING #2

Mix flaked tuna with chopped celery and chopped nuts. Moisten with mayonnaise.

FLAKED FISH FILLING #3

Mix flaked tuna with chopped pickle and crushed pineapple. Moisten with French dressing.

FLAKED FISH FILLING #4

Combine 1 cup salmon, tuna, or other canned seafood with 1/2 cup chopped celery. Moisten with mayonnaise.

TUNA AND EGG FILLING

Combine 1 cup flaked tuna, 2 chopped hard-cooked eggs, and 1/4 cup chopped stuffed olives. Moisten with mayonnaise.

SALMON SALAD FILLING

- 1 1/2 cups flaked salmon
- 1/4 cup chopped celery
- 1 tablespoon chopped green pepper
- 2 tablespoons salad dressing

Combine salmon, celery, and green pepper. Add salad dressing and mix thoroughly. Makes 1 1/2 cups filling, enough for 6 sandwiches.

TUNA-SLAW SUBMARINES

- 2 tablespoons mayonnaise or salad dressing
- 2 tablespoons chili sauce
- 1 tablespoon lemon juice
- Dash of salt
- 1 can (7 ounces) tuna, drained and flaked
- 2 small loaves or 1 large loaf French bread
- 1 cup cole slaw, well drained

Blend mayonnaise or salad dressing, chili sauce, lemon juice, and salt; add tuna; toss lightly.

Split French bread lengthwise almost through; spread with additional mayonnaise or salad dressing; line with lettuce, if desired.

Fill first with tuna mixture, then with slaw. Cut in serving-sized slices. Serves 4.

SARDINE-EGG FILLING

Combine 1 can drained, mashed sardines and 2 chopped hard-cooked eggs. Moisten with lemon juice to taste.

SALAD FILLED ROLLS

- 2/3 cup ripe olives
- 2 hard-cooked eggs
- 1 7-ounce can tuna
- 3/4 cup chopped celery
- 1/2 cup mayonnaise
- 6 finger rolls
- Butter or margarine
- Lettuce

Cut olives into large pieces. Dice eggs. Drain oil from tuna and flake coarsely. Combine olives, eggs, tuna, and celery and blend lightly with mayonnaise.

Cut rolls in half leaving one side attached, and hollow slightly. Butter insides, and heap with filling. Tuck a crisp lettuce leaf inside each roll. Serves 6.

Salad Filled Rolls

Arrangement for make-your-own sandwich tray.

TUNA-APPLE FILLING

1 cup flaked tuna
¾ cup diced apple
1 tablespoon lemon juice
½ teaspoon salt
⅛ teaspoon pepper
½ cup finely minced celery
4 tablespoons mayonnaise

To flaked tuna add diced apple, lemon juice, salt, pepper, and celery. Mix well.

Add mayonnaise and keep in refrigerator. Makes 2½ cups filling.

SARDINE-PICKLE FILLING

1 4-ounce can sardines, packed in oil, drained, flaked
1 dill pickle, chopped or 2 tablespoons plus 1 teaspoon sweet pickle relish
1 tablespoon softened butter or margarine
1 teaspoon prepared mustard
1 tablespoon salad dressing or mayonnaise

Combine ingredients and spread on toast. Makes spread for 4 sandwiches.

SARDINE FILLING #1

Cream sardines with melted butter, flavored with salt, cayenne, and a generous amount of horseradish. Moisten with lemon juice.

SARDINE FILLING #2

Combine 1 can of mashed drained sardines, ½ cup finely chopped peeled cucumber (seeds removed), and lemon juice to taste.

SARDINE FILLING #3

Mix sardines with chopped hard-cooked eggs, grated cheese, butter, and lemon juice. Season with curry powder.

SHRIMP BUTTER FILLING

½ pound shrimp, cooked and cleaned
½ cup soft butter or margarine
Salt and pepper to taste
1 tablespoon lemon juice
½ teaspoon Tabasco or 1 teaspoon Worcestershire (if desired)

Grind shrimp using meat chopper or blender. Combine with remaining ingredients.

SALMON BOATS

1 can (7¾ or 8 ounces) salmon, drained and flaked
1 cup diced celery
¼ cup salad dressing
2 hard-cooked eggs, chopped
½ teaspoon onion salt
⅛ teaspoon pepper
6 frankfurter rolls
Lettuce

Combine salmon, celery, salad dressing, eggs, and seasonings.

Split 6 frankfurter rolls; line with lettuce; spoon salmon salad into rolls. Makes 6 salad rolls.

EGG-ANCHOVY FILLING

Cream yolks of hard-cooked eggs with butter and anchovy paste.

Egg Sandwiches

Prepare hearty sandwich stacks in advance; store in refrigerator until serving time. To prevent soaking of the bread spread the rounds with butter between each filling.

DEVILED EGG FILLING

3 hard-cooked eggs
3 teaspoons chopped parsley
3 teaspoons vinegar
1/8 teaspoon dry mustard
1/4 teaspoon salt
1/8 teaspoon pepper

Chop hard-cooked eggs fine. Combine with parsley, vinegar, dry mustard, salt, and pepper. Blend well.

EGG-BACON FILLING

4 chopped hard-cooked eggs
6 slices chopped crisp bacon
3 tablespoons chopped olives
1/4 teaspoon salt
Mayonnaise

Combine hard-cooked eggs, bacon, olives, and salt. Moisten with mayonnaise.

EGGS AND LIVER FILLING

4 chopped, hard-cooked eggs
1/2 cup minced cooked liver
Salt and pepper
Prepared horseradish
Mayonnaise

Combine hard-cooked eggs with minced cooked liver. Season with salt and pepper and prepared horseradish. Moisten with mayonnaise.

EGG-FRANKFURTER FILLING

2 hard-cooked eggs
2 cooked frankfurters, ground
1 cup finely cut celery
1 teaspoon salt
1/3 cup salad dressing

Chop hard-cooked eggs. Combine with frankfurters, celery, salt, and salad dressing. Chill. Makes 1 1/2 cups.

EGG AND WATERCRESS FILLING

Mix chopped hard-cooked egg, watercress, and mayonnaise.

EGG-CELERY FILLING

3 hard-cooked eggs
Salt and pepper
1/2 cup finely chopped celery
Mayonnaise or prepared sandwich spread

Chop hard-cooked eggs well. Season with salt and pepper. Mix with celery and mayonnaise or prepared sandwich spread. Makes 4 sandwiches.

EGGS AND SPINACH FILLING

Mix ground hard-cooked eggs with half the amount of spinach.

EGG-HAM FILLING

Combine 4 chopped hard-cooked eggs and 1/4 to 1/2 cup chopped boiled ham. Moisten with mayonnaise.

EGGS AND KETCHUP FILLING

Moisten ground hard-cooked eggs with ketchup.

EGG SALAD FILLING

3 hard-cooked eggs
1/4 cup chopped ripe olives
1/4 cup mayonnaise
1/4 teaspoon prepared mustard
1/4 teaspoon salt
Black pepper to taste

Chop eggs and blend with remaining ingredients. Makes about 1 cup.

"Ranch Foreman" Sandwich

Fruit and Vegetable Sandwiches

"RANCH FOREMAN" SANDWICH

Snip dried figs into small pieces right onto bread richly spread with peanut butter, and sprinkled with broken peanut or walnut meats. Sprinkle lightly with brown sugar if desired.

DRIED FRUIT-NUT FILLING

1/2 cup finely chopped raisins, figs, and dates
1/2 cup chopped nuts
1/8 teaspoon salt
5 teaspoons mayonnaise
Few drops lemon juice

Combine all ingredients well. Store in covered jar in refrigerator. Makes 4 sandwiches.

CARROT-PEANUT FILLING

1 cup finely grated carrots
1/2 cup finely chopped salted peanuts
3 tablespoons mayonnaise
1/4 teaspoon salt

Combine all the ingredients. Spread generously between buttered slices of whole wheat bread.

CELERY-ALMOND FILLING

Mix chopped celery and chopped almonds. Moisten with mayonnaise.

COTTAGE CHEESE-RAISIN FILLING

Chop 1/2 cup seedless raisins and mix with 1 cup cream-style cottage cheese. Good on white bread.

CARROT-RAISIN FILLING

Chop 1/3 cup seedless raisins and blend with 1 cup grated carrot and 3 tablespoons mayonnaise. Good on very dark wheat bread.

CHEESE-RAISIN FILLING

Chop 1/2 cup seedless raisins and mix with 1 cup grated American cheese and 1/4 cup mayonnaise. Good on rye bread.

RED KIDNEY OR LIMA BEAN FILLING

2 cups cooked beans, well drained and pressed through a colander
2 tablespoons pickle relish
1 teaspoon salt
Paprika
1 tablespoon mayonnaise

Mix well and spread on buttered bread, rye, whole wheat or soya. Makes 6 sandwiches.

FRUIT AND VEGETABLE SANDWICHES

BANANA RAISIN SANDWICHES

1 cup chopped raisins
1 teaspoon salt
Mayonnaise or salad dressing
8 slices bread
2 fully-ripe bananas
Butter or margarine

Mix together raisins and salt in mixing bowl. Add enough mayonnaise or salad dressing to moisten.

Spread 4 slices of bread with raisin mixture. Peel bananas and slice on top of raisin mixture.

Cover with remaining slices of bread spread with butter or margarine. Makes 4 sandwiches.

CUCUMBER-RADISH FILLING

Slice cucumbers thin. Top with thinly sliced radishes. Moisten with mayonnaise.

MUSHROOM FILLING

4   6-ounce packages mushrooms
4   tablespoons butter or margarine
2   tablespoons chopped onion
$1\frac{1}{2}$ tablespoons chopped green pepper
2   to 4 tablespoons flour
2   tablespoons cream

Chop mushrooms fine. Pan fry mushrooms in butter with the onion and green pepper. Add just enough flour to take up the butter.

When they begin to brown, add cream. Season with salt and pepper. Cool. Makes 8 to 10 sandwiches.

RAW VEGETABLE FILLING

1 cup chopped raisins
$\frac{1}{2}$ cup shredded cabbage
$\frac{1}{2}$ cup shredded carrots
$\frac{1}{2}$ cup chopped apple
1 tablespoon lemon juice
4 tablespoons salad dressing

Combine all ingredients well. Makes 4 sandwiches.

DATE-NUT FILLING

Mix ground dates and chopped nuts. Moisten with orange juice.

COMBINATION FILLING

$\frac{1}{2}$ cup seedless raisins
$\frac{1}{2}$ cup shredded carrots
$\frac{1}{2}$ cup cottage cheese
$\frac{1}{8}$ teaspoon salt
1 tablespoon mayonnaise

Combine all ingredients well. Makes 4 sandwiches.

OLIVE-NUT FILLING

$\frac{1}{2}$ cup chopped ripe olives
$\frac{1}{2}$ cup finely chopped nuts
$\frac{1}{4}$ cup mayonnaise
Salt to taste

Combine olives, nuts, mayonnaise, and salt.

Finely chopped celery may also be added if desired.

Makes about 1 cup.

Ripe bananas—decorative and satisfying—when used with a variety of spreads.

Whole-Meal Sandwich

Meat and Poultry Sandwiches

WHOLE-MEAL SANDWICH

For each serving, butter a large round slice of rye bread. Place butter-side-up on dinner plate.

First put on several leaves of head lettuce, then a layer of thin slices of Swiss cheese.

Then add large lettuce cup, reverse side up. Cover it with slices of white meat of chicken. Now pour Thousand Island dressing over all.

Top with a tomato slice, then a hard-cooked egg slice. Garnish sandwich with crisp, hot bacon slices, ripe olives, and topper of parsley.

CHICKEN-RIPE OLIVE FILLING #1

Combine 1 cup chopped cooked chicken with ½ cup chopped celery and ¼ cup chopped olives. Moisten with mayonnaise.

CHICKEN-RIPE OLIVE FILLING #2

Chop cold cooked chicken. Add chopped ripe olives. Moisten with mayonnaise.

CHICKEN-ALMOND FILLING

1 cup chopped cooked chicken
3 tablespoons chopped toasted almonds
2 tablespoons salad dressing
1 tablespoon lemon juice
Salt and pepper

Combine all ingredients. Spread on slices of white bread. Makes 4 sandwiches.

MOCK PÂTÉ FILLING

Blend liverwurst with cream cheese. Season with grated onion.

MOCK CHICKEN FILLING

1 cup coarsely ground cooked veal
½ cup chopped or shredded raw carrots
½ cup chopped celery
2 tablespoons chow chow
3 tablespoons mayonnaise
Salt to taste

Combine all ingredients and mix thoroughly. Makes 5 sandwiches.

CHICKEN SALAD FILLING #1

1 cup minced, cooked or canned chicken
½ cup minced celery
¼ cup mayonnaise or salad dressing
½ teaspoon salt
⅛ teaspoon pepper
Pinch of Ac'cent
¼ teaspoon prepared mustard

Combine all ingredients. Makes 4 sandwiches.

CHICKEN SALAD FILLING #2

3 cups minced cooked chicken or turkey
1 cup minced celery
1 pimiento, minced
6 large stuffed olives, minced
Salad dressing to moisten

Mix all ingredients and season to taste.

Spread liberally between slices of light or dark bread. A leaf of lettuce may be added. Spreads 12 whole sandwiches.

Note: The same mixture may be used for salad if meat and celery is cubed rather than minced.

MARMALADE CHICKEN FILLING

¼ cup orange marmalade
2 tablespoons mayonnaise
1½ cups chopped cooked chicken
2 tablespoons finely chopped nuts

Blend orange marmalade and mayonnaise together. Carefully stir in chicken and nuts; mix. May be stored in a covered refrigerator jar. Makes 1¾ cups.

CHICKEN OR TURKEY-ALMOND FILLING #2

Moisten chopped, cooked chicken or turkey with mayonnaise or salad dressing. Add finely chopped almonds. Season with salt and pepper.

ZESTY CHICKEN LIVER FILLING

3 slices bacon
½ pound chicken livers
¼ pound chopped mushrooms
1 tablespoon minced onion
¾ teaspoon salt
Dash of pepper
8 slices rye bread

Fry bacon until crisp. Remove from skillet.

In bacon drippings, sauté chicken livers with mushrooms until tender.

Turn into chopping bowl with bacon; chop fine. Add onion, salt, and pepper. Blend well. Makes 4 sandwiches.

LIVER-EGG FILLING

⅔ pound steamed pork liver
2 hard-cooked eggs
1 small chopped onion
1 tablespoon shortening
½ cup cream or top milk
Salt and pepper
Few drops Tabasco sauce

Steam liver 25 minutes in deep-well cooker or large kettle.

Cool, put through food grinder. Chop eggs coarsely. Brown onion in the shortening. Mix all ingredients well. Keep in a cool place.

GROUND LIVER FILLING

1 cup ground, cooked liver
1 teaspoon chopped pickle
1 tablespoon pickle juice
4 tablespoons mayonnaise
Dash of Tabasco (optional)
Salt and pepper to taste

Combine all ingredients and mix thoroughly. Makes 5 sandwiches.

HAM-CABBAGE FILLING

Combine chopped cooked or canned ham and chopped or finely shredded cabbage. Moisten with mayonnaise or salad dressing. Season with prepared mustard.

HAM-CUCUMBER FILLING

Combine 1 cup ground, cooked ham, 1/4 cup diced cucumber, 3 tablespoons mayonnaise, and salt to taste. Mix well.

HAM-CHUTNEY FILLING

Combine ground cooked or canned ham and chutney. Moisten with mayonnaise or salad dressing.

GROUND HAM FILLING

1/2 cup vinegar
1 teaspoon prepared mustard
1/2 teaspoon salt
1/4 cup light brown sugar
1 egg, well beaten
1/2 pound ground, cooked ham

Combine all ingredients except ham, and cook, stirring constantly, until boiling. Boil 5 minutes.

Cool, then add ham and mix well. Spread between buttered slices of enriched white or whole wheat bread. Serve with pickle.

SALAMI-EGG FILLING

Combine chopped salami and hard-cooked egg. Top with sliced onion or tomato.

HAM-CHEESE FILLING

2 cups process American cheese
1/2 teaspoon Ac'cent
About 1/2 cup ketchup
2 or 3 slices boiled ham

Coarsely grate cheese. Add Ac'cent and enough ketchup for spreading consistency. Cut ham into 1/4-inch strips and use for tops. Makes filling for 4 to 6 sandwiches.

BOLOGNA-EGG FILLING

1/2 pound bologna
1/4 cup chopped pickles
1/2 cup mayonnaise
1/2 teaspoon minced onion
Dash of Tabasco sauce
2 tablespoons pickle juice
3 chopped hard-cooked eggs
1/2 teaspoon salt

Grind bologna and mix well with remaining ingredients.
Makes 7 sandwiches.

SALAMI-BEAN FILLING

1/2 pound salami, finely chopped
3/4 cup canned baked beans with tomato sauce, drained
2 teaspoons minced onion
2 tablespoons chili sauce
2 teaspoons prepared mustard
1 teaspoon prepared horseradish

Place salami, baked beans, onion, chili sauce, mustard, and horseradish in mixing bowl. Mash well with fork. Makes 2 1/2 cups.

DRIED BEEF FILLING

1 2 1/2-ounce jar dried beef
1 3-ounce package cream cheese
1 teaspoon horseradish
1 tablespoon minced onion
Pepper, if desired

Cut dried beef into thin strips with scissors. Combine with remaining ingredients. Makes 4 sandwiches.

GROUND BEEF FILLINGS

1. Cook ground beef with chopped celery and onion. Mix with a little horseradish and salad dressing.

2. Cook ground beef with a little chopped onion. Mix with chili sauce and mayonnaise.

3. Cooked ground beef mixed with pickle relish and mayonnaise.

4. Slice each of meat loaf, tomato, and cheese, spread with prepared mustard.

5. Slice meat loaf, pickle relish, sliced hard-cooked egg, and salad dressing.

MEAT AND POULTRY SANDWICHES 2375

DRIED BEEF-HORSERADISH FILLING

Moisten shredded dried beef with mayonnaise or salad dressing. Season with prepared horseradish.

TURKEY OR CHICKEN CLUB SANDWICHES

Spread a slice of toast with butter and mayonnaise. Add layer of thin sliced cooked chicken or turkey. Top with another buttered slice of toast.

Then add strips of crisp bacon, slices of tomato and a leaf of lettuce. Cover with third slice of toast. Skewer together with wooden picks and cut into quarters.

BACON-PICKLE FILLING

Fry 6 slices of bacon crisp. Crumble and combine with $1/2$ cup chopped dill pickle, and $1/4$ cup mayonnaise. Makes 4 sandwiches.

TONGUE-OLIVE FILLING

Combine 1 cup chopped cooked or canned tongue with $1/2$ cup chopped stuffed olives. Moisten with mayonnaise or salad dressing.

CLUB HOUSE SANDWICH WITH SPECIAL SAUCE

Start first with 2 slices of hot, buttery toast securely placed on a good-sized plate.

On one slice, place crisp leaf, bib, or head lettuce, then generous uniformly cut slices of light and dark turkey.

On the second slice, place more crisp lettuce and thin slices of tomato topped with 3 savory slices of crisp bacon.

For the salad dressing: Here's your chance to excel. Start with 1 cup of cooked dressing for 2 sandwiches.

Add finely chopped onion, green pepper, and green olives or tart pickle.

Look to the herbs for the subtle fooler, but be content with one—curry powder, chili, powdered tarragon, or thyme. Next, add a dash of Tabasco or other hot sauce. You may insist on chili sauce or ketchup, but use judiciously to avoid overpowering the other flavors.

Now thin this mixture with zesty French dressing. Stir to blend and literally blanket both halves of the sandwich.

Club House Sandwich with Special Sauce

Keep frozen sandwiches on hand for quick lunch-box packing.

ROLLED CHICKEN SANDWICHES
(For a Crowd)

- 3 3-ounce packages soft cream cheese
- 2 cups firmly packed, very finely ground cooked chicken
- 1/2 cup firmly packed, finely ground celery
- 1/4 cup chopped parsley
- 1/2 cup sauterne or other dry white wine
- 2 teaspoons grated onion
- 1 teaspoon Worcestershire sauce
- Salt to taste
- Softened butter or margarine
- 36 to 40 thin slices very fresh white bread, crusts trimmed

Blend cheese, chicken, celery, and parsley. Gradually beat in wine. Add onion and seasonings.

Spread bread with butter after rolling lightly with rolling pin, and spread with filling. Roll up like jelly roll.

Place seam-side-down on platter or shallow pan. Cover with waxed paper, then wrap in damp towel and chill 1/2 hour or longer before serving. Makes 36 to 40.

CORNED BEEF FILLING

- 4 tablespoons sharp American cheese
- 2 tablespoons mayonnaise
- 1/4 pound cooked corned beef
- 6 tablespoons minced sweet pickle
- 2 teaspoons finely minced onion
- 1 teaspoon prepared mustard
- 1/4 teaspoon salt
- 1/8 teaspoon pepper

Cut cheese into small pieces and blend thoroughly with mayonnaise until smooth and soft. Add shredded corned beef and other ingredients.

Spread on half slices of buttered whole wheat and white bread. A slice of tomato and crisp lettuce may be added to each sandwich. Makes 12 sandwiches.

LIVERWURST FILLING

- 1/4 cup sweet pickle relish
- 1/4 cup liverwurst
- 1/4 cup cream cheese

Blend ingredients well. Makes spread for 3 to 4 sandwiches.

PORK-EGG-PICKLE RELISH FILLING

Combine chopped canned spiced pork, chopped hard-cooked egg, and pickle relish. Moisten with mayonnaise or salad dressing.

HAM SALAD FILLING

- 1/2 pound (1 1/2 cups) baked ham or minced ham (luncheon meat)
- 1 cup sweet pickles or pickle relish
- 4 hard-cooked eggs
- 1 teaspoon lemon juice
- About 1/2 cup mayonnaise

Grind meat and sweet pickles; chop hard-cooked eggs (chop whites **very** fine). Add lemon juice. Mix with mayonnaise. Makes 6 to 8 sandwiches.

MEAT-FILLED SANDWICH BUNS

- 1 cup ground, cooked meat
- 1/4 teaspoons Ac'cent
- 1/2 teaspoon Worcestershire sauce
- 1/4 cup minced green pepper
- 1 tablespoon pickle relish
- 1/2 teaspoon onion salt
- Few grains cayenne
- 2 tablespoons chili sauce
- 3 tablespoons mayonnaise

Combine all ingredients. Makes enough filling for 4 large buns.

Peanut Butter Sandwiches

PEANUT BUTTER-BACON FILLING

    6 tablespoons butter or margarine
    6 tablespoons peanut butter
    ¼ cup finely chopped celery
    2 slices crisp bacon, chopped

Blend all ingredients to spreading consistency. Makes 1 cup.

PEANUT BUTTER-BACON FILLING #2

Combine ½ cup peanut butter, 4 slices crisply fried bacon cut into fine pieces, and 2 tablespoons mayonnaise. Makes ½ cup.

PEANUT BUTTER-RAISIN FILLING

Chop ¼ cup seedless raisins and mix with ½ cup peanut butter. Good on corn bread.

PEANUT BUTTER-CELERY FILLING

Mix well ½ cup peanut butter, ⅓ cup diced celery, and 4 tablespoons mayonnaise. Makes 1 cup.

PEANUT BUTTER-OLIVE FILLING

Combine and mix well ½ cup peanut butter, ½ cup finely chopped celery, ½ cup chopped stuffed olives, ½ cup salad dressing, 1 tablespoon lemon juice, and salt to taste. Makes 2 cups.

PEANUT BUTTER-MARMALADE FILLING

Mix well ½ cup peanut butter with ¼ cup orange marmalade. Makes ¾ cup.

A variety of fillings may be prepared in advance and stored in the refrigerator.

PEANUT BUTTER AND CHOW CHOW OR CHILI SAUCE FILLING

    ½ cup peanut butter
    2 tablespoons chow chow
    2 tablespoons mayonnaise

Combine peanut butter, chow chow, and mayonnaise. Or combine 1 cup of peanut butter or peanut crush with ⅓ cup chili sauce.

PEANUT BUTTER-PRUNE FILLING

Chop finely 6 pitted prunes and 1 cup seedless raisins.

Add ½ cup peanut butter, ¼ cup evaporated milk, 1 tablespoon lemon juice, and ⅓ teaspoon salt. Mix well. Makes 2 cups.

PEANUT BUTTER-WHOLE BRAN FILLING

Mix well ½ cup whole bran, 2 teaspoons butter, ¼ cup peanut butter, and 1 tablespoon honey. Use on white bread. Makes ¾ cup.

PEANUT BUTTER-HONEY FILLING

Mix 6 tablespoons peanut butter with 2 tablespoons honey. Spread on slices of buttered bread.

Hot Sandwiches

Egg 'N' Bacon Square   Yankee Pizza Sandwich

EGG 'N' BACON SQUARE

Combine 4 chopped hard-cooked eggs, ¼ cup chopped green pepper, ½ teaspoon salt, and enough Thousand Island salad dressing to moisten.

Spread egg mixture over 4 slices whole wheat bread. Top with ⅓ cup crumbled cooked bacon.

Broil 3 inches from broiling unit 3 minutes.

DENVER OR WESTERN SANDWICH

For each sandwich, fry 1 tablespoon minced onion in butter until slightly browned.

Add 1 tablespoon minced cooked ham and stir in 1 slightly beaten egg.

Cook slowly until firm and season with salt and pepper. Serve hot.

CRANBERRY MEAT SANDWICH

Toast bread. Place a slice of broiled or roast meat on each slice of bread. Pour over gravy, if desired. Top with generous spoonful of hot cranberry sauce.

YANKEE PIZZA SANDWICH

Split 4 soft rolls. Top bottom halves with canned spaghetti sauce with meat.

Arrange process American cheese strips over sauce. Broil 3 inches from broiling unit 5 to 8 minutes. Serve with remaining roll halves.

PIZZA-STYLE CHEESE TOMATO SNACK

- 6 English muffins
- 3 ripe tomatoes or 1¼ cups drained stewed tomatoes
- 24 anchovy fillets
- 12 thin slices of cheese
- Olive oil
- Salt and pepper

Break apart muffins. Toast until slightly crisp.

Thinly slice tomatoes. Place 1 slice of tomato or 2 tablespoons stewed tomatoes on each muffin half. Add 2 anchovy fillets.

Add another layer of tomato or stewed tomatoes. Top with slice of cheese. Sprinkle with olive oil, salt, and pepper. Broil until cheese melts.

Serves 4 to 6.

Garden Ham Sandwich *Swiss Puppies*

GARDEN HAM SANDWICH

Top 4 slices rye bread with boiled ham slices.

Combine 1½ cups shredded cabbage, ¼ cup grated carrot, ¼ cup sliced radishes, 2 tablespoons chopped green pepper, 2 tablespoons grated onion, 2 teaspoons prepared mustard, and enough mayonnaise to moisten.

Top ham slices with vegetable mixture.

Broil 3 inches from broiling unit about 7 minutes.

BAKED BEANS AND SALAMI

¼ pound salami
1½ cups canned baked beans with tomato sauce
2 tablespoons chili sauce
2 tablespoons prepared mustard
½ teaspoon minced onion

Cut salami into small bits and combine with remaining ingredients. Mash with a fork.

Spread between slices of bread. Broil the sandwiches, turning to brown both sides.

SWISS PUPPIES

Slash 4 frankfurters diagonally and stuff with slices of process Swiss cheese.

Broil 3 inches from broiling unit until cheese melts. Serve on frankfurter rolls.

GOLDEN EGG AND TOMATO

⅓ cup butter or margarine
⅓ cup flour
1½ cups milk
¾ teaspoon salt
¾ teaspoon Worcestershire sauce
⅛ teaspoon white pepper
6 hard-cooked eggs, quartered
1 cup cooked peas
4 thinly sliced tomatoes
6 slices toast

Melt butter in top of double boiler. Add flour, blend thoroughly and add milk gradually, stirring constantly. Add seasoning. Cook over hot water 5 minutes, or until thickened. Add eggs and peas. Continue cooking 5 minutes.

Place tomato slices on each piece of toast. Cover with sauce. Garnish with parsley. Serves 6.

Brown Bean Sandwiches

BROWN BEAN SANDWICHES

Butter or margarine
6   slices bread
1   jar or can brown beans
1   cup grated cheese
6   slices bacon

Butter bread. Top each slice with brown beans and sprinkle with grated cheese.

Cut bacon slices in half. Top each sandwich with 2 slices of bacon in crisscross fashion.

Bake or broil until cheese melts and bacon is crisp. Serve with pickles. Makes 6 sandwiches.

LIMA SOUFFLÉ SANDWICHES

3   egg whites
1/4 teaspoon cream of tartar
1   cup grated sharp American cheese
1/2 cup mayonnaise
1   tablespoon prepared mustard
6   drops Tabasco sauce
1   tablespoon grated onion
1   teaspoon salt
2 1/2 cups hot cooked large dry limas (1 cup before cooking)
4   slices buttered toast
Bacon curls

Beat egg whites with cream of tartar until stiff. Carefully fold in cheese, mayonnaise, and seasonings.

Spoon drained limas over toast on baking sheet.

Spread soufflé mixture completely over limas. Broil until puffed and golden brown. Serve with bacon curls. Makes 4 sandwiches.

CHEESE SAUCE OVER MEAT SANDWICHES

Melt 1 cup grated American cheese in 1 cup medium white sauce. Pour over any meat sandwich.

EGG SAUSAGEBURGERS

1   pound pork sausage
2   tablespoons finely chopped green pepper
2   tablespoons finely chopped onion
2   tablespoons sausage fat for cooking
8   eggs, beaten slightly
1/2 teaspoon salt
1/8 teaspoon pepper
8   buns

Mold sausage into 8 patties to fit buns and fry.

Meanwhile, cook green pepper and onion in fat until onion is transparent but not browned.

Blend eggs and seasoning and add to onions and green pepper. Scramble over low heat.

Place 1 sausage patty, topped with a tablespoon of scrambled egg, between split bun. Serve hot with relishes. Makes 8.

Egg-Cheeseburger: Omit sausage in above. Cut buns and place cut-side-up on baking sheet. Top half of the buns with sliced cheese.

Broil or bake in hot oven until cheese begins to melt and plain halves are toasted. Place scrambled eggs on toasted half. Serve promptly.

Lima Soufflé Sandwiches

Bacon, Cheese and Tomato Double Deckers

Hot Cheese Sandwiches

BACON, CHEESE AND TOMATO DOUBLE DECKERS

- 12 slices white bread
- 1/3 cup butter or margarine
- 12 slices American cheese
- 6 tomato slices
- Salt
- 12 bacon slices

Trim crusts from white bread slices and toast on one side. Spread untoasted side generously with butter.

Cover 6 slices each with a slice of cheese and remaining 6 slices of bread, double-decker fashion.

Put slices of peeled tomato on top of bread, salt, and then top with a slice of cheese.

Place in moderate oven until cheese begins to soften.

Place 2 slices of partially broiled bacon on top. Place under low broiler heat until cheese is thoroughly melted and bacon is crisp.

Makes 6 double-decker sandwiches.

Serve with a variety of spring vegetables arranged in lettuce cups so that everyone may make their own salad to suit the individual's taste.

CHEESE BARBECUE

Grind together 1 pound Cheddar cheese, 1/2 green pepper, 1 medium onion, 2 hard-cooked eggs, and 1 cup stuffed olives.

Add 1/2 can condensed tomato soup and 2 tablespoons melted butter. Mix well.

Spread on bun halves or rye bread and broil.

CHEESE PUFFS

Cut 4 dinner rolls in half. Cream 1/2 cup butter or margarine, and mix in 1 cup shredded sharp Cheddar cheese.

Stir in 1 stiffly beaten egg white.

Top rolls with a generous spoonful of the mixture. Bake in hot oven (400°F.) 15 minutes, or until puffy.

Waffle-Grilled Cheese Sandwiches

WAFFLE-GRILLED CHEESE SANDWICHES

For each sandwich, place 1 slice of process American cheese between 2 slices of bread.

Brush top and bottom of sandwich with melted buter or margarine.

Put sandwiches in waffle iron until bread is golden brown, and cheese is melted.

BARBECUED CHEESE BUNS

6 sandwich buns
1½ cups (½ pound) finely diced American cheese
3 chopped, hard-cooked eggs
¾ cup finely cut green pepper
1½ teaspoons grated onion
⅓ cup evaporated milk
3 tablespoons ketchup
¾ teaspoon salt
⅛ teaspoon pepper

Split buns. Put in shallow baking pan cut-side-up.

Combine remaining ingredients and mix thoroughly. Arrange on buns, using about ¼ cup mixture for each.

Bake on top shelf in hot oven (400°F.) 7 minutes, until cheese melts and buns are toasted. Serve with radishes, if desired. Serves 6.

Note: Slices of bread can be used instead of sandwich buns.

To Fix Buns Ahead of Time: Combine above cheese mixture and keep chilled. When ready to use, mix well, arrange on split buns and toast.

GRILLED CHEESE DELIGHTS

¾ pound American cheese
½ to ¾ cup chopped stuffed olives
12 slices enriched bread
⅓ cup butter or margarine, creamed

Grate cheese into mixing bowl and mix with chopped olives. Spread mixture on 6 of the slices of buttered bread.

Cover with remaining slices of buttered bread, and trim off crusts if desired. Spread butter generously on outside of sandwiches, both sides.

Brown sandwiches immediately on griddle or in a large skillet, turning carefully. By the time both sides are browned, the cheese will be melted.

Serve hot, with mustard sauce if desired. Serves 6.

Mustard Sauce:

3 tablespoons butter or margarine
3 tablespoons flour
Few grains pepper
¾ teaspoon salt
1½ cups milk
¼ cup prepared mustard
1½ tablespoons Worcestershire sauce

Melt butter in saucepan; stir in flour and seasonings and blend thoroughly.

Add milk gradually while stirring, and cook until smooth and thickened, stirring constantly.

Add mustard and Worcestershire sauce. Makes 1½ cups sauce.

CHEESEWICH

Cut day-old bread in ¼-inch slices. Cut thin slices of American cheese.

Make sandwiches, seasoning with salt, paprika, and a light covering of mixed English mustard.

Press sandwiches gently together and trim off crusts. Cut sandwiches in quarters or triangles.

Melt some butter in frying pan. Fry sandwiches over very low heat until lightly browned, taking care in turning that they do not separate.

Serve hot.

Olive-Cheese Sandwiches

OLIVE-CHEESE SANDWICHES

1 cup ripe olives
1½ cups grated American cheese
⅓ cup mayonnaise
½ teaspoon grated onion
½ teaspoon Worcestershire sauce
6 round French rolls
Butter or margarine
Tomatoes

Cut olives in small pieces. Blend with cheese, mayonnaise, onion, and Worcestershire sauce.

Make 2 cuts part way through each roll from top to bottom, and spread cut edges lightly with butter, then quickly with cheese-olive mixture.

Cut tomatoes in halves and then into thin slices. Put a half slice in each cut.

Place rolls on baking sheet. Bake in moderate oven (375°F.) about 15 minutes. Serve at once. Makes 6 rolls.

Cheese Strata

CHEESE STRATA

Arrange 6 slices of bread (crusts trimmed) in bottom of rectangular dish.

Place a slice of pasteurized process American cheese on each slice of bread. Cover with 6 slices of bread (crusts trimmed).

Beat 4 eggs. Add 2½ cups milk and salt and pepper.

Pour egg and milk mixture over bread and cheese sandwiches. Let stand an hour.

Bake in slow oven (325°F.) about 40 minutes. Serve plain or with your favorite jelly.

SAUTÉED TOMATO AND CHEESE

Spread slices of bread with nippy mayonnaise.

Put a slice of tomato and a slice of American cheese between each 2 slices.

Dip in an egg-milk mixture; fry as for French toast.

BROILED COTTAGE CHEESE SANDWICHES

Season cottage cheese with salt and paprika.

Spread on buttered toast. Top with bacon strips and broil slowly until bacon is crisp.

SWISS LOAF

- 1 1-pound loaf unsliced bread
- 1/4 cup butter or margarine
- 1/2 cup finely chopped onion
- 1/4 cup chili sauce
- 1 tablespoon celery seeds
- 8 slices (1/2 pound) Swiss cheese

With a sharp knife, make 9 equal diagonal slices, almost through to the bottom crust.

Melt butter in a skillet; add onion and sauté about 5 minutes. Add chili sauce and celery seeds and heat 5 minutes. Remove from heat.

Spread onion mixture and 1 slice of cheese between each slice of bread. Place loaf on cookie sheet. Pour remaining onion mixture over top.

Bake in a moderate oven (350°F.) for 20 minutes. Serves 8.

For a hearty party luncheon: toasted cheese sandwiches, stuffed eggs, and individual ring molds filled with vegetable salad.

CHEESE CLUB SANDWICH

Melt 1/2 pound (2 cups) sharp Cheddar cheese in chafing dish or top of double boiler. Add 1/3 cup milk gradually, stirring until sauce is smooth.

Add 1/2 teaspoon salt, 1/4 teaspoon pepper, 1 teaspoon Worcestershire sauce, and 1/8 teaspoon dry mustard.

Trim crusts from 12 slices white bread and toast slices on both sides.

For each sandwich, spread toast slice with mayonnaise, cover with peeled sliced tomatoes, and second toast slice spread with mayonnaise on both sides; add 2 slices broiled bacon and a lettuce leaf. Cover with third toast slice spread with mayonnaise.

Cut diagonally and serve each sandwich with generous amount of hot cheese sauce. Garnish with pickle fan. Makes 4.

CHEESE FRENCH TOASTWICHES

- 12 slices day-old white bread
- 2 cups freshly grated American cheese
- 1/2 cup chopped green or stuffed olives
- 2 tablespoons minced onion or chives (optional)
- 2 eggs, well beaten
- 1/2 teaspoon salt
- 1/2 cup milk

Spread one side of 12 slices of bread with softened butter.

Blend grated American cheese, chopped olives, and onion and spread on 6 buttered slices.

Make into sandwiches and cut in halves diagonally.

Beat eggs; add salt and milk and blend. Pour into shallow dish.

Dip each sandwich in egg mixture, turning it to coat both sides thoroughly.

Brown on both sides in butter in a moderately hot skillet. Makes 12 Toastwiches.

Serve hot with a variety of vegetable relishes.

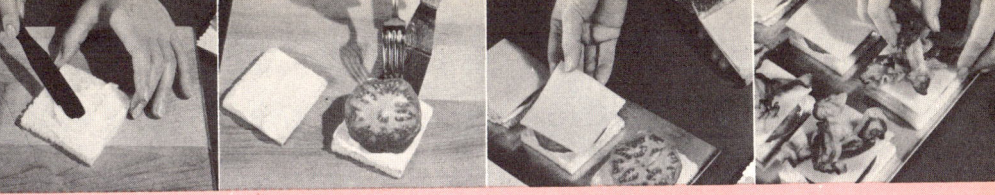

BACON, CHEESE AND TOMATO SANDWICHES

Trim the crusts from slices of bread and toast them on one side. Spread the untoasted sides with mayonnaise.

Place a slice of peeled tomato on each slice of toast.

Place a slice of pasteurized process American cheese on each slice of tomato.

Arrange two slices of partially broiled bacon on each slice of cheese. Place under moderate broiler heat until the cheese melts.

Serve piping hot, and see why it's called America's favorite sandwich.

SOUFFLÉED CHEESE SANDWICH #1

4 to 6 slices of bread
$\frac{1}{2}$ teaspoon salt
3 eggs, separated
Dash of pepper
Dash of paprika
$\frac{1}{2}$ cup grated sharp cheese

Toast bread (crust removed, if desired) on one side.

Add salt to egg whites and beat until stiff, but **not dry**.

Add pepper and paprika to yolks. Beat until light. Add cheese and fold into beaten egg whites.

Heap on untoasted side of bread. Place on greased baking sheet. Bake in moderate oven (350°F.) for 15 minutes or until puffy and delicately browned. Serve at once.

Makes 4 to 6 sandwiches, depending upon size of slice and thickness of egg mixture desired.

SOUFFLÉED CHEESE SANDWICH #2

6 slices bread
Sliced cheese to cover bread
$\frac{1}{4}$ teaspoon salt
3 eggs, separated
$\frac{1}{4}$ cup salad dressing

Toast bread on 1 side. Cover untoasted side with cheese.

Add salt to egg whites and beat until shiny and whites leave peaks when beater is withdrawn.

Add salad dressing to yolks and beat until light. Fold yolk mixture into whites. Heap on top of cheese.

Bake in moderate oven (350°F.) until puffy and brown, about 15 minutes. Serve promptly. Makes 6.

Variation: Place thin slice of cooked ham on toast. Top with cheese and proceed as above.

CHEESE BARBECUE #2

$1\frac{1}{2}$ cups grated processed cheese
3 tablespoons chopped green pepper
$\frac{1}{2}$ cup chopped onion
2 hard-cooked eggs, chopped
3 tablespoons chopped stuffed olives
$\frac{1}{2}$ teaspoon Worcestershire sauce
3 tablespoons ketchup
1 tablespoon melted butter or margarine
6 buns, split open

Combine all ingredients and place $\frac{1}{4}$ cup in each bun. Toast under preheated broiler about 5 minutes. Makes 6.

Salmon Sandwich Fondue

Hot Fish and Shellfish Sandwiches

SALMON SANDWICH FONDUE

1	8-ounce can salmon
1	cup minced celery
¼	cup mayonnaise
1	tablespoon prepared mustard
¼	teaspoon salt
12	thin slices whole wheat bread
6	slices American Cheddar cheese
3	beaten eggs
2½	cups milk
2	teaspoons Worcestershire sauce
½	teaspoon Ac'cent

Drain salmon; flake, removing bones; add celery.

Blend mayonnaise, mustard, and salt; add to salmon mixture; mix well.

Spread between bread slices to make 6 sandwiches. Arrange sandwiches in shallow baking dish; top each with slice of cheese.

Combine eggs, milk, Worcestershire sauce, and Ac'cent. Pour over sandwiches.

Bake in slow oven (325°F.) 45 minutes. Makes 6 sandwiches.

BARBECUED TUNA BURGERS

1	clove garlic, minced
1	tablespoon butter or margarine
1	can (8 ounces) tomato sauce
2	tablespoons vinegar
1	tablespoon brown sugar
½	teaspoon salt
½	teaspoon dry mustard
½	teaspoon chili powder
1	can (7 ounces) tuna, drained and flaked
4	hamburger buns, split

Cook garlic in butter or margarine 1 minute; add remaining ingredients, except tuna and buns; simmer 5 minutes. Add tuna; heat thoroughly.

Toast buns; spoon barbecued tuna over buns. Makes 4 sandwiches.

SUPER TUNA TOASTWICHES

1	can (7 ounces) tuna, drained and flaked
2	hard-cooked eggs, chopped
½	cup diced celery
¼	cup chopped olives
1	tablespoon chopped chives or onion
1	tablespoon chopped parsley
2	teaspoons capers
¼	cup mayonnaise or salad dressing
16	slices bread
2	eggs, slightly beaten
⅓	cup milk
	Butter or margarine

Combine tuna, eggs, celery, olives, chives or onion, parsley, capers, and mayonnaise or salad dressing.

Spread tuna mixture over 8 bread slices; top with remaining bread.

Blend eggs and milk. Dip each sandwich in egg mixture, turning it to coat well.

Brown sandwiches slowly on both sides in small amount of butter or margarine in frying pan. Serve at once. Makes 8 toastwiches.

OYSTER CLUB SANDWICHES

 12 slices bacon
  1 pint oysters
 1/2 cup flour
 1/2 teaspoon salt
 1/8 teaspoon pepper
 12 lettuce leaves
 12 slices tomato
 1/2 cup mayonnaise
 18 slices buttered toast

Fry bacon and drain on absorbent paper.

Drain oysters, roll in flour seasoned with salt and pepper. Fry in bacon fat. When brown on one side, turn and brown on other side. Cooking time is about 5 minutes. Drain on absorbent paper.

Arrange lettuce, oysters, bacon, tomatoes, and mayonnaise between 3 slices of toast. Fasten with wooden picks. Serves 6.

HOT FISH SANDWICHES

  1 tablespoon fat
 1 1/2 tablespoons minced green pepper
  1 tablespoon minced onion
  2 slightly beaten eggs
 1/4 cup milk
 1/2 teaspoon salt
 3/4 cup flaked canned or cooked fish
 Toasted rolls

Heat fat and cook green pepper and onion in it until they are tender.

Combine remaining ingredients and add to vegetables. Cook over low heat or boiling water, stirring constantly, until thick and creamy. Serve hot on toasted rolls. Makes 4.

NEW MOON SANDWICHES

  1 8-ounce can salmon
  3 hard-cooked eggs, chopped
 1/4 teaspoon Worcestershire sauce
  2 tablespoons drained pickle relish
  3 tablespoons mayonnaise
 1/4 cup chopped peanuts
 1/2 teaspoon Ac'cent
 12 to 16 slices enriched bread
  2 eggs, slightly beaten
 2/3 cup milk
  2 teaspoons sugar

Drain, bone, and flake salmon; combine with eggs, Worcestershire sauce, pickle relish, mayonnaise, peanuts, and Ac'cent; mix well.

Spread between slices of bread, making 6 to 8 sandwiches.

Combine beaten eggs, milk, and sugar; dip sandwiches in this mixture and fry in little butter or margarine until golden brown on both sides. Garnish with pickle fans and olives. Makes 6 to 8 sandwiches.

New Moon Sandwiches

Souffléed Shrimp Sandwich

SOUFFLÉED SHRIMP SANDWICH

  8 slices enriched bread
  2 eggs, separated
  4 ounces Cheddar cheese, grated
Dash of pepper
Dash of paprika
  1 pound shrimp, cleaned

Trim crusts from bread; toast lightly and cut in half. Beat egg yolks.

Melt cheese in top of double boiler. Gradually add to the beaten egg yolks. Add seasonings and fold this mixture into stiffly beaten egg whites.

Arrange toast points in 4 individual or 1 large greased baking dish. Top with cleaned shrimp, then the sauce.

Bake in slow oven (325°F.) until brown and puffy. Serves 4.

FRENCH-TOASTED SALMON SANDWICHES

  1 7½-ounce can salmon
  ¼ cup finely diced cucumber
  ¼ teaspoon Ac'cent
Few drops Tabasco sauce
  2 teaspoons prepared horseradish
Mayonnaise or salad dressing
  8 slices bread
  3 eggs
  ½ teaspoon salt
  ¼ teaspoon Ac'cent
  1 tablespoon sugar
  1 cup milk
Butter or margarine

Flake salmon; add cucumber, Ac'cent, Tabasco, and horseradish with enough mayonnaise or salad dressing to make spreading consistency.

Spread on 4 slices bread; top with remaining slices.

Beat eggs slightly; add salt, Ac'cent, sugar, and milk; blend well.

Dip sandwiches in egg mixture; sauté in a little butter or margarine until golden brown on both sides, turning once. Or cook on a table grill, according to manufacturer's directions. Makes 4 sandwiches.

FRENCH-TOASTED TUNA CHEESE SANDWICHES

  1 7-ounce can tuna flakes
  1 teaspoon lemon juice
  ½ cup diced celery
  3 tablespoons mayonnaise
  4 tablespoons butter or margarine
 12 slices bread
  6 slices American cheese
  2 eggs, beaten
  ½ teaspoon salt
  1 cup milk
  2 tablespoons butter or margarine

Combine tuna flakes, lemon juice, celery, and mayonnaise.

Butter slices of bread on one side; spread 6 buttered slices with tuna mixture.

Top each with a slice of cheese and place remaining slices on top; chill.

Combine eggs, salt, and milk; stir to blend. Dip each sandwich in mixture to coat both sides.

Melt butter in frying pan or on griddle over medium heat and lightly brown sandwiches on both sides, turning only once. Serve immediately. Serves 6.

Hot Meat and Poultry Sandwiches

CHEESE-HAM ROLLS

- 1 tablespoon finely chopped onion
- 2 tablespoons chili sauce
- 2 tablespoons chopped green pepper
- 2 tablespoons sweet piccalilli
- 1/4 cup deviled ham
- 1 1/2 cups grated process cheese, firmly packed
- 8 frankfurter buns

Combine onion, chili sauce, green pepper, piccalilli, ham, and cheese. Cut buns in half and place 3 tablespoons cheese-ham mixture between matched bun halves.

Wrap and seal each filled bun in aluminum foil. Heat in moderate oven (350°F.) for 8 to 10 minutes, or until cheese melts. Makes 8 cheese-ham rolls.

SAUTÉED MEAT SANDWICHES

Moisten ground leftover meat with thick white sauce or gravy. Put between slices of bread. Brown on each side in hot fat.

HOT CHICKEN SALAD IN BUNS

- 1 5-ounce can chicken
- 1/2 cup diced celery
- 1/4 cup chopped green peppers
- 1/4 cup chopped pimientos
- Salt and pepper to taste
- 1 tablespoon mayonnaise
- 4 frankfurter rolls
- Grated Parmesan cheese
- Butter or margarine

Toss chicken with celery, green pepper, and pimientos. Season and mix in mayonnaise.

Slice tops off rolls and scoop out bread.

Fill with chicken salad. Sprinkle tops generously with Parmesan cheese and dot with butter or margarine.

Wrap each roll in square of aluminum foil. Refrigerate until serving time.

Place on baking sheet and heat through in very hot oven (450°F.) about 10 minutes. Remove foil to serve. Serves 4.

Cheese-Ham Rolls

Frenched Avocado Chicken Sandwiches

FRENCHED AVOCADO CHICKEN SANDWICHES

½ cup seedless grapes
2 cups finely diced cooked chicken or turkey
½ cup finely diced celery
1 cup diced avocado
½ cup mayonnaise
1 tablespoon lemon juice
Salt
12 slices bread
2 eggs
½ cup milk
¼ cup melted butter or margarine

Cut grapes into small pieces and combine with chicken, celery, and avocado.

Blend mayonnaise, lemon juice, and ½ teaspoon salt, and mix lightly with chicken mixture.

Spread thickly on 6 slices bread. Top with remaining bread.

Beat eggs lightly and combine with milk, butter, and ¼ teaspoon salt. Turn into flat dish or pie pan.

Dip sandwiches quickly into egg mixture on both sides. Place on flat well greased pan. Place under broiler until well browned, turning with broad spatula to brown second side.

Garnish with additional avocado slices if desired. Makes 6 very thick sandwiches.

BARBECUED SANDWICH

1½ cups cooked leftover meat, chopped fine
1 cup thick barbecue sauce

Use beef, veal, lamb, pork, or chicken. Add meat to sauce. Heat.

Cut round flat buns in half. Toast on cut side. Spread with heated meat. Serve hot. Makes 6.

CURRY FRIED PORK SANDWICHES

¼ cup vinegar
4 to 6 slices cooked pork
3 tablespoons flour
2 teaspoons curry powder
½ teaspoon salt
1 tablespoon shortening
4 slices bread
Butter or margarine

Pour vinegar over pork. Let stand 15 to 30 minutes.

Combine flour, curry powder, and salt. Drain pork slices and dip in flour mixture. Fry in melted shortening until crisp.

Place between slices of buttered bread. Serve hot. Serves 2.

BROILED HAM, CHICKEN AND PICKLE SANDWICHES

4 slices bread, toasted on 1 side
Butter or margarine
4 slices cooked or canned chicken
4 slices cooked or canned ham
Thin sliced dill pickles
4 slices process cheese

Spread untoasted side of bread with butter or margarine.

Place slice of chicken, then slice of ham on each.

Cover with a layer of pickle, then slice of cheese. Broil until cheese melts. Serve hot. Makes 4.

For Chicken Rabbit Sandwiches, arrange toast in a shallow baking dish; top with thick slices of chicken. Cover with cheese sauce; sprinkle lightly with paprika. Heat under broiler only until cheese sauce begins to brown lightly.

HOT SANDWICHES **2391**

Sautéed chicken livers, grilled tomatoes, and crisp bacon are a popular and satisfying sandwich combination.

OPEN-FACE SANDWICHES (Italian Style)

½ pound ground beef
½ pound sausage meat
8 thin slices Mozzarella or Muenster cheese
8 slices brown-and-serve French bread
Oregano

Mix beef and sausage and shape in 8 thin patties. Broil under medium heat until well browned on both sides.

Put a slice of cheese on each slice of bread. Sprinkle with oregano. Broil until cheese is slightly melted.

While still hot, press a meat patty on each slice.

Makes 8 small sandwiches.

HOT ROAST BEEF SANDWICHES

Make sandwiches with toasted bread and slices of roast beef.

Serve on hot plates, with hot gravy poured over the sandwiches. Garnish with a sprig of parsley and a pickle.

CHICKEN SANDWICH ROYAL

8 slices buttered toast
Slices of cooked chicken
Slices of tomato
Salt
1 cup grated Cheddar cheese
2 teaspoons Worcestershire sauce

Lay slices of buttered toast in shallow baking pan. Place sliced chicken on toast. Place slices of tomato on the chicken. Sprinkle with salt.

Spread thickly with grated cheese mixed with Worcestershire sauce.

Broil quickly until cheese is melted and browned. Serve at once. Makes 8.

CRANBERRY SUPPER SANDWICHES

6 slices boiled ham or cold sliced turkey
1½ tablespoons bacon drippings
6 slices buttered toast
1 1-pound can jellied cranberry sauce
¼ pound sharp American cheese, grated
Parsley
Sweet pickles

Heat the ham or turkey slightly in bacon drippings in skillet.

Place a slice of turkey on each slice of buttered toast.

Top with a slice of jellied cranberry sauce. Then sprinkle grated cheese over all.

Arrange sandwiches on broiler pan and place under broiler to melt cheese. Serve immediately with parsley and sweet pickle garnish. Serves 6.

Cranberry Supper Sandwiches

HOT MEAT AND POULTRY SANDWICHES

HOT DOG TOASTIES

  8 frankfurters
  8 slices sandwich bread
Melted butter or margarine
Prepared mustard
Wooden picks

Pour boiling water over frankfurters and let stand 8 minutes.

Spread bread with butter and mustard.

Place frankfurters cornerwise on bread and fasten opposite corners together with wooden picks.

Brush with melted butter and broil until toast is golden brown. Serve with French fried onion rings. Serves 8.

CHEESE AND FRANKFURTERS

  1 pound frankfurters
  1 cup grated sharp natural Cheddar cheese
$\frac{1}{2}$ cup chopped peanuts
  2 tablespoons salad dressing
Frankfurter buns

Cut a long slit in each frankfurter. Combine cheese, peanuts, and salad dressing. Fill each frankfurter with cheese mixture.

Place frankfurters on cooky sheet. Bake in slow oven (325°F.) 10 minutes or until cheese is melted and frankfurters are heated through. Serve in warmed **buns**.

TURKEY RED DEVILS

Buttered toast
Sliced sharp cheese
Sliced tomatoes
Sliced cooked turkey
  1 can condensed cream of mushroom soup
$\frac{1}{2}$ can of broth, milk, or water
Cayenne and mustard (optional)
Paprika

Arrange on a shallow baking pan for individual servings—toast topped with the cheese, tomato seasoned with salt and pepper, and the turkey.

Blend soup with broth and season with cayenne and mustard if desired.

Top each sandwich with 3 or 4 spoonfuls of the soup. Sprinkle with paprika.

Place in hot oven (425°F.) until cheese begins to melt and top is browned, about 15 minutes. The diluted mushroom soup is enough for 4 or 5 sandwiches.

CHICKEN-CHEESE SANDWICHES

  2 tablespoons butter or margarine
  2 tablespoons flour
$\frac{1}{2}$ teaspoon salt
$\frac{1}{4}$ teaspoon dry mustard
  1 cup milk
  1 cup grated process Cheddar cheese
  6 slices hot toast
  1 peeled large avocado or tomato, cut into slices
12 slices cooked or canned chicken
Paprika

Melt butter; blend in flour, salt, and mustard. Add milk; cook, stirring, until mixture thickens and boils.

Add cheese; stir over very low heat until melted.

Arrange hot toast in bottom of shallow pan. Cover with slices of avocado, then chicken slices. Pour cheese sauce over all. Sprinkle with paprika.

Heat in preheated broiler 1 or 2 minutes, or until lightly browned. Serves 6.

Jiffy Special: Omit sauce. Top chicken with thin cheese slices; broil. Serve with canned condensed cream of mushroom soup, heated with $\frac{1}{2}$ cup milk.

CHEESE AND CHIPPED BEEF SANDWICHES

$\frac{1}{4}$ pound chipped beef, ground or chopped
  1 clove garlic, finely minced
  1 8-ounce can tomato sauce
$\frac{1}{4}$ pound cheese, grated
  1 slightly beaten egg
Dash of cayenne pepper

Combine all ingredients in top of double boiler and cook until cheese melts, stirring constantly. Serve on toasted bread. Serves 6.

For whole meal sandwiches in casseroles: place 1/2 inch thick, oblong slices of whole wheat bread on a baking sheet in moderate oven (350° F.) and bake until crisp and toasted. Then place a slice of toast in a shallow casserole, cover with slice of cooked turkey, then a crisp, cooked bacon slice. Cover all with about 1/3 cup thick, well seasoned cheese sauce. Bake in moderate oven (350° F.) until cheese is bubbly, 15 to 20 minutes. Serve at once.

CHILI CLUB SANDWICHES

- 4 hamburger buns
- 1 can chili con carne, heated
- 4 thin slices American cheese
- 4 slices bacon
- 4 thin slices Bermuda onion

Split and butter buns. Spread bottom halves with hot chili con carne.

Arrange a slice of cheese and a slice of bacon on top of each.

Broil under moderate heat until bacon is crisp and cheese bubbling.

Add onion slices and remaining halves and buns. Serve very hot. Serves 4.

CHICKEN AND HAM SANDWICH

- 1/4 cup chopped fresh mushrooms or 1 3-ounce can chopped mushrooms, drained
- 1 tablespoon butter or margarine
- 2 cups minced, cooked or canned chicken
- 1/2 cup heavy cream
- 1/2- to 3/4-pound ready-to-eat ham, 1/4-inch thick

Paprika

- 1/2 cup sherry
- 4 slices hot toast

Cook mushrooms in butter 5 minutes. Add chicken and cream; set aside.

Cut ham into 4 pieces; sprinkle both sides generously with paprika. Brown ham slightly on both sides in hot skillet. Add sherry; simmer, turning frequently, until sherry cooks down to small amount of rich sauce. Place ham on toast; keep hot. Add chicken mixture to sauce in skillet; heat quickly, stirring. Heap on top of ham. Serves 4.

TURKEY SANDWICH GRILL

- 1 cup chopped cooked turkey
- 1 cup finely diced celery
- 1 tablespoon sweet pickle relish
- 1/3 cup mayonnaise or salad dressing

Salt and pepper

- 6 slices buttered toast
- 1 cup (1/4 pound) grated cheese

Combine turkey, celery, pickle relish, and mayonnaise. Season to taste with salt and pepper.

Spread turkey mixture atop toast. Sprinkle cheese over each.

Place in hot oven (425° F.) or under broiler to melt cheese, 2 to 5 minutes.

Serve with a dot of chili sauce and a sprig of parsley atop each sandwich.

If desired, serve with triangles of additional toast, grilled tomatoes and crisp bacon. Makes 6 sandwiches.

2394

Open-Face Cheeseburgers

Hamburger Sandwiches

OPEN-FACE CHEESEBURGERS

Place on cooky sheet the lower halves of large round buns which have been spread liberally with butter, mixed with prepared mustard if desired.

Toast under broiler until golden brown. Keep hot in oven until needed.

In the meantime, quickly cook seasoned hamburger patties on griddle or under broiler.

Arrange on each bun half a crisp lettuce leaf, onion rings or thin slices, thinly sliced tomato, a spoonful of hot baked beans—any one or all as fancy and taste dictate.

Top each with a hot hamburger patty.

Place on each:

(1) A slice of American Cheddar cheese, or—

(2) A mixture of blue cheese, $\frac{1}{2}$ cup, mixed with $\frac{1}{4}$ cup butter, 2 teaspoons Worcestershire sauce, or—

(3) $\frac{1}{2}$ cup sharp Cheddar cheese spread mixed with 2 teaspoons Worcestershire sauce.

Place low under broiler until the cheese is bubbly, browned, and melted. Serve at once.

Have the hot butter-toasted bun tops handy to clap on the sandwich, if you like, but this creation is more easily eaten with a fork than as a portable meal!

HAMBURGER SANDWICHES

BROILED DEVILED HAMBURGERS
- 1 pound ground beef
- 4 tablespoons ketchup
- 1½ teaspoons Worcestershire sauce
- 1 teaspoon salt
- Dash of pepper
- 6 hamburger buns, split

Combine all ingredients except buns.
Toast uncut surfaces of buns under broiler and spread with meat mixture.
Broil about 6 minutes, with meat surface about 3 inches from the unit. Serves 3.

HURRY-UP BURGERS
- 1 pound hamburger
- 1 cup diced celery
- 1 teaspoon salt
- 1 tablespoon fat
- 1 tablespoon Worcestershire sauce
- 4 hamburger buns, split and buttered

Brown and cook hamburger, celery, and salt in fat in a heavy skillet.
Add Worcestershire sauce. Heap meat mixture on halves of large round buns. Serves 6.

Cheese Hurry-Ups: Follow the above recipe. After heaping each bun with meat mixture, top with a slice of cheese food. Broil until cheese melts. Serve hot.

WIENERBURGERS ON ROLLS
- 2 pounds ground beef
- 1 tablespoon chopped onion
- 2 tablespoons cream
- 1 teaspoon Worcestershire sauce
- 1 teaspoon salt
- ¼ teaspoon pepper
- 3 dill pickles
- 12 frankfurter rolls, split and toasted

Mix beef, onion, cream, Worcestershire, salt, and pepper.
Cut dill pickles in quarters, lengthwise.
Shape meat mixture around pieces of pickle to form wiener shape.
Bake in hot oven (425°F.) about 15 minutes. Serve on frankfurter rolls. Makes 12.

SLOPPY JOES
- ¼ cup sliced onions
- ½ cup chopped green pepper
- 2 tablespoons fat
- 2 medium-sized tomatoes, peeled
- ¾ cup sliced mushrooms
- ½ pound ground beef
- 1 cup tomato juice
- ¾ teaspoon salt
- ¼ teaspoon pepper
- ¼ teaspoon paprika

Cook onion and green pepper in hot fat until lightly browned.
Cut tomatoes into eighths and add.
Add mushrooms, beef, tomato juice, salt, pepper, and paprika.
Cover and cook over very low heat 15 to 20 minutes.
If desired, thicken sauce by sprinkling in a little flour and cooking until well blended. Serve over split toasted hamburger buns. Serves 6.

PEPPERBURGERS
- 1½ pounds ground beef
- 1 teaspoon salt
- ¼ teaspoon pepper
- 4 green peppers, halved
- 8 sandwich rolls

Mix ground beef with salt and pepper. Shape into 8 patties. Broil or cook in hot, greased skillet to degree of doneness desired.
Fry or boil green peppers until tender. Place on top of patties. Serve between split, heated rolls. Makes 8.

HAMBURGER ROLLS
- 3 pounds ground beef
- 2 10½-ounce cans tomato soup
- 1 cup pickle relish
- 1 tablespoon salt
- ½ teaspoon pepper
- 24 frankfurter or sandwich rolls, split and heated

Cook beef until browned, stirring with fork.
Add soup, relish, salt, and pepper; simmer about 15 minutes. Serve on rolls. Makes 24.

For an easy cheeseburger, place a spoonful of soft cheese spread on each hot hamburger just before serving.

"ORIENTAL" HAMBURGER SANDWICH

1 tablespoon finely chopped fresh ginger root (or 2 teaspoons powdered ginger)
2 cloves garlic, chopped fine
½ cup chopped onion
2 tablespoons sugar
½ cup soy sauce
¼ cup water
1 pound hamburger

Make sauce from ginger root, garlic, onion, sugar, soy sauce, and water. Pour over meat. Let stand 1 to 2 hours in refrigerator.

Spread mixture on 6 hamburger buns. Broil about 3 inches from heat source, 3 to 5 minutes. Serves 6.

HAMBURGER WESTERN SANDWICHES

¼ pound ground beef
1 small onion, chopped
½ medium green pepper, chopped
Salt and pepper
4 eggs, slightly beaten
Butter or margarine
8 slices bread or toast

Cook beef, onion, and green pepper, stirring with fork, until meat loses its red color. Sprinkle with salt and pepper.

Pour eggs over mixture. Reduce heat to medium, and cook until eggs are set; do not stir.

Cut in quarters; turn, and brown on other side. Serve hot between buttered bread or toast. Serves 4.

HAMBURGER SHORTCAKES

1 pound hamburger
2 teaspoons prepared mustard
1 teaspoon salt
¼ teaspoon savory
2 cups biscuit mix
About ½ cup milk
Ketchup or tomato sauce

Combine hamburger, mustard, salt, and savory. Shape into 6 patties.

Combine biscuit mix and milk. Turn out onto sheet of waxed paper. Knead 6 times. Roll out ¼ inch thick on a lightly floured pastry cloth or board. Cut 12 circles the size of the patties (a No. 2 can is about right).

Place 2 biscuit circles together shortcake fashion. Place patties and biscuits on a baking sheet or jelly roll pan.

Bake in a hot oven (400°F.) for 15 minutes. Serve patties between biscuit shortcakes with ketchup or tomato sauce. Serves 6.

BEEF AND MUSHROOMS ON TOAST

1 pound ground beef
1 medium onion, minced
½ cup diced celery
½ medium green pepper, minced
1 cup sliced mushrooms
1½ teaspoons salt
⅛ teaspoon pepper
Dash of cayenne
2 tablespoons quick-cooking tapioca
8 slices toast

Brown beef, stirring with fork. Add onion, celery, green pepper, mushrooms, seasonings, and 2 cups water.

Cover, and simmer 25 minutes. Add tapioca, and cook until gravy thickens slightly and tapioca is clear. Serve on toast. Serves 4.

SAUCE AND GRAVY COOKBOOK

One thinks of sauces in connection with French cookery especially, for it is the French who have perfected the sauce and from whose language we derive the word. Sauce is the delightful finishing touch that distinguishes just an average cook from a master.

Master Sauces with Variations

MASTER WHITE SAUCE

Thin White Sauce:

- 1 tablespoon butter or fat
- 1 tablespoon flour
- ¼ teaspoon salt
- 1 cup milk, cream, or stock

Medium White Sauce:

- 2 tablespoons butter or fat
- 2 tablespoons flour
- ¼ teaspoon salt
- 1 cup milk, cream, or stock

Thick White Sauce:

- 3 tablespoons butter or fat
- 3 to 4 tablespoons flour
- ¼ teaspoon or more salt
- 1 cup milk, cream, or stock

Use methods 1, 2, or 3 (below). Makes about 1 cup sauce.

1. Melt butter; stir in flour and salt.

2. Add milk gradually; stir until smooth.

3. A perfect white sauce is smooth, glossy, satiny.

FOR A PERFECT WHITE SAUCE

WHITE SAUCE USES

Thin Sauce: Use as base for cream soups and other sauces.

Medium Sauce: Use for creamed and scalloped dishes, and gravies.

Thick Sauce: Use for croquettes and soufflés.

   Method 1: Melt fat, stir in flour and salt. Cook until mixture bubbles.
   Remove from heat; add liquid, and stir until smooth.
   Cook in double boiler or over low heat until mixture thickens, stirring constantly or not at all.

   Method 2: Melt fat and remove from heat. Add flour and salt. Stir until smooth.
   Add liquid gradually, stirring constantly over low heat until mixture thickens.

   Method 3: Stir enough liquid into flour and salt to form a thin smooth paste.
   Scald remainder of liquid in double boiler. Add flour paste to hot liquid, stirring constantly until mixture thickens.
   Cover and cook 20 minutes longer. Stir in fat just before serving.
   To keep hot and prevent crust from forming over sauce, place over hot water and cover tightly.

WHITE SAUCE VARIATIONS

Asparagus Sauce: Add $\frac{1}{2}$ cup cooked or canned asparagus, cut into small pieces, to hot medium white sauce. Serve with omelets or soufflés.

Caper Sauce: Add 3 to 4 tablespoons chopped capers and 1 teaspoon lemon juice to white sauce. Serve with fish.

Cheese Sauce: Add $\frac{1}{2}$ to 1 cup chopped or grated American cheese and a dash of Worcestershire sauce or paprika (optional) to white sauce.
   Stir over hot, not boiling, water until cheese is melted. Serve with fish, eggs, macaroni, or rice.

Cheese Olive Sauce: Prepare thin white sauce and omit salt. Add $\frac{1}{2}$ to 1 cup chopped or grated American cheese and $\frac{1}{2}$ cup sliced stuffed olives to white sauce.
   Stir over hot, not boiling, water until cheese is melted. Serve with macaroni, rice, or vegetables.

Cheese Tomato Sauce: Use $\frac{1}{2}$ cup tomato juice or strained tomatoes and $\frac{1}{2}$ cup milk in preparing medium sauce.
   Add $\frac{1}{4}$ cup grated or finely cut American cheese to hot sauce. Stir until melted. Serve over cauliflower.

Crabmeat Sauce: Remove bony particles from crabmeat and add $\frac{1}{2}$ to 1 cup flaked canned crabmeat to seasoned medium white sauce.

Flavor with 1 tablespoon dry white wine if desired.

Cream Onion or Celery Sauce: Sauté ¼ cup finely chopped onion or celery in 1 tablespoon butter or margarine. Add to 1 cup medium white sauce.

Creole Sauce: Use tomato juice or strained tomatoes for the liquid.

Sauté minced onion, chopped green pepper, and minced celery in the butter before flour is added.

Curry Sauce: Add ¼ to ½ teaspoon curry powder with dry ingredients. Serve with chicken, lamb, rice or fish.

Dill Sauce: Add 3 tablespoons minced fresh dill to 1 cup hot, seasoned medium white sauce.

Egg Sauce: Add 2 chopped hard-cooked eggs to white sauce, additional salt, and a dash of paprika. Serve with fish.

Goldenrod Sauce: Add 2 chopped hard-cooked egg whites to 1 cup seasoned medium white sauce. Pour over fish and sprinkle with chopped hard-cooked egg yolks.

Green Pea Sauce: Add ½ cup hot cooked or canned peas and 1 tablespoon chopped pimiento to hot medium white sauce. Serve with omelets or salmon or tuna loaf.

Horseradish Sauce: Add 2 to 4 tablespoons prepared drained horseradish, and ¼ to ½ teaspoon prepared mustard to white sauce. Serve with boiled beef or corned beef.

Lobster or Shrimp Sauce: Add ½ to 1 cup canned or cooked lobster meat or shrimp, cut into small pieces to seasoned medium white sauce.

For added flavor, add a tablespoon dry white wine. Serve with omelets, baked, broiled, or poached fish.

Milanese Sauce: Use ½ cup veal stock and ½ cup milk in preparing medium white sauce.

Add 2 tablespoons grated Parmesan cheese to the thickened sauce. Serve with veal.

Mock Hollandaise Sauce: To ½ cup well seasoned white sauce, add equal amount of mayonnaise and enough lemon juice to sharpen. Serve on asparagus and other green vegetables.

Mushroom Sauce: Add ½ to 1 cup sliced cooked or canned mushrooms to white sauce. Serve with chicken or vegetables.

Mustard Sauce: Add 1 tablespoon prepared mustard to white sauce. Serve with fish or tongue.

Oyster Sauce: Gently cook ½ cup small oysters in their own liquid until they plump and the edges begin to curl, about 3 minutes.

Add to hot medium white sauce. Serve with omelets, fish patties, and timbales.

Paprika Sauce: Add ½ to 1 teaspoon paprika with dry ingredients. Season with ¼ teaspoon onion juice, if desired. Serve with noodles, macaroni, or chicken.

Pimiento Sauce: Add ¼ cup chopped pimiento to white sauce; ¼ cup chopped green pepper may be added, if desired. Serve with fish or vegetables.

Wine Egg Sauce: To 1½ cups medium white sauce, add 1 teaspoon Worcestershire sauce, 4 chopped hard-cooked eggs, and 2 tablespoons sherry or other white wine. Blend thoroughly and serve hot on fish.

Yellow Sauce: Add a little cold water to a slightly beaten egg yolk, and stir slowly into the white sauce.

Cook for a minute over hot water, stirring constantly. Serve over vegetables, meat or poultry.

Asparagus Ham Rolls with Cheese Sauce

WHITE SAUCE MIX WITH DRY MILK
(Master Recipe)

- 2 cups nonfat dry milk solids
- 1 cup enriched flour
- 1 cup butter or margarine

Combine all ingredients with pastry blender until mixture is consistency of coarse corn meal.

Store in covered jars in refrigerator. Makes about 2 quarts medium sauce.

This master mix can be used for thin, medium, or thick white sauces. Just measure the required amount into a saucepan; add water and cook until thickened, adding the desired seasonings.

Thin White Sauce: Use 1/4 cup mix with 1 cup water.

Medium White Sauce: Use 1/2 cup mix with 1 cup water.

Thick White Sauce: Use 3/4 cup mix with 1 cup water.

CHEESE SAUCE #2

- 2 tablespoons butter or margarine
- 2 tablespoons flour
- 1 cup milk
- 1 egg yolk, well beaten
- 1/2 teaspoon dry mustard
- 1/8 teaspoon pepper
- 3/4 teaspoon salt
- Few grains cayenne or paprika
- 2 tablespoons grated Parmesan cheese

Melt butter and blend in flour. Add milk slowly, stirring constantly. Cook over hot water until smooth and thick.

Pour over egg yolk, stirring constantly.

Season to taste. Add cheese. Serve with vegetables, fish, macaroni, or rice.

RICH CREAM SAUCE
(Master Recipe)

- 2 tablespoons butter or margarine
- 2 tablespoons flour
- 1 cup light cream
- 1/4 teaspoon salt
- Dash of pepper

Melt butter and remove from heat. Blend in flour; stir until smooth and gradually add cream.

Cook over hot water, stirring constantly until thick. Add salt and dash of pepper, if desired. Cook 5 minutes longer, stirring constantly.

Place over hot water. Cover tightly to keep hot. Serve with fish, croquettes, etc. Makes about 1 1/4 cups sauce.

Rich Cream Sauce Variations

Cream Gravy: In preparing master recipe for cream sauce substitute 2 tablespoons meat drippings for butter.

Horseradish Cream Sauce: Add 1/3 to 1/2 cup drained prepared horseradish to cream sauce.

Mushroom Cream Sauce: Add 1/4 to 1/3 cup sliced cooked or canned mushrooms to cream sauce.

Savory Cream Sauce: Add 1 teaspoon each of chopped parsley, onion, celery, and canned pimiento to cream sauce.

Truffle Sauce: Prepare cream sauce. At the end add 1 tablespoon chopped truffle and 1 tablespoon Madeira wine.

Yellow Cream Sauce: Combine 1 slightly beaten egg with 1/4 cup light cream, then stir slowly into cream sauce.

SPANISH SAUCE

1 tablespoon minced onion
1 tablespoon chopped green pepper
¼ cup sliced mushrooms
2 tablespoons fat
2 cups canned tomatoes
½ teaspoon salt
½ teaspoon chili powder

Sauté onion, green pepper, and mushrooms in hot fat over low heat about 5 minutes.

Add remaining ingredients and simmer until thickened. Makes about 1½ cups sauce.

SOUR CREAM CHEESE SAUCE

1 egg
1 teaspoon cornstarch
1 teaspoon salt
1 teaspoon Worcestershire sauce
¼ teaspoon dry mustard
¼ cup sour cream
1 cup diced Cheddar cheese
1½ cups milk, scalded

Beat egg; stir in cornstarch and seasonings. Add sour cream and cheese and mix well.

Gradually stir mixture into scalded milk and cook until thickened over hot water. Makes about 2 cups.

MUSHROOM SAUCE

½ cup butter or margarine
1 large can mushrooms or ¼ pound fresh mushrooms
¼ cup flour
2 cups chicken stock or 2 bouillon cubes and water
¼ cup cream or evaporated milk
⅛ teaspoon paprika
About ½ teaspoon salt
1 teaspoon lemon juice
1 teaspoon chopped parsley (optional)

Wash fresh mushrooms or drain canned mushrooms; cook in butter for 5 minutes.

Add flour and stir to blend well. Add stock and cook, stirring constantly, until thickened.

Add cream and mushroom liquid (if any). Add seasonings to taste.

Stir in lemon juice and parsley just before serving. Keep hot over water. Serve with chicken, sweetbreads, omelets, etc. Makes about 3 cups.

Meat Balls with Mushroom Sauce

Hollandaise Sauce

BECHAMEL SAUCE
(Master Recipe)

1½ cups chicken or veal stock
1 sprig parsley
6 celery leaves
½ small onion
¼ bay leaf
6 whole black peppers
3 tablespoons butter or margarine
3 tablespoons flour
Few grains cayenne
¼ teaspoon salt
Few grains nutmeg
1 cup scalded milk

Simmer stock with parsley, celery leaves, onion, bay leaf, and whole black peppers for 20 minutes.

Strain and measure. If necessary, add water to make 1 cup.

Melt butter over low heat and blend in flour and seasonings. Gradually add hot stock and scalded milk.

Bring to boiling point and let boil 2 minutes or until thick and smooth.

Strain through fine sieve. Serve on chicken croquettes, chicken mousse, or fried chicken. Makes about 2 cups.

Bechamel Sauce Variations

Fish Bechamel Sauce: Substitute fish stock for chicken or veal stock.

Stir a little hot stock into 1 slightly beaten egg and beat into remaining sauce. Blend in 1 tablespoon lemon juice.

Mornay Sauce: Add 2 to 4 tablespoons grated Parmesan cheese to sauce. Serve with vegetables or fish.

Yellow Bechamel Sauce: Stir 1 slightly beaten egg yolk into sauce.

Mushroom Bechamel Sauce: Sauté 1 cup sliced mushrooms in butter 5 minutes before blending in flour.

HOLLANDAISE SAUCE
(Master Recipe)

½ cup butter or margarine
4 egg yolks
2 tablespoons lemon juice
¼ teaspoon salt
Dash of cayenne
¼ cup boiling water

Divide butter into 3 portions. Beat egg yolks and lemon juice together. Add 1 piece of butter and cook in double boiler, stirring constantly until mixture begins to thicken.

Remove from range, add second piece of butter, and stir rapidly.

Then add remaining butter and continue to stir until mixture is completely blended. Add salt, cayenne, and boiling water.

Return to double boiler; cook until thickened, stirring constantly. Serve at once.

Note: Sauce may separate if cooked too long, or at too high a temperature, or if permitted to stand too long before serving. To smooth, beat in 1 tablespoon boiling water and a little lemon juice drop by drop, with a rotary beater.

Hollandaise Sauce Variations

Bearnaise Sauce: Reduce lemon juice to 1½ tablespoons. Add 1 teaspoon each chopped tarragon and chopped parsley, 1 tablespoon tarragon vinegar, and 1 teaspoon onion juice or ½ teaspoon onion salt. Serve with baked or broiled fish.

Chive Hollandaise Sauce: Add 1½ tablespoons finely chopped chives to sauce. Serve with vegetables.

Cucumber Hollandaise Sauce: Add 1 cup drained, chopped cucumber to sauce. Serve with fish.

Dill Hollandaise Sauce: Add 1 tablespoon chopped dill to sauce.

Mint Hollandaise Sauce: Add 1 tablespoon finely chopped mint to sauce.

BASIC À LA KING RECIPE

2 cups medium white sauce (made from stock if desired)
1 egg yolk, slightly beaten
1 cup cooked, diced meat, poultry, or fish
1 cup peas, canned or fresh
½ cup cooked celery, diced
2 tablespoons butter or margarine
¼ cup chopped green pepper and pimiento, mixed
½ pound mushrooms, diced
Salt and pepper

Make sauce in the top of a double boiler and when cooked and smooth, blend in egg yolk. Add meat, cooked peas, and celery.

Cook pepper, pimiento, and mushrooms in butter over low heat until tender. Add to cream sauce. A few drops of onion juice may be added, if desired. Serves 6.

MASTER BROWN SAUCE

4 tablespoons butter or fat
4 tablespoons flour
2 cups meat, vegetable, or fish stock
1 teaspoon salt
⅛ teaspoon pepper

Melt butter, blend in flour and cook until browned, stirring constantly.

Gradually add stock, stirring constantly, until mixture boils and thickens.

Add salt and pepper; cook 3 minutes longer, stirring constantly.

Serve with meat, poultry, fish or vegetables. Makes 2 cups.

Brown Sauce Variations

Creole Brown Sauce: Sauté ¼ cup chopped onion and ½ cup chopped green pepper in fat before adding flour.

Dill Brown Sauce: Add to brown sauce 2 tablespoons wine or cider vinegar and chopped dill to taste. Serve with veal or lamb.

Giblet Gravy #2: Substitute pan drippings for other fat. Add chopped cooked chicken or turkey giblets to gravy.

Mushroom Brown Sauce: Sauté 1 cup sliced mushrooms and 1 teaspoon chopped onion in fat before adding flour.

Olive Brown Sauce: Add about 12 sliced pitted green or ripe olives to brown sauce.

Pan Gravy: In Master Brown Sauce substitute pan drippings for other fat. Use water or stock.

Piquant Brown Sauce: Simmer together for a few minutes 2 tablespoons each tarragon vinegar and finely chopped green pepper, 1 teaspoon each chopped onion and chopped capers. Add to brown sauce with 2 tablespoons chopped pickle.

Serve with fish, beef, veal, or tongue. If used with fish, use fish stock when preparing master brown sauce.

Port Wine Brown Sauce: To 1 cup of brown sauce add 2 tablespoons port wine. Simmer about 5 minutes.

Savory Horseradish Brown Sauce: Add 3 to 4 tablespoons prepared horseradish and 1 tablespoon prepared mustard to brown sauce.

Spanish Brown Sauce: Sauté ¼ cup chopped onion, ½ cup chopped green pepper, ½ cup sliced mushrooms in fat before adding flour.

Substitute 1 cut tomato juice or stewed tomatoes for 1 cup stock. Serve with rice, spaghetti, or meat balls.

Use the Basic À La King recipe to prepare Chicken À La King; serve with corn meal pancakes.

The right sauce is a cook's best friend. It changes the most ordinary dish into a culinary triumph.

CREOLE SAUCE #2

- 2 tablespoons chopped onion
- 2 tablespoons butter or margarine
- 1 tablespoon flour
- 2 cups canned tomatoes
- 1/2 cup chopped celery
- 1 green pepper, chopped
- 4 tablespoons chopped cooked ham or bacon
- Chopped parsley
- Salt and pepper to taste

Cook onion in butter for a few minutes. Sprinkle flour over onion and quickly stir in tomatoes, celery, and green pepper. Simmer about 20 minutes.

Add ham or bacon, parsley, and salt and pepper. Serve with omelets, spaghetti and fish. Makes about 2 1/2 cups sauce.

VELOUTÉ SAUCE
(Master Recipe)

- 2 tablespoons butter or margarine
- 2 tablespoons flour
- 1 cup fish, chicken, or veal stock
- Salt to taste
- Dash of white pepper
- 1/8 teaspoon nutmeg (optional)

Melt butter over low heat. Blend in flour. Remove from heat and gradually stir in stock.

Return to heat and cook, stirring constantly, until smooth and thick. Blend in seasonings.

If desired, strain through a very fine sieve. Serve hot over croquettes, baked fish, etc. Makes about 1 cup.

Velouté Sauce Variations

Allemande Sauce: Stir into strained velouté sauce 1 well beaten egg, 1 teaspoon lemon juice, and 2 tablespoons cream or finely grated Parmesan cheese.

Anchovy Velouté Sauce: Omit salt and use fish stock in master recipe.

Blend 1 1/2 teaspoons anchovy paste into flour and butter mixture.

Add 1 tablespoon finely minced parsley just before serving.

Caper Velouté Sauce: Prepare master recipe. Add 1 teaspoon capers to strained sauce. Serve with lamb or vegetables.

If serving with fish, substitute fish stock for chicken or veal stock.

Fish Velouté Sauce: Use fish stock in master recipe.

Normandy Sauce: Use fish stock in master recipe. Beat a little hot sauce into 2 slightly beaten egg yolks and beat into remaining sauce. Blend in 1 tablespoon lemon juice, salt, pepper, and cayenne to taste.

Parsley Sauce: Add 2 tablespoons finely chopped parsley to strained Allemande Sauce.

Soubise Sauce (Onion Sauce): Cover 3 medium-sized onions with boiling water and cook until soft. Drain and rub onion pulp through a sieve into Velouté Sauce.

Add 1/2 cup cream and stir until boiling point is reached.

Remove from heat and stir in 1 tablespoon butter. Season with salt to taste. Serve with mutton, pork, or hard-cooked eggs.

Sauce Poulette: Add 1/2 cup sliced cooked mushrooms to strained Allemande Sauce.

BORDELAISE SAUCE

2 tablespoons butter or margarine
2 tablespoons flour
2 cups brown stock or consommé
2 cloves garlic, chopped fine
2 tablespoons chopped onion
Bit of bay leaf
2 tablespoons chopped ham
2 slices carrot
2 tablespoons chopped parsley
8 whole black peppers
1 tablespoon Worcestershire sauce
1 tablespoon ketchup
2 tablespoons sherry

Melt butter. Stir in flour until lightly browned. Add remaining ingredients except sherry and simmer 8 minutes.

Strain sauce and season with sherry, salt and pepper to taste. Makes about 2 cups.

Sauces for Meats and Poultry

ENGLISH BREAD SAUCE

1 onion
6 whole cloves
2 cups milk
Few grains cayenne
1 teaspoon salt
1 cup fresh fine breadcrumbs

Stud onion with cloves. Place onion and milk in a saucepan. Add cayenne and salt. Bring to boiling point. Cook 5 minutes.

Strain and add breadcrumbs. Taste and add more salt if necessary.

Serve with roast poultry or game. If a richer sauce is desired, add a little butter or cream at the end.

HOT STEAK SAUCE

$1/2$ cup butter or margarine
2 to 4 tablespoons minced green onions
3 tablespoons ketchup
3 tablespoons Worcestershire sauce
$1/4$ teaspoon dry English mustard
Salt, pepper, paprika to taste

Melt butter and add rest of ingredients. Heat through and serve hot with steak. Makes about 1 cup.

ORANGE SAUCE FOR ROAST DUCK

$2/3$ cup sugar
$1/4$ teaspoon salt
2 teaspoons cornstarch
1 cup boiling water
1 teaspoon butter or margarine
Juice and grated rind of 2 oranges

Mix sugar, salt, and cornstarch. Pour hot water over mixture, stirring constantly. Cook until thick and clear.

Add butter, orange juice, and grated rind just before removing from heat. Stir well and serve with duck. Makes about 2 cups.

CURRANT JELLY SAUCE

1 8-ounce glass currant jelly
2 tablespoons vinegar
1 teaspoon dry mustard
$1/4$ teaspoon ground cloves
$1/4$ teaspoon cinnamon

Heat jelly until melted. Add other ingredients and simmer 10 minutes. Serve hot with ham or baked canned meats. Makes about 1 cup.

MINT SAUCE FOR LAMB

2 to 3 tablespoons sugar
$1/4$ cup hot water
$1/2$ cup mild vinegar
$1/2$ cup chopped fresh mint leaves
3 tablespoons lemon juice
$1/2$ teaspoon salt

Dissolve sugar in water. Add vinegar. Bring to boil.

Pour over fresh mint leaves. Add lemon juice and salt.

Let stand $1/2$ to 1 hour before straining and serving with lamb. Makes about 1 cup sauce.

Smoked Tongue with Raisin Sauce

CURRY SAUCE

- 2 tablespoons butter or margarine
- 1 medium onion, chopped
- 2 tablespoons flour
- ½ teaspoon curry powder
- 1 cup beef broth, bouillon, or consommé

Melt butter; add onion and let cook until tender.

Stir in flour; let it brown slightly, then add curry and liquid. Cook and stir until sauce is thickened and smooth.

A hint of garlic may be added to this sauce by cooking a clove with onion for 1 minute. Serve with veal, lamb, or poultry. Makes 1 cup.

RAISIN SAUCE FOR TONGUE AND HAM

- ½ cup brown sugar
- 1½ teaspoons dry mustard
- 1 tablespoon cornstarch
- 1½ cups water
- ¼ cup vinegar
- ⅓ cup raisins
- 1 tablespoon butter or margarine

Combine dry ingredients; slowly add water and vinegar.

Add raisins and cook over low heat, stirring constantly, until thickened.

Cook 10 minutes longer to plump raisins, then add butter or margarine.

PARSLEY SAUCE FOR BROILED STEAK

- ½ cup chopped parsley
- 1 tablespoon Worcestershire sauce
- Salt and pepper
- ½ teaspoon dry mustard
- 2 tablespoons butter or margarine
- Grated rind of ¼ lemon

Combine parsley, Worcestershire sauce, salt and pepper to taste, and mustard.

After broiling steaks, add butter to drippings and allow to melt. Combine with parsley mixture and add lemon rind.

Pour over steaks while very hot. Makes about ½ cup.

HORSERADISH SAUCE

- 1 tablespoon butter or margarine
- 1 tablespoon flour
- 1 cup milk
- ½ cup prepared horseradish
- 1 tablespoon lemon juice
- Salt and pepper
- 1 tablespoon minced pimiento

Melt butter and blend in flour. Slowly add milk, stirring constantly until the mixture boils.

Add drained horseradish to lemon juice, seasonings, and pimiento. Add to cream sauce and serve hot. Serve with "boiled" meats and poultry. Makes 1½ cups.

GINGERSNAP SAUCE

- 5 crushed gingersnaps
- ½ cup brown sugar
- ¼ cup vinegar
- 1 teaspoon onion juice
- 1 cup hot water
- 1 lemon, sliced
- ¼ cup raisins

Mix ingredients in saucepan and heat, stirring constantly, until smooth and fairly thick. Serve with boiled tongue. Makes 1½ cups.

Gravies

FLOUR PASTE FOR THICKENING SAUCES AND GRAVIES

A thin paste will give better results. The usual proportions are about 1 part water to 2 parts flour.

Blend flour and cold water together, then stir as much as required into boiling stock or drippings. Cook until sauce thickens.

HOW TO BROWN FLOUR FOR GRAVY

Spread flour on pan and place in slow oven (300°F.). Stir frequently to prevent burning; 20 to 25 minutes are required to brown 3 cups.

Flour may be browned in a skillet on top of range. Watch carefully to avoid burning flour.

Store browned flour in a tightly covered receptacle.

POT ROAST GRAVY

Measure amount of pot roast liquid left in the cooking pan. Add to this enough water, soup, stock, or water in which vegetables have been cooked to make the desired amount of gravy.

For each cup of liquid, measure 2 tablespoons flour and make a smooth paste by adding enough cold water to blend. The water must be cold to prevent lumping. Use a spoon or egg beater to thin flour paste.

Add paste gradually to pot roast liquid, stirring constantly over moderate heat. Bring to a boil and simmer 2 or 3 minutes.

PAN GRAVY

Measure 1 cup pan drippings. Add ½ cup boiling water. Season to taste with salt, pepper, and Worcestershire sauce. Heat. Serve just enough over meat to moisten well.

TO PREPARE GRAVY WITH PAN DRIPPINGS

1. Measure the fat and drippings to be used.

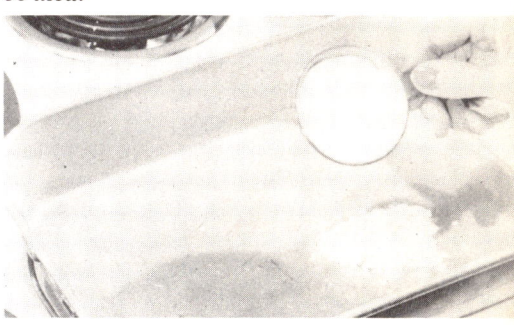

2. Measure and add flour, stirring until well blended.

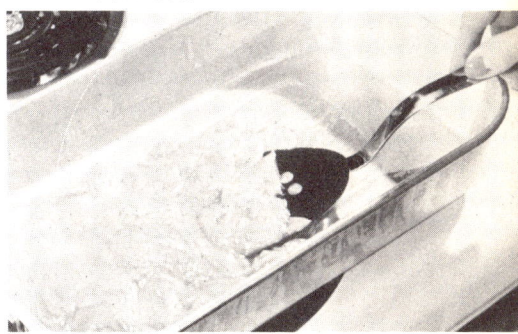

3. Gradually add broth or other liquid called for in recipe.

4. Cook over low heat, stirring until thick and smooth.

Chicken with Country Gravy

ROAST BEEF GRAVY

Skim fat from the roast drippings, leaving about 4 tablespoons in pan. Add 6 to 8 tablespoons flour and stir over moderate heat until flour is thoroughly browned. Do not add water until the flour is thoroughly browned.

Gradually add 2 cups water or stock. Cook, stirring until gravy is smooth and thickened. Season to taste with salt and pepper.

GIBLET GRAVY

Chop cooked giblets fine and save broth in which they were cooked.

Skim off excess fat in roasting pan, leaving about ½ cup for quart of gravy.

Add ½ cup flour and stir until smooth over low heat.

Gradually add 4 cups broth, using water if there isn't enough broth. Stir constantly to keep gravy smooth as it thickens.

Add chopped giblets, and salt and pepper, to season. For thinner gravy, add more liquid. Makes 1 quart.

SAVORY ONION GRAVY FOR STEAKS

- 4 cups sliced onions
- 2 tablespoons fat
- 2 tablespoons flour
- 2 cups meat stock
- 1 tablespoon Worcestershire sauce
- Salt and pepper to taste

Cook onions in hot fat until golden; stir in flour.

Add meat stock, Worcestershire, salt and pepper, and cook, stirring constantly, over low heat until thick. Cover and simmer 10 minutes. Makes 6 to 8 servings.

Note: 2 bouillon cubes dissolved in 2 cups hot water may be used instead of meat stock.

COUNTRY GRAVY

- 2 cups milk
- ¼ cup flour
- ¼ cup drippings
- Salt and pepper

This is milk gravy made after frying chicken, salt pork, or sausage.

Make a smooth thin paste with a little of the milk and flour.

Add paste to hot drippings, stirring constantly.

Add remaining milk, stir and cook until gravy is smooth and thickened. Season to taste.

WINE GRAVY

Make gravy according to any of given recipes. Add 2 tablespoons wine for each cup of gravy and cook only long enough to heat through.

Use red wine for beef gravy and white wine for veal.

SOUR CREAM GRAVY

Prepare gravy according to any of given recipes. Add ½ cup sour cream for each cup of gravy, just before removing from heat.

Cook just long enough to heat sour cream. Do not boil as sour cream will curdle.

Steak with Savory Onion Gravy

Sauces for Fish and Shellfish

BLACK BUTTER
(Buerre Noir)

- 4 tablespoons butter or margarine
- 4 sprigs parsley, stripped of stems
- 2 tablespoons lemon juice

Melt butter and when very hot add parsley. Fry until crisp and brown.

When butter is brown but not burnt, pour into serving dish.

Heat lemon juice very hot and add to butter before serving.

DRAWN BUTTER SAUCE

- 1/3 cup butter or margarine
- 3 tablespoons flour
- 1 1/2 cups vegetable or fish stock
- 1/2 teaspoon salt
- 1/8 teaspoon pepper
- 1 teaspoon lemon juice

Melt half the butter. Add flour and blend until smooth. Gradually add stock.

Bring to boiling point, stirring constantly. Cook 3 minutes. Add seasonings and remaining butter.

Drawn Butter Sauce Variations

Drawn Butter with Anchovy: Season Drawn Butter Sauce to taste with anchovy paste.

Drawn Butter with Capers: Add 1 tablespoon drained capers to Drawn Butter Sauce.

Drawn Butter with Egg: Add 2 sliced hard-cooked eggs to Drawn Butter Sauce.

Drawn Butter with Seafood: Add 1/2 cup cooked or canned shrimp or other seafood to Drawn Butter Sauce.

LEMON SAUCE FOR FISH

- 2 cups hot fish stock
- Juice of 2 lemons
- 1/4 cup chopped blanched almonds
- 3 beaten egg yolks
- Sugar

Mix lemon juice, almonds, and fish stock. Cook over boiling water 15 minutes.

Add a little cold water to the beaten egg yolks and stir slowly into the sauce. Add sugar to taste. Serve at once, hot.

CUCUMBER SAUCE FOR FISH

- 1 cup diced cucumber
- 1/2 cup water
- 2 tablespoons butter or margarine
- 2 tablespoons flour
- 2 teaspoons lemon juice
- 1 teaspoon grated lemon rind
- 1 teaspoon grated onion
- 1/2 teaspoon salt
- 1/2 teaspoon Ac'cent
- Few grains pepper

Cook cucumber in water until clear and tender; drain and save cooking water.

Melt butter or margarine; blend in flour.

Measure cooking water; add enough more water to make 1 cup; add to flour mixture; stir over low heat until smooth and thickened.

Add remaining ingredients; blend well. Add cooked cucumber. Serve with broiled fish. Makes about 2 cups.

SOY BUTTER SAUCE

Heat 1/4 cup butter or margarine and add 3 tablespoons soy sauce.

HOT TARTAR SAUCE

- 3/4 cup medium white sauce
- 1/4 cup mayonnaise
- 1 tablespoon lemon juice
- 1 teaspoon minced onion
- 2 tablespoons minced parsley
- 3 tablespoons minced dill pickle
- Salt and pepper

Combine and heat together, seasoning to taste.

Flavored butter sauces take fish out of the ordinary and make it a specialty dish.

PARSLEY BUTTER SAUCE

Combine 2 to 3 teaspoons finely chopped parsley with 1/2 cup melted butter or margarine.

Add 1 teaspoon lemon juice, 1/2 teaspoon salt, and 1/8 teaspoon pepper.

BROWN BUTTER SAUCE

Brown slowly but do not burn, 1/4 cup butter or margarine, stirring constantly. Add 2 teaspoons lemon juice and 1/4 teaspoon salt.

OLIVE BUTTER SAUCE

Heat 1/4 cup butter or margarine and add 2 tablespoons minced stuffed olives.

SAUCE MEUNIÈRE

Heat 4 to 5 tablespoons butter or margarine until it is brown.

Stir in 1 teaspoon lemon juice and pour over food already sprinkled with chopped parsley.

MINT BUTTER SAUCE

Combine 2 to 3 tablespoons finely chopped mint with 1/2 cup melted butter or margarine.

ALMOND BUTTER SAUCE

Sauté 1/4 cup shredded blanched almonds in 1/4 cup butter or margarine until lightly browned, stirring constantly. Serve with fish. Makes about 1/3 cup.

PIMIENTO BUTTER SAUCE

Heat 1/4 cup butter or margarine and add 1 minced pimiento.

CHIVES OR CHERVIL BUTTER SAUCE

Heat 1/4 cup butter or margarine and add 2 tablespoons minced chervil or 1 tablespoon minced chives.

GARLIC OR ONION BUTTER SAUCE

Heat 1/4 cup butter or margarine and 1 clove garlic or 1 very small minced onion. Strain.

HORSERADISH BUTTER SAUCE

Combine 2 to 4 tablespoons horseradish with 1/2 cup melted butter or margarine.

LEMON BUTTER

Combine 2 to 3 tablespoons lemon juice with 1/2 cup melted butter or margarine. Add 1 tablespoon chopped parsley and a dash of paprika.

CHILI SAUCE BUTTER

Heat 1/4 cup butter or margarine. Add 2 tablespoons chili sauce and 1 tablespoon lemon juice.

LEMON CHIVE BUTTER SAUCE

Combine 1 tablespoon chopped chives and 2 tablespoons lemon juice with 1/2 cup melted butter or margarine.

MAÎTRE D'HÔTEL BUTTER

Cream 1/2 cup butter. Add 1 tablespoon chopped parsley and gradually blend in 3 tablespoons lemon juice, 1/2 teaspoon salt, and 1/8 teaspoon pepper. Serve with broiled fish. Makes 2/3 cup sauce.

ANCHOVY BUTTER SAUCE

Add 1 tablespoon anchovy paste to Maître D'Hôtel Butter with the lemon juice.

Fresh Fruit Salad

Make-A-Meal Salad

Shrimp a la New Orleans

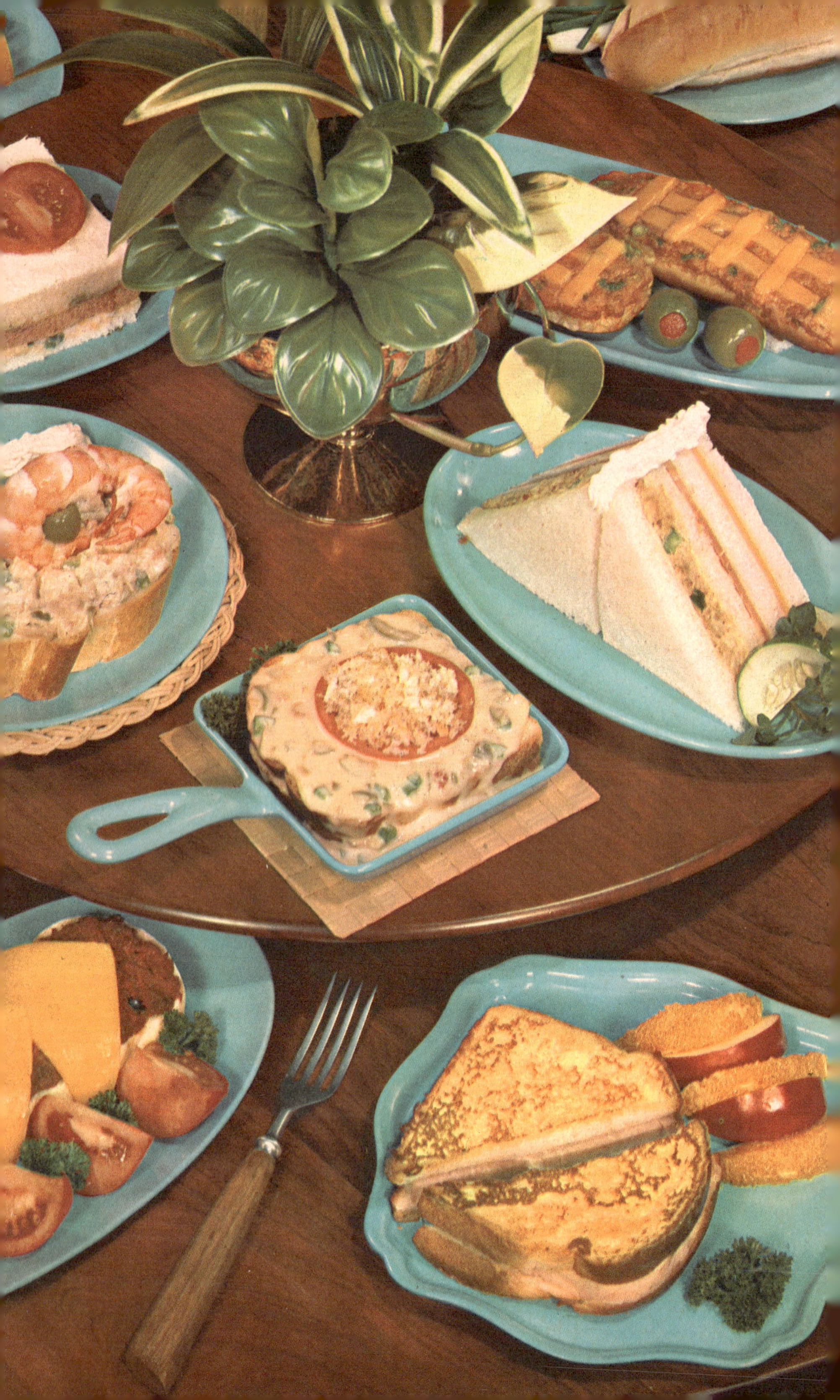

Sauces for Vegetables

SAVORY BUTTER SAUCE

You can make this with a variety of seasonings to pep up vegetables.

To about 1/4 cup melted butter or margarine add 1 teaspoon lemon juice and your choice of these: 1 teaspoon celery, poppy or caraway seed; 1/2 teaspoon garlic salt or 1/4 teaspoon each of powdered rosemary and marjoram.

PARSLEY-BUTTER SAUCE

1/2 cup melted butter or margarine
3 to 4 tablespoons chopped parsley

Wash and dry parsley. Chop parsley fine and add to hot melted butter; pour over cooked potatoes and serve immediately.

ALMOND BUTTER FOR VEGETABLES

To 1/4 cup melted butter or margarine, add 2 tablespoons chopped salted almonds and 1 tablespoon lemon juice.

Serve over green beans, Brussels sprouts, or broccoli.

MINT BUTTER FOR VEGETABLES

To 1/4 cup butter or margarine, add 1 tablespoon chopped fresh mint leaves. Serve on peas, carrots, or a combination of the two.

ORANGE BUTTER FOR BEETS

To 1/4 cup butter or margarine, add 3 tablespoons orange juice and 1 tablespoon grated orange rind.

Simmer for a few minutes over low heat and serve over beets.

GREEK LEMON-EGG SAUCE FOR VEGETABLES

3 tablespoons lemon juice
2 tablespoons flour
1/4 teaspoon salt
1/8 teaspoon black pepper
2 cups vegetable water or meat stock
2 beaten eggs

Combine lemon juice, flour, salt, and black pepper.

Add this to a heated mixture of vegetable water or meat stock. Bring to boil and let cook until slightly thickened.

Pour some of this hot mixture over eggs in a bowl. Return to main mixture, but do not have it boiling and do not let it boil or eggs will curdle.

To use, pour over baked or cooked vegetables.

SOUR CREAM SAUCE
(Mock Hollandaise)

2 egg yolks
3/4 cup sour cream
1 tablespoon lemon juice
1/2 teaspoon minced parsley
1/8 teaspoon salt
1/4 teaspoon paprika

Beat egg yolks and cream together in top part of double boiler.

Place over simmering water and cook, stirring constantly, until mixture is of custard consistency.

Remove from heat and add remaining ingredients. Serve at once with vegetables or fish.

Flavored butters are perfect for adding zest to the mildest tasting vegetables.

MOCK HOLLANDAISE SAUCE

1. Place an 8-ounce package of cream cheese (which has been standing at room temperature until soft) in the top of double boiler. Cream it with a spoon.

2. Add 2 egg yolks, one at a time, blending thoroughly after each addition.

Slowly add 2 tablespoons lemon juice and a dash of salt.

3. Place over hot water just until the sauce is heated through. Pour over hot cooked asparagus spears placed on toast points.

4. Serve hot. A delicious sauce, too, for broccoli and cauliflower.

SNAPPY MOCK HOLLANDAISE SAUCE

Heat ½ cup mayonnaise over very low heat; stir in 1 teaspoon lemon juice and ⅛ teaspoon Tabasco.

Adds glamour to asparagus, broccoli, green beans, and other vegetables. Serves 4.

VINAIGRETTE SAUCE

- 1 teaspoon salt
- ½ teaspoon paprika
- ⅛ teaspoon pepper
- ½ tablespoon dry mustard
- ½ teaspoon sugar
- 1 tablespoon tarragon vinegar
- 2 tablespoons cider vinegar
- ⅓ cup olive oil or salad oil
- 1 tablespoon chopped pickles
- 1 tablespoon chopped stuffed olives
- 1 teaspoon minced onion

Mix all ingredients together and beat well.

Heat to boiling point and serve with vegetables such as spinach, broccoli, artichokes, and asparagus.

Tomato Sauces

TOMATO SAUCE
(Master Recipe)

- 2 cups canned tomatoes
- 2 slices onion
- 1 teaspoon sugar
- 1 bay leaf
- 2 whole allspice
- 2 whole cloves
- Butter or other fat
- Flour
- Salt and pepper

Simmer tomato, onion, sugar, and spices 10 minutes. Strain through fine sieve and measure the liquid.

For each cup liquid blend 2 tablespoons flour and 2 tablespoons melted fat. Add to tomato juice with salt and pepper to season, and stir until thickened.

Continue to cook over hot water 5 to 10 minutes. Serve hot over croquettes, meat loaf, or spaghetti.

Tomato Sauce Variations

Tomato Cheese Sauce: Add ½ cup grated cheese to tomato sauce. Cook until cheese is melted.

Tomato Lobster Sauce: Add 1 cup chopped cooked or canned lobster meat to tomato sauce. Use shrimp or lobster sauces over cooked spaghetti or macaroni.

Tomato Meat Sauce: Brown tiny meat balls in fat before blending in flour. Serve with spaghetti or noodles in casserole.

Tomato Shrimp Sauce: Add 1 cup canned or cooked cleaned shrimp to tomato sauce.

Tomato Wine Sauce: Add 1/4 cup sherry to tomato sauce.

TOMATO SAUCE
(Italian Style)

- 2 cups chopped onion
- 3 cloves garlic, chopped
- 3 tablespoons olive oil
- 1 No. 2 1/2 can (3 1/2 cups) Italian style plum tomatoes
- 2 6-ounce cans tomato paste
- About 2 cups water or meat broth
- 1 bay leaf
- 1/2 teaspoon salt
- 1/2 teaspoon oregano or 1/4 teaspoon each oregano and basil

Sauté onion and garlic in olive oil until brown, stirring often.

Add tomatoes, tomato paste, water or broth, bay leaf, salt, and pepper. Simmer, uncovered, stirring occasionally, about 2 hours. Add additional water as needed.

Add oregano and basil and continue cooking about 15 minutes. The sauce should be thick. Makes about 1 1/2 quarts.

SPANISH MEAT SAUCE

- 1/2 pound hamburger
- 3 tablespoons fat
- 2 tablespoons chopped onion
- 1/2 cup chopped celery
- 2 tablespoons flour
- 1 cup water
- 2 tablespoons chopped green pepper
- 1/2 teaspoon chili powder
- 1/2 teaspoon salt
- 1/8 teaspoon black pepper
- 2 cups cooked tomatoes

Brown meat slightly in hot fat in heavy skillet. Add onion and celery and continue cooking until well browned. Add flour and blend. Add remaining ingredients. Simmer 1 hour or longer.

Serve over hot fluffy rice, noodles, or toast points. Serves 6.

BARBECUE SAUCE

- 1 medium onion, chopped
- 2 tablespoons fat
- 2 tablespoons lemon juice
- 1 cup water
- 1/2 cup chopped celery
- 1/2 teaspoon dry mustard
- 2 tablespoons vinegar
- 2 tablespoons brown sugar
- 1 cup ketchup
- 2 tablespoons Worcestershire sauce
- 1/8 teaspoon pepper
- 1 teaspoon salt

Brown onion in hot fat. Add remaining ingredients and simmer gently 20 to 30 minutes. Pour over meat before cooking or baste meat during roasting.

Use over baked or broiled chicken, frankfurters, braised beef, steaks, hamburgers, etc. Makes about 2 cups sauce.

ZIPPY TOMATO SAUCE

Combine 1 8-ounce can tomato sauce, 3 tablespoons brown sugar, 1 tablespoon vinegar, 1 teaspoon onion flakes, 1 teaspoon Worcestershire sauce; simmer 5 minutes.

Serve over meat loaf, ground beef patties, stuffed peppers, cabbage rolls, omelet. Makes 1 cup.

For a barbecued touch, spoon barbecue sauce over chicken toward end of broiling.

Omelets with Quick Spanish Sauce

Quick Sauces with Canned Soups

Condensed soups when heated may be the right consistency for the sauce you want. Use such soups as asparagus, celery, mushroom, tomato, etc.

Vary the seasonings by using about 2 tablespoons sherry wine, a little salt, pepper, chili powder, cayenne or Tabasco sauce, Worcestershire sauce, curry powder, dry mustard, etc.

If the sauce is too thick, dilute with a little milk or stock.

Ready-to-serve soups may be thickened with a roux made of flour blended into melted butter, but be sure to cook several minutes after blending in the roux. Specific examples of such sauces are given in this section.

QUICK TOMATO SAUCE

1 can (1¼ cups) condensed tomato soup
¼ bay leaf
4 whole cloves
1 sprig parsley

Combine and heat thoroughly. Strain before serving.

QUICK À LA KING SAUCE

1 finely chopped green pepper
1 tablespoon butter or margarine
1 can (1¼ cups) condensed cream of mushroom soup
1 pimiento, chopped

Sauté green pepper in melted butter. Add to heated mushroom soup with pimiento.

QUICK SPANISH SAUCE

2 tablespoons finely chopped onion
1 tablespoon finely chopped green pepper
2 tablespoons shortening or bacon drippings
1 can (1¼ cups) condensed tomato soup
½ cup cooked mushrooms, if desired

Cook onion and green pepper until tender in shortening.

Stir in soup and mushrooms; continue cooking over low heat about 5 minutes.

This sauce is especially good on omelets, meat, or cooked rice. Makes about 2 cups.

QUICK ONION SAUCE

Heat 1 can ready-to-serve onion soup. Blend in a little flour to thicken it and cook a few minutes.

If desired, add a little grated cheese just before serving.

QUICK MUSHROOM SAUCE

Combine 1 can (1¼ cups) condensed cream of mushroom soup with ½ cup hot milk. Heat thoroughly. Serve at once.

QUICK HOT MUSTARD SAUCE

Blend 1 can (1¼ cups) condensed cream of celery soup, ½ cup milk, and 2 tablespoons prepared mustard; heat well.

Serve over broccoli, asparagus, cauliflower, carrots, or with tongue, ham, corned beef. Makes 2 cups.

QUICK BARBECUE SAUCE

1 can (1¼ cups) condensed cream of tomato soup, undiluted
½ cup India relish
¼ cup finely chopped onion
1 tablespoon Worcestershire sauce
1 tablespoon flour

Combine soup, relish, onion, and Worcestershire. Blend in flour, stirring constantly, over low heat.

Bring to boiling point and simmer 3 minutes.

Use for barbecued meat, poultry, or fish, or serve hot with meat or fish loaf, on frankfurters, etc.

QUICK BARBECUE SAUCE #2

⅓ cup finely chopped onion
⅓ cup finely chopped celery
½ clove garlic, minced
3 tablespoons melted shortening or oil
1 can (1¼ cups) condensed tomato soup
2 tablespoons brown sugar
2 tablespoons Worcestershire sauce
2 tablespoons lemon juice or vinegar
2 teaspoons prepared mustard
4 drops Tabasco sauce, if desired

Cook onion, celery, and garlic until soft in shortening in heavy skillet.

Add remaining ingredients; stir well and simmer 10 minutes.

Excellent on broiled steaks, chops, chicken, baked spareribs, meat loaf or with hot dogs or hamburgers. Makes about 2½ cups.

QUICK CREOLE SAUCE

¼ cup finely chopped onion
¼ cup finely chopped green pepper
2 tablespoons melted shortening or oil
½ cup water
1 can (1¼ cups) condensed tomato soup
1 teaspoon vinegar
Black or cayenne pepper to taste
Dash of Tabasco sauce

Cook onion and green pepper until tender in shortening in heavy skillet.

Add remaining ingredients and cook over low heat about 10 minutes.

Use on rice, seafood, roast meats, or as a hot "dunking" sauce. Makes about 2 cups.

QUICK MEAT SAUCE

To a can of condensed tomato soup add canned luncheon meat which has been finely chopped or cut in small cubes.

Heat thoroughly and season to taste. Serve over cooked macaroni, spaghetti, noodles, or rice.

Cold Sauces

MAYONNAISE CHAUD-FROID

2 tablespoons (2 envelopes) unflavored gelatin
½ cup cold water
2 cups mayonnaise

Soften gelatin in cold water for 5 minutes and stir over hot water until the gelatin is dissolved.

Add mayonnaise and blend well. This sauce is used to bind salad mixtures which are to be molded.

It is used to coat cold fish, lobster, poultry, and meats, and fix decorations on them.

HORSERADISH
(Home Prepared)

Wash horseradish root, scrape or cut off thick peel. Grate. Mix well with enough white vinegar to cover.

Add sugar to taste and cover tightly to keep in strength.

Horseradish with Mayonnaise: Mix ¼ cup grated horseradish with 1 cup mayonnaise.

Horseradish with Sour Apples: Add grated sour apples and a few ground almonds to plain horseradish.

For zestful eating, select a tasty sauce to accompany baked or broiled fish.

SOUR CREAM-CUCUMBER SAUCE

½ cup thick sour cream
1 cup diced, unpeeled cucumber
½ teaspoon salt
4 drops onion juice

Whip sour cream until smooth; add cucumber, salt, and onion juice. Serve with fish. Makes 1¼ cups.

RAVIGOTE OR VINAIGRETTE SAUCE

1 cup salad oil
⅓ cup tarragon vinegar
1 tablespoon capers
1 tablespoon minced onion
2 tablespoons minced parsley
Salt and pepper
1 hard-cooked egg, sieved or chopped fine

Combine ingredients and mix thoroughly.
Serve with cold meats, vegetables, vegetable salads, and fish. Makes about 1½ cups.

REMOULADE SAUCE

½ cup finely chopped sour pickles
2 tablespoons finely chopped capers
1 tablespoon prepared mustard
1 tablespoon mixed finely chopped parsley, tarragon, chervil, and chives
2 cups mayonnaise

Press all moisture out of pickles and capers. Add with remaining ingredients to mayonnaise.

ASPIC GLAZE FOR MEATS

1 tablespoon (1 envelope) unflavored gelatin
½ cup cold meat or vegetable stock
2 cups hot meat or vegetable stock
Seasoning to taste

Soften gelatin in cold stock. Dissolve it over hot water and add to hot stock. Season to taste.
Chill until somewhat thickened, then use as a glaze for cold meats, fish, and hors d'oeuvres.

CUCUMBER SAUCE

½ cup mayonnaise
½ cup whipped cream
1 cup diced, drained cucumber
Salt, pepper, paprika

Mix mayonnaise with whipped cream. Add cucumber and season to taste. Makes 2¼ cups.

TARTAR SAUCE

1 cup mayonnaise or cooked dressing
¼ cup chopped pickles
1 teaspoon minced onion
1 tablespoon capers (optional)
1 tablespoon chopped ripe olives
1 tablespoon minced parsley
1 hard-cooked egg, chopped
1 tablespoon chopped green pepper
Lemon juice

Blend ingredients and add lemon juice to thin slightly and point up flavors. Makes about 1½ cups.

SWEDISH DILL SAUCE

½ cup olive oil
½ cup vinegar
1 teaspoon dry mustard
1 tablespoon sugar
1 tablespoon chopped fresh dill or 1 teaspoon dried dill seed
Salt and pepper

Combine ingredients and serve with cold fish (lobster, crabmeat, or plain boiled fish of any kind). Makes about 1 cup.

SOUFFLÉ MANUAL

Soufflé means puffed and that is an exact description of what happens to this dish in cooking. The proudly light and puffed main dish or dessert soufflé rises because air beaten into the egg whites expands in the oven's warmth.

Long considered the final test of an accomplished cook, the soufflé is often held in awe by many people who entertain an exaggerated idea of the difficulties of its composition. The classic French soufflé is actually easy to prepare and has a simple, even thrifty base: butter, flour, and milk for cream sauce, a cup of cheese or almost any leftover, and eggs.

Today, we Americans often simplify this dish even more: a can of condensed soup, cheese, and eggs make a main dish soufflé; a package of prepared pudding mix, some milk, and eggs make the most delectable—and impressive—of desserts.

SOUFFLÉ SECRETS

- The secret of a soufflé is primarily the proper beating of the eggs and the incorporation of these beaten eggs into the basic mixture.
- Use eggs at room temperature; however yolks aren't as likely to break if you separate them from the whites while still cold from the refrigerator.
- If you let egg whites warm up to room temperature before beating, they'll fluff up better.

SOUFFLÉ HINTS

- French chefs always beat an extra egg white into a soufflé for lightness, that is, 4 whites to every 3 yolks.
- Many good cooks add ¼ teaspoon cream of tartar to whites while beating—as insurance for a well risen soufflé.
- Egg yolks are beaten until thick and lemon-colored.
- Egg whites are beaten until stiff but still glossy—never until dry.
- Underbeaten eggs make a small, unstable soufflé; overbeaten eggs will cause a tough product.
- The ready and waiting hot sauce is slowly stirred into the beaten egg yolks. This way the yolks are smoothly blended with the sauce.
- The *cooled* sauce mixture is *folded* very gently into the beaten egg whites. A blending fork or metal spoon is just the thing for this. Take your time, and gently lift up-and-over in high strokes.
- Soufflés may be prepared in advance, with the exception of the beating of the egg whites, which must be done immediately before the soufflé is put into the oven.
- The size, shape, and preparation of the baking dish will influence the quality of a soufflé.
- A straight-sided dish gives maximum volume.
- For a 3- or 4-egg soufflé, use a 1½-quart dish; for a large soufflé with more than 4 eggs, use a 2-quart dish.
- For highest rise, butter or oil the bottom only, but not the sides of a baking dish. The mixture will cling to the dry sides and make a taller and more uniform product.
- For extra height, tie a folded strip of waxed paper around the outside of soufflé dish like a collar to support the rise. Pour soufflé mixture in almost to the top of dish.
- To bake a soufflé with a "top hat," pour the soufflé mixture into the baking dish, then run a teaspoon all around, 1 inch from the edge and about 1 inch deep. This crease will cause the crust to break at this point and form a taller center.
- For a sweet crust dessert soufflé, butter the baking dish and sprinkle with sugar before filling.
- The baking of a soufflé has much to do with its quality. Do not place the dish in hot water unless the recipe calls for it. The water will keep the soufflé moist and soft, and in some cases it is preferable to have it crisp and crusty.
- When making a soufflé in a ring mold with the intention of inverting the contents when done, butter the ring pan well. Then fill with soufflé mixture and set in larger pan with 1 inch of hot, not boiling, water. This will facilitate turning out the soufflé from the mold and will give it a uniform consistency. For serving, fill the center of the turned out, inverted mold.

Testing for doneness

- Once done, serve soufflés promptly, because they start falling as soon as they start cooling. It is better to let your family or guests wait for the soufflé than to let the soufflé do the waiting. If your meal is delayed, turn the oven temperature to very low (250°F.) and leave the soufflé in the oven—but not more than an extra 10 or 15 minutes.
- Soufflés may be cooked in a double boiler over, not in, simmering water. Grease well both the pot and the lid. Pour in the soufflé mixture. Cover it and cook about 45 minutes to 1 hour. Turn out onto a hot platter.

Savory Soufflés

Easy Asparagus-Cheese Soufflé

EASY ASPARAGUS-CHEESE SOUFFLÉ

(Short-Cut Main Dish Soufflé)

- 1 can (1¼ cups) condensed cream of asparagus soup
- 1 cup shredded American cheese
- 6 eggs, separated

Heat soup slowly; add cheese and cook, stirring constantly until cheese is melted. Add slightly beaten egg yolks; cool. Fold stiffly beaten egg whites into soup mixture.

Pour into an ungreased 2-quart casserole. Bake in a slow oven (300°F.) for 1 to 1¼ hours or until soufflé is golden brown. Serve immediately. Serves 6.

Easy Chicken Soufflé: Follow recipe for Easy Asparagus Cheese Soufflé except use cream of chicken soup instead of asparagus; omit cheese and use instead 1 cup finely diced cooked chicken.

Easy Celery Salmon Soufflé: Follow recipe for Easy Asparagus Cheese Soufflé except use cream of celery soup instead of asparagus; omit cheese and use instead, 1 cup finely flaked salmon, drained.

Easy Mushroom Cheese Soufflé: Follow recipe for Easy Asparagus Cheese Soufflé except use cream of mushroom soup instead of cream of asparagus.

OYSTER SOUFFLÉ

- 1 pint oysters
- 3 tablespoons butter or margarine
- 3 tablespoons flour
- 1 cup milk
- 1 teaspoon salt
- ⅛ teaspoon pepper
- Dash of nutmeg
- 3 eggs, separated

Drain and chop oysters. Melt butter and blend in flour. Add milk and bring to boiling point, stirring constantly. Cook 3 minutes.

Add oysters, seasonings, and beaten egg yolks.

Beat egg whites until stiff but not dry. Fold into oyster mixture. Pour into buttered casserole.

Set in pan of hot water and bake in moderate oven (350°F.) until brown, about 30 minutes. Serves 6.

TOP-OF-THE-RANGE SOUFFLÉ

- 1½ cups milk
- 2 tablespoons butter or margarine
- ¾ teaspoon salt
- ¼ teaspoon pepper
- 6 eggs, beaten
- Chopped parsley

Heat milk and butter in upper part of double boiler.

Add seasonings to eggs and beat until very light.

Add the hot milk to eggs and beat to combine thoroughly. Return to upper part of double boiler and cook for 30 minutes over gently simmering water. Do not disturb by stirring.

Serve on warm plates by scooping out enough for 1 serving with a large spoon. Garnish with a sprig of or finely chopped parsley. Serve plain or with mushroom sauce. Serves 6.

1. Make a cream sauce, using the butter, flour, milk, salt, and cayenne.

2. When the sauce is thickened and smooth, add the sliced cheese; stir until cheese melts.

3. Remove from the heat and add the beaten egg yolks while stirring constantly. Cool the mixture slightly.

4. Fold the cheese sauce into the egg whites beaten until stiff but not dry, cutting and folding the mixture thoroughly together.

5. Pour into ungreased 2-quart casserole. With a teaspoon draw a line around the casserole one inch in from the edge to form a "top hat."

6. Bake 1¼ hours in a slow oven (300° F.) and serve immediately.

"TOP HAT" CHEESE SOUFFLÉ

"TOP HAT" CHEESE SOUFFLÉ

- 4 tablespoons butter or margarine
- 4 tablespoons flour
- 1 teaspoon salt
- Dash of cayenne
- 1½ cups milk
- ½ pound process American cheese, or "Old English" cheese, sliced
- 6 eggs, separated

Melt the butter or margarine in the top of a double boiler placed over boiling water. Remove from the boiling water, and blend in the flour, salt, and cayenne.

Gradually add the milk, blending well. Return to the boiling water and cook, stirring constantly, until the sauce is thick and smooth.

Add the sliced cheese and continue cooking, stirring frequently, until the cheese has melted.

Remove from the heat and slowly add the beaten egg yolks, blending them in well.

Slightly cool the mixture, then pour onto the stiffly beaten whites of the eggs, cutting and folding the mixture thoroughly together. Pour into an *ungreased* 2-quart casserole.

Run the tip of a teaspoon around in the mixture one inch from the edge of the casserole, making a slight "track" or depression. This forms the "top hat" on the soufflé as it bakes and puffs up.

Bake in a slow oven (300°F.) 1¼ hours. Serve immediately. Serves 6.

BACON SOUFFLÉ

- 1 cup diced fried bacon (½ to ¾ pound)
- 6 slices bread
- 5 beaten eggs
- ¾ teaspoon salt or more*
- ¼ teaspoon dry mustard
- Paprika
- 2 cups milk

Dice bacon and cook until light brown. Drain, if very fat.

Grease casserole with bacon fat. Arrange bread in layers in casserole, sprinkling the cooked bacon and some bacon fat over each layer. Reserve some bacon for the top.

Add seasonings and milk to eggs and pour over bread. Sprinkle reserved bacon over top.

Bake in moderate oven (350°F.) until puffy and knife inserted in center comes out clean, about 1 hour. Serve from casserole. Serves 6 to 8.

*Note: Saltiness will depend upon saltiness of bacon.

VEGETABLE SOUFFLÉ RING

- 3 cups leftover cooked vegetables
- 1 cup meat, fish, poultry, or vegetable stock (depending upon the filling to be used in the ring)
- 3 egg yolks
- ½ cup cold milk
- ½ cup sieved breadcrumbs
- 2 teaspoons lemon juice
- 2 teaspoons onion juice
- Salt, pepper, and nutmeg to taste
- 3 egg whites
- Salt

Cook leftover cooked vegetables in stock over low heat for 15 minutes, or until the liquid is almost absorbed.

Rub both vegetables and liquid through a fine sieve. There should be 3 cups of moist vegetable pulp.

Beat egg yolks well and stir into them the vegetable pulp, cold milk, breadcrumbs, lemon juice, onion juice, salt, pepper, and nutmeg to taste.

Blend very thoroughly and fold in egg whites, beaten stiff with a few grains of salt.

Pour into a buttered ring mold and bake in hot oven (400°F.) 30 to 35 minutes, or until firm to the touch.

Let it stand for a minute, then turn out on a hot round platter. Fill center with a creamed mixture made with meat, chicken, poultry, or eggs.

Serves 6 to 8.

CHESTNUT SOUFFLÉ

- 2 tablespoons flour
- ½ teaspoon salt
- ⅛ teaspoon pepper
- 1 cup mashed or riced cooked chestnuts
- ½ cup milk
- 3 egg whites

Mix the flour, salt, and pepper and add to the chestnuts. Mix well. Add the milk, stirring until smooth.

Beat the egg whites stiff and fold lightly into the chestnut mixture.

Pour the mixture into a 1-quart ungreased casserole. Bake in slow oven (325°F.) about 30 minutes, or until firm. Serves 4.

HAM SOUFFLÉ

- 2 tablespoons melted butter or margarine
- 2 tablespoons flour
- 2 cups milk
- 3 eggs, separated
- 1 cup dry breadcrumbs
- 2 cups ground cooked ham
- 1 tablespoon chopped parsley
- Salt and pepper to taste

Prepare a sauce of butter, flour, and milk.

Beat yolks and mix with crumbs, ham, and sauce. Add parsley, salt, and pepper.

Fold in stiffly beaten egg whites. Turn into greased baking dish.

Bake in slow oven (300°F.) until set in center, about 1 hour. Serves 6.

MASTER CHEESE SOUFFLÉ

- 4 tablespoons butter or margarine
- 4 tablespoons flour
- 1 cup milk
- 1/4 pound sharp cheese, chopped
- 1/4 teaspoon dry mustard
- 1/8 teaspoon pepper
- 3/4 teaspoon salt
- 4 eggs, separated

Melt butter, add flour, blend well and cook over low heat until bubbly.

Add cold milk all at once and cook, stirring constantly, until thickened throughout. Add cheese to white sauce and stir until melted and well blended.

Add mustard, pepper, and sauce to egg yolks beating constantly.

Add salt to egg whites and beat until shiny and whites leave peaks that fold over when beater is withdrawn.

Pour yolk-cheese mixture gradually over egg whites folding at the same time. Pour into an *ungreased* 1½-quart casserole.

Circle mixture with a spoon about 1-inch from side of casserole and about 1-inch deep.

Set in a pan of hot water and bake in slow oven (325°F.) until puffy, delicately browned, and knife inserted in center comes out clean, 60 to 75 minutes. Serve promptly. Serves 4.

Variations of Cheese Soufflé

Chicken, Turkey, Salmon, or Tuna Soufflé: Omit cheese. Stir 1 cup finely chopped cooked meat and 1 tablespoon minced onion into yolks before combining with hot sauce.

Increase seasonings as needed with salt and add grated rind of 1 lemon and 1 tablespoon lemon juice. Serve plain or with gravy, or mushroom sauce.

Chive Cheese Soufflé: Add ½ teaspoon finely chopped chives and 1 teaspoon finely chopped parsley with the stiffly beaten egg whites.

Mushroom Cheese Soufflé: Sauté ½ cup finely chopped mushrooms in butter for a few minutes. Add with stiffly beaten egg whites.

Spinach or Carrot Soufflé: Omit cheese. Stir 1 cup finely chopped raw spinach or grated raw carrot and 1 tablespoon chopped onion into yolks before combining with hot sauce. Increase salt to 1¼ teaspoons. Cheese, parsley, or tomato sauce is a good accompaniment.

INDIVIDUAL CHEESE CRUMB SOUFFLÉS

- 1 cup milk, scalded
- 1¼ cups fine, soft breadcrumbs
- 1½ cups grated sharp American cheese
- ½ teaspoon salt
- ¼ teaspoon paprika (optional)
- ½ teaspoon baking powder
- 4 eggs, separated

Pour scalded milk over crumbs and cheese. Add seasoning and baking powder.

Pour part of mixture into beaten egg yolks. Add egg mixture to remainder of sauce.

Fold in stiffly beaten egg whites. Turn into individual baking dishes.

Bake in moderate oven (350°F.) until delicately browned and firm to touch, about 30 minutes. Serve at once. Serves 6.

Variations of Cheese Crumb Soufflé

Chicken or Veal Soufflé: Substitute finely chopped cooked chicken or veal for cheese and add ¼ cup finely chopped celery, if desired.

Ham Soufflé: Substitute finely chopped ham for cheese and add ¼ teaspoon mustard, if desired.

Salmon Soufflé: Substitute 1½ cups finely flaked canned salmon for cheese. Add ¼ cup minced green pepper, 2 teaspoons lemon juice, and ½ teaspoon onion juice.

LOBSTER SOUFFLÉ

- 5 tablespoons butter or margarine
- 5 tablespoons flour
- 1/2 teaspoon salt
- 1/2 teaspoon paprika
- 1 1/2 cups milk
- 5 eggs, separated
- 1 1/2 cups finely flaked, cooked lobster meat
- 1 tablespoon ketchup
- 1 teaspoon Worcestershire sauce

Melt butter. Blend in flour, salt, and paprika. Add milk gradually and cook, stirring constantly, until smooth and thickened.

Remove from heat and beat in egg yolks, one at a time.

Stir in lobster meat, ketchup, and Worcestershire sauce. Fold in stiffly beaten egg whites.

Turn into greased 1 1/2-quart casserole. Bake in hot oven (425°F.) about 25 minutes. Serve at once. Serves 4 to 6.

OLIVE RICE SOUFFLÉ

- 1 cup ripe olives
- 3 eggs, separated
- 1/2 cup milk
- 1 teaspoon salt
- 1 teaspoon Worcestershire sauce
- 1 teaspoon grated onion
- 1 cup chopped raw spinach
- 1 cup grated American cheese
- 3 cups cooked rice
- 1/4 cup melted butter or margarine

Cut olives into large pieces. Separate eggs and beat yolks slightly. Combine with olives and all remaining ingredients except egg whites.

Fold in stiffly beaten egg whites.

Turn into 1 1/2-quart baking dish. Bake in moderate oven (350°F.) about 35 minutes. Serves 5 to 6.

Olive Rice Soufflé

Budget Chicken Soufflé

INDIVIDUAL CHEESE SOUFFLÉS

- 2 tablespoons butter or margarine
- 2 tablespoons flour
- 1/3 teaspoon baking soda
- 1 teaspoon salt
- 2 teaspoons Worcestershire sauce
- 1/4 teaspoon paprika
- 1/2 cup milk
- 1 cup grated cheese
- 4 eggs, separated

Melt butter; add flour, soda, salt, Worcestershire sauce, and paprika and stir until well blended.

Add milk gradually, stirring constantly over boiling water until sauce thickens.

Remove from heat and stir in grated cheese and egg yolks, beaten until thick and lemon colored. Then fold in stiffly beaten egg whites.

Bake in individual paper cases or in well buttered custard cups which can be sent to the table. Bake in moderate oven (350°–375°F.) about 12 minutes. Serve immediately. Makes 8 to 10 soufflés of custard-cup size.

BUDGET CHICKEN SOUFFLÉ

- 2 tablespoons butter or margarine
- 2 tablespoons flour
- 1 10 3/4-ounce can cream of chicken soup, undiluted
- 3 eggs, separated

Melt butter in saucepan; stir in flour. Add soup; heat slowly, stirring until mixture bubbles and is thickened. Cool slightly.

Beat egg whites until stiff but not dry.

Add soup mixture gradually to slightly beaten egg yolks. Fold in egg whites.

Spoon into 1-quart casserole. Place casserole in pan of warm water.

Bake in slow oven (325°F.) for 1 hour or until knife, when inserted, comes out clean. Serves 4 to 5.

Note: For 4 to 5 individual casseroles: Bake as above for 30 to 45 minutes.

CHICKEN-RICE SOUFFLÉ DELUXE

- 3 tablespoons butter or margarine
- 3 tablespoons flour
- 1 cup heavy cream
- Salt and pepper
- 3 eggs, separated
- 1 cup cooked rice
- 1 cup diced cooked or canned chicken
- 1/3 cup finely chopped ham
- 1 small onion, finely chopped
- 1/2 cup grated Swiss or Parmesan cheese

Melt the butter; blend in flour and add cream slowly, cooking until smooth and thickened.

Remove from the heat and stir in the egg yolks and then the rice, chicken, ham, onion, and cheese. Season.

Whip the egg whites until stiff and fold in gently.

Turn into a greased baking dish, preferably one with straight sides, and bake in a moderate oven (350°F.) until the top is lightly browned and springs back when gently touched with the finger. Serves 4 to 6.

CRABMEAT SOUFFLÉ

- 1 cup (6½-ounce can) crabmeat
- 1 cup thick white sauce
- 1 tablespoon lemon juice
- 4 eggs, separated
- 1½ teaspoons grated onion
- 1 tablespoon finely chopped parsley
- 1/2 teaspoon paprika
- 1/4 teaspoon cream of tartar

Pick over crabmeat to remove cartilage and shred fine.

To white sauce add crabmeat, lemon juice, egg yolks beaten until thick and lemon-colored, onion, parsley, and paprika. Cool.

Beat egg whites until frothy; add cream of tartar and continue beating until stiff but not dry. Fold into crabmeat mixture.

Turn into a 1½-quart greased casserole. Bake in slow oven (325°F.) about 1 hour. Serves 4 to 6.

TOMATO SOUFFLÉ

- 2 slices bread
- 1/2 cup milk
- 5 fresh tomatoes
- 2 tablespoons butter or margarine
- 1 teaspoon onion juice
- Salt and pepper
- 4 egg yolks, slightly beaten
- 5 egg whites, stiffly beaten
- 2 tablespoons grated cheese

Trim crusts from bread and soak in the milk. Mix bread and milk to a paste.

Peel, seed, and finely chop the tomatoes.

Melt the butter in a saucepan. Add tomatoes, onion juice, bread, and salt and pepper to taste. Cook, stirring until ingredients are thoroughly incorporated.

Remove from heat, stir in beaten egg yolks, and cool.

Fold in egg whites and pour into a well buttered soufflé dish.

Sprinkle grated cheese on top. Bake in moderate oven (350°F.) for 35 to 40 minutes. Sprinkle with paprika.

Serves 4.

POTATO SOUFFLÉ WITH CHEESE

- 3 cups hot mashed potatoes
- 2 egg yolks
- 2 tablespoons butter or margarine
- 1/2 cup hot cream
- 1 teaspoon salt
- 1/8 teaspoon paprika
- 2 egg whites
- 1/8 teaspoon salt
- 1/3 cup dry grated cheese, preferably Parmesan

Combine mashed potatoes, egg yolks, butter, cream, 1 teaspoon salt, and paprika; beat well.

Shape these ingredients into a mound on an oven-proof dish.

Whip egg whites and 1/8 teaspoon salt until stiff. Fold in grated cheese. Spread this mixture lightly over the mound.

Bake in slow oven (325°F.) about 15 minutes. Serves 6.

SAVORY SOUFFLÉS

CHICKEN LIVER SOUFFLÉ

½ pound chicken livers
1 tablespoon finely chopped onion
5 tablespoons butter or margarine
3 slices crumbled cooked bacon
3 tablespoons flour
1 cup milk or chicken broth
3 eggs, separated
Salt and pepper

Sauté chicken livers with onion in 2 tablespoons butter. Mash slightly with a fork and add bacon.

Melt the other 3 tablespoons butter in another pan; stir in flour and blend well. Add the milk or chicken broth and stir constantly until thickened and smooth.

Remove from the heat. Add chicken-livers-and-bacon mixture and beaten egg yolks.

Fold in stiffly beaten egg whites and turn into a greased baking dish with straight sides.

Bake in a moderate oven (350°F.) 45 to 50 minutes or until the top is delicately brown and springs back when gently touched. Serves 4.

CORN MEAL SOUFFLÉ

2 cups milk
⅓ cup white or yellow corn meal
1 tablespoon butter or margarine
3 tablespoons or more grated cheese
1 teaspoon salt
¼ teaspoon paprika
Few grains cayenne
3 eggs, separated

Heat milk to boiling point and stir in corn meal and butter. Reduce heat and stir in cheese. Cook these ingredients to consistency of mush.

Season them with salt, paprika, and cayenne. Add beaten egg yolks. Cook and stir for 1 minute longer to permit the yolks to thicken. Cool these ingredients.

Whip egg whites until stiff, then fold in.

Bake in an ungreased 7-inch baking dish in moderate oven (350°F.) until it is slightly crusty, about 45 minutes. In Italy bits of ham and seafood are added to the batter which is baked until it is very crisp. Serves 3.

RICE AND CHEESE SOUFFLÉ

2 cups cooked rice
⅛ to ¼ pound finely diced or grated Cheddar cheese
1 tablespoon melted butter or margarine
2 beaten egg yolks
1 cup milk
½ teaspoon salt
⅛ teaspoon paprika
Few grains cayenne
1 tablespoon grated onion (optional)
1 teaspoon Worcestershire sauce (optional)
3 tablespoons chopped parsley (optional)
2 egg whites
⅛ teaspoon salt

Combine rice, cheese, butter, egg yolks, milk, salt, paprika, cayenne, onion, Worcestershire sauce, and parsley.

Beat egg whites and salt until stiff.

Fold them into the rice mixture. Bake the soufflé in a moderate oven (350°F.) for about 25 minutes. Serves 4.

SWEET POTATO SOUFFLÉ

2 cups cooked, mashed sweet potatoes
¾ cup hot milk
⅓ cup butter or margarine
1 teaspoon grated lemon rind
¾ teaspoon salt
Few grains pepper
3 stiffly beaten egg whites

To mashed sweet potatoes add hot milk and butter; beat until fluffy. Add lemon rind, salt and pepper.

Fold in egg whites beaten stiff but not dry.

Pile lightly into a greased casserole. Bake in a hot oven (400°F.) 30 to 35 minutes, or until puffy and browned. Serves 6.

"Top Hat" Spinach Soufflé

"TOP HAT" SPINACH SOUFFLÉ

1 cup packed, chopped fresh spinach, uncooked (1/2 cup chopped frozen spinach, thawed but uncooked, may also be used)
1/4 cup butter or margarine
1/4 cup enriched flour
1 cup milk
1/3 cup shredded sharp cheese
3 beaten egg yolks
1/2 teaspoon salt
1/16 teaspoon pepper
3 egg whites
1/4 teaspoon salt

Prepare spinach, wash and drain thoroughly.

Melt butter or margarine in top of double boiler. Blend in flour. Add milk. Cook over hot water, stirring constantly, until thick. Stir in cheese. Remove from heat.

Blend in egg yolks to which a little of the hot mixture has been added. Fold in 1/2 teaspoon salt, pepper, and drained spinach. Place over hot water.

Beat egg whites with 1/4 teaspoon salt until stiff but not dry. Fold in hot spinach mixture gently but thoroughly.

Pour into ungreased 1 1/2-quart casserole. Place casserole inside pan of hot water; water should be level with top of soufflé mixture. With spatula or knife, mark a circle around top of soufflé about 1 inch in from edge and 1/2 inch deep.

Bake in moderate oven (375°F.) 35 to 40 minutes or until firm to the touch. Serve immediately or, if it must wait a few minutes, leave in oven with heat turned off. Serves 4 to 6.

MUSHROOM AND HAM SOUFFLÉ

2 cups thick white sauce
1/3 cup grated American cheese
3/4 cup minced celery
1 1/2 tablespoons minced pimiento
1 cup mushrooms, cooked
3/4 cup chopped boiled ham
4 eggs, separated
3/4 teaspoon curry powder
1 1/2 teaspoons grated onion

To white sauce add cheese, celery, pimiento, mushrooms, ham, well beaten egg yolks, curry powder, and onion. Mix well, then fold in egg whites beaten stiffly but not dry.

Turn into a greased casserole and place in a pan of hot water.

Bake in moderate oven (350°F.) about 30 to 45 minutes, or until nicely browned. Serves 6.

Vegetable Soufflé

FISH SOUFFLÉ

2½ cups leftover cooked fish, flaked (or use drained canned salmon, tuna, or bonito)
1 tablespoon lemon juice
Salt and pepper to taste
½ teaspoon paprika
Pinch of nutmeg
¾ cup breadcrumbs
¾ cup milk
4 eggs, separated

Sprinkle flaked fish with lemon juice and mix in seasonings.

Combine breadcrumbs and milk; heat to just boiling point, and add to fish.

Beat egg yolks until light yellow in color; combine with fish and breadcrumb mixture.

Finally, add egg whites which have been beaten until stiff but not dry.

Pour into buttered baking dish. Set into a pan with hot water and bake in moderate oven (350°F.) until set, about 40 to 45 minutes.

Serve immediately in baking dish with an egg sauce, tomato sauce, or lobster sauce. Serves 6.

VEGETABLE SOUFFLÉ

½ tablespoon finely chopped onion
½ tablespoon finely chopped green pepper
1 tablespoon finely chopped celery
2 tablespoons melted fat
2 tablespoons flour
½ cup milk
½ teaspoon salt
Pepper to taste
¾ cup diced cooked vegetables
2 eggs, separated

Brown onion, green pepper, and celery lightly in fat.

Blend in flour and add milk. Cook over low heat, stirring constantly, until thickened. Season with salt and pepper.

Stir vegetables into sauce; add hot mixture to beaten egg yolks.

Beat egg whites stiff but not dry. Fold in vegetable mixture. Pour into greased baking dish.

Bake in slow oven (325°F.) 40 to 50 minutes or until set. Serves 4.

Dessert Soufflés

SHORT-CUT DESSERT SOUFFLÉ

1 package pudding or pie filling (vanilla, butterscotch, or chocolate flavor)
1 cup milk
3 eggs, separated
Pinch of salt

Combine in saucepan the pudding or pie filling and milk. Cook and stir over medium heat until mixture thickens and boils. Remove from heat.

Beat egg yolks and add pudding gradually, stirring constantly.

Beat egg whites with a pinch of salt until stiff enough to stand in soft peaks. Carefully fold in egg yolk mixture.

Pour into greased and sugar-sprinkled 1½-quart baking dish. Bake in moderate oven (350°F.) for 45 minutes, or until firm. Serves 6 to 8.

TOP-OF-RANGE CHOCOLATE SOUFFLÉ

⅔ cup milk
⅓ cup granulated sugar
1 ounce (1 square) unsweetened chocolate
⅛ teaspoon salt
½ teaspoon vanilla
2 eggs, unbeaten

In double boiler, heat milk with sugar, chocolate, salt, and vanilla until chocolate melts. With egg beater, beat until smooth.

Break eggs into cup; add to chocolate mixture, beating 1 minute.

Cook, covered, over boiling water 35 minutes without removing cover. Serve hot or cold, as is or with light cream. Serves 4.

PRUNE SOUFFLÉ
(Master Recipe)

4 tablespoons sugar
1 cup prune pulp
2 teaspoons lemon juice
5 egg whites

Combine sugar and prune pulp and heat until sugar has dissolved. Add lemon juice.

Beat egg whites until frothy. Fold in.

Turn into a baking dish and bake in moderate oven (350°F.) about 40 minutes.

When done, sprinkle with powdered sugar. Serve at once from baking dish with cream. Serves 4.

Variations of Prune Soufflé

Apple Soufflé: Substitute 1 cup thick applesauce for prune pulp.

Apricot Soufflé: Substitute 1 cup apricot pulp for prune pulp. Add ¼ teaspoon almond extract with lemon juice.

Cherry Soufflé: Substitute sweet cherry pulp for prunes and cherry brandy for lemon juice.

Peach Soufflé: Substitute 1 cup peach pulp for prune pulp. Add ¼ teaspoon almond extract with lemon juice.

FRESH PEACH SOUFFLÉ

1 cup peach pulp
1½ tablespoons lemon juice
¼ cup sugar
4 beaten egg yolks
⅛ teaspooon salt
1 tablespoon grated orange rind
4 stiffly beaten egg whites
Cream

Peel and mash ripe peaches to make 1 cup peach pulp. (Or use an equal amount of canned puréed baby food peaches or other raw or canned fruit pulp.)

Add lemon juice, sugar, egg yolks, salt, and orange rind to peach pulp. Fold in egg whites.

Place the mixture in a 7-inch baking dish. Bake in slow oven (325°F.) for about 45 minutes. Serve hot with cream. Serves 5.

VANILLA SOUFFLÉ
(Master Recipe)

⅓ cup enriched flour
½ cup sugar
⅛ teaspoon salt
1 cup milk
4 eggs, separated
¼ teaspoon cream of tartar
1 teaspoon vanilla

Combine flour, sugar, and salt in a saucepan. Stir in milk a little at a time. Cook over low heat, stirring constantly, until mixture is smooth and thick.

Beat egg yolks until thick and yellow; slowly fold in the milk mixture.

Beat egg whites until foamy; sprinkle the cream of tartar over them and continue beating until stiff but not dry. Fold into the first mixture with vanilla.

Pour into an ungreased 1½-quart casserole. Bake in slow oven (325°F.) 50 to 60 minutes, or in a hot oven (425°F.) about 25 minutes or until well browned, using a lower shelf in the oven.

The long slow baking makes a soufflé of even moistness throughout; quick baking gives a thicker crust and a soft moist interior. Serve immediately from the baking dish. Serves 6.

Vanilla Soufflé Variations

Butterscotch Pecan Soufflé: In Vanilla Soufflé, substitute ⅔ cup firmly packed brown sugar for granulated sugar; add 2 tablespoons butter or margarine.

Fold in 1 cup finely chopped pecans with the thickened milk mixture.

Chocolate Soufflé: In Vanilla Soufflé, stir 2 squares (2 ounces) melted unsweetened chocolate into thickened milk mixture before stirring into egg yolks.

Pineapple Soufflé: In Vanilla Soufflé, substitute 1 cup pineapple juice for milk. Omit vanilla; add 1 tablespoon lemon juice and ½ teaspoon lemon rind. Fold in ⅔ cup well drained crushed pineapple with the thickened milk mixture.

Lemon Soufflé: In Vanilla Soufflé, reduce milk to ⅔ cup. Add ⅓ cup lemon juice when thickened. Omit vanilla; add 1 teaspoon grated lemon rind.

Orange Soufflé: In Vanilla Soufflé, substitute 1 cup orange juice for milk. Omit vanilla; add 1 tablespoon lemon juice and 1 tablespoon grated orange rind.

APPLE ZWIEBACK SOUFFLÉ

5 to 6 apples
2 tablespoons sugar
4 beaten eggs
1 cup milk
12 slices zwieback

Peel, core and slice apples. Mix with 1 tablespoon sugar.

Combine eggs, milk, and remaining tablespoon sugar.

Grease baking dish; place a layer of zwieback on bottom, next a layer of apples, then part of egg-milk mixture.

Repeat until dish is filled and cover with egg-milk mixture.

Cover and bake in moderate oven (350°F.) 45 minutes, or until apples are tender. Serves 6.

LEMON SOUFFLÉ #2

4 eggs, separated
¼ cup hot water
1 cup sugar
½ teaspoon salt
2 teaspoons grated lemon rind
¼ cup lemon juice

Beat yolks until thick; add water gradually and continue beating. Add sugar gradually, beating thoroughly after each addition.

Add salt and lemon rind and juice; fold in stiffly beaten egg whites.

Turn into 1½-quart dish, buttered on the bottom.

Place in pan of hot water and bake in moderate oven (350°F.) 30 to 45 minutes, or until firm. Serve at once with lemon sauce. Serves 6.

STRAWBERRY SOUFFLÉ

1 pint strawberries
½ cup sugar
2 tablespoons kirsch or brandy
¼ cup butter or margarine
3 eggs, separated
1 cup soft breadcrumbs

Slice strawberries; add ¼ cup sugar and liquor and let stand until needed. Drain berries, reserving 1 cup for soufflé and remainder of berries and juice for sauce.

Cream butter with remaining ¼ cup sugar until fluffy. Add well beaten egg yolks, then crumbs and cup of strained berries.

Beat egg whites until stiff and fold into mixture.

Turn into 1½-quart casserole which has been greased only on the bottom or which has been buttered all over and sprinkled with sugar.

Set in pan of hot water and bake in moderate oven (350°F.) until firm, about 45 minutes. Serve with reserved berry and juice mixture. Serves 4 to 5.

HAZELNUT SOUFFLÉ

3 eggs, separated
3 tablespoons sugar
3 tablespoons flour
⅛ teaspoon salt
¾ cup hazelnuts
1 cup milk
3 tablespoons butter or margarine
½ teaspoon vanilla or 1 tablespoon rum
1 cup heavy cream, whipped
Caramel or coffee flavoring

Beat egg yolks until light. Gradually beat in sugar, flour, and salt.

Put hazelnuts through a nut grinder. Pour milk over them and heat to just below the boiling point.

Stir in egg mixture. Stir and cook these ingredients over low heat to permit the yolks to thicken slightly. Stir in butter.

Cool, then beat in vanilla or rum.

Beat egg whites until stiff; fold into first mixture.

Mocha Soufflé

Bake in a buttered dish in slow oven (325°F.) for about 30 minutes. Serve hot or cold with whipped cream flavored with caramel or coffee. Serves 4 to 5.

MOCHA SOUFFLÉ

3 tablespoons butter or margarine
¼ cup enriched flour
5 tablespoons sugar
2 teaspoons cocoa
⅔ cup milk
⅓ cup strong fresh coffee
4 eggs, separated
¼ teaspoon salt
¼ teaspoon vanilla

Melt butter in saucepan; gradually stir in flour combined with sugar and cocoa. Cook, stirring constantly, until mixture bubbles.

Then slowly stir in milk mixed with coffee. Cook, stirring constantly, until thick and smooth. Let cool.

Then stir in well beaten egg yolks, salt, and vanilla. Gently fold in stiffly beaten egg whites.

Turn into 1½-quart casserole, greased on bottom only. Put casserole in pan of hot water.

Bake in slow oven (325°F.) until done, 50 to 60 minutes. Serve at once. Serves 6.

DESSERT SOUFFLÉS

PINEAPPLE MACAROON SOUFFLÉ

- 3 tablespoons butter or margarine
- 3 tablespoons flour
- 1 cup crushed pineapple
- 2/3 cup dry crushed macaroons
- 3 eggs, separated
- 1/8 teaspoon salt
- 2 tablespoons sugar
- 1/2 teaspoon vanilla

Melt butter over low heat. Stir in flour. When blended, stir in pineapple.

Then when thick and smooth, stir in macaroons and egg yolks. Permit the yolks to thicken slightly. Cool the mixture.

Beat egg whites with salt until stiff. Gradually beat in sugar and vanilla. Fold this into the soufflé mixture.

Bake it in a 7-inch baking dish in a slow oven (325°F.) for about 30 minutes. Serves 4.

ALMOND AND STRAWBERRY SOUFFLÉ

- 3/4 cup almonds
- 1 tablespoon sugar
- 1 cup crushed strawberries
- 1/3 cup sugar
- 3/4 cup hot milk
- 2 tablespoons flour
- 1/4 cup cold milk
- 1 tablespoon sweet butter or margarine
- 4 egg yolks, well beaten
- 6 egg whites, stiffly beaten

Blanch almonds by steeping in boiling water for 5 minutes, then cut lengthwise into slivers.

Add 1 tablespoon sugar to crushed strawberries. Dissolve 1/3 cup sugar in hot milk.

Blend flour in cold milk and add gradually to the hot milk, stirring over the heat for about 2 minutes, or until thick and creamy.

Remove from heat and stir in butter and well beaten egg yolks. Cool.

Fold in strawberries and three quarters of the almonds, then fold in egg whites. Pour into greased baking dish; sprinkle top with remaining almonds. Bake in moderate oven (350°F.) for 30 minutes. Sprinkle top with powdered sugar. Serves 6.

ORANGE SOUFFLÉ #2

- 1/4 cup butter or margarine
- 6 tablespoons enriched flour
- Dash of salt
- 1 cup milk
- 1 6-ounce can frozen orange juice concentrate
- 1/2 cup water
- 1 1/2 teaspoons grated lemon rind
- 6 eggs, separated
- 1/4 cup sugar
- 1 recipe orange sauce (below)

Melt butter; blend in flour and salt. Gradually stir in milk; cook over low heat, stirring constantly, until thick.

Combine 1/4 cup of the orange juice concentrate (reserve remainder for orange sauce), water, and lemon rind. Stir into hot mixture.

Beat egg yolks until thick and lemon colored; gradually add hot mixture; mix well.

Beat egg whites until soft peaks form; gradually add sugar, beating until stiff peaks form.

Fold yolk mixture into egg whites. Pour into ungreased straight-sided 1 1/2-quart casserole around which has been tied a 6-inch collar of greased waxed paper.

Set baking dish in shallow pan, filling pan to 1 inch with hot water.

Bake in slow oven (325°F.) about 1 1/2 hours, or until mixture doesn't adhere to knife. Serve at once with orange sauce. Serves 8.

Orange Sauce: Combine 1/2 cup sugar, 1 1/2 tablespoons cornstarch, and dash of salt.

Stir in reserved orange juice concentrate (1/2 cup) and 1 cup water. **Cook**, stirring constantly, until thick.

Remove from heat; stir in 1 tablespoon butter or margarine. Serve warm in pitcher or bowl. Makes about 1 1/2 cups.

SOUPS AND CHOWDERS

Of all the calls to dinner, "Soup's on" rings as invitingly today as ever. Families around the world think of the soup kettle as a symbol of home and pleasant hours together. Soup favorites vary from country to country—onion soup in France, Italy's beloved minestrone with beans and macaroni, England's mulligatawny, the clear broths of China and Japan, and tomato and vegetable soups in the United States.

SOUP-MAKING HINTS

There are innumerable ways to vary soups and there are many enticing names but, basically, soups are divided into just a few groups.

Soups made from white stock have veal or poultry as a base.

Soups made from brown stock have dark meats as a base.

Bouillon is a clear soup made from beef stock.

Consommé is made from beef, chicken, veal, and vegetables.

Chowders are thick soups made from fish, meat, and vegetables.

Broth is the liquid resulting from meat which has been simmered slowly in water.

The cream soups (purées and bisques) contain both milk and butter, as well as the vegetables after which they are named.

Soups should be an important part of any low-cost menus, not only because they are highly nutritious, but because to delicious soups may be added food ingredients which the average homemaker may normally discard.

The water in which meats, fish, and vegetables are simmered, as well as the liquids from canned vegetables, contain much of the precious vitamins and minerals and should be used as a liquid in the preparation of soups. They can be saved and stored in the refrigerator for future use.

Scraps of raw or cooked vegetables, fish, meats, and bones should be used in soups together with the addition of the lower-priced cuts of meats. Inexpensive meat cuts have essentially the same nutritive values as the higher-priced cuts. To obtain the full flavor from such soups, always simmer or boil these soups in closely covered kettles. A helpful hint to keep in mind is that soups made from these leftover ingredients may very often be improved with the addition of a can of prepared soup.

Stocks and Soups Made with Meat

BEEF OR BROWN SOUP STOCK
(Master Recipe)

- 5 pounds beef knuckle
- 3 quarts cold water
- 1 medium onion, sliced
- 2 carrots, sliced
- 1 medium turnip, diced
- 4 pieces celery (with leaves), cut into 1/2-inch pieces
- 1/2 teaspoon whole black peppers
- 5 whole cloves
- 1 small bay leaf
- 3 sprigs parsley
- 1 tablespoon salt

Have beef knuckle cut in several pieces. Cut meat from bone and cut in cubes. Brown meat cubes.

Put meat and bone into soup kettle; add water and let stand 1 hour to draw out juices.

Bring to boil; skim and reduce heat to simmering. Cook slowly 4 to 5 hours.

Add vegetables and seasonings during last hour of cooking.

Strain stock. Chill. Remove layer of fat when stock is chilled. Makes about 2 quarts.

LAMB OR MUTTON STOCK

Follow recipe for Beef or Brown Soup Stock and substitute 4 to 5 pounds of lamb or mutton for beef.

Do not brown meat. Remove any excess fat from meat before cooking.

VEAL OR WHITE STOCK

Follow recipe for Beef or Brown Soup Stock and substitute 4 to 5 pounds of knuckle of veal or poultry or a combination of both for beef.

Do not brown meat. Cover with cold water and proceed as directed.

BOUILLON

Prepare brown stock. Cool and clarify as directed.

TOMATO BOUILLON

Combine 2 cups bouillon and 2 cups tomato juice; stir well and heat to boiling point. Pour into cups. Top with slightly salted whipped cream. Sprinkle with chopped parsley.

BEEF BROTH

Use 3 to 4 pounds beef (shin, chuck, or neck); cut in pieces and crack bone. Combine with 1 quart cold water; bring slowly to a boil, skim, then cover and simmer about 4 hours. Add 1/2 teaspoon salt after 2 hours of cooking.

Remove fat and strain. Reheat and serve in hot cups, or chill and serve as a jelly. Makes about 2 cups broth.

HOW TO CLARIFY STOCK

For 1 quart of stock, combine 2 tablespoons water with 1 egg white and shell. Add to cold stock. Heat stock and stir constantly until it boils. Boil 5 to 10 minutes without stirring.

Let stand 15 to 20 minutes at back of range for stock to settle. Strain through two thicknesses of cheesecloth.

VEGETABLE SOUP, FAMILY STYLE

Bones and scraps from rib roast or leg of lamb
2½ quarts cold water
1 medium onion, sliced
2 stalks celery (with leaves), sliced

Place above ingredients in large kettle. Simmer 1¼ hours.

½ cup barley
2 medium white turnips, diced
2 medium potatoes, diced
4 medium carrots, diced
1½ cups sliced celery
½ cup minced parsley
2 teaspoons salt
¼ teaspoon pepper
1 to 1½ teaspoons Ac'cent
⅛ teaspoon powdered cloves (optional)
⅛ teaspoon thyme

At end of 1¼-hour first simmering add barley. Continue cooking, at a gentle boil, until barley is swollen and tender, about 1 to 1¼ hours.

Remove bones from stock. If soup is not to be finished for immediate serving, chill stock to congeal fat on top, then remove it. Otherwise skim off fat from stock; bring to boil and add all remaining ingredients.

Simmer gently until vegetables are tender, about 15 minutes.

Meanwhile remove all meat from bones; chop or dice.

Soup meat
2 cans condensed tomato sup
1 teaspoon sugar
Ac'cent, as needed

Add soup meat, tomato soup, and sugar. Heat soup thoroughly. Correct seasoning with Ac'cent. Makes 2 to 2½ quarts.

Vegetable Soup, Family Style

CONSOMMÉ

Follow recipe for Brown Soup Stock. Substitute 2 pounds lean beef (cut in 1-inch cubes), 1 pound marrowbone (cracked), and 2 pounds veal knuckle (cut in pieces), for beef knuckle.

Sauté vegetables in 1 tablespoon butter until lightly browned before adding to stock.

Chicken stock or chicken bones may be added to soup kettle. Makes about 2 quarts consommé.

CONSOMMÉ ROYALE

Garnish each serving of consommé with royal custard (see Index) diced or cut in fancy shapes.

CONSOMMÉ MACEDOINE

Add cubed cooked vegetables in various colors to stock and reheat.

CONSOMMÉ PRINCESS

Serve consommé with shredded chicken and new green peas.

CONSOMMÉ JARDINIERE

Cut vegetables into fancy shapes with vegetable cutters.

Cook and serve in the consommé, allowing about 1 cup vegetables to 1 quart stock.

TOMATO-RICE SOUP

Cook ½ cup rice and ¼ cup diced celery in 4 cups chicken broth until tender.

Add 1 can condensed tomato soup, 1 red pepper pod, and salt to taste. Heat and remove pepper pod before serving. Serves 6.

WHAT TO DO IF SOUP IS TOO SALTY

Add a few slices raw potato to the soup. Let the soup boil until potatoes are done. They will absorb excess salt.

JIFFY STOCK, BOUILLON, OR CONSOMMÉ

For quick stock, bouillon, or consommé, use one of the following: canned light soup directly from the can; canned condensed soup diluted with an equal amount of water; 1 or 2 bouillon cubes dissolved in 1 cup boiling water, or 1 to 2 teaspoons beef extract or meat concentrate dissolved in 1 cup boiling water.

MUSHROOM CONSOMMÉ

¾ pound mushrooms
6 cups brown stock or 2 cans condensed consommé diluted with 3 cups water

Wash mushrooms. Remove stems and chop fine; slice caps.

Place chopped stems and stock in a saucepan; cover and simmer about 30 minutes. Strain, chill and remove excess fat.

Simmer sliced mushroom caps in 1 cup of the stock until tender, about 10 minutes. Combine with remaining stock and reheat. Serves 6 to 8.

CLARET BOUILLON

Heat 2½ cups beef bouillon to boiling point. Remove from heat and add ¾ cup claret wine. Serve at once in bouillon cups and garnish with chopped parsley.

MADRILÈNE

1½ cups chicken stock or bouillon
1½ cups beef stock or bouillon or use cube or canned bouillon
1½ cups tomato juice
1 cup chopped celery
½ cup chopped carrot
1 cup chopped leeks
Salt and pepper

Mix bouillons and tomato juice; bring to a boil.

Add vegetables and simmer 30 minutes. Taste, and add more salt and pepper if needed. Strain. Reheat. Serve hot or chilled. Serves 5 to 6.

French Onion Soup

FRENCH ONION SOUP

- 2 tablespoons butter or margarine
- 1¼ to 2½ cups thinly sliced onions (depending upon desired thickness)
- 5 cups meat stock, canned bouillon, or diluted bouillon cubes
- Salt and pepper to taste
- 1 cup finely grated aged Cheddar or Parmesan cheese
- Croutons or French bread

Melt butter in a saucepan; add onions and sauté until lightly browned, about 5 minutes.

Add stock and simmer, covered, about 20 minutes or until onions are just tender.

Season with salt and pepper. Pour into soup bowls; sprinkle with grated cheese and place croutons on top. If using French bread place slices around edge of soup. Makes about 6 8-ounce cups of soup.

QUEBEC PEA SOUP

- 1 pound dried whole peas (2½ cups)
- 5 quarts cold water
- ½ pound fat back salt pork or 1 ham bone
- ⅓ cup chopped onion
- Salt and pepper

Wash peas and soak overnight in cold water.

Add salt pork and chopped onion. Bring soup gradually to boiling point. Then simmer slowly about 3 hours or until peas are tender and mealy, which gives a thick, velvety soup.

Remove pork. Before serving, add salt, if needed, pepper, and parsley or savory to taste. Makes 12 servings (about 1 cup each).

Note: If pea soup is made in pressure cooker, use the recipe given above, reducing water to 8 cups and cooking 1 hour at 10-pound pressure. Remove from heat and allow pressure to drop gradually until it is completely down.

AVOCADO SOUP

- 4 cups beef or chicken stock, (canned or cubes and water may be used)
- 1 large avocado, peeled
- 3 tablespoons finely minced parsley
- Salt
- 4 tablespoons sherry

Heat stock to boiling point in top part of double boiler over direct heat. Keep hot over hot water.

Put avocado pulp through ricer or sieve.

Stir avocado pulp, minced parsley, salt to taste, and sherry into hot stock just before serving. Serves 4.

Note: Do not heat soup with avocado pulp over direct heat. Flavor of avocado is hurt by too much heat.

Mushroom and Barley Soup

BEEF AND VEGETABLE SOUP

1 beef soup bone
1 pound soup beef, cubed
Salt
½ teaspoon whole black peppers
1 bay leaf
1 medium onion, sliced
1 large carrot, diced
3 stalks celery, sliced
1 cup each cut green beans, corn, green peas, and diced potato
1 No. 2 can tomatoes
1 medium green pepper, diced
Pepper

Put bone, meat, 1 tablespoon salt, whole black peppers, bay leaf, and 2 quarts water in large kettle. Bring to boil. Cover and simmer 1 hour.

Add vegetables and bring to boil. Cover and simmer 1 hour longer, or until meat is tender.

Remove meat from bone and put back in soup. Season with salt and pepper to taste. Makes about 2½ quarts.

Variations: Other vegetables, such as diced yellow turnip, cauliflower, lima beans, chopped cabbage, etc., can be substituted for those listed above.

MUSHROOM AND BARLEY SOUP
(With Dried Mushrooms)

¼ pound barley
1 quart bouillon
1 ounce dried mushrooms
1 onion, diced
1 carrot, diced
Few sprigs of parsley
Few sprigs of dill
2 bay leaves
½ cup diced cooked soup meat

Cook the barley in water until tender. Combine bouillon, cooked barley, and dried mushrooms which have been washed and cut into pieces, onion, and carrot.

Wrap the parsley and dill around the bay leaves and tie into a bouquet; add to soup kettle.

Simmer gently until vegetables are tender, then remove bouquet. Add the soup meat and serve hot. Serves 4 to 6.

HOW TO REMOVE EXCESS FAT FROM SOUP

Method #1: This is the easiest method. Chill the soup and remove the excess fat which has hardened.

Method #2: Put a lettuce leaf in the hot soup. When it has absorbed the fat, remove it.

Method #3: Float a paper towel on the surface of the soup until it has absorbed as much fat as it will take. Or roll up a paper towel and use one end to skim off fat. When the end is coated with fat, cut it off and continue the process.

Method #4: Put an ice cube in a clean cloth and move it about just under the surface of the soup until the cloth absorbs the fat.

CHICKEN SOUP STOCK

1 4- to 4½-pound chicken, cut up
6 cups cold water
2 small onions, sliced
2 pieces celery, diced
1 carrot, sliced
3 sprigs parsley
1 teaspoon salt
Dash of pepper
4 whole black peppers

Put chicken in soup kettle and cover with cold water. Bring to boiling point and skim.

Add vegetables and seasonings, and simmer until meat is tender.

Remove chicken and strain stock. Cool. Place in refrigerator until needed.

Before using chicken stock, remove fat film from top. The chicken stock may be used for sauces or as a soup base.

Use the chicken meat in chicken salad, chicken loaf, or soufflé. Makes about 1 quart.

CHICKEN NOODLE SOUP

Heat 4 cups chicken stock in top of double boiler.

Add 1½ cups noodles and cook until noodles are tender, about 25 to 30 minutes. Serves 6.

CHICKEN RICE SOUP

Heat 4 cups chicken stock in top of double boiler. Add 1 cup rice; cook until rice is fluffy, about 40 minutes. Serves 6.

COCK-A-LEEKIE (From Scotland)

2 bunches leeks
1 3½- to 4-pound chicken
1½ teaspoons salt
½ teaspoon pepper
½ teaspoon nutmeg
2 quarts veal stock or water
1 dozen prunes

Wash leeks and cut off green tops. Slice white parts in ½-inch pieces. Place half the sliced leeks in a large kettle with closely fitting cover.

Cut chicken into serving pieces and place on top of leeks. Add remaining leeks and seasonings. Cover with stock. Bring to rolling boil and skim the top.

Cover well and simmer until chicken is tender, about 1½ hours.

Add prunes 30 minutes before end of cooking time.

Remove meat from bones and place in soup bowls. Pour soup over chicken. Serves 6 to 8.

SPLIT PEA SOUP

2 cups dried split peas
3 quarts water
1 large onion, chopped
2 stalks celery
Sprig of parsley (optional)
Ham bones or small shank end of ham
Salt and pepper

Soak peas overnight in cold water to cover.

Combine peas, onion, celery, parsley, ham bones or shank, and additional water to make 3 quarts. Cover and simmer until peas are tender, 3 to 4 hours.

Rub vegetables through a sieve or leave some of the peas whole. Skim off excess fat. Season to taste with salt and pepper.

If desired, thicken soup with a paste made of 3 tablespoon flour and 3 tablespoons butter. If desired, dilute with additional water or milk.

Serve with croutons or slices of frankfurters or Vienna sausage if desired. Garnish with julienne strips of cooked carrot. Serves 6 to 8.

Variations of Split Pea Soup

Purée Mongole: Use yellow split peas and at end dilute with strained cooked tomatoes instead of water or milk.

Black Bean Soup: Use dried black beans instead of peas. Garnish each portion with a slice of lemon and a slice of hard-cooked egg.

Soup St. Germain: Add 3 or 4 lettuce leaves with the peas. Serve with croutons.

Clear Tomato Soup with Cheese

POT-AU-FEU
(French Boiled Dinner)

- 4 pounds lean beef with bone (brisket, rump, shin, plate, chuck, or round)
- 3 quarts cold water
- 1 tablespoon salt
- Bouquet Garni (see below)
- 2 cups chopped mixed vegetables
- 3 large carrots, quartered
- 6 cabbage wedges
- 6 leeks, white part only
- 6 potatoes, whole or quartered

For the bouquet garni, tie in a cheesecloth bag 1 bay leaf, ¼ teaspoon thyme, ½ teaspoon whole black peppers, 3 cloves, 4 sprigs parsley, and a few celery leaves.

For the 2 cups mixed vegetables, use onion, carrots, white turnips, and parsnips.

Place meat, water, salt, and bouquet garni in a large soup kettle. Bring to boiling point, skimming often. Lower heat and simmer until meat is almost tender, 4 hours or longer.

Add chopped vegetables and those cut into larger pieces. Simmer until larger pieces are tender, about 45 minutes.

To serve, remove meat to hot serving platter and surround with large pieces of vegetables. Keep warm.

Serve the broth with chopped vegetables as a first course. Refrigerate the balance. Chill and remove fat. Use for stock. Serves 6 or more.

Note: If a fatty piece of meat is used, it is better to make it a day earlier. Chill and remove fat before serving.

CLEAR TOMATO SOUP WITH CHEESE

- 1½ cups sliced onions
- 3 tablespoons butter or margarine
- 1 No. 2 can (2½ cups) tomatoes
- ½ teaspoon salt
- ¼ teaspoon pepper
- ½ teaspoon oregano
- 3 cups beef bouillon or beef stock
- 1 cup shredded sharp Cheddar cheese

Sauté onion in butter until clear. Add tomatoes and cook 5 minutes longer.

Add seasonings and bouillon or stock. Simmer for 10 minutes.

Strain. Serve with shredded Cheddar cheese. Serve 4.

Note: If 3 cups of meat stock are not available, prepare bouillon using 3 cups of boiling water and 3 beef bouillon cubes.

BEEF JUICE OR TEA FOR INVALIDS AND CHILDREN

Cut 1 pound lean round steak into small cubes. Put in a quart glass jar. Add 1 cup cold water and a pinch of salt.

Cover jar tightly and place in a pan of cold water, using as much water a possible without upsetting the jar.

Slowly bring the water in pan to a boil and boil gently for 1 hour.

Remove jar and place on a rack to cool as quickly as possible.

Strain the juice and store in refrigerator until ready to heat and serve.

MINESTRONE
(Italian Vegetable Soup)

¼ pound bacon or bacon ends, chopped
2 medium onions, sliced
1 clove garlic, minced
½ cup chopped celery and leaves
1 carrot, sliced
¼ cup chopped parsley
1 cup chopped escarole
1 cup chopped cabbage
1½ cups cooked dried beans
1 No. 2 can tomatoes
½ cup canned chickpeas
½ teaspoon dried basil
¼ teaspoon oregano
Salt
½ teaspoon Ac'cent (optional)
½ cup elbow macaroni
Cayenne
1 pound hot Italian sausage, sliced and cooked
Grated Parmesan cheese

Brown bacon and onions in large kettle. Add remaining raw vegetables; cook 10 minutes, stirring occasionally.

Add 6 cups water, beans, tomatoes, chickpeas, herbs, ½ teaspoon Ac'cent, and 2 teaspoons salt. Bring to boil; cover and simmer 30 minutes.

Add macaroni, and cook 10 minutes, or until tender. Add salt and cayenne to taste. Serve topped with sausage and cheese. Makes 3 quarts.

CHICKEN CORN SOUP
(Pennsylvania-Dutch)

1 chicken (a 4-pound hen is a good size), cut up
1 onion, chopped fine
4 quarts cold water
1 teaspoon salt
10 ears of corn
½ cup chopped celery and leaves
¼ teaspoon pepper
2 hard-cooked eggs

Combine chicken, onion, and cold water. Cook chicken slowly until tender; add salt during last 30 minutes of cooking.

Remove chicken and strain broth through a fine sieve. Take meat from bones and chop fine, now add to broth.

Cut corn from the cob and add to soup. Add celery and seasoning to taste.

Ten minutes before serving, add 2 chopped hard-cooked eggs. **Cover and cook slowly for 8 minutes.** Serves 6.

Minestrone

CHICKEN AND RICE SOUP
(Brazilian Style)

1 plump stewing chicken, 2½ to 4 pounds, disjointed
Salt and pepper
1 medium onion
1 garlic clove, minced
2 tablespoons fat
½ cup uncooked rice
2 quarts (8 cups) boiling water
1 herb bouquet (see below)
¼ pound ham, diced

Sprinkle chicken with salt and pepper and let stand about 30 minutes.

Cook onion and garlic in fat until onion is delicately browned. Lift out onion and garlic and set aside. Add chicken and cook to nice brown, turning to brown evenly.

Transfer chicken to large kettle. Add onion and garlic, rice, water, and herb bouquet. Add ham and simmer until chicken is tender, 2½ to 3½ hours.

Lift out chicken, remove bones, and cut meat into convenient-sized pieces. Return meat to broth. Taste for seasoning. Serve very hot. Serves 6 generously.

Herb Bouquet: Use 2 sprigs parsley, 1 small bay leaf, and 1 sprig marjoram or thyme. Tie into cheesecloth bag for easy removal before serving.

PETITE MARMITE PARISIENNE

2 quarts meat stock
6 to 8 chicken wings or pieces of chicken
6 cubes of beef (¾ inch)
1 small onion, split and toasted with a clove in each half
2 carrots
2 sticks celery
1 white turnip
1 bunch leeks, cut 1-inch long and thick as a pencil
⅛ head cabbage
Salt and pepper to taste
1 tablespoon Ac'cent
6 marrow bone rings (have meatman saw ¼-inch thick)
French bread crusts, toasted
Grated Parmesan cheese
Sprinkle of chopped chervil

Put meat stock in stew pot and bring slowly to boil. Add chicken, beef, and onion; simmer about 30 minutes.

Add carrots, celery, turnip, and leeks, and continue to simmer.

Parboil cabbage in salted water; drain and wash in cold water. When rest of vegetables are nearly cooked, add cabbage, correct seasoning and add Ac'cent.

Remove from heat and place in earthen pot designed for petite marmite.

You can float marrow bone rings in pot or bring slowly to boil in more shallow dish with stock, to be lifted later to individual serving.

Serve with bread crust and cheese. Sprinkle with chervil. Serves 6 to 8.

MULLIGATAWNY SOUP

¼ cup butter or other fat
1 cup raw diced chicken
1 apple, thinly sliced
1 small onion, diced
⅓ cup diced celery
⅓ cup diced carrot
1 green pepper, chopped fine
¼ cup flour
1 teaspoon curry powder
1 blade mace
3 cloves
1 cup canned tomatoes
2 tablespoons minced parsley
1 teaspoon salt
½ teaspoon pepper
1½ quarts chicken stock
1 cup cooked rice

Cook chicken, apple, and vegetables (except tomatoes and parsley) in butter until brown.

Add remaining ingredients (except rice) in order given. Simmer gently 1 hour.

Strain and pick out pieces of chicken. Press vegetables through a sieve.

Return chicken and vegetables to soup. Adjust seasoning. Serve very hot over cooked rice. Serves 6 to 8.

LOW CALORIE APPLE CIDER SALAD

1½ tablespoons (1½ envelopes) unflavored gelatin
⅓ cup cold water
2 teaspoons Sucaryl solution or 16 tablets, crushed
2 cups apple cider or juice
2 tablespoons lemon juice
½ teaspoon salt
2 medium apples, finely chopped

Soften gelatin in cold water. Combine Sucaryl, cider, lemon juice, and salt. Heat and add to the softened gelatin, stirring until gelatin dissolves.

Cool until mixture begins to thicken. Fold in apples. Chill until set in a 3-cup mold. Makes 8 servings, each containing 57 calories.

LOW CALORIE FRUIT SALAD DRESSING

- 1 tablespoon (1 envelope) unflavored gelatin
- 1 tablespoon cold water
- 1/4 cup boiling water
- 1 tablespoon Sucaryl solution or 24 tablets, crushed
- 1/4 teaspoon salt
- 1/4 cup lemon juice
- 1/8 teaspoon dry mustard
- 1/2 teaspoon paprika

Soften gelatin in cold water; dissolve in boiling water.

Combine remaining ingredients and mix with dissolved gelatin. Store in refrigerator. (Becomes firm when cold. Reheat to soften.) Makes 1/2 cup; each tablespoon contains 6 calories.

GUATEMALAN BREAD SOUP

1 tablespoon butter or margarine
1½ cups canned tomatoes
1 medium onion, chopped
1 tablespoon flour
1½ cups water
¼ teaspoon pepper
1 teaspoon Ac'cent
6 slices bread
3 tablespoons butter or margarine
6 cups chicken bouillon
2 hard-cooked eggs, sliced
Grated Parmesan cheese

Melt 1 tablespoon butter in saucepan; add tomatoes and onion. Cook until onion is soft.

Mix flour to a smooth paste with a little of the water. Add with remaining water, pepper, and Ac'cent. Stir until blended. Simmer until mixture is thickened to consistency of tomato sauce.

Cut bread in ½-inch strips; brown in 3 tablespoons butter.

Add bouillon to tomato mixture; mix well. Pour into soup bowls; top with bread strips. Garnish with egg slices. Serve with grated Parmesan cheese if desired. Makes 6 generous portions.

Guatemalan Bread Soup

SCOTCH BROTH

½ cup barley
3 pounds lamb or mutton
2 tablespoons butter or margarine
¼ cup each celery, carrots, turnips, onions, or leeks, diced
Salt and pepper
Minced parsley

Soak barley for 2 hours or overnight in cold water.

Combine meat and cold water to cover in kettle. Bring to boiling point and add barley. Simmer until meat is tender, about 1½ to 2 hours.

Sauté vegetables in butter and add to soup for last half hour. Add salt and pepper to taste. Add more boiling water if soup is too thick. Add parsley just before serving. Serves 6 to 8.

Note: For the meat, use the inexpensive cuts such as breast, neck, or flank. Soaked split peas may be added with the barley. Rice may be substituted for barley. Add with the vegetables.

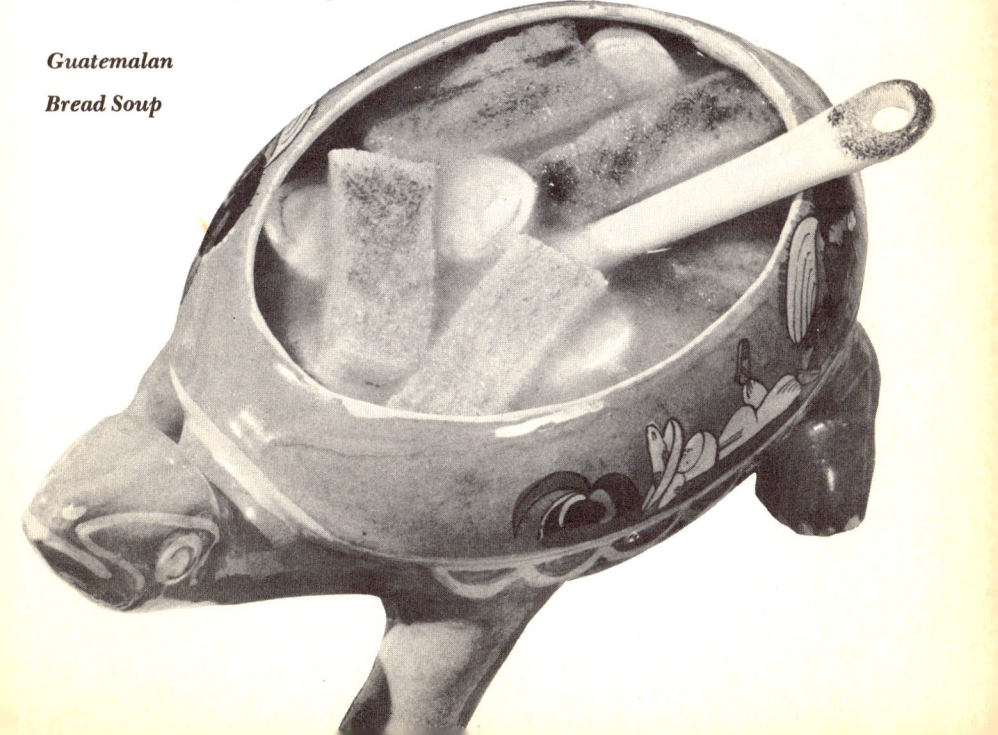

Chicken Okra Gumbo

CHICKEN OKRA GUMBO
(Creole)

2 tablespoons butter or margarine
1 3- to 3½-pound chicken
1½ to 2 pounds ham slices
1 onion, chopped
½ pod hot red pepper, seeded
1 sprig thyme or parsley, chopped
6 large tomatoes, peeled and chopped
1 quart (1 pound) okra
3 quarts boiling water
1 bay leaf
Salt and cayenne
2½ cups rice, boiled

Heat butter. Add the chicken and ham, both of which have been cut up into pieces. Cook, covered, about 10 minutes.

Add onion, red pepper, thyme, and solid part of tomatoes, reserving juice. Simmer a few minutes; stir often.

Wash okra well, remove stems and cut into ½-inch slices. Add to onion mixture and simmer, stirring constantly until brown.

Add the reserved tomato juice, boiling water, and bay leaf. Add salt and cayenne to taste. Simmer about 1 hour. Serve with boiled rice. Serves 8 to 10.

Note: Okra quickly burns, and should be watched and often stirred during browning. The traditional New Orleans gumbo is highly seasoned, so add cayenne generously.

The Creoles of the Crescent City make many different gumbos, thickening them wtih powdered filé (sassafras) or with okra. Chicken gumbo, like the above, is done with either. Okra often is preferred to the filé in crab and shrimp gumbos.

Of the thick soup that is the gumbo, it has been said:

"It is an original conception, a something *sui generis* in cooking, peculiar to New Orleans alone, and to the manner born."

TURKEY BONE SOUP

Bones of 1 turkey
2 quarts cold water
1 carrot, sliced
1 stalk celery, chopped
1 teaspoon chopped onion
1 sprig parsley
¼ bay leaf
3 whole black peppers
½ teaspoon salt

Place all ingredients in large kettle. Bring to a boil and simmer, covered, 2 hours; strain. Makes about 1½ quarts soup.

RUSSIAN CABBAGE SOUP

1½ pounds flank steak
2½ quarts water
1 tablespoon salt
Pepper to taste
1 No. 2 can tomatoes or 2½ cups chopped fresh tomatoes
1 large onion
1 bay leaf (optional)
½ clove garlic, cut fine (optional)
1 medium head cabbage
2 tablespoons sugar
1 tablespoon vinegar or lemon juice

Place meat and water in 5-quart soup kettle. Add salt, pepper, tomatoes, onion, bay leaf, and garlic. Bring to boiling point; reduce heat and simmer 1½ hours.

Shred cabbage coarsely and add. Add sugar, vinegar, and a little more salt to taste. Simmer gently for another 1½ hours. Serve hot. Serves 4 to 6.

Note: If desired, top each portion with a heaping tablespoon of sour cream.

PHILADELPHIA PEPPER POT

- 1 pound fresh honeycomb tripe
- 3 tablespoons butter or drippings
- 3 quarts cold water
- 1 pound stewing lamb or mutton, trimmed of fat
- 1/4 pound lean salt pork
- 1 small bay leaf
- 1 clove
- 1 sprig each parsley, thyme, and marjoram
- 2 cups mixed vegetables
- 1 cup diced potatoes

Use a variety of vegetables in season, making up the 2 cups of equal parts of beans, carrots, and celery; peas, onions, and beans; tomato, eggplant, and onion, etc.

Wash tripe, drain well, and cut into cubes. Brown in soup kettle in butter or drippings.

Add water, meat (cut into small pieces), salt pork, and seasonings tied together in a piece of cheesecloth. Cover tightly, bring to boiling point and simmer 2 hours.

Add vegetables and potatoes and cook until tender.

Cool, skim off fat and season to taste with salt and pepper. Thicken with a paste made of 3 to 5 tablespoons flour blended with 3 to 5 tablespoons butter. Bring to boiling point.

If a rich effect is desired, pour boiling soup over 2 egg yolks, while stirring constantly. Serves 6 to 8.

EGG AND LEMON SOUP
(Greece)

- 8 cups soup stock (below)
- 1/2 to 1 cup uncooked rice
- 3 egg yolks
- 1 tablespoon cornstarch
- 1 cup milk
- Juice of 1/2 lemon
- 1 tablespoon butter or margarine, melted
- 1 teaspoon chopped parsley
- Salt and pepper to taste

(To make stock: Cut 1 1/2 to 2 pounds of lean lamb in pieces, add 2 quarts water, 3 teaspoons salt, 4 carrots, 1 onion, 2 potatoes, and 1 celery root (celeriac) if available. The vegetables should be sliced or cut in pieces before adding. Simmer until meat is tender, then strain off the stock and chill.)

Remove fat from stock, measure, and add water to make 8 cups. Heat to boiling. Wash rice and add to hot stock. Cook until rice is tender (about 30 minutes). Mix egg yolks with cornstarch and milk and stir into soup. When the mixture has thickened slightly, remove from heat and stir in lemon juice slowly to avoid curdling. Add butter, chopped parsley, salt, and pepper to soup and serve immediately. Serves 8 to 12.

OXTAIL SOUP

- 2 oxtails
- Flour
- 3 tablespoons fat
- 1 teaspoon salt
- 1/2 teaspoon whole black peppers
- Dash of cayenne
- 1 bay leaf
- 1/2 cup chopped celery
- 1 medium onion or leek, chopped
- 1 carrot, diced
- 1/2 cup tomato purée
- 1 teaspoon Worcestershire sauce
- Chopped parsley
- Salt and pepper

Have oxtails cut in pieces and roll in 1/2 cup flour. Brown in 2 tablespoons fat in large kettle.

Add 2 quarts water, salt, pepper, cayenne, and bay leaf. Bring to boil and skim. Cover and simmer 3 hours, or until meat is tender.

Strain broth. Cool and remove fat. Separate meat from bones.

To broth and meat, add celery, onion, and carrot. Bring to boil. Reduce heat and simmer 30 minutes.

Add tomato purée and simmer 10 minutes.

In skillet, brown 2 tablespoons flour; blend in remaining 1 tablespoon fat. Add to soup and bring to boil.

Add Worcestershire and parsley. Season to taste. Makes about 2 quarts.

FILIPINO CHICKEN SOUP

1 3-pound stewing chicken
1 tablespoon fat
2 cloves garlic, mashed
2 tablespoons minced fresh or dried ginger root
Salt and pepper to taste
6 cups boiling water
3 pounds very green papaya (substitute white squash here)

Clean chicken and cut meat into 1-inch pieces.

Heat fat in saucepan and brown garlic in it. Remove garlic and discard.

Add ginger root and chicken. Brown chicken all over.

Add salt and pepper to taste. Add boiling water. Cover pan tightly and let simmer until chicken is nearly tender.

Add papaya or white squash cut into 1-inch cubes (about 8 cups). Cook until chicken is tender.

Serve as soup or stew—if stew is desired, use less water (4 cups in all).

In the Philippines and in Hawaii, 1/2 teaspoon of Ajinomoto (*monsodium glutamate*) is usually added with the salt. Serves 6 to 8.

CANADIAN CHEESE BISQUE

4 cups clear chicken or veal stock
1 tablespoon minced carrot
1 tablespoon minced celery
2 tablespoons flour
2 tablespoons butter or margarine
1/2 pound strong Cheddar cheese, 2 years old, grated
1/8 teaspoon pepper
1/2 teaspoon salt
1/2 teaspoon Worcestershire sauce
1 tablespoon minced green pepper
1 cup strong ale, heated

To the stock add the minced carrot and celery.

Make a roux by blending the flour, butter, and cheese. Stir into the stock and whip until smooth and blended.

Season with pepper, salt, and Worcestershire sauce.

Lastly add the green pepper, then set on top of stove until ready to serve, whereupon add the strong ale, heated. Blend together and serve. Serves 6.

GREEN KERN SOUP

1/2 cup green kern*
4 cups water
2 stalks celery, with leaves
3 sprigs parsley
2 quarts soup stock
1 tablespoon butter or margarine
1 tablespoon flour

Soak the green kern in the water for 30 minutes.

Tie the celery and parsley in a bunch and add to the kern and water. Cook gently until the water is absorbed, watching it carefully.

Remove the bunch of celery and parsley. Add the soup stock and cook in a double boiler until the kern is very tender, about 2 hours.

Stir and blend the butter and flour over heat, then stir this slowly into the soup. Bring to a boil.

If desired, add 1/2 cup or more warm cream and seasoning to taste. Makes about 2 quarts.

*Note: Kern is dried green wheat used to make this favorite European soup.

CHICKEN BROTH

Use a 3- to 4-pound ready-to-cook stewing chicken. Clean, remove skin and fat and cut in pieces.

Cover with 2 quarts cold water; heat slowly to a boil. Skim, then cover and simmer until tender, about 3 hours. Add 1 teaspoon salt after 2 hours of cooking.

Remove fat and strain as for clear soup. Season to taste and serve hot. Makes about 1 quart broth.

Note: If desired, 2 tablespoons tapioca, sago, rice, or barley soaked overnight, may be cooked with the broth.

Meat cut from bones may be used in salads, creamed, or in other dishes calling for cooked chicken meat.

UKRAINIAN BORSHT

2½ pounds soup meat
Soup bones
1 bunch beets, cleaned and quartered
1 large onion
1 can tomato paste
3 cloves garlic, crushed
2 tablespoons lemon juice
¼ cup sugar
2 to 3 tablespoons salt
½ teaspoon paprika
⅛ teaspoon pepper
2 quarts water
3 pounds cabbage, quartered

Combine all ingredients, except cabbage, in large pot. Cover and simmer slowly for 2 hours or until meat is tender.

Put cabbage wedges on top and simmer about another hour until cabbage is done.

Serve with sour cream and plenty of crisp crackers. Makes about 10 servings but most people will want more than one. If there's any left, it's just as delicious reheated for another meal.

QUICK CHICKEN GUMBO

3 tablespoons butter or margarine
1 onion, chopped fine
½ green pepper, chopped fine
4 cups chicken stock or consommé
1½ cups cooked or canned okra
1 No. 2 can tomatoes
About 1½ teaspoons salt
About ¼ teaspoon pepper
1 cup finely diced cooked or canned chicken

Cook onion and green pepper in melted butter until tender, about 5 minutes.

Add stock and remaining ingredients. Simmer gently about 20 minutes. Serves 6.

Miscellaneous Creamed Soups

RICE CREAM SOUP

2½ quarts chicken or veal stock, strained
¼ cup uncooked rice
Salt and pepper to taste
Dash of Tabasco sauce
4 tablespoons butter or margarine
4 tablespoons flour
2 cups milk
2 egg yolks, beaten
3 tablespoons milk
Nutmeg

Put the 2½ quarts of strained chicken stock or veal stock into a saucepan, or soup kettle. Bring to a boil. Add the uncooked rice. Add salt, pepper, and Tabasco sauce. Bring to a vigorous boil.

Turn the heat as low as possible. Cover and leave over this low heat for 20 minutes.

In a saucepan over a low heat, melt butter or margarine. Blend in flour and mix until smooth. Add 2 cups milk, stirring constantly until the mixture thickens.

Stir some of stock and rice mixture into milk mixture. Return to soup kettle.

When ready to serve, beat the 3 tablespoons of milk into the egg yolks. Slowly pour some of the hot soup over the egg yolks, stirring vigorously.

Return soup and egg yolk mixture to the soup kettle. Add a sprinkling of nutmeg and serve piping hot. Makes 11 cups soup.

Rice Cream Soup

Almond Cream Soup

CREAM OF CHICKEN SOUP

- 2 tablespoons butter or margarine
- 2 tablespoons flour
- 2 cups heated chicken stock
- 1 cup scalded milk or cream
- Salt and pepper

Melt butter and blend in flour. Add stock and milk or cream. Cook 5 minutes, stirring constantly.

Season to taste and remove from heat to avoid curdling. Serves 4.

With Egg Yolk: Use only 1 tablespoon flour. Beat an egg yolk slightly. Slowly pour hot soup over it. Strain and serve at once.

DUCHESS SOUP

- 1/4 cup butter or margarine
- 1/4 cup enriched flour
- 1 teaspoon salt
- Dash of pepper
- 4 chicken bouillon cubes
- 4 cups hot water
- 2 slices onion
- 2 cups heavy cream
- 1/2 cup grated process American cheese
- 2 hard-cooked eggs, sieved
- Croutons

Melt butter, blend in flour, salt, and pepper.

Dissolve bouillon cubes in the hot water; gradually stir into flour mixture. Cook, stirring constantly, until slightly thick.

Add onion and cream. Simmer gently 25 to 30 minutes, stirring occasionally. Remove onion.

Just before serving, stir in cheese and egg; top with croutons.

Serves 6 to 8.

ALMOND CREAM SOUP

- 3 tablespoons butter or margarine
- 1/2 cup finely diced onion
- 1 cup finely diced celery
- 4 tablespoons flour
- 2 teaspoons salt
- 1/8 teaspoon pepper
- 1/2 teaspoon Worcestershire sauce
- 4 cups milk
- 2 chicken bouillon cubes
- 1/2 cup blanched, chopped almonds
- Slivered, toasted almonds for garnish

Melt butter, add onions and celery and cook over low heat until tender.

Add flour, seasonings, and Worcestershire sauce; blend.

Stir in milk and cook over low heat, until smooth and thickened.

Add bouillon cubes and stir to dissolve. Stir in blanched almonds.

Turn into hot soup bowls and sprinkle with almonds. Serves 6.

HAM AND CORN CHOWDER

- 1/2 cup onion slices
- 1/2 cup melted butter or margarine
- 1 No. 2 can cream-style corn
- 1/2 cup light cream
- 1 cup chopped cooked ham
- 1/4 teaspoon salt
- 1/8 teaspoon pepper

Sauté onion slices in melted butter until tender. Add corn, light cream, cooked ham, salt, and pepper. Heat to serving temperature. Serve with celery croutons. Serves 4 to 5.

Creamed Vegetable Soups

CREAM OF VEGETABLE SOUP
(Master Recipe)

- 3 tablespoons butter or margarine
- 2 or 3 medium-sized onion slices
- 3 tablespoons flour
- 1½ teaspoons salt
- Few grains pepper
- 3 cups milk
- About 2 cups vegetables and cooking liquid (see below)
- ⅓ cup cream (optional)

Melt butter in saucepan; add onion and cook gently until soft but not browned, about 5 minutes.

Stir in flour and seasonings. Remove from heat and slowly add milk, stirring until well blended.

Place over low heat and cook until smooth and thick, stirring constantly.

Add vegetable and cooking liquid prepared as directed below.

Heat thoroughly and add cream if desired. Sprinkle each portion with chopped parsley, watercress, or chives or a dash of paprika. Serves 6.

Cream of Vegetable Soup Variations

With Leftover Vegetables: Reheat vegetables singly or in combination in vegetable cooking liquid or in milk until soft enough to put through electric blender.

Measure pureé or finely chopped vegetables and add cooking liquid or milk to make 2 cups.

Cream of Asparagus Soup: Follow master recipe, increasing butter and flour to 4 tablespoons each.

Use 2 pounds of asparagus cut in 1-inch lengths. Cook covered in ¾ cup boiling salted water until very tender.

Save tips for garnish and put remainder through a sieve. Add cooking liquid to make 2 cups purée.

Cream of Carrot Soup: Follow master recipe. Use 3 cups finely shredded carrots which have been cooked covered in 1 cup boiling salted water for 5 to 10 minutes.

Cream of Celery Soup: Follow master recipe. Use 2 cups finely chopped or diced celery. Cook covered in 1 cup milk in top of double boiler or over low heat until very tender. Add cooking liquid to measure 2 cups.

Cream of Corn Soup: Follow master recipe. Use 1 No. 2 can cream-style corn, or cook 2½ cups chopped fresh corn in 1 cup of milk until tender. Press canned or cooked corn through sieve.

Cream of Spinach Soup: Use 1 pound raw spinach. Cook until tender covered in water which clings to leaves after washing.

Put through sieve. Follow master recipe, increasing butter and flour to 4 tablespoons each.

Cream of Spinach Soup

CREAMED VEGETABLE SOUPS

Cream of Vegetable Soup Variations

Cream of Watercress Soup: Use 2 bunches of watercress. Wash and chop coarsely. Cook covered in 1 cup boiling salted water until tender.

Put through sieve and add cooking liquid to make 2 cups. Follow master recipe, increasing butter and flour to 4 tablespoons each.

Cream of Mushroom Soup: Use 1/4 pound fresh mushrooms. Wash and chop fine; cook gently in 1/4 cup butter with 1 teaspoon grated onion until tender, about 10 minutes.

Follow master recipe, adding 1 to 2 teaspoons lemon juice, if desired.

Cream of Lima Bean Soup: Use 1 1/2 to 2 cups cooked or canned lima beans and liquid. Put through sieve and follow master recipe.

Cream of Onion Soup: Use 2 1/2 cups very finely sliced or chopped onions. Cook gently in 1/4 cup butter until tender, about 15 minutes, but do not brown. If desired put through sieve. Follow master recipe.

Cream of Pea Soup: Use 2 cups fresh or frozen peas or 1 No. 2 can peas. Cook fresh peas in 1 cup boiling salted water, frozen peas according to package directions until very tender.

Heat canned peas in their own liquid about 10 minutes. Put peas through a sieve. Follow master recipe.

Cream of Potato Soup: Use 2 cups diced, cooked potatoes and 1 tablespoon chopped pimiento. Do not put through sieve. Follow master recipe.

CREAM OF CAULIFLOWER SOUP

Follow master recipe for Cream of Vegetable Soup. Use 1 medium head of cauliflower; cut into tiny flowerets to make about 1 quart.

Wash, drain, and cook in 1 to 1 1/2 cups salted milk in top of double boiler or over very low heat until very tender.

Reserve about 1/3 of the flowerets for garnish and press remainder through sieve. Add the cooking liquid to purée.

Garnish each serving with a few tiny flowerets and sprinkle with a dash of paprika. Serves 6.

CREAM OF TOMATO SOUP

1   No. 2 can (2 1/2 cups) tomatoes
2   slices onion
1   bay leaf
1   teaspoon salt
1/4 teaspoon pepper
1/4 teaspoon cinnamon
1/8 teaspoon cloves
2   tablespoons butter or margarine
2   tablespoons flour
2   cups milk

Combine tomatoes, onion, and seasonings. Simmer 10 minutes, then strain.

Make white sauce: melt butter; blend in flour. Gradually add milk and cook over low heat until slightly thick, stirring constantly.

Just before serving, slowly add hot, strained tomatoes to white sauce, stirring constantly. Do not reheat. Serves 6.

MUSHROOM BISQUE

1   pound mushrooms
3   cups water
1   slice onion
1/2 teaspoon salt
3   tablespoons butter or margarine
1/4 cup flour
2   cups milk
Salt and pepper
Paprika
1   egg yolk
1/3 cup heavy cream, whipped

Clean and chop mushrooms. Add water, onion, and 1/2 teaspoon salt. Simmer 1/2 hour. Press through a medium sieve.

Melt butter and blend in flour. Gradually add milk and cook over hot water, stirring occasionally until thick.

Add the sieved mushrooms, season with salt, pepper, and paprika to taste.

Beat egg yolk and gradually add to mushroom mixture. Serve with garnish of whipped cream. Serves 4 to 6.

CORN AND POTATO CHOWDER
(Master Recipe)

- 1 medium onion, chopped fine
- 3 tablespoons fat
- 3 cups boiling water
- 3 medium-sized potatoes, cubed
- Dash of pepper
- 1½ teaspoons salt
- 1½ cups canned corn
- 3 cups scalded milk

Sauté onions in fat until lightly browned. Add boiling water, potatoes, and seasonings. Cook until potatoes are tender, about 15 minutes.

Add corn and milk. Heat to boiling point, but do not boil. Serves 6.

Variations of Corn and Potato Chowder

Bean Chowder: Substitute 1½ cups canned lima beans for corn and diced carrots for potatoes.

Fish Chowder: Substitute 1½ pounds fish (haddock or cod) for corn. Add fish with potatoes and cook until both are tender. Then add milk, heat, and serve.

Additional fish bones or heads may be used, if desired.

Potato Soup: Omit corn. Cook 2 tablespoons chopped celery leaves with potatoes.

Garnish each serving with a little butter and dash of paprika.

POTATO CARROT CHOWDER

- 1 white onion, minced
- ¼ cup butter or margarine
- 2 cups diced raw potatoes
- 3 cups boiling water
- 1 teaspoon salt
- ¼ teaspoon paprika
- 1 tablespoon flour
- 2 cups milk, scalded
- 2 carrots, diced and cooked

Sauté onion in 2 tablespoons butter in large saucepan until lightly browned.

Add potatoes, boiling water, salt, and paprika. Boil about 15 minutes or until potatoes are soft.

Blend flour with remaining butter and gradually add milk stirring constantly, until smooth and thickened.

Add to potato mixture. Add carrots. Cook 5 minutes, stirring until smooth. Serves 6.

Corn and Potato Chowder

Veloutine de Crustaces

Fish and Seafood Soups, Chowders, and Bisques

VELOUTINE DE CRUSTACES

- 6 medium blue point oysters with liquid (or small to medium oysters)
- 1 cup diced scallops
- 10 cherrystone clams (or canned little neck clams)
- 5 or 6 celery leaves
- 2 cups chicken broth
- 2 tablespoons quick-cooking tapioca
- 2 egg yolks
- ½ cup light cream
- Salt to taste
- ½ teaspoon Ac'cent
- Dash of pepper
- 1 tablespoon butter or margarine

Cook oysters, scallops, clams (if fresh), and celery leaves in oyster liquid for 5 minutes; strain.

Skim liquid; add chicken broth; heat to boiling. Add tapioca; **cook** until thickened (about 10 minutes).

Beat egg yolks with cream; add to chicken broth while stirring. Add remaining ingredients with oysters, scallops, and clams; heat to boiling but do not boil.

Serve hot in soup bowls; keep hot if for sauce; spoon hot into pastry shells if for entrée.

Garnish with finely chopped chives or sprinkle of paprika. Makes 3½ cups, or 4 to 6 servings.

FISH BISQUE
(Master Recipe)

- 1½ cups thin white sauce
- 1 slice onion
- ½ to ¾ cup canned or cooked fish
- Lemon juice
- Whipped cream (optional)

Add onion to white sauce. Add flaked or chopped fish and heat thoroughly.

Press through a sieve. Heat carefully. Season to taste.

Just before serving, add a few drops lemon juice. If desired, garnish with whipped cream to which a few grains of salt has been added, and, if desired, a bit of paprika. Serves 3.

Variations: Vary by adding a dash of Tabasco sauce or 1/2 teaspoon Worcestershire sauce. If desired, 1/2 cup cooked celery may be added before pressing through sieve.

NEW ENGLAND CLAM CHOWDER

- 1 quart shucked clams
- 6 tablespoons chopped bacon
- 1 cup sliced onions
- 3 cups diced potatoes
- 1/2 teaspoon salt
- 1/4 teaspoon pepper
- 2 cups hot water
- 1 quart milk
- 8 soda crackers

Drain clams, saving juice. Chop clams.

Cook bacon in large saucepan until crisp. Add onions and brown slightly.

Add potatoes, salt, pepper, and water; cook 10 minutes.

Add clams, milk, and clam juice; cook until potatoes are tender, about 10 minutes.

Pour chowder over plain or crumbled crackers in serving bowls. Serves 6.

Manhattan Clam Chowder: Follow recipe for New England Clam Chowder, substituting 1 cup diced celery for potatoes, and 4 cups canned tomatoes or tomato juice for milk. Add 1 teaspoon thyme.

CLAM BROTH

Wash and scrub clams in shell with a brush. Place in deep saucepan. Add 1/2 cup water for each quart clams. Cover tightly and cook until clams open wide, 20 to 30 minutes.

Let stand 10 to 15 minutes so any sediment will settle. Strain through cheesecloth. Season to taste.

Serve hot or cold. Chop clams and use for canapé spread or other recipes.

Clam Broth Variations

Clam and Tomato Broth: Combine equal quantities of clam broth and tomato juice or tomato bouillon. Season with celery salt.

Clam and Chicken Frappé: Combine 1 1/2 cups clam broth and 2 1/2 cups highly seasoned chicken stock. Freeze to mush. Serve in chilled cups.

Clam and Chicken Broth: Combine equal quantities of clam broth and chicken stock. Either or both may be fresh or canned. Season to taste with salt and pepper. Garnish with chopped chives or parsley.

LOBSTER BISQUE
(Master Recipe)

- 3 tablespoons butter or margarine
- 4 tablespoons flour
- 1 teaspoon salt
- 1/8 teaspoon pepper
- 3 cups milk
- 1 cup bouillon
- 1 6-ounce can lobster meat
- 1 medium-sized onion, sliced
- 1 sprig parsley
- 1/2 cup light cream

Melt butter in saucepan. Stir in flour, salt, and pepper. Add milk and bouillon gradually, stirring constantly, and simmer over low heat until mixture thickens.

Add lobster, onion, and parsley. Cover and simmer 10 minutes. Remove from heat.

Strain, pressing as much of the meat as possible through a sieve. Add cream and reheat. Serves 6.

Lobster Bisque Variations

Crab Bisque: Substitute canned crabmeat for lobster.

Shrimp Bisque: Remove black line and wash 1 cup canned or cooked shrimp. Substitute in Lobster Bisque.

Clam Bisque: Substitute canned minced clams for lobster.

BOUILLABAISSE

2/3 cup salad oil
1 carrot, minced
3 onions, minced
3 pounds fish fillets
1 bay leaf
1 cup tomato pulp
3 cups fish stock or water
1 dozen oysters or clams
1 cup cooked shrimp or lobster meat
2 pimientos, minced
2 teaspoons salt
1/3 teaspoon paprika
2 tablespoons lemon juice
Toast
2 tablespoons minced parsley

Use a combination of several kinds of fish such as flounder, haddock, perch, sole, whiting, or whitefish.

Heat oil in large heavy saucepan and cook carrot and onions 5 minutes. Add fish, cut into small pieces, and bay leaf. Cook 5 minutes then add tomato pulp and fish stock.

Cover and simmer, without actually boiling, about 20 minutes or until fish is tender.

Add oysters or clams, shrimp or lobster meat, pimientos, seasonings, and lemon juice. Heat thoroughly.

Serve in soup plates, ladling the Bouillabaisse over toast in plates and sprinkling parsley over the surface. Serves 6.

NEW ENGLAND LOBSTER CHOWDER

1 small onion
1/2 cup diced salt pork
3 soda crackers, rolled fine
1 quart milk, scalded
2 6-ounce cans lobster or 2 1/2 cups fresh, cooked lobster
Salt, pepper, and cayenne pepper
1/4 cup butter or margarine
1 1/2 cups hot cream

Chop onion and cook with salt pork until golden in color. Strain and discard onion and pork.

To 4 tablespoons of the fat, add soda cracker crumbs.

Pour in hot milk gradually, stirring constantly until smooth; add lobster and heat in double boiler for 15 minutes.

Season to taste, then add butter and hot cream. Serve with crisp crackers. Makes 2 quarts.

Note: The cracker crumbs are a good way to prevent fat separation. In this rich, creamy chowder the onion is only a hint, with the delicate lobster flavor predominating.

TURTLE SOUP

1 1/2 cups diced fresh turtle meat
2 quarts beef stock
1 bay leaf
1 1/2 tablespoons lemon juice
1 clove mace
Few drops Tabasco sauce
Salt and pepper
Sherry wine
2 hard-cooked egg whites, chopped

Combine turtle meat, stock, bay leaf, mace, lemon juice, and Tabasco sauce. Bring to boiling point. Simmer until turtle meat is tender.

Remove bay leaf and mace. Season with salt and pepper.

Add 1 tablespoon sherry to each serving and garnish with chopped egg white. Serves 8.

GULF STATES OYSTER GUMBO

4 tablespoons butter or margarine
1 1/2 tablespoons minced onion
1 pint oysters
4 cups fish stock or canned clam broth
1 cup cooked or canned okra
2 cups cooked or canned tomatoes
Salt and pepper
2 tablespoons flour

Cook onion in 2 tablespoons melted butter until lightly browned.

Add oysters and their liquid, stock, okra, tomatoes, and salt and pepper to taste. Bring slowly to boiling point.

Add a smooth paste made of 2 tablespoons butter and 2 tablespoons flour. Stir until smooth. Serves 4 to 6.

SHRIMP CHOWDER
(Peru's National Chowder)

1 pound small fresh shrimp
1¼ cups cold water
1 tablespoon salt
2 potatoes, cubed
1 cup fresh peas (1 pound)
1 tablespoon chopped onion
1 teaspoon salt
1⅓ cups boiling water
1 cup milk
3 tablespoons butter or margarine, melted
¼ cup flour

Remove shell and sand vein from shrimp. Wash thoroughly. Add cold water and 1 tablespoon of salt; cover, bring to a boil, simmer for 8 minutes.

Cook potatoes, peas, and onion in boiling, salted water until tender; water should be almost evaporated at the end of cooking time.

Combine shrimp and vegetable mixture, including liquids and the milk; heat.

Blend the butter and flour and add a little of the warm liquid to make a paste. Add it to the chowder gradually. Simmer for 3 minutes, stirring occasionally. Serves 4 (6½ cups).

OYSTER STEW

4 tablespoons butter or margarine
1 pint shelled oysters with liquid
1 quart (4 cups) milk
1 teaspoon salt
⅛ teaspoon pepper
1½ tablespoons flour

Heat 2 tablespoons butter with oysters and oyster liquid in top part of a double boiler.

Combine 3½ cups milk, 2 tablespoons butter, salt, and pepper in a saucepan; heat to scald milk.

Stir flour into remaining ½ cup milk and blend well. Add to the scalded milk mixture; cook over low heat, stirring constantly, until it thickens.

Pour over the hot oysters and place stew over, not in, hot water for 15 minutes before serving. Serves 4 to 6.

Shrimp Chowder

FISH SOUPS, CHOWDERS, BISQUES

SOUTHERN CRAWFISH BISQUE

- 2 dozen crawfish
- 1 quart water
- 2 onions
- 2 carrots
- 2 ribs celery
- 4 sprigs parsley
- 1/4 teaspoon thyme
- 6 tablespoons cracker crumbs
- Milk
- 3 tablespoons butter or margarine
- 2 tablespoons flour
- Salt and pepper
- 1 beaten egg

Prepare crawfish for soup by soaking in cold salted water (1 tablespoon salt to 4 cups water) for 30 minutes. Wash and scrub under running water to remove all the dirt.

When cleaned, place in a soup kettle with the water, 1 onion, the carrots, celery, half the quantity of parsley, and the thyme. Allow to come to a boil and simmer for 25 minutes.

Drain off the water from the crawfish and set aside for later use.

Remove the meat from the heads and bodies of the crawfish; set aside the heads which are to be stuffed.

Moisten cracker crumbs with milk. Chop crawfish meat and add to the moistened crumbs.

Mince the remaining onion; melt the butter, add the onion and 1 tablespoon of flour. Add 1 tablespoon of the broth and the remainder of the parsley. Season with salt and pepper to taste.

Simmer slowly for a few minutes; add the crawfish and cracker crumb mixture and cook 2 minutes longer.

Remove from range and let cool slightly. Stir in the beaten egg. Fill the heads with this mixture.

Roll the heads in flour and fry in butter until nicely browned. Drain on paper and keep warm while preparing the stock.

Melt the balance of the butter; add the remainder of the flour and stir until smooth.

Strain reserved stock in order to remove celery and carrots. Add the broth to the butter and flour. Cook slowly for 12 minutes; season with more salt and pepper if desired. Before serving, add the stuffed crawfish heads.

Serves 4 to 5.

PORTUGUESE PRINCES' CHOWDER

- 1/4 pound butter or margarine
- 2 onions, sliced
- 1/4 pound raw ham, minced
- 1 large tomato, chopped
- 6 sorrel leaves, minced
- 1 small eel, skinned and sliced
- 8 raw shrimp, shelled
- 1 slice each of 4 varieties of fish (4 slices in all)
- 24 mussels
- 1/4 bay leaf
- 1/4 teaspoon freshly ground black pepper
- Salt
- 8 large oysters
- 2 tablespoons lemon juice

Melt butter in saucepan. Add onions; cook until limp and yellow.

Add ham, tomato, sorrel leaves, eel, shrimp, and fish slices. Cook a minute or two, shaking pan, until heated through and boiling.

Meanwhile, put mussels into a steamer; steam until shells open; remove from shells; remove beards from mussels and discard them.

Add to the mussel water, enough to make 1 1/2 quarts. Add mussel meats to it and cook 15 minutes.

Strain; pour liquid over cooking fish mixture. Put over low heat and let simmer 10 minutes. after adding bay leaf, pepper, and salt to taste.

Then add oysters with their liquid. Cook only until edges of oysters curl, then add lemon juice and serve at once, adding to each plate a little of each kind of fish and seafood.

The mussels are discarded, not being eaten. Serves 6.

NEW ENGLAND FISH CHOWDER

- 1½ pounds fresh cod, haddock, or any other large fish
- 2 cups diced potatoes
- 1 cup diced carrots
- 1 quart water
- ¼ pound salt pork, diced
- 1 onion, chopped
- 2 tablespoons flour
- 2 cups milk
- ½ teaspoon Ac'cent
- Salt and pepper
- 6 soda crackers
- 2 tablespoons butter or margarine

Cut fish into small pieces; remove bones and skin. Cook fish, potatoes, and carrots in water 15 minutes.

Fry salt pork until crisp; remove and drain.

Sauté onion in drippings; add flour and stir until well blended. Gradually add milk. Add to fish mixture. Add Ac'cent and salt and pepper to taste. Stir frequently and simmer 10 minutes longer.

Add more seasoning if necessary. Add crackers and butter. Serve at once. Serves 6.

QUICK SHRIMP GUMBO

- 1 medium-sized onion, chopped
- ½ green pepper, chopped
- 3 tablespoons butter or margarine
- 4 cups chicken stock or consommé
- 1½ cups cooked or canned okra, cut in small pieces
- 1 No. 2 can tomatoes
- 1 cup cooked or canned shrimp
- ½ teaspoon filé powder

Cook onion and green pepper in melted butter until soft, about 5 minutes. Add stock, okra, and tomatoes and simmer gently 20 minutes.

Add shrimp and filé powder. Heat thoroughly. *Do not boil* after adding filé powder.

Season to taste with salt and pepper. Garnish with minced parsley. **Serves 6.**

Quick Crab Gumbo: Substitute canned crabmeat for shrimp.

CREOLE SHRIMP GUMBO

- 1 slice (½ pound) raw ham, cut in small pieces
- 2 pounds okra, cut in ¾-inch pieces
- 1½ cups chopped onion
- 2 stalks celery with leaves, chopped
- ½ chopped green pepper, seeds and membrane removed
- 2 cloves garlic, minced
- 1 sprig fresh thyme or ⅓ teaspoon dried thyme
- 1 bay leaf
- 1½ cups skinned fresh tomatoes or 1 No. 1 can tomatoes
- 6 cups water
- 2 pounds fresh shrimp
- 2 tablespoons chopped parsley
- Boiled rice

Sauté ham lightly in a skillet. Sauté okra slowly in ham drippings for 10 minutes. (If you use canned okra, omit the sautéing.) Add onion and sauté for the last 2 minutes.

Add celery, green pepper, garlic, thyme, bay leaf, tomatoes, and water. If a thick gumbo is desired use less water.

Shell and remove black sand veins from shrimp. Let the soup boil then reduce heat and add ham, shrimp, and parsley. Simmer 30 minutes.

Serve with boiled rice. **Serves 8 to 10** as a main dish or 10 to 12 as a soup.

New England Fish Chowder

FISH SOUPS, CHOWDERS, BISQUES

CLAM CHOWDER À LA CAPE COD

- 4 dozen medium hard-shelled clams
- 6 cups cold water
- 1 2-inch cube salt pork, diced
- 1 large onion, chopped very fine
- 4 medium-sized potatoes, diced
- Salt and pepper
- 2 cups milk
- 1 cup light cream

Wash and scrub clams thoroughly. Place in deep saucepan with cold water. (Water should almost cover clams.) Let boil gently until shells open, about 10 minutes.

Strain broth through cheesecloth and save. Remove clams from shells, clean and chop fine.

Fry out salt pork in deep saucepan. Add onion and let cook slowly until it begins to turn golden brown.

Add clams and broth. Skim well, if necessary. Add potatoes and season to taste with salt and pepper. Cook until potatoes are tender.

Remove from heat and slowly add milk and cream which have been heated. Serve at once. Serves 8 to 10.

PACIFIC COAST CLAM CHOWDER

- ½ cup diced salt pork, ham, or bacon
- 1 small onion, finely chopped
- 1 cup boiling water
- 2 cups diced raw potatoes
- 2 to 3 cups milk
- 1 cup fresh or canned minced clams with liquid
- ½ cup cream-style corn (optional)
- Salt, pepper, celery salt to taste

Brown the salt pork in soup kettle, then add onion and cook gently until transparent.

Add water and potatoes; cover kettle and cook until potatoes are tender.

Add milk, clams, and corn. (If fresh clams are used, heat them in their own liquid before combining with milk mixture.)

Season to taste. Heat thoroughly and serve. Serves 4 to 6.

Variations: Canned tomatoes, put through a fine sieve, may be substituted for the milk. A tiny bit of thyme may be added to either the milk or tomato chowder.

Miscellaneous Meatless Soups

MUSHROOM STOCK

This is a good way to use up mushroom skins and ends. Combine with chopped onion, celery pieces and leaves, sliced carrots, and chopped parsley.

Cover with cold water; simmer for 30 minutes.

Strain the stock and when ready to use season with salt, pepper, and sherry.

ESSENCE OF TOMATO

- 1 quart canned tomatoes
- ¾ cup diced celery
- ½ cup diced carrots
- 1 small onion, diced
- Parsley
- 1 green pepper, diced
- 3 whole cloves
- 1 teaspoon whole black peppers
- 1 teaspoon salt
- Dash of cayenne
- Dash of mace
- ¾ cup heavy cream, whipped

Put tomatoes in saucepan and add vegetables and seasonings. Simmer 45 minutes to 1 hour or until vegetables are cooked.

Strain but do not force vegetables through sieve, as the tomato essence should be clear.

Reheat and serve hot in bouillon cups. Top with teaspoon of whipped cream. Serves 6 to 8.

MEATLESS LENTIL SOUP

- 2 cups lentils
- 1 onion, diced
- 2 tablespoons fat
- 1 carrot, diced
- 3 stalks celery, diced
- 1 teaspoon salt
- 1/4 teaspoon pepper
- 2 quarts hot water
- Minced parsley

Soak lentils overnight in cold water to cover.

Drain and add diced onion browned in fat. Stir over heat 5 minutes.

Add carrot, celery, salt, and pepper and 2 quarts hot water. Simmer slowly until lentils are tender, about 45 minutes.

Rub through a sieve. Bring to boil and serve hot garnished with parsley. Serves 6 to 8.

Lentil Soup Variatons

Lentil and Barley Soup: Add 1/2 cup barley with the lentils.

Lentil Soup With Frankfurters: Slice frankfurters into pieces about 1/2-inch thick. Cook in a few cups of soup stock. Serve soup with sliced frankfurters.

Lentil Soup With Meat: Add soup bone and 1 1/2 to 2 pounds soup meat. Simmer until meat is tender.

FRENCH VEGETABLE SOUP
(Potage Julienne)

- 2 potatoes
- 2 turnips
- 2 carrots
- 2 celery sticks
- 3 cabbage leaves
- 2 green onions
- 1/2 pound string beans
- 1 cup sweet green peas
- 1 1/2 quarts (6 cups) water
- 1 1/2 teaspoons salt
- 2 tablespoons butter or margarine

Cut the vegetables in thin, matchlike strips; cook all vegetables for 1 hour in boiling water to which you have added salt and butter. Liquid should be reduced to half its volume.

For a *créme julienne,* press the cooked vegetables through a sieve and add 1/2 to 1 cup of thin cream or rich milk just before serving. Serves 6 to 8.

Meatless Minestrone

MEATLESS MINESTRONE
(Italian Vegetable Soup)

- 1 cup navy beans or garbanzos
- 5 cups cold water
- 1/4 teaspoon salt
- 1/4 cup oil or butter
- 1 clove garlic, chopped fine
- 1 tablespoon onion, chopped fine
- 2 tablespoons parsley, chopped fine
- 3/4 cup or more celery, chopped fine
- 1/4 teaspoon salt
- 1/3 teaspoon pepper
- 1 cup fresh or canned tomato pulp
- 1 cup coarsely chopped cabbage
- 1 cup cooked macaroni
- Salt and paprika
- 1/4 cup or more grated Parmesan cheese

Soak navy beans or garbanzos. Drain and add cold water. Simmer the beans until tender.

Add boiling water, if needed, and 1/4 teaspoon salt.

Heat oil or butter in a saucepan. Sauté the garlic, onion, parsley, and celery in the oil until golden brown. Add 1/4 teaspoon salt, pepper, tomato pulp, and cabbage. Bring to boiling point and combine with the cooked beans.

Add cooked macaroni. Simmer 15 minutes longer. Add salt and paprika, if needed. Serve in bowls and sprinkle with Parmesan cheese. Makes about 6 cups soup.

Orange Jellied Soup

Some canned bouillons and consommés will jell when thoroughly chilled in the refrigerator. Others require the addition of gelatin. If a canned bouillon or consommé, ready-to-serve or condensed will jell upon chilling, it is usually so stated on the label.

The cans should be stored in the refrigerator for several hours or preferably overnight. Most rich, concentrated homemade bouillons or consommés will jell when thoroughly chilled.

JELLIED CONSOMMÉ OR BOUILLON

When using a consommé or bouillon which requires the addition of gelatin, allow 1 teaspoon (1/3 envelope) unflavored gelatin for each measuring cup of bouillon or consommé.

Soften the gelatin in a little cold water (1 tablespoon to a teaspoon gelatin). Then add hot bouillon or consommé and stir until gelatin is dissolved. Season to taste.

Pour into a pan; chill until firm. Just before serving, cut into cubes or break up lightly with a fork. Pile lightly in chilled serving cups. Serve with lemon slices.

CANNED MADRILÈNE

Chill in the can. Turn out into a chilled bowl, whip with a fork and serve at once in chilled cups.

Top each serving with 1½ to 2 tablespoons sour cream, or a little chopped parsley, chives or fresh dill, basil or chervil.

Jellied Soups

JELLIED TOMATO BOUILLON

- 6 fresh tomatoes, sliced
- 1 onion, sliced
- 2 stalks celery, chopped
- 1/4 green pepper, chopped
- 1 tablespoon chopped parsley
- 1 3/4 cups water
- 1/2 teaspoon salt
- 1 teaspoon sugar
- 4 whole cloves
- 1 bay leaf
- 1 tablespoon (1 envelope) unflavored gelatin

Bring to a boil vegetables, 1½ cups water, and seasonings; simmer, covered, 20 minutes, then strain.

Soften gelatin in remaining 1/4 cup cold water; add to hot tomato liquid, stirring until dissolved.

Chill until firm. Arrange by spoonfuls in bouillon cups. Serves 6.

Note: If desired, use 2 cups stewed tomatoes and reduce water to 1/4 cup.

ORANGE JELLIED SOUP

- 1/2 tablespoon (1/2 envelope) unflavored gelatin
- 2 tablespoons cold water
- 1/3 cup boiling water
- 1/4 cup sugar
- 1 cup orange juice (about 2 oranges)
- 1/8 teaspoon salt
- 2 teaspoons lemon juice
- 2 whole oranges

Soften gelatin in cold water for 5 minutes and dissolve in boiling water.

Add sugar, orange juice, salt, and lemon juice.

Section oranges and add to gelatin mixture. Fill bouillon cups about half full and place in refrigerator to chill. Serves 6 to 8.

Fruit Soups

Fruit soups are an old world invention especially favored in the Scandinavian countries and in Israel. Colorful, tart, and appetizing, they are particularly delightful for summer meals.

When served cold, they should be thoroughly chilled. Serve hot fruit soups when the remainder of the menu consists of cold food.

CHILLED FRUIT SOUP
(Master Recipe)

2 tablespoons quick-cooking tapioca
1½ cups water
1 tablespoon sugar
Dash of salt
½ cup quick-frozen concentrated orange juice
2½ cups diced fresh fruits (peaches, cherries, apples, bananas, etc.)

Place tapioca and water in saucepan. Bring to boil, stirring constantly. Remove from heat.

Add sugar, salt, and concentrated orange juice; blend. Cool, stirring once after 15 to 20 minutes. Cover and chill.

Before serving, add fruits. If thinner soup is desired, add more juice or less fruit.

Garnish bowl with fruit such as halved strawberries, orange sections, cherries, blueberries, bananas.

Serves 5 to 6.

Chilled Fruit Soup

SWEDISH FRUIT SOUP

½ pound mixed dried fruits (prunes, peaches, apricots)
½ cup dried apples
¼ cup currants
¼ cup seedless raisins
2 quarts cold water
¼ cup red sago (roda sago-gryn)
1 inch stick cinnamon
⅛ teaspoon salt
2 tablespoons sugar
1 tablespoon grated lemon rind
2 cups raspberry juice

Wash dried fruits thoroughly. Cover with cold water; let stand overnight.

In the morning add sago (or tapioca) and cinnamon. Bring to boiling point; cover, reduce heat and simmer 1¼ hours. Add remaining ingredients.

Chill soup. Serve very cold as dessert, sprinkled with finely sliced almonds. Serves 6.

BERRY SOUP

1 pint blueberries, raspberries, or other berries
3½ cups water
2 cups apple juice
¼ teaspoon salt
⅛ teaspoon nutmeg
Sugar to taste
2 tablespoons cornstarch
¼ cup lemon juice

Combine berries and water in saucepan; bring to boil. Cover and cook 20 minutes or until soft; put through sieve.

Add apple juice, salt, nutmeg, and sugar to taste. Add cornstarch dissolved in 2 tablespoons cold water. Cook until clear, stirring constantly. Chill and add lemon juice.

Top each serving with a spoonful of whipped cream if desired. Sprinkle with chopped mint. Serves 6.

Berry Cream Soup: After chilling add 1 cup thick sour cream.

Chilled Soups

To most people at one time, a cold creamed soup meant Vichyssoise in the most elegant, high-priced restaurants or made with lots of trouble at home. It is not only possible but easy to make good cold soups at home with little effort and at slight expense—in infinite varieties. Many of the recipes given below require only a few minutes preparation.

There are a few points to remember. Canned soups, served cold, are much lighter in flavor than when heated. In some cases they can take double the usual amount of seasoning to make them delicious.

Chill the ingredients thoroughly and use a rotary beater, electric blender, or electric mixer for combining.

Use the soup can for measuring.

To keep the soup cold on the table, put it in a bowl and set in a larger bowl filled with ice. Bowls or serving dishes of copper are ideal because they hold cold well.

VICHYSSOISE
(Cream of Potato and Leek Soup)

- 4 large potatoes
- 3 leeks
- 2 cups chicken stock
- 1 tablespoon butter or margarine
- 2 teaspoons salt
- 1/4 teaspoon white pepper
- 2 cups milk
- 1 cup cream
- 4 tablespoons chopped chives
- 1/2 teaspoon paprika

Peel and dice potatoes; cook with diced leeks (using green tops also) in stock until very soft (about 20 minutes). Put through a fine strainer.

To this purée add butter, seasonings, milk, and cream and reheat.

Serve cold or hot with minced chives on top and a garnish of paprika. If served cold, more milk or cream may need to be added on serving. Two medium white onions may be used instead of leeks. Serves 6.

BORSHT (Chilled Beet Soup)

- 2 bunches young beets
- 2 quarts water
- Salt and pepper to taste
- Juice of 1 lemon
- Sugar to taste
- 2 eggs

Use dark red beets. Wash, peel, and grate. Add to water with salt and pepper, to taste. Cook until tender.

Add lemon juice and about 1 tablespoon sugar. Cool. Soup should have distinctly sweet-sour taste. Since beets vary in sugar content, amount of seasonings is added accordingly. Beat eggs slightly and blend slowly with cooled borsht. May be served hot or ice cold topped with a tablespoon of sour cream.

Sliced hard-cooked eggs and chopped cucumber are also used as a garnish. A small sprig of fresh dill added to beets while cooking enhances flavor. If desired, serve with hot boiled potatoes. Serves 8.

SCHAV BORSHT

- 1 1/2 pounds sorrel (sour grass or schav)
- 1 quart water
- 1/3 cup sugar
- 1 tablespoon vinegar
- 2 tablespoons lemon juice
- 1 teaspoon salt
- 2 lightly beaten eggs
- 1/2 cup heavy sour cream

Wash sorrel thoroughly in cold water; remove stems and chop fine. Combine sorrel, water, and sugar in kettle; bring to boiling point. Lower heat and simmer 10 minutes. Add vinegar, lemon juice, and salt. Let cool.

Mix eggs and sour cream until blended. Add to schav and mix thoroughly. Chill and serve very cold with a hot boiled potato per serving, or sliced hard-cooked eggs. Makes about 1 1/2 quarts.

Spinach Borsht: Substitute spinach for sorrel.

CHILLED CREAM OF ASPARAGUS SOUP

Combine 2 cans condensed cream of asparagus soup and 2 cans light cream or rich milk.

Season with ¼ teaspoon each of paprika, garlic salt, and marjoram, and freshly ground pepper to taste. Garnish with minced chives. Serves 6.

CHILLED BLACK BEAN SOUP

Stir 1 can condensed black bean soup well and add 1 can condensed consommé. Stir in 1 can water and 1½ teaspoons sherry.

Chill 4 hours. Garnish each serving with a lemon slice. Serves 4.

CHILLED CREAM OF CHICKEN SOUP

Combine 2 cans condensed cream of chicken soup and 2 cans light cream or rich milk.

Season with salt and freshly ground pepper to taste. Garnish with minced chives. Serves 6.

Chilled Cream of Chicken Soup

CHILLED TOMATO SOUP

Stir 2 cans condensed tomato soup; add 1 can light cream and 1 can milk gradually, stirring constantly.

Chill 4 hours. Garnish with parsley. Serves 4.

QUICK BORSHT

Mix 1 can consommé and a 3½-ounce jar junior beets. Season and serve hot or cold with sour cream and chopped chives or green onions. Serves 3.

CHILLED CHICKEN AND MUSHROOM SOUP

Combine 1 can condensed cream of chicken soup and 1 can condensed cream of mushroom soup and stir; gradually add 2 cans water.

Chill 4 hours. Serves 4.

Quick Changes with Canned Soups

Many new soups are made possible by combining two prepared soups of different yet harmonizing flavors. The addition of herbs, cream, or perhaps wine (madeira or sherry), finely chopped onions, chives, parsley, etc., will improve the flavors as well as seasoning such as curry, Worcestershire, or Tabasco sauce.

Delightful, appetizing combinations result from personal experimentation in "mixing and matching" these soups.

Condensed soups are also used as cooking sauces and in preparing main dishes such as casseroles and meat loaves, to enhance the flavor of homemade soups and in recipes calling for soup stock.

The "can" measure in preparing "Quick Change" combinations is your soup can.

ASPARAGUS AND MUSHROOM SOUP

Combine 1 can each asparagus and mushroom soups. Dilute condensed soups with milk. Heat and garnish with chopped pimiento.

BEEF-CELERY SOUP

Mix 1 can cream of celery soup and 1 can beef soup. Stir well.

Blend in 2 cans of water. Simmer about 5 minutes.

BLACK BEAN SOUP

Combine 1 can each bouillon or consommé and black bean soup; heat.

Add a dash of sherry if desired. Garnish each bowl with a thin slice each of lemon and hard-cooked egg.

QUICK CHANGES WITH CANNED SOUPS

BACON-CLAM CHOWDER

Combine 1 can each clam chowder and cream of celery soup.

Add 1 can milk, ½ teaspoon grated onion, 1 tablespoon chopped parsley, and pinch of thyme. Heat to boiling and simmer a few minutes.

Garnish with generous spoonful of crumbled cooked bacon.

CHICKEN WATERCRESS SOUP

Combine 1 can cream of chicken soup with 1 can milk; heat almost to boiling.

Add ½ cup chopped watercress; simmer a few minutes.

CLAM CHOWDER CREOLE

Combine equal parts clam chowder and chicken gumbo creole.

CREAM OF TOMATO AND BEAN SOUP WITH FRANKFURTERS

Combine 1 can each tomato and bean soup.

Add 2 cans milk and ¼ pound frankfurters, sliced. Heat.

OLD-FASHIONED VELVET

Stir 1 can cream of mushroom soup; add 2 cans water slowly, stirring constantly.

Blend in 1 can chicken noodle soup. Heat, don't boil.

CREOLE TOMATO SOUP

Combine 1 can tomato soup, 1 can chicken gumbo soup, and 2 cans water. Simmer about 5 minutes.

Vegetable Soup, Peasant Style

TOMATO CHICKEN-NOODLE SOUP

Combine 1 can each tomato and chicken noodle soup. Add 1 can water and dash of garlic salt.

Heat to boiling and simmer a few minutes.

FISH MONGOLE SOUP

Combine 1 can each tomato and pea soup. Add 2 cans milk or water and 1 cup flaked cooked fish.

Bring to boil and add 2 tablespoons sherry, if desired.

GREEN PEA AND MUSHROOM SOUP

Mix 1 can green pea soup and 1 can cream of mushroom soup. Stir well.

Slowly add 1 can water, then 1 can milk. Heat thoroughly, but don't boil.

HIGHLAND PEA SOUP

Combine 1 can green pea soup and 2 cans water. Stir well.

Add 1 can Scotch broth. Simmer 5 minutes.

VEGETABLE AND BEEF NOODLE

Combine 1 can vegetable soup, 1 can beef noodle soup and 1½ cans water. Simmer about 5 minutes.

VEGETABLE SOUP, PEASANT STYLE

Combine 1 can vegetable soup, 1 can bean with bacon soup, and 2 cans water. Simmer about 5 minutes.

QUICK MINESTRONE

1 can vegetable soup
2 cans hot water
1 can baked beans in tomato sauce
2 tablespoons elbow macaroni
1 clove garlic, finely sliced
Grated Parmesan cheese

Combine all ingredients. Cook until macaroni is tender, about 12 minutes.

Serve with grated Parmesan cheese sprinkled over each bowl.

Serve soups with imaginative accompaniments like piping hot bacon-wrapped saltine crackers and colorful crisp vegetables.

Soup Garnishes and Accompaniments

SOUP GARNISHING HINTS

The finishing touch—a bit of colorful garnish—is liked by everyone and should not be forgotten when serving soups. Here are some suggestions.

For Chowders and Meat Soups: Chopped parsley, thin slices of lemon for fish chowder; thin slices of frankfurters in bean and pea soups. See other suggestions with specific recipes.

For Clear Soups: Finely minced parsley, chives, thin slices of lemon, balls or slices of avocado, thin cooked celery rings or celery leaves, sautéed mushroom slices, thinly sliced olive rings, julienned carrots, string beans, rice, macaroni in small shapes.

For Cream Soups: Salted whipped cream alone or with minced parsley or chopped nuts, toast croutons, chopped pimiento, chopped chives, puffed cereals, raw grated carrots, thick sour cream, crumbled crisp bacon, grated cheese.

RADISH WHEELS

Cut into paper thin circles. Serve several slices on cream soups or green pea soup.

CHIVED PARSLEY

Mix 1 tablespoon minced parsley with 1 teaspoon chopped chives. Appetizing on all soups.

CRISPY DRY CEREAL

Choose any dry cereal that comes in interesting small shapes. Sprinkle or float on soup. Good with many soups.

FRITTER GARNISH FOR SOUP

1 egg
$3/4$ teaspoon salt
$1/2$ cup flour
2 tablespoons milk or water

Beat egg until light. Add salt, flour, and milk.

Put through colander into deep hot fat (365°F.). Fry until brown. Drain on paper. Serve in hot soup.

FARINA PUFFS FOR SOUP

2 tablespoons butter or margarine
3 tablespoons uncooked farina
$1/2$ teaspoon baking powder
1 well beaten egg yolk
$1/8$ teaspoon salt
$1/8$ teaspoon nutmeg
Boiling water or soup

Cream the butter or margarine. Mix farina with baking powder and work into the creamed butter. Add egg yolk, salt, and nutmeg.

Drop by $1/4$ teaspoonfuls into simmering water or soup. Cook about 10 minutes.

Remove with a slotted spoon if cooked in water. The puffs will double or triple in size. Makes 20 small puffs.

Croutons

CROUTONS

Cut bread into $\frac{1}{4}$- to $\frac{1}{2}$-inch cubes. Sauté in butter or other fat until golden brown.

Or they may be dropped into deep fat hot enough to brown one cube in 30 seconds (370°F.).

Or spread the cubes on a greased baking sheet and brown them in a moderate oven (350°F.), 10 to 15 minutes.

Herb Croutons: Sprinkle hot browned croutons with onion salt and celery salt.

CHEESE PUFF BALLS

$\frac{1}{2}$ cup grated Parmesan cheese
1 tablespoon flour
$\frac{1}{4}$ teaspoon salt
Dash of cayenne or paprika
2 egg whites, stiffly beaten
3 tablespoons cracker crumbs

Mix cheese, flour, salt, and pepper; fold into egg whites. If too crumbly to mold, add a few drops of milk.

Shape in small balls; roll in crumbs and fry in hot deep fat (375°F.) about 1 minute, or until golden brown. Drain on absorbent paper. Makes 1$\frac{1}{2}$ dozen balls.

ALMOND BALLS FOR SOUP

1 egg yolk
$\frac{1}{2}$ cup ground blanched almonds
$\frac{1}{8}$ teaspoon salt
$\frac{1}{8}$ teaspoon grated lemon rind
1 stiffly beaten egg white

Beat egg yolk, almonds, salt, and lemon rind. Fold in stiffly beaten egg white.

Drop the batter from a teaspoon into hot fat; brown lightly.

Drain well on absorbent paper. Add to clear soup immediately before serving.

CHICKEN FORCEMEAT FOR SOUP
(Quenelles)

$\frac{1}{2}$ cup fine stale breadcrumbs
$\frac{1}{2}$ cup milk
2 tablespoons butter or margarine
1 stiffly beaten egg white
Salt
Few grains cayenne
Slight grating of nutmeg
$\frac{2}{3}$ cup raw breast of chicken

Cook breadcrumbs and milk to paste. Add butter, egg white, and seasonings.

Add chicken which has been pounded and forced through a purée strainer or food chopper. Form into small balls and cook in soup.

EGG BALLS FOR SOUP

2 hard-cooked egg yolks
$\frac{1}{4}$ teaspoon salt
Dash of pepper
About 1 egg white
1 tablespoon flour
2 tablespoons fat

Force egg yolks through sieve; add seasonings and enough egg white to moisten.

Shape in small balls about $\frac{1}{4}$ inch in diameter; roll in flour and sauté in fat until lightly browned.

Add to soup just before serving. Makes about 10 small balls.

MARROW BALLS FOR SOUP

1/4 cup fresh marrow
2 tablespoons butter or margarine
3 eggs
1/4 teaspoon salt
1/8 teaspoon paprika
2 tablespoons chopped parsley
Cracker crumbs

Combine marrow and butter and beat until creamy.

Add eggs, salt, paprika, parsley, and just enough cracker crumbs to make the right consistency to shape into balls.

Cook in simmering soup 15 minutes.

PIROGEN OR PIROSHKI
(Baked Meat Dumplings)

Filling:

3/4 pound cooked beef
2 broiled chicken livers
1 onion, sliced and fried
1 egg
Salt, pepper, cinnamon

Dough:

1 1/2 cups sifted enriched flour
1 1/2 teaspoons baking powder
1 slightly beaten egg
1/4 cup chicken fat or shortening
Pinch of salt
About 1/4 cup water

Put the cooked beef, chicken livers, and onion through the food chopper. Add the egg; season to taste and mix well.

Combine the dough ingredients, adding just enough water to make a soft dough.

Roll out about 1/8-inch thick and cut in 3 1/2-inch rounds.

Fill each round with 1 tablespoon meat mixture. Shape in half moons by folding the edges together over the filling. Pinch the edges together securely.

Bake on a greased baking sheet in hot oven (400°F.) until nicely browned, 25 to 30 minutes. Serve with clear soups.

Variations: These old-time European baked dumplings or turnovers may also

Matzo Balls for Soup

be made with a yeast dough or pie crust (homemade or packaged mix).

If a yeast dough is used, allow the filled pirogen to rise 1 to 1 1/2 hours on the greased baking sheet, then brush with chicken fat, melted shortening, or egg yolk diluted with equal amount of water.

Bake in moderate oven (375°F.) until nicely browned, 20 to 25 minutes.

Other well seasoned fillings such as cooked liver, or poultry, or kasha (cooked buckwheat groats) may be used.

MATZO BALLS FOR SOUP

3 tablespoons melted chicken fat
2 eggs, separated
3/4 to 7/8 cup matzo meal
1/2 cup hot water
Salt
1/8 teaspoon ginger (optional)

Place chicken fat and egg yolks in a large bowl; beat until well blended.

Add 3/4 cup matzo meal alternately with hot water (3 additions of each).

Taste and add up to 1 teaspoon salt; stir in ginger.

Form a trial ball, about 1 inch in diameter. Drop into a pan of simmering water. Cover and cook 5 minutes. It should hold its shape. If it crumbles, add a little more matzo meal (1 to 3 tablespoonfuls) and make another trial ball.

When consistency is satisfactory, chill mixture from 1 to 3 hours.

Then form into small balls and simmer 15 to 20 minutes in hot water or hot soup. For larger balls, use a longer period of time, up to 25 minutes. Serves 6.

Funnyface Garnishes

EGG DROP FOR SOUP

1 beaten egg
Dash of salt
3 tablespoons flour
¼ cup cold water

Stir all ingredients together until smooth. Drop slowly from end of spoon into boiling soup.

Cover. Cook 5 minutes and serve hot.

Variation: Pour well beaten egg gradually into boiling soup just before serving.

DRIED CELERY AND PARSLEY FOR SOUP

Place celery leaves or parsley on a rack in a very slow oven (250°F.) or less. Dry until brittle. Then store in a tightly covered container.

CUSTARD FOR SOUP

1 egg
½ cup milk or stock
⅛ teaspoon salt
⅛ teaspoon nutmeg (optional)
⅛ teaspoon paprika

Beat egg slightly. Add milk or stock and seasonings. Pour into small buttered cup.

Set in pan of hot water and bake in slow oven (325°F.) until it is set.

Remove from bowl and cut into diamonds or fancy shapes. Drop into soup just before serving it.

Royal Custard: Add 3 egg yolks and proceed as above.

NOCKERLN

4 tablespoons butter or margarine
1 egg
1 cup enriched flour
Pinch of salt
6 tablespoons milk

Cream together the butter and egg.

Stir in flour and a pinch of salt. Moisten to form a stiff batter by adding milk gradually.

Cut out the batter with a teaspoon to form small balls or Nockerln.

Drop them into boiling soup stock; cover the pan, and cook for 10 minutes.

MOCK ALMONDS FOR SOUP

Cut stale bread into ⅓-inch slices. Cut slices with round cutter 2 inches in diameter, then cut in almond-shaped pieces.

Brush with melted butter; put on cooky sheet. Place in hot oven (425°F.) or under broiler until lightly browned.

WHIPPED CREAM GARNISH

½ cup cream
2 tablespoons horseradish
⅛ teaspoon paprika

Whip cream. Fold in horseradish and paprika.

Place a spoonful on top of an individual serving of soup.

Variations: Omit horseradish and paprika; place a spoonful of whipped cream on top of each serving and garnish with paprika and chopped parsley.

Or add ⅛ teaspoon cayenne or curry to the whipped cream instead of horseradish and paprika.

With Eggs: Fold equal amount of whipped cream into stiffly beaten egg whites to make a fluffy and less rich garnish for soups.

With Color: Add 1 tablespoon tomato paste or puréed pimiento to give whipped cream garnish an attractive pink color. Use with white or green soups.

SPECIAL DIETS

One of the most important secrets for helping a patient to recover and get well is the correct preparation and serving of attractive and properly selected foods. It is an important part of medical treatment.

In order to understand how to choose foods to keep the whole family in good health and for a better understanding of the correct selection and preparation of foods for the ill and convalescent, every homemaker should read the basic information given in **Meal Planning and Nutrition** (see Index).

While it is the doctor's responsibility to decide what kind of diet is to be prescribed for a patient, it is, nevertheless, the homemaker's responsibility to see that the food is prepared so that its nutritive values are retained and that the food is so well prepared and so attractively served that the ill or convalescent patient will want to eat it.

General Hints for Preparing and Serving Meals to the Ill and Convalescent

- Use as little as possible high seasonings and rich sauces. Irritating foods should never be served.
- Avoid foods with a strong flavor such as onions, cabbage, cauliflower, and turnips.
- Unless advised otherwise by the doctor, give sparingly such excessively sweet foods as candies, jams, jellies, preserves, and very sweet desserts and concentrated foods such as fats.
- Since the sight, aroma, and taste of food that the patient likes aids him in his digestion, try to include such foods, if the diet prescribed by the doctor permits it.
- Select fresh foods with variety in texture and color.
- Cook vegetables in a very small amount of water and just before serving.
- Foods may be more quickly and easily digested if given in liquid form. Such foods include milk and milk drinks, fruit juices, cereal gruels, broths, and raw eggs.
- If foods are to be finely divided, scrape or chop meat, and chop or mash vegetables.
- If foods are to be given in bland form, strain out cellulose and large particles from such foods as vegetables and cereals, or use finely milled, rather than coarse cereals.
- Use low or moderate temperatures in cooking such protein foods as eggs, cheese, fish, and meat to make them more readily digestible. Eggs, for example, should never be "boiled." Cook eggs in simmering water until done to desired consistency.
- Arrange trays attractively in a planned order for the convenience of the patient. The appearance of the tray may do much in favorably affecting the appetite of the patient. That means attractive dishes, related to the size of the tray, colorful napkins, and occasionally a surprise in the form of a favor, a flower, or some other pleasing item.
- Serve foods when they are hot and most palatable, even if this means preparing and serving the food before the family meal is to be served.
- Remember that one objective in feeding a patient is to avoid the gain of too much weight. Dietary requirements depend on age, sex, height, and activity (metabolic and physical) of the patient. The objective is to achieve and maintain the "ideal" weight of the patient.
- Remove the tray as soon as the food is eaten; food should never be allowed to stand in the patient's room.

Diabetic Diet

A person with diabetes need no longer cause a flurry of extra work in the kitchen even though the meal plan must be under the guidance of a physician. Nearly all diabetic menus may be planned around the family meals with little extra preparation. The number and size of the servings may be different. Meals should be on time, and the carbohydrate allowance should be divided appropriately among the three meals with a good source of protein in each. The physician often advises an afternoon or bedtime snack.

Here are three different plans easily adapted from the family meals. Ask your physician if you may follow one of these plans, or if he could adapt one for you. Meal plan No. 1 is for the adult on a low-calorie diet. Plans No. 2 and No. 3 include more milk and are suitable for children and adults requiring more calories.

All foods for the meal plans have been divided into six groups called *Exchange Lists*. The amount or serving of each food included on the same list has approximately equal food value, and so you may exchange one food for another on the *same* list.

DIABETIC DIET—PLAN NO 1

(*Approximate composition: Carbohydrate, 150 grams; protein, 70 grams; fat, 70 grams, and calories, 1500.*)

Use only as your physician prescribes.

Include these foods daily:

*A. Milk

Include 1 pint whole milk or 2 milk exchanges from List #1. (If permitted, you may also drink coffee or tea, without sugar. Be sure to substract any milk used in beverage or in cooking from allowance. If you use cream, subtract amount used from fat allowance.)

*B. Vegetable

Select 1 cup (approximately 2 average servings) or less from Group A, List #2, each meal, if desired. In addition, ½ cup (approximately 1 average serving) from Group B, List #2, should be included daily. One serving should be high in vitamin A.

*C. Fruit

Select 3 servings or exchanges from List #3, including 1 high in ascorbic acid.

*D. Bread

Select 6 servings or exchanges from List #4.

*E. Meat

Select 6 exchanges from List #5.

*F. Fat

Include 4 servings or exchanges from List #6.

Note: Your physician may include other foods in your menu plan. See List #7.

* Sample menus in Diabetic Meal Plan No. 1 show how exchanges may be divided among 3 meals and a bedtime snack.

DIABETIC MEAL PLAN NO. 1— SAMPLE MENUS

Note: Letters preceding menu items refer to food groups; see Diabetic Diet, Plan No. 1, above.

DP refers to dietetic-packed canned foods.

MENU NO. 1

Breakfast
- C   Tomato juice—1 cup—lemon
- D   Puffed wheat—3/4 cup
- E   Soft-cooked egg—1
- D   Toast—1 slice
- F   Butter—1 teaspoon
- A**Milk—1/2 cup

Lunch at Home
- E, B, F   *Chicken and Mushroom Salad
- D   Round, thin crackers—6 to 8
- C   Purple plums (DP)—2 medium
- A**Milk—3/4 cup

Dinner
- E   Baked ham—3 ounces
- D   Parsley potato—1 small
- B   Green beans—1/2 cup
- B   *Pickled beets
- D   Bread—1 slice
- F   Butter—1 teaspoon
- C   *Fruit Cocktail Whip (DP)

Bedtime
- D   Graham crackers—2
- A**Milk—3/4 cup

* Recipes included in this section.

** The total milk allowance may be divided among the meals and used as a beverage, on cereal or in recipes.

MENU NO. 2

Breakfast
- C   Grapefruit sections (DP)—1/2 cup
- E   Poached egg—1
- D   Toast—1 slice (whole wheat)
- F   Butter—1 teaspoon
- A**Milk—1/4 cup

Lunch Box
Tuna salad sandwich:
- E   tuna—2 ounces
- B   lettuce
- F   mayonnaise—2 teaspoons
- D   bread—2 slices
- B   Celery—2 large stalks
- C   Orange—1
- A**Milk—1 cup

Dinner
- E   Fried liver—3 ounces
- D   Mexican corn—1/3 cup
- B   Steamed onion rings—1/2 cup
- B   Cucumber (6 slices)—lettuce salad—vinegar
- D   Bread—1 slice
- F   Butter—1 teaspoon
- C   *Spiced Applesauce (DP)

Bedtime
- D   Spongecake—1 1/2-inch cube
- A**Milk—3/4 cup

* Recipes included in this section.

** The total milk allowance may be divided among the meals and used as a beverage, on cereal or in recipes.

MENU NO. 3

Breakfast
- C   Orange juice, unsweetened—1/2 cup
- D   Cooked rolled oats—1/2 cup
- E   Soft-cooked egg—1
- D   Toast—1 slice
- F   Butter—2 teaspoons
- A**Milk—1/4 cup

Lunch in a Restaurant
- E   Grilled chopped steak—3 ounces
- B   Green peas—1/2 cup
- B   Tossed salad—vinegar
- D   Bread—1 slice or 1 roll
- F   Butter—1 teaspoon
- C   Grapefruit—1/2 small

Dinner
- E, D, A**, B*   Noodle Bake
- B   Stewed tomatoes—1/2 cup
- D   Bread—1 slice
- F   Butter—1 teaspoon
- C   Peach halves (DP)—2 medium
- A**Milk—3/4 cup

Bedtime
- D   Soda crackers—3
- A**Milk—3/4 cup

* Recipes included in this section.

** The total milk allowance may be divided among the meals and used as a beverage, on cereal or in recipes.

DIABETIC DIET—PLAN NO. 2

(Approximate Composition: Carbohydrate, 180 grams; protein, 80 grams; fat, 80 grams, and calories, 1800.)

Use only as your physician prescribes.

Include these foods daily:

*A. Milk

Include 1 quart whole milk or 4 milk exchanges from List #1. (If permitted, you may also drink coffee or tea, without sugar. Be sure to subtract any milk used in beverage or in cooking from allowance. If you use cream, subtract amount used from fat allowance.)

*B. Vegetable

Select 1 cup (approximately 2 average servings) or less from Group A, List #2, each meal, if desired. In addition, ½ cup (approximately 1 average serving) from Group B, List #2, should be included daily. One serving should be high in vitamin A.

*C. Fruit

Select 3 servings or exchanges from List #3, including 1 high in ascorbic acid.

*D. Bread

Select 6 servings or exchanges from List #4.

*E. Meat

Select 5 exchanges from List #5.

*F. Fat

Include 3 servings or exchanges from List #6.

Note: Your physician may include other foods in your menu plan. See List #7.

* Sample menus in Diabetic Meal Plan No. 2 show how exchanges may be divided among 3 meals and a bedtime snack.

DIABETIC MEAL PLAN NO. 2— SAMPLE MENUS

Note: Letters preceding menu items refer to food groups; see Diabetic Diet, Plan No. 2, above.

DP refers to dietetic-packed canned foods.

MENU NO. 1

Breakfast

- C Grapefruit sections (DP)—½ cup
- D Cooked rolled oats—½ cup
- E Soft-cooked egg—1
- D Toast—1 slice
- F Butter—1 teaspoon
- A**Milk—1 cup

Lunch at Home

Peanut butter sandwich:
- E peanut butter—2 tablespoons
- D Bread—1 slice
- F butter—1 teaspoon

Pineapple salad:
- C pineapple (DP)—2 slices
- B watercress
- B Celery sticks
- E, B, A,** *Pumpkin custard
- A**Milk—¾ cup

Dinner

- E Grilled chopped steak—2 ounces
- D Curried spaghetti—½ cup
- B Green beans—½ cup
- B Cabbage-vinegar slaw—½ cup
- D Roll—1
- F Butter—1 teaspoon
- C *Ginger Pears (DP)
- A**Milk—¾ cup

Bedtime

- D Spongecake—1½-inch cube
- A**Milk—1 cup

* Recipes included in this section.

** The total milk allowance may be divided among the meals and used as a beverage, on cereal or in recipes.

MENU NO. 2

Breakfast

- C   Pineapple juice (DP)—1/3 cup
- D   Cooked wheat cereal—1/2 cup
- E   Poached egg—1
- D   Toast—1 slice
- F   Butter—1 teaspoon
- A**Milk—1 cup

Lunch Box

    Cheddar cheese sandwich:
- E   Cheddar cheese shredded—2 ounces
- B   chopped pimiento—2 teaspoons
- B   lettuce
- F   mayonnaise—1 teaspoon
- D   bread—2 slices
- C   Orange—1
- A**Milk—1 cup

Dinner

- B   Tomato juice—1/2 cup
- E   Baked ham—2 ounces
- D   Mashed potatoes—1/2 cup
- B   Brussels sprouts—1/2 cup
- B   Winter squash—1/2 cup
- F   Butter—1 teaspoon
- C   *Fruit Cocktail Whip (DP)
- A**Milk—1 cup

Bedtime

- D   Graham crackers—2
- A**Milk—1 cup

* Recipes included in this section.

** The total milk allowance may be divided among the meals and used as a beverage, on cereal or in recipes.

MENU NO. 3

Breakfast

- C   Orange juice, unsweetened—1/2 cup

Timesaver tip for feeding special diets. Strained and chopped canned baby foods supply fine textured, bland foods for many special diets as well as for older folks with food problems.

- D   Corn flakes—3/4 cup
- E   Soft-cooked egg—1
- D   Toast—1 slice
- F   Butter—1 teaspoon
- A**Milk—1 cup

Lunch in a Restaurant

- E   Broiled halibut—2 ounces
- D   Parsley potato—1 small
- B   Peas and carrots—1/2 cup
- B   Lettuce—1/8 head—vinegar
- D, F   Ice cream—1/2 cup
- A**Milk—1 cup

Dinner

- C   Grapefruit—1/2 small
- E   Scrambled eggs—2
- D   on toast—1 slice
- B   Pimiento asparagus—6 spears
- C   Dark, sweet cherries (DP)—1/3 cup
- A**Milk—1 cup

Bedtime

- D   Round, thin crackers—6 to 8
- A**Milk—1 cup

* Recipes included in this section.

** The total milk allowance may be divided among the meals and used as a beverage, on cereal or in recipes.

DIABETIC DIET—PLAN NO. 3

(*Approximate composition: Carbohydrate, 250 grams; protein, 100 grams; fat, 130 grams, and calories, 2600.*)

Use only as your physician prescribes.

Include these foods daily:

***A. Milk**

Include 1 quart whole milk or 4 milk exchanges from List #1. (If permitted, you may also drink coffee or tea, without sugar. Be sure to subtract any milk used in beverage or in cooking from allowance. If cream is used, subtract amount used from fat allowance.)

***B. Vegetable**

Select 1 cup (approximately 2 average servings) or less from Group A, List #2, each meal, if desired. In addition, 1/2 cup (approximately 1 average serving) from Group B, List #2, included daily. One serving should be high in vitamin A.

***C. Fruit**

Select 4 servings or exchanges from List #3, including 1 high in ascorbic acid.

***D. Bread**

Select 10 servings or exchanges from List #4.

***E. Meat**

Select 7 exchanges from List #5.

***F. Fat**

Include 11 servings or exchanges from List #6.

Note: Your physician may include other foods in your menu plan. See List #7.

* Sample menus in Diabetic Meal Plan No. 3 show how exchanges may be divided among 3 meals and a bedtime snack.

DIABETIC MEAL PLAN NO. 3—SAMPLE MENUS

Note: Letters preceding menu items refer to food groups; see Diabetic Diet, Plan No. 3, above.

DP refers to dietetic-packed canned foods.

MENU NO. 1

Breakfast

- C Pineapple juice (DP)—1/3 cup
- D Puffed wheat—3/4 cup
- E Poached eggs—2
- D Toast—2 slices
- F Butter—2 teaspoons
- A** Milk—1 cup

Lunch at Home

- D, E, B, A** *Noodle Bake
- C *Spiced Hot Applesauce (DP)
- D Bread—2 slices
- F Butter—2 teaspoons
- C Apricot halves (DP)—4
- A** Milk—1 cup

Dinner

- D, E, F *Salmon Cakes
- B Nutmeg carrots—1/2 cup
- D Green lima beans—1/2 cup
- B Tossed green salad:
- F   French dressing—1 tablespoon
- D Bread or roll—1
- F Butter—2 teaspoons
- E, A** *Baked Custard

Bedtime

- C Orange and grapefruit sections (DP)—1/2 cup
- D Saltines—5
- F Cream cheese—1 tablespoon
- A** Milk—1 cup

* Recipes included in this section.

** The total milk allowance may be divided among the meals and used as a beverage, on cereal or in recipes.

MENU NO. 2

Breakfast

- C Tomato juice—1 cup—lemon
- D Cooked farina—1/2 cup
- E Scrambled eggs—2
- D Toast—2 slices
- F Butter—3 teaspoons
- A**Milk—1 cup

Lunch Box

Meat sandwich:
- E luncheon meat—2 ounces
- B lettuce
- F mayonnaise—3 teaspoons
- D bread—2 slices
- B Celery sticks
- C Orange—1
- D Spongecake—1 1/2-inch cube
- A**Milk—1 cup

Dinner

- E Broiled liver—3 ounces
- F Crisp bacon—1 slice
- D Parsley potatoes—2 small
- B Peas and carrots—1/2 cup
- B Lettuce—1/8 head;
- F French dressing—1 tablespoon
- D Bread—1 slice
- F Butter—2 teaspoons
- C *Fruit Cocktail Whip (DP)
- A**Milk—1 cup

Bedtime

- C Apricot halves (DP)—4
- D Cinnamon toast—1 slice;
- F butter—1 teaspoon
- A**Milk—1 cup

* Recipes included in this section.

** The total milk allowance may be divided among the meals and used as a beverage, on cereal or in recipes.

MENU NO. 3

Breakfast

- C Grapefruit juice, unsweetened—1/2 cup
- D Wholewheat flakes—3/4 cup
- E Soft-cooked eggs—2

In all diets a good breakfast should supply 1/4 to 1/3 of the day's food needs.

- D Toast—2 slices
- F Butter—2 teaspoons
- A**Milk—1 cup

Lunch in a Restaurant

- E Pot roast (no gravy)—3 ounces
- D Baked potato—1 medium
- B Sliced beets—1/2 cup
- B Lettuce—1/8 head
- F mayonnaise—2 teaspoons
- D Bread or roll—1
- F Butter—1 teaspoon
- D, F Ice cream—1/2 cup
- A**Milk—1 cup

Dinner

- E Baked ham—2 ounces
- D Sweet potatoes—1/2 cup
- B Pimiento asparagus—6 spears
  Pineapple-cream cheese salad:
- C pineapple (DP)—2 slices
- F cream cheese—1 tablespoon
- B lettuce
- D Bread—1 slice
- F Butter—3 teaspoons
- C Purple plums (DP)—2 medium
- A**Milk—1 cup

Bedtime

- C Blackberries (DP)—1/2 cup
- D Round, thin crackers—6 to 8
- A**Milk—1 cup

* Recipes included in this section.

** The total milk allowance may be divided among the meals and used as a beverage, on cereal or in recipes.

Food Exchange Lists for Diabetic Diets

LIST 1—MILK EXCHANGES

(Each serving or exchange contains: Carbohydrate, 12 grams; protein, 8 grams; fat, 10 grams, and calories, 170, and is equal to ½ pint or 1 cup (8 ounces) whole milk.)

Type of Milk	Approximate Measure
Whole milk (plain or homogenized)	1 cup
Skim milk**	1 cup
Evaporated milk	½ cup
Powdered whole milk	¼ cup
Powdered skim milk (nonfat dried milk)**	¼ cup
Buttermilk (from whole milk)	1 cup
Buttermilk (from skim milk)**	1 cup

** Contains no fat; add 2 fat exchanges to the diet when used.

LIST 2—VEGETABLE EXCHANGES

Group A

(One cup or less contains negligible carbohydrate, protein and calories. Canned, fresh or frozen vegetables may be used.)

Asparagus
Beans (green or wax)
*Broccoli
Brussels sprouts
Cabbage
Cauliflower
Celery
*Chicory
Cucumbers
Eggplant
*Escarole
*Greens:
  Beet
  Chard, Swiss
  Collard
  Dandelion
  Kale
  Mustard
  Spinach
  Turnip
Lettuce
Mushrooms
Okra
*Peppers
Radishes
Sauerkraut
Squash (summer)
*Tomatoes
*Watercress

Group B

(One-half cup serving contains: Carbohydrate, 7 grams; protein, 2 grams, and calories, 35.)

Beets
*Carrots
Onions
Peas (green)
*Pumpkin
Rutabaga
*Squash (winter)
Turnip

* High in vitamin A; include at least 1 serving each day.

LIST 3—FRUIT EXCHANGES

(Each serving or exchange of unsweetened fruit listed below contains about 10 grams carbohydrate and 40 calories from carbohydrates.)

Fruit	Quantity
Apple (2-in. diameter)	1
Apple Juice**	⅓ cup
Applesauce**	½ cup
Apricots (fresh or dried)**	2 medium
Banana	½ small
Blackberries**	1 cup
Blueberries**	⅔ cup
Boysenberries**	½ cup
*Cantaloupe (6-in. diameter)	¼
Cherries, sweet (dark or light); red, tart**	10 large or ⅓ cup
Cranberry Sauce**	⅓ cup
Dates	2
Figs, Kadota**	3 medium or ⅓ cup
Figs (dried)	1 small
Fruit Cocktail**	½ cup
Fruits for Salad**	½ cup
*Grapefruit	½ small
Sections or Juice**	½ cup
Grape Juice**	¼ cup
Grapes (white)**	12 or ⅓ cup
Honeydew Melon (7-in diameter)	⅛
*Lemon Juice**	½ cup
*Loganberries**	⅔ cup
Mango	½
*Orange	1 small
*Orange Juice**	½ cup
*Orange and Grapefruit Juice**	½ cup
*Papaya	⅓ medium
Peaches**	1 medium
Pears**	1 small
Pineapple	2 slices or ½ cup
Pineapple Juice**	⅓ cup

Fruit	Quantity
Plums (Greengage or Purple)**	2 medium
Prunes (dried)	2 medium
Raisins	2 tablespoons
*Raspberries**	½ cup
*Strawberries**	1 cup
*Tangerine	1 large
*Tangerine Juice**	½ cup
*Tomato Juice**	1 cup
Watermelon	1 cup
Youngberries**	½ cup

* High in ascorbic acid.

** Unsweetened canned fruit or fruit juice may be substituted in the same amount. (When canned fruit is used, quantity includes liquid.)

LIST 4—BREAD EXCHANGES

(Each serving or exchange contains: Carbohydrate, 15 grams; protein, 2 grams; calories, 70.)

Bread—1 slice; biscuit, roll or muffin (2-inch diameter)—1; corn bread—1½-inch cube

Flour—2½ tablespoons

Cereal (cooked), rice, grits—½ cup; (dry) flaked or puffed—¾ cup

Spaghetti, noodles (cooked)—½ cup

Crackers—graham (2½ inches square)—2; oysterettes—20 (½ cup); soda (2½ inches square)—3; round, thin (1½ inches in diameter)—6 to 8; saltines (2 inches square)—5

Vegetables—beans and peas, dried and cooked—½ cup
  Lima beans, fresh—½ cup; baked beans (no pork)—¼ cup
  Corn, sweet—⅓ cup
  Parsnips—⅔ cup
  Potatoes, white (2-inch diameter) baked or boiled—1; mashed—½ cup

Sweet potatoes or yams—¼ cup

Sponge cake, plain (1½-inch cube)—1

Ice Cream (omit 2 fat exchange)—½ cup

Corn, popped—1 cup

LIST 5—MEAT EXCHANGES

(Each exchange contains: Protein, 7 grams; fat, 5 grams; calories, 75.)

Food	Approximate Measure
Meat and poultry, medium fat (beef, lamb, pork, liver, chicken)	1 ounce
Cold cuts (4½-inch square, ⅛-inch thick)	1 slice
Frankfurter (8 to 9 per pound)	1
Fish—cod, mackerel	1 ounce
salmon, tuna, crab	¼ cup
oysters, shrimp, clams	5 medium
sardines	3 medium
Cheese, Cheddar or American	1 ounce
cottage	¼ cup
Egg	1
Peanut Butter*	2 tbsps.

*Limit use to one exchange per day; or deduct 5 grams carbohydrate per serving when more than one exchange is used.

LIST 6—FAT EXCHANGES

(Each serving or exchange contains: Fat, 5 grams; calories, 45.)

Food	Approximate Measure
Bacon, crisp	1 slice
Butter, margarine, mayonnaise, oil, cooking fat	1 teaspoon
Cream, light (20%)	2 tablespoons
heavy (40%)	1 tablespoon
Cream cheese	1 tablespoon
French dressing	1 tablespoon
Nuts	6 small
Olives	5 small
Avocado (4-inches diameter)	⅛

LIST 7

Foods to use as desired (check with physician)

Bouillon	Rennet tablets
Clear broth	Rhubarb
Coffee	Spices
Gelatin, unflavored	Tea
Lemon	Vinegar
Mustard, dry	
Non-caloric sweeteners	
Pepper	
Pickles, sour or dill, unsweetened	

Recipes for Diabetic Menus

Note: Recipes for one serving may be increased. Be sure to take your correct portion.

CHICKEN AND MUSHROOM SALAD

(2 Meat Exchanges, 2 Fat Exchanges, 2 Vegetable Group A servings.)

- 2 ounces canned chicken,* diced
- 1/2 cup drained canned mushrooms, stems and pieces
- 1/2 cup diced celery
- 2 teaspoons mayonnaise
- 1/2 teaspoon lemon juice or vinegar
- Salt and pepper
- Lettuce

Combine all ingredients except lettuce; toss lightly. Serve on lettuce.

*Note: Shrimp, tuna, salmon, or turkey may be substituted for the chicken.

SALMON CAKES

(2 Meat Exchanges, 1 Bread Exchange, 3 Fat Exchanges.)

- 2 ounces canned salmon
- 1/2 cup mashed potatoes
- 1/4 teaspoon salt
- Pepper
- 1/2 teaspoon grated onion
- 5 small stuffed olives, sliced
- 2 teaspoons butter

Combine all ingredients, except butter; shape into 2 cakes. Brown in butter. Serve hot.

NOODLE BAKE

(2 Meat Exchanges, 1 Vegetable Group A serving, 1 Bread Exchange, 1/4 cup milk.)

- 2 ounces Cheddar cheese, cubed
- 1/4 cup milk
- 1/2 cup drained canned green beans
- 1/2 cup cooked noodles*
- Salt and pepper
- Paprika

Melt cheese in milk in small saucepan over low heat; blend until smooth. Combine with beans, noodles, salt, and pepper.

Place in individual casserole; sprinkle with paprika.

Bake in moderate oven (350°F.) 25 minutes, or until brown.

*Note: Macaroni, rice, or spaghetti may be substituted for noodles.

SPICED APPLESAUCE

(1 Fruit Exchange)

- 1/2 cup canned applesauce (DP)
- 2 saccharin tablets** (1/4-grain each) dissolved in 1 tablespoon warm water
- 1/4 teaspoon nutmeg
- Dash of cloves
- Dash of ginger

Combine all ingredients; heat thoroughly. Serve hot or cold.

BAKED CUSTARD

(1 Meat Exchange, 3/4 cup milk)

- 3 saccharin tablets** (1/4-grain each)
- 1 tablespoon warm water
- 1 egg, well beaten
- 3/4 cup milk
- 1/2 teaspoon vanilla
- Nutmeg

Dissolve saccharin in water; combine with remaining ingredients except nutmeg.

Pour into large custard cup; sprinkle with nutmeg.

Place in shallow pan of hot water. Bake in moderate oven (350°F.) 50 minutes, or until knife inserted near edge of custard comes out clean.

Note: Any non-caloric sweetener approved by your physician may be substituted for saccharin (1/4-grain tablet equals 1 teaspoon sugar.)

PUMPKIN CUSTARD

(1 Meat Exchange, 1 Vegetable Group B serving, ½ cup milk.)

3   saccharin tablets** (¼-grain each)
1   tablespoon warm water
1   egg, beaten
½   cup milk
½   cup canned pumpkin
⅛   teaspoon salt
¼   teaspoon nutmeg
¼   teaspoon cinnamon
    Dash of ginger

Dissolve saccharin in warm water. Combine with remaining ingredients; pour into custard cup.

Place in shallow pan of hot water. Bake in moderate oven (350°F.) 45 minutes, or until knife inserted near edge of custard comes out clean.

FRUIT COCKTAIL WHIP

(1 Fruit Exchange)

1   teaspoon unflavored gelatin
2   tablespoons cold water
½   cup boiling water
1   tablespoon lemon juice
3   saccharin tablets** (¼-grain each)
½   cup drained fruit cocktail* (DP)

Sprinkle gelatin over cold water; let stand 5 minutes.

Add boiling water; stir until dissolved. Add lemon juice and saccharin.

Chill until mixture begins to set.

Beat until fluffy with rotary beater; fold in fruit cocktail. Chill until firm.

*****Note:** Other dietetic-packed *Fruit Exchanges* may be substituted for fruit cocktail. Liquid drained from fruit may be brought to boil and substituted for boiling water.

For Jellied Fruit Salad, omit beating, if preferred.

GINGER PEAR HALVES

(1 Fruit Exchange)

½   cup liquid drained from canned pears (DP)
1   saccharin tablet** (¼-grain each)
¼   teaspoon ginger
2   pear halves, drained

Combine all ingredients except pear halves; heat to boiling.

Add pear halves. Cover and let stand in hot liquid for at least a half hour. Serve hot or chilled.

PICKLED BEETS

(½ cup equals 1 Vegetable Group B serving.)

1   No. 2 can (1 pound 4 ounces) sliced beets
⅓   cup vinegar
½   teaspoon salt
4   whole cloves
1   bay leaf
4   saccharin tablets** (¼-grain each)

Drain liquid from beets into saucepan; add remaining ingredients and bring to boil. Pour over beets.

Chill about 6 hours before serving. Serve cold or reheat. Serves 5.

Pickled Beets

****Note:** Any non-caloric sweetener approved by your physician may be substituted for saccharin (¼-grain tablet equals 1 teaspoon sugar).

Low-Sodium Diet

Perhaps your physician has restricted the salt (sodium) in your food. All foods and even water contain some natural sodium. Your physician will tell you how much sodium you may have. Perhaps you need eliminate only salt in cooking, or you may have to limit foods which are naturally high in sodium or are processed with sodium.

Here you will find two low-sodium meal plans. Both restrict sodium to about 500 milligrams (.5 grams). Your physician may allow more sodium or restrict it further depending on your particular requirements. If your physician recommends that you lose weight also, he may suggest the low-calorie diet. If you are maintaining your weight, he may prefer the higher calorie diet. You will find menus, recipes and also food groups from which you can plan your own menus. You will soon realize that you can enjoy a variety of delicious foods. But remember to omit:

1. Salt in cooking or at the table.
2. Smoked or prepared meats and fish, such as ham, bacon, corned beef, cold cuts, and anchovies.
3. Meat extracts, bouillon cubes, and meat sauces.
4. Bread or bakery products unless prepared without salt and other sources of sodium.
5. Salted foods, such as potato chips and nuts.
6. Prepared condiments, relishes, Worcestershire sauce, ketchup, pickles, and olives.
7. Frozen fish fillets and shellfish, except oysters.
8. Frozen peas and lima beans.
9. Prepared flour and flour mixes, baking powder, and soda.
10. All canned meat and vegetable products unless prepared without salt (dietetic pack).
11. Canned pears, figs, and applesauce unless prepared without salt (dietetic pack).
12. Butter, cheese, and peanut butter unless prepared without salt.
13. Vegetable salts, such as onion, garlic, or celery salt.
14. Sodium in any form, such as sodium benzoate, sodium bicarbonate, monosodium glutamate.

Read all labels carefully.

SALT SUBSTITUTES

Discuss with your physician the salt substitutes on the market. If he approves, try several to find the one you like best. Omit salt when preparing food. When cooked, remove your portion and season with substitute; add regular salt to the rest for family eating.

FLAVOR TOUCHES

Whether you can use salt substitutes or not, all is not lost. Now's the time to be adventurous and try some of the herbs, spices, and seasonings you may not have used before. Go lightly—a little goes a long way. Enhance the food flavor—don't overwhelm it! Don't limit yourself to one or two—experiment with several. Here are suggestions for a start:

Allspice: ground meats, stews, tomatoes, peaches

Almond Extract: puddings, fruits

Basil: eggs, fish, lamb, ground meats, liver, stews, salads, soup, sauces, fish cocktails

Bay Leaves: meats, stews, poultry, soup, tomatoes

Caraway Seeds: meats, stews, soups, salads, breads, cabbage, asparagus, noodles

Chives: salads, eggs, sauces, soups, meat dishes, vegetables

Cider Vinegar: salads, vegetables, sauces

Cinnamon: fruits (especially apples), breads, pie crust

Curry Powder: meats (especially lamb), chicken, fish, tomatoes, tomato soup

Dill: fish sauces, soups, tomatoes, salads, macaroni

Garlic (not garlic salt): meats, soups, salads, vegetables, tomatoes

Ginger: chicken, fruits

Lemon Juice: meats, fish, poultry, salads, vegetables

Mace: hot breads

Mustard (dry): ground meats, salads, sauces

Nutmeg: fruits, cottage cheese, pie crust, potatoes

Onion (not onion salt): meats, vegetables, salads

Paprika: meats, fish, stews, sauces, soups, vegetables

Parsley: meats, fish, soups, salads, sauces, vegetables

Peppermint Extract: puddings, fruits

Pimiento: salads, vegetables, casserole dishes

Rosemary: chicken, veal, meat loaf, beef, pork, sauces, stuffings, potatoes, peas, lima beans

Sage: meats, stews, biscuits, tomatoes, green beans

Savory: salads, egg dishes, pork, ground meats, soup, green beans, squash, tomatoes, lima beans, peas

Thyme: eggs, meats (especially veal, pork), sauces, soups, onions, peas, tomatoes, salads

Turmeric: meats, eggs, fish, sauce, rice

LOW-SODIUM DIET—PLAN #1

(500 milligrams sodium, approximately 1500 calories.)

Use only as your physician prescribes.

Include these foods daily:

*A. Fruit

Select three servings from List #1—Fruit Group, including one high in ascorbic acid.

*B. Vegetable

Select four servings from List #3—Vegetable Group. One serving should be high in vitamin A.

*C. Milk

Include one pint of whole milk. (If permitted, you may also drink coffee or tea, without sugar. Be sure to subtract any milk used in beverage or in cooking from allowance. If you use cream, subtract amount used from fat allowance.)

*D. Meat, Poultry and Fish

Select two 3-ounce servings from List #2—Meat, Poultry and Fish Group—or make equivalent substitution.

*E. Egg

Include one egg.

*F. Bread and Cereal

Select three servings from List #4—Bread and Cereal Group.

*G. Fat and Oil

Include two servings from List #5—Fat and Oil Group.

*Sample menus Low-Sodium Meal Plan #1 below show how servings may be divided among 3 meals.

SPECIAL DIETS

LOW-SODIUM MEAL PLAN #1— SAMPLE MENUS

Note: Letters preceding menu items refer to food groups; see Low-Sodium Diet—Plan No. 1 above.

DP means dietetic-packed canned foods. L.S. means low sodium.

MENU #1

Breakfast

- B Tomato juice (DP)—½ cup—lemon
- F Unsalted cooked rolled oats—½ cup
- E Poached egg—1
- F L.S. toast—1 slice
- G Sweet butter—1 teaspoon
- C **Milk—½ cup

Lunch at Home

- D Sliced turkey (DP)—3 ounces
- A Cranberry sauce (DP)—⅓ cup
- Cabbage and fruit slaw:
- B   shredded cabbage—1 cup
- A   fruit cocktail (DP)—½ cup
- G *L.S. French dressing—2 teaspoons
- F Cinnamon L.S. toast—1 slice
- C **Milk—1 cup

Dinner

- D Broiled liver—3 ounces
- B Paprika potatoes (DP)—2 small
- B Steamed onion rings—½ cup
- A Purple plums (DP)—2 medium
- C **Milk—½ cup

*Note: Recipes included in this section.

**The total milk allowance may be divided among the meals and used as a beverage, on cereal or in recipes.

MENU #2

Breakfast

- A Orange juice (DP)—½ cup
- F Shredded wheat—1 biscuit
- E Soft-cooked egg—1
- C **Milk—1 cup

Lunch Box

Tuna sandwich:
- D tuna (DP)—2 ounces
- B tomato—1 small
- G *L.S. mayonnaise—2 teaspoons
- F L.S. bread—2 slices
- A Apple—1 small
- C **Milk—1 cup

Dinner

- D Unsalted pot roast (no gravy)—4 ounces
- B Winter squash (DP)—½ cup
- B *Herb green beans (DP)—½ cup
- B Lettuce-cucumber salad—vinegar
- A *Apricot-Rum Whip

*Note: Recipes included in this section.

**The total milk allowance may be divided among the meals and used as a beverage, on cereal or in recipes.

MENU #3

Breakfast

- A Pineapple juice (DP)—⅓ cup
- F Puffed rice—1 cup
- E Poached egg—1
- F L.S. toast—1 slice
- G Sweet butter—1 teaspoon
- C **Milk—½ cup

Lunch in a Restaurant

- D Unsalted roast lamb (no gravy)—3 ounces
- B Baked potato—1 small
- B Green salad—vinegar
- A Grapefruit—½ small
- C **Milk—1 cup

Dinner

Peach and cottage cheese salad:
- A   peach halves (DP)—2
- D   L.S. cottage cheese—¾ cup
- B   lettuce
- B Brussels sprouts—½ cup—lemon juice
- F L.S. toast—1 slice
- G Sweet butter—1 teaspoon
- C **Milk—½ cup

*Note: Recipes included in this section.

**The total milk allowance may be divided among the meals and used as a beverage, on cereal or in recipes.

SPECIAL DIETS **2483**

LOW-SODIUM DIET—PLAN #2

(500 milligrams sodium, approximately 2500 calories)

Use only as your physician prescribes.

Include these foods daily:

*A. Fruit

Select four servings from List #1—Fruit Group—including one high in ascorbic acid. (You may use syrup-packed fruits in place of dietetic-packed fruits, with the exception of applesauce, figs, and pears.)

*B. Vegetable

Select five servings from List #3—Vegetable Group. One serving should be high in vitamin A.

*C. Milk

Include 1 pint of whole milk. (If permitted, you may also drink coffee or tea. Be sure to subtract any milk used in beverage or in cooking from milk allowance; any cream used from fat allowance; any sugar used from sugar allowance.)

*D. Meat, Poultry and Fish

Select two 3-ounce servings from List #2—Meat Group—or make equivalent substitution.

*E. Egg

Include one egg.

*F. Bread and Cereal

Select six servings from List #4—Bread and Cereal Group.

*G. Fat and Oil

Include twelve servings from List #5—Fat and Oil Group.

*H. Sugar, Jam, Jelly, or Honey

Include nine teaspoons

*Note: Sample menus in Low Sodium Meal Plan No. 2 below show how servings may be divided among 3 meals.

LOW-SODIUM MEAL PLAN #2—SAMPLE MENUS

Note: Letters preceding menu items refer to food groups; see Low-Sodium Diet—Plan #2—above.

DP means dietetic-packed canned foods. L.S. means low sodium.

MENU #1

Breakfast

- A Orange juice—½ cup
- F Unsalted cooked wheat cereal—½ cup
- E Soft-cooked egg—1
- F L.S. toast—1 slice
- G Sweet butter—3 teaspoons
- H Sugar—2 teaspoons
- C **Milk—1 cup

Lunch at Home

Fruit and cottage cheese salad:
- A pineapple—2 slices
- A apricots—4 halves
- D L.S. cottage cheese—¾ cup
- B lettuce
- G *L.S. mayonnaise—2 teaspoons
- F L.S. toast—2 slices
- G Sweet butter—2 teaspoons
- H Jelly—3 teaspoons
- C **Milk—1 cup

Dinner

- B Tomato juice (DP)—½ cup—lemon
- D Unsalted broiled liver—3 ounces
- B Parsley potatoes (DP)—2 small
- B *Curried corn (DP)—⅓ cup
- B Steamed onion rings—½ cup
- F L.S. bread—2 slices
- G Sweet butter—3 teaspoons
- H Jelly—2 teaspoons
- H, A *Spiced applesauce (DP)
- G heavy cream—2 tablespoons

*Note: Recipes included in this section.

**The total milk allowance may be divided among the meals and used as a beverage, on cereal or in recipes.

SPECIAL DIETS

Plan the carried lunch carefully to supply 1/3 of the daily food needs.

MENU #2

Breakfast

A Grapefruit sections—1/2 cup
F Puffed rice—1 cup
E Scrambled egg—1 (use part of milk and butter allowance)
F L.S. toast—1 slice
G Sweet butter—3 teaspoons
H Jelly—3 teaspoons
H Sugar—3 teaspoons
G Light cream—2 tablespoons
C **Milk—1 cup

Lunch Box

Chicken sandwich:
D   chicken (DP)—2 ounces
B   lettuce
G   sweet butter—2 teaspoons
G   *L.S. mayonnaise—2 teaspoons
F   L.S. bread—2 slices
D Hard-cooked egg—1
A Orange—1
C **Milk—1 cup

Dinner

D Unsalted roast veal (no gravy)—3 ounces
A Cranberry sauce—1/3 cup
B Paprika potato—1 small
B Green lima beans (DP)—1/2 cup
B Winter squash (DP)—1/2 cup
B Lettuce and tomato salad
G *L.S. mayonnaise—2 teaspoons
F L.S. bread—2 slices
G Sweet butter—2 teaspoons
H Jelly—3 teaspoons
A Sweet, light cherries—1/3 cup

*Note: Recipes included in this section.

**The total milk allowance may be divided among the meals and used as a beverage, on cereal or in recipes.

MENU #3

Breakfast

A Pineapple juice—1/3 cup
F Shredded wheat—1 biscuit
E Poached egg—1
F L.S. toast—2 slices
G Sweet butter—4 teaspoons
H Jelly—3 teaspoons
G Heavy cream—4 tablespoons
H Sugar—3 teaspoons
C **Milk—1 cup

Lunch in a Restaurant

D Unsalted broiled steak—3 ounces or scrambled eggs—3
B Baked potato—1 small
B Tossed green salad—tomatoes, vinegar-oil dressing
A Peach halves—2

Dinner

A Chilled fruit cocktail—1/2 cup
D, F, B, C** *Tuna and mushrooms on macaroni
B *Minted Peas (DP)—1/2 cup
B Cucumber-vinegar salad
F L.S. bread—1 slice
G Sweet butter—4 teaspoons
H Jelly—3 teaspoons
A *Apricot—rum whip

*Note: Recipes included in this section.

**The total milk allowance may be divided among the meals and used as a beverage, on cereal or in recipes.

Food Groups for Low-Sodium Diets

LIST 1—FRUIT GROUP

(Each serving contains less than 5 milligrams sodium and 45 calories. Cup measures of canned fruits include liquid.)

Fruit	Quantity
Apple (2-in. diameter), F	1
Apple Juice (DP)	1/3 cup
Applesauce (DP)	1/2 cup
Apricots (DP)	4 halves
Fresh	2 medium
Banana	1/2 small
Blackberries (DP), F	1/2 cup
Blueberries (DP), F	1/2 cup
Boysenberries (DP)	1/2 cup
Cherries, sweet (dark or light); red, tart (DP)	1/3 cup
Cranberries, F	1/3 cup
Cranberry Sauce (DP)	1/3 cup
Currants, F	1/2 cup
Dates	2
Figs, kadota (DP), F	3 medium
Fruit Cocktail (DP)	1/2 cup
Fruits for Salad (DP)	1/2 cup
Grape Juice (DP)	1/4 cup
*Grapefruit Juice, unsweetened or Sections (DP)	1/2 cup
Fresh	1/2 small
Grapes, white (DP)	1/3 cup
Fresh	12
*Lemon Juice (DP)	1/2 cup
*Loganberries (DP)	2/3 cup
*Orange Juice, unsweetened, F	1/2 cup
*Orange and Grapefruit Juice, unsweetened	1/2 cup
Nectarine, F	1 medium
Peaches (DP), F	2 halves
Pears (DP), F	2 halves
Pineapple (DP), F	1/2 cup
Pineapple Juice (DP)	1/3 cup
Plums, greengage or purple (DP), F	2 medium
*Raspberries (DP), F	1/2 cup
*Strawberries (DP), F	1 cup
*Tangerine, F	1 large
*Tomato Juice (DP)	1 cup

Fruit	Quantity
Watermelon, F	1 cup
Youngberries (DP)	1/2 cup

*High in ascorbic acid; (DP)—dietetic pack; F—fresh.

LIST 2—MEAT, POULTRY AND FISH GROUP

(3-ounce servings contain less than 90 milligrams sodium and from 100–350 calories.)

Beef	Duck
Beef heart	Goose
Lamb	Turkey (DP) or cooked
Liver	Cod
Pork	Halibut
Sweetbreads	Oysters (6 to 8)
Veal	Salmon (DP) or cooked
Chicken (DP) or cooked	Tuna (DP) or cooked

You may substitute for 1 ounce meat: 1 egg; 1/4 cup low-sodium cottage cheese; 1 ounce low-sodium Cheddar cheese.

LIST 3—VEGETABLE GROUP

Dietetic-packed or unsalted, fresh or frozen vegetables may be used. (Each serving contains less than 10 milligrams sodium.)

Low Calorie Content

(Contains less than 10 calories.)

*Chicory or endive—5 large leaves
Cucumber, pared, 6 to 8 1/8-inch slices
Lettuce—1/8 head
*Parsley, chopped—4 tablespoons
*Peppers (empty pod,) sweet green—1 small

Medium Calorie Content

(1/2 cup serving contains 20–40 calories.)

Asparagus (6 med. spears or 1/2 cup)
Beans, green or wax

Brussels sprouts (5 to 6 or ½ cup)
Cabbage, cooked—½ cup
   raw—1 cup
Eggplant
Mushrooms
Okra
Onions
*Pumpkin
Squash, summer
*Squash, winter
*Tomatoes
Turnip, yellow

**High Calorie Content

(*Each serving contains 50–80 calories.*)

Beans, green lima—½ cup
Corn, sweet—⅓ cup
Parsnips—½ cup
Peas—½ cup
Potatoes, raw—1 small (3 ounces)
   canned (DP)—2 very small
*Sweet potatoes, raw—½ small
   canned (DP)—¼ cup

   *High in vitamin A: include at least 1 serving each day.

   **High in calories: For the 1500 calorie diet, include only one serving from this group each day; for the 2500 calorie diet, include two servings.

LIST 4—BREAD AND CEREAL GROUP

(*Each serving contains less than 5 milligrams sodium.*)

   Consult your physician for information about other low-sodium cereals.

Medium Calorie Content

(*Each serving contains 50–75 calories.*)

Bread, low-sodium	1 slice
Corn meal, farina, wild rice, cooked	½ cup
Rolled oats, whole wheat, brown rice, cooked	½ cup
Puffed rice and wheat	1 cup
Noodles, low-sodium, cooked	½ cup
Flour, enriched	2 tablespoons

High Calorie Content

(*Each serving contains 80–120 calories.*)

Barley, tapioca, polished rice, cooked	½ cup
Beans, dried-navy, lima and soy, cooked	½ cup
Macaroni, spaghetti, cooked	½ cup
Matzos, Passover, unsalted	1
Shredded wheat	1 biscuit

LIST 5—FAT AND OIL GROUP

(*Each serving contains less than 5 milligrams sodium and about 45 calories.*)

Fats	*Quantity*
Sweet or unsalted butter	1 teaspoon
Corn, olive, or peanut oil	1 teaspoon
Lard or vegetable shortening	1 teaspoon
Low-sodium mayonnaise	1 teaspoon
Low-sodium French dressing	2 teaspoons
Light cream* (20%)	2 tablespoons
Heavy cream* (40%)	1 tablespoon

   *About 5 milligrams sodium per tablespoon; do not use more than 4 tablespoons daily.

Recipes for Low-Sodium Menus

SPICED APPLESAUCE

(*1 fruit serving, 2 sugar servings.*)

½ cup canned applesauce (DP)
2 teaspoons honey
⅛ teaspoon nutmeg
Dash of cinnamon
Dash of ginger

   Combine all ingredients; heat thoroughly. Serve hot or chilled.

SPECIAL DIETS 2487

LOW-SODIUM FRENCH DRESSING

1/2 cup salad oil
1/4 cup cider vinegar
1/4 cup water
2 teaspoons sugar
1 teaspoon dry mustard
1/2 teaspoon paprika
Dash of pepper

Combine all ingredients; beat well with rotary beater or shake well in jar with tight-fitting cover. Makes 1 cup.

LOW-SODIUM MAYONNAISE

1 egg yolk
1/2 teaspoon dry mustard
1 teaspoon sugar
2 tablespoons lemon juice or cider vinegar
1 cup salad oil

Beat together egg yolk, mustard, sugar, and 1 tablespoon lemon juice.

Add salad oil very slowly, beating constantly.

Beat in remaining tablespoon lemon juice.

Chill in refrigerator. Makes 1 cup.

TUNA AND MUSHROOMS ON MACARONI

(1 meat serving, 2 bread servings, 1 vegetable serving, 1 cup milk.)

2 tablespoons flour
1 cup milk
1 teaspoon grated onion
Dash of white pepper
2 teaspoons chopped pimiento
3 ounces canned tuna (DP)
1/2 cup drained canned mushrooms (DP)
1/2 cup hot cooked macaroni

Blend flour with part of milk to make smooth paste; add remaining milk, onion, pepper and pimiento.

Cook in small saucepan over low heat until thickened, stirring constantly.

Add tuna and mushrooms. Heat thoroughly. Serve over macaroni.

HERB GREEN BEANS

(1/2 cup equals 1 vegetable serving.)

1 No. 2 can (1 pound, 4 ounces) green beans (DP)
1 tablespoon chopped chives or onion
Dash of thyme
Dash of pepper

Drain liquid from beans into small saucepan. Boil quickly until liquid is reduced to about 1/3 cup.

Add beans and seasonings; heat thoroughly. Makes 5 servings.

CURRIED CORN

(1/3 cup equals 1 vegetable serving.)

1 No. 2 can (1 pound, 4 ounces) whole kernel corn (DP)
2 teaspoons chopped pimiento
1/4 to 1/2 teaspoon curry powder
Dash of pepper

Drain liquid from corn into small saucepan. Boil quickly until liquid is reduced to about 1/3 cup.

Add corn, pimiento, and seasonings. Heat thoroughly; toss lightly. Makes 7 servings.

MINTED PEAS

(1/2 cup equals 1 vegetable serving.)

1 No. 2 can (1 pound, 4 ounces) peas (DP)
1/2 teaspon sugar
1 tablespoon chopped fresh mint

Drain liquid from peas into small saucepan. Add sugar; boil quickly until liquid is reduced to about 1/3 cup.

Add peas; heat thoroughly. Just before serving, add mint and toss lightly. Makes 5 servings.

APRICOT-RUM WHIP*

(1 fruit serving)

1 teaspoon unflavored gelatin
2 tablespoons cold water
1/2 cup boiling water or apricot liquid
3 saccharin tablets** (1/4-grain each)

½ tablespoon lemon juice
¼ to ½ teaspoon rum extract
4 apricot halves (DP) drained and chopped

Sprinkle gelatin over cold water; let stand 5 minutes.

Add boiling water; stir until dissolved. Add saccharin, lemon juice, and extract.

Chill until mixture begins to set.

Beat until fluffy with rotary beater; fold in apricots. Chill until firm.

*Note: For 2500 calorie, low-sodium diet use syrup-packed fruit and 1 tablespoon sugar in place of saccharin.

**Any non-caloric sweetener approved by your physician may be substituted for saccharin (¼-grain tablet equals 1 teaspoon sugar).

Miscellaneous Diets

SOFT DIET

A soft diet is sometimes prescribed to provide essential nutrients in a form which is low in residue and easily digested. The following foods are permitted in a soft diet:

Fruits: Fruit juices, ripe bananas, cooked or canned fruit without coarse skins, seeds, or fibers.

Cereal and Cereal Products: Dry or well cooked cereals, not very highly seasoned macaroni or spaghetti.

Breads: Whole wheat or enriched white bread, plain white crackers.

Soups: Broth and strained cream soup.

Eggs: Soft-cooked ("boiled") eggs.

Fish, Meat and Poultry: Lightly seasoned, tender fish, ground beef and lamb, tender chicken, sweetbreads.

Dairy Products: Milk (sweet or buttermilk), cream, butter, cottage or cream cheese, Cheddar cheese used in cooking.

Vegetables: Cooked vegetables only: asparagus, beets, carrots, peas, string beans, spinach, squash; boiled, mashed, creamed, au gratin, or baked potatoes.

Desserts: Ice cream, ices, sherbets, cereal puddings, custard, gelatin, plain cakes and cookies.

Beverages: Coffee or coffee substitutes, tea, cocoa, carbonated beverages, milk and milk drinks.

SAMPLE MENU FOR SOFT DIET

Breakfast: Orange juice, fine cereal with milk or cream, soft scrambled eggs, buttered whole wheat or enriched white toast, coffee with **cream and sugar.**

Lunch or Supper: Strained vegetable soup, ground beef, mashed potato, buttered carrots, whole wheat or enriched white bread and butter or enriched margarine, plain ice cream and chocolate sauce, or cooked fruit, milk.

Dinner: Cream of pea soup with plain white crackers, macaroni au gratin, buttered beets, whole **wheat bread or enriched white bread and butter or** enriched margarine, plain gelatin with whipped cream, tea with **cream and sugar.**

LIGHT DIET

The following foods are permitted in a light diet:

Fruits: All cooked and canned fruits, citrus fruits, ripe bananas.

Cereals and Cereal Products: Dry or well cooked cereals; not very highly seasoned, macaroni and spaghetti.

Breads: Whole wheat or enriched white bread, plain white crackers.

Soups: All soups and broths.

Fish, Meat, and Poultry: Lean ground or tender beef, tender lamb or veal, chicken, liver, fish, and bacon.

Eggs: Soft-cooked ("boiled") eggs.

Dairy Products: Milk (sweet or buttermilk), cream, butter, cottage or cream cheese, Cheddar cheese used in cooking.

Vegetables: Cooked vegetables: asparagus, beets, carrots, peas, string beans, spinach, squash; boiled, mashed, creamed, au gratin, or baked potatoes.

Salads: Tomato and lettuce.

Desserts: Ice cream, ices, sherbets, cereal puddings, custard, gelatin, plain cakes or cookies.

Beverages: Coffee or coffee substitutes, tea, cocoa, carbonated beverages, and milk and milk drinks.

SAMPLE MENU FOR LIGHT DIET

Breakfast: Orange juice; cereal with milk or cream; soft scrambled eggs; whole wheat or enriched white bread toast with butter or enriched margarine; coffee with cream and sugar.

Lunch or Supper: Cream of pea soup with plain crackers; macaroni au gratin; shredded lettuce with dressing; whole wheat or enriched white bread with butter or enriched margarine; fruit gelatin; coffee or tea with cream and sugar.

Dinner: Vegetable soup; roast lean lamb or veal; mashed potato; buttered cooked carrots; sliced tomatoes with dressing; whole wheat or enriched white bread with butter or enriched margarine; ice cream; milk.

LIQUID DIET

A liquid diet consists of any food which can be served in strained or liquid form plus such foods as soft-cooked ("boiled") eggs, soft custards, plain puddings, plain gelatin, tapioca, and plain ice cream or sherbets. All foods in solid form are avoided.

Foods allowed include:

Beverages: Coffee or coffee substitutes, tea, milk, buttermilk, milk drinks, strained fruit juices.

Cereals: Strained cereals, thin gruels, and cereal waters.

Eggs: Soft-cooked ("boiled") or beaten in beverages.

Soups: Cream soups made with strained vegetables, all clear soups, and strained vegetable soup.

Vegetables: Strained vegetable juices or strained vegetables.

Desserts: Soft custard, plain pudding, gelatin, tapioca, plain ice cream, plain sherbet, ices, or strained fruit.

SAMPLE MENU FOR LIQUID DIET

Breakfast: Strained fruit juice; strained cereal with milk and sugar; soft-cooked ("boiled") egg with butter; beverage with cream and sugar.

Lunch or Supper: Strained fruit juice; cream soup with butter or enriched margarine; strained vegetables (two); strained fruit; milk.

Dinner: Strained cream soup with butter or enriched margarine; strained vegtables; dessert; milk.

Snacks for Between Meals and at Bedtime: Strained fruit juice, milk, malted milk, or eggnog.

HIGH PROTEIN DIET

For a high protein diet the normal diet is supplemented with protein-rich foods such as lean meat, fish, poultry, egg white, cheese, and milk.

A normal diet should include the essential foods indicated in **Nutrition** (see Index).

LOW PROTEIN DIET

In a low protein diet the normal diet is followed but there is a reduction in certain foods. Meat is usually cut down to about 1 to 2 ounces, only 1 egg a day is permitted, and not more than 1 pint of milk is permitted.

Some foods should be avoided such as cheese, gelatin, beans, lentils, peas nuts, and desserts containing milk or egg in excess of the amounts allowed.

For essential foods in a normal diet see **Nutrition** (see Index).

LOW CALORIE DIET

See reducing diets, calorie charts, and suggestions for eating to lose weight in **Weight Control** (see Index).

HIGH CALORIE DIET

See suggestions for gaining weight in **Weight Control** (see Index).

LOW FAT DIET

A low fat diet is used in various liver and gallbladder diseases. Foods permitted include:

Beverages: Coffee, tea, skim milk, or fruit juices.

Bread: Whole wheat or enriched white bread preferred; however, there is no restriction except breads containing much fat.

Cereals: Ready-to-eat whole grain or enriched.

Eggs and Cheese: Egg yolk and all cheese except cottage cheese should be restricted. Limit the diet to one whole egg daily prepared without fat. Cottage cheese and egg white are permitted freely.

Fats: None.

Meats, Fish, and Poultry: The amount consumed should be restricted; use lean beef, liver, lamb, veal, chicken, turkey, and lean fish.

Soup: Skimmed chicken, meat, or vegetable soups.

Vegetables: Vegetables are allowed to the limit of tolerance, fresh or cooked. Use no fats in preparing vegetables. Use no fats in salad dressings. Use bland vegetables; avoid broccoli, Brussels sprouts, cabbage, cauliflower, corn, onions, parsnips, and turnips.

Fruits: All fruits permitted except melons.

Desserts: Plain desserts made without fat and egg; also fruit ices, jams, jellies, preserves, and hard candies.

Vitamin Supplement: Vitamin A supplement usually required, especially if all butter is omitted and skim milk is used.

SAMPLE LOW FAT MENU

Breakfast: Fruit or fruit juice; ready-to-eat whole wheat or enriched cereal with skim milk and sugar; egg, prepared without fat; whole wheat or enriched bread toast; jelly or jam, and coffee or tea with skim milk and sugar, if desired.

Lunch or Supper: Soup, fruit juice, etc., if desired; lean fish, meat, or other main dish; cooked or raw vegetables; whole wheat or enriched white bread and jelly or jam; dessert or fruit, and beverage.

Dinner: Soup, fruit juice, etc., if desired; lean fish, meat, or poultry; cooked or raw vegetable; potato; whole wheat or enriched bread or roll with jam or jelly; milk, and dessert.

Between-Meal Snacks, If Desired: Fruit juices; fresh fruit; ready-to-eat cereals with skim milk and sugar, or bread and jelly sandwich.

DIET FOR ANEMIA

The diet for anemic patients must contain a variety of foods which will aid the body in storing hemoglobin and red blood corpuscles. Such a diet, therefore, must contain a generous amount of foods which have a high iron content. Outstanding, of course, is liver; however, other organ meats such as beef heart, kidneys, and sweetbreads are valuable in this respect. Liver should be served at least three times a week and, in addition, other organ meats.

Other foods that should be served include: one large serving each day of steak, lamb chops, roast beef, or roast lamb; at least three servings daily of green vegetables (green leafy vegetables, cabbage, and potatoes are especially valuable); eggs; milk should be included daily; at least three servings of fruit daily (with one raw); prunes and raisins are especially valuable; and whole-grain breads and cereals.

All fried or warmed-over foods should be avoided as well as fancy desserts and rich pastries. Fruit desserts are preferred.

BLAND DIET

A bland diet is frequently prescribed for ulcer patients.

The purpose of such a diet is to dilute the gastric juices often by giving several feedings daily of easily digested non-irritating foods.

Milk is the basis of such a bland diet and other foods are gradually added as they can be tolerated by the patient.

No irritating fruits, vegetables, or seasonings are permitted.

Breakfast: Cereal with milk and sugar; soft-cooked egg; enriched white bread and butter or enriched margarine; coffee or tea with milk and sugar, and strained fruit or fruit juice at the end of meal.

Lunch or Supper: Cream soup; small serving of lean meat; potato, rice, or spaghetti; enriched white bread and butter or enriched margarine, and strained fruit or juice at the end of meal.

Dinner: Small serving of lean meat, fish, or poultry; potato; two strained cooked vegetables; enriched white bread and butter or enriched margarine, and strained fruit or juice at end of meal.

Snacks for Between Meals and at Bedtime: Milk and plain white crackers.

DIET FOR ORDINARY CONSTIPATION

Note that a doctor should be consulted to make sure there is no actual disease of the intestinal tract.

Drink lots of fluid, including up to $2\frac{1}{2}$ to $3\frac{1}{2}$ quarts per day because water keeps the food masses in semi-fluid condition. Chew your food well. Relax and establish regular bowel habits.

When constipation in an adult has a long history and extends back many years, it may not respond immediately to good food and elimination habits. Nevertheless with proper diet, adequate fluid intake, and a continued effort towards mental and physical relaxation in developing good bowel habits, good results are usually attained in overcoming the problem.

A diet to relieve ordinary constipation must supply material which will pass on into the colon without too much absorption in the small intestines. Most fruits and vegetables as well as whole-grain cereals contain cellulose which will give bulk to the material in the bowel. Some cellulose is tender enough to be partially digested, but in general cellulose is not utilized by the human body except to give bulk.

When water acts on cellulose, it may swell up somewhat and additionally increase the bulk. The danger of a diet containing too much cellulose is that it can interfere with normal digestion of other materials as well as irritate the intestinal tract.

Foods to choose from in correcting ordinary constipation include:

Vegetables: Adequate amounts (especially green vegetables) which will with fruits provide bulk; cabbage, celery, carrots, Brussels sprouts, asparagus, beets, lettuce, tomatoes, onions, baked potatoes with skin on, spinach, and turnips.

Breads and Cereals: Whole-grain breads and cereals and those containing bran.

Fruits: Adequate amounts of raw fruit with the skins on to provide bulk and fruit acids which are laxative; apples (especially at bedtime), berries, prunes, oranges, plums, pears, peaches, figs, and melons.

Honey and Molasses: Used in moderation they are helpful because they tend to cause gases which are a slight stimulant to bowel movement; too much of either may cause digestive disturbances.

Milk or Buttermilk: Drink two glasses daily; buttermilk may be somewhat more helpful.

Meat, Fish, and Poultry: At least once a day.

Sugars and Sweets: Use in moderation.

Fats: Butter or enriched margarine, and oil on salads.

Avoid: All fried foods and warmed-over foods, pastries and sweets.

SAMPLE MENU FOR RELIEF OF ORDINARY CONSTIPATION

Before Breakfast: Many people find that a glass of hot water taken 1 hour before breakfast is helpful.

Breakfast: 1 orange or ½ grapefruit with pulp; stewed fruit; whole-grain or enriched cereal with milk and sugar; 1 or 2 eggs; 1 slice whole-grain or enriched bread with butter or enriched margarine, and beverage with cream and sugar, if desired.

Right After Breakfast: Go to the toilet. Relax and sit there until you move your bowels. If necessary, your doctor may advise a suppository for the first few days in order to help you definitely establish a movement at this time. A habit can be created to move your bowels at this time every day.

Lunch or Supper: Lean meat; potato; 2 vegetables (spinach and cauliflower); lettuce and tomato salad with French dressing; 1 slice bread with butter; baked apple with cream, and a glass of buttermilk.

Dinner: Vegetable soup; omelet or lean meat or fish; potato, rice, or spaghetti; 2 green or yellow vegetables; vegetable or fruit salad with oil dressing; 1 slice bread with butter; stewed figs with cream, and milk or buttermilk.

Facts about Food

The tables that follow give the food values in common portions. These compact food composition tables will enable you to compare quickly the nutritive value of foods and to estimate the nutritive value of diets.

Data are given in quantities that can be readily adjusted to servings of different sizes. Values for prepared foods and food mixtures have been calculated from typical recipes. Values for cooked vegetables are without added fat.

A table showing recommended amounts of key nutrients is included. These are a goal, subject to revision, toward which to aim in planning practical dietaries. These allowances can be attained with a good variety of common foods which will also provide other minerals and vitamins for which requirements are less well known.

The tables were adapted from a publication, AIB–36, of the Bureau of Human Nutrition and Home Economics of the United States Department of Agriculture.

The following abbreviations are used: Gm. for gram; mg. for milligram; I.U. for International Unit; cal. for calories; Tr. for trace. Ounce refers to weight; fluid ounce to measure.

FACTS ABOUT FOOD

Food and approximate measure or common weight	Water	Food energy	Protein	Fat	Total carbohydrate	Calcium	Iron	Vitamin A value	Thiamine	Riboflavin	Niacin value	Ascorbic acid
	Pct.	Cal.	Gm.	Gm.	Gm.	Mg.	Mg.	I.U.	Mg.	Mg.	Mg.	Mg.
MILK AND MILK PRODUCTS:												
Buttermilk, from skim milk, 1 cup	90	85	9	Tr.	12	288	0.2	10	0.09	0.43	0.3	3
Milk, cow:												
Fluid, whole, 1 cup	87	165	9	10	12	288	.2	390	.09	.42	.3	3
Fluid, nonfat (skim), 1 cup	90	85	9	Tr.	13	303	.2	10	.09	.44	.3	3
Evaporated (undiluted), 1 cup	74	345	18	20	25	612	.4	1,010	.12	.91	.5	3
Condensed (undiluted), 1 cup	27	980	25	26	168	835	.6	1,300	.16	1.19	.6	3
Dry, whole. 1 tablespoon	4	40	2	2	3	76	0	110	.02	.12	.1	1
Dry, nonfat solids, 1 tablespoon	4	30	3	Tr.	4	98	0	Tr.	.03	.15	.1	1
Milk, goat, fluid, 1 cup	87	165	8	10	11	315	.2	390	.10	.26	.7	2
Cheese, 1 ounce:												
Cheddar (1 in. cube)	37	115	7	9	1	206	.3	400	.01	.12	Tr.	0
Cheddar, processed	40	105	7	8	1	191	.3	370	Tr.	.12	Tr.	0
Cheese foods, Cheddar	43	90	6	7	2	162	.2	300	.01	.16	Tr.	0
Cottage, from skim milk	76	25	6	Tr.	1	27	.1	10	.01	.09	Tr.	0
Cream	51	105	3	10	1	19	.1	410	Tr.	.06	Tr.	0
Swiss	39	105	8	8	Tr.	262	.3	410	Tr.	.11	Tr.	0
Cream, 1 tablespoon:												
Light	72	30	Tr.	3	1	15	0	120	Tr.	.02	Tr.	Tr.
Heavy	59	50	Tr.	5	Tr.	12	0	220	Tr.	.02	Tr.	Tr.
Beverages, 1 cup:												
Chocolate (all milk)	80	240	8	12	26	260	.5	350	.08	.40	.3	2
Cocoa (all milk)	79	235	10	12	27	298	1.0	400	.10	.46	.5	3
Chocolate flavored milk	83	185	8	6	26	272	.2	230	.08	.40	.2	2
Malted milk	78	280	12	12	32	364	.8	680	.18	.56	—	3
Desserts:												
Blanc mange, 1 cup	76	275	9	10	39	290	.2	390	.08	.40	.2	2
Custard, baked, 1 cup	77	285	13	13	28	283	1.2	840	.11	.49	.2	1
Custard pudding, canned, strained (infant food), 1 ounce	75	30	1	1	5	26	.1	60	Tr.	.04	Tr.	Tr.
Ice cream, plain:												
1/7 of quart brick	62	165	3	10	17	100	.1	420	.03	.15	.1	1
8 fluid ounces	62	295	6	18	29	175	.1	740	.06	.27	.1	1

FACTS ABOUT FOOD

Food and approximate measure or common weight	Water	Food energy	Protein	Fat	Total carbohydrate	Calcium	Iron	Vitamin A value	Thiamine	Riboflavin	Niacin value	Ascorbic acid
	Pct.	Cal.	Gm.	Gm.	Gm.	Mg.	Mg.	I.U.	Mg.	Mg.	Mg.	Mg.
FATS, OILS, RELATED PRODUCTS:												
Bacon, medium fat, broiled or fried 2 slices	13	95	4	9	Tr.	4	0.5	0	0.08	0.05	0.8	0
Butter, 1 tablespoon	16	100	Tr.	11	Tr.	3	0	460	Tr.	Tr.	Tr.	0
Fats, cooking (vegetable fats):												
1 cup	0	1,770	0	200	0	0	0	0	0	0	0	0
1 tablespoon	0	110	0	12	0	0	0	0	0	0	0	0
Lard, 1 tablespoon	0	125	0	14	0	0	0	0	0	0	0	0
Margarine, 1 tablespoon	16	100	Tr.	11	Tr.	3	0	460	0	0	0	0
Oils, salad or cooking, 1 tablespoon	0	125	0	14	0	0	0	0	0	0	0	0
Salad dressings, 1 tablespoon:												
French	40	60	Tr.	5	3	0	0	0	0	0	0	0
Home-cooked	68	30	1	2	3	15	.1	80	.01	.03	Tr.	Tr.
Mayonnaise	16	90	Tr.	10	Tr.	2	.1	30	Tr.	Tr.	0	0
EGGS:												
Eggs, raw, medium:												
1 whole	74	75	6	6	Tr.	26	1.3	550	.05	.14	Tr.	0
1 white	88	15	3	0	Tr.	2	.1	0	0	.08	Tr.	0
1 yolk	49	60	3	5	Tr.	25	1.2	550	.05	.06	Tr.	0
Eggs, dried, whole, 1 cup	5	640	51	45	3	205	9.5	4,040	.36	1.14	.3	0
MEAT, POULTRY, FISH:												
Beef, 3 ounces, without bone, cooked:												
Chuck	51	265	22	19	0	9	2.6	0	.04	.17	3.5	0
Hamburger	47	315	19	26	0	8	2.4	0	.07	.16	4.1	0
Sirloin	54	255	20	19	0	9	2.5	0	.06	.16	4.1	0
Beef, canned:												
Corned beef, medium fat, 3 ounces	59	180	22	10	0	17	3.7	0	.01	.20	2.9	0
Corned beef hash, 3 ounces	70	120	12	5	6	22	1.1	Tr.	.02	.11	2.4	0
Strained (infant food), 1 ounce	78	30	5	1	0	3	1.2	0	Tr.	.06	.9	0
Beef, dried, 2 ounces	48	115	19	4	0	11	2.9	0	.04	.18	2.2	0
Beef and vegetable stew, 1 cup	79	250	13	19	17	31	2.6	2,520	.12	.15	3.4	15
Chicken, canned, boned, 3 ounces	62	170	25	7	0	12	1.5	0	.03	.14	5.4	0

FACTS ABOUT FOOD 2495

Food and approximate measure or common weight	Water	Food energy	Protein	Fat	Total carbohydrate	Calcium	Iron	Vitamin A value	Thiamine	Riboflavin	Niacin value	Ascorbic acid
	Pct.	Cal.	Gm.	Gm.	Gm.	Mg.	Mg.	I.U.	Mg.	Mg.	Mg.	Mg.
MEAT, POULTRY, FISH—Continued												
Chile con carne, canned (without beans) ½ cup.	67	170	9	13	5	32	1.2	130	.01	.10	1.9	—
Clams, raw, meat only, 4 ounces	80	90	15	2	4	109	7.9	120	.11	.20	1.8	—
Cod, dried, 1 ounce	12	105	23	1	0	14	1.0	0	.02	.13	3.1	0
Crab meat, canned or cooked, 3 ounces	77	90	14	2	1	38	.8	—	.04	.05	2.1	—
Flounder, raw, 4 ounces	83	80	17	1	0	69	.9	—	.07	.06	1.9	—
Haddock, fried, 1 fillet (4 by 3 by ½ in.)	67	160	19	6	7	18	.6	—	.04	.09	2.6	—
Halibut, broiled, 1 steak (4 by 3 by ½ in.)	64	230	33	10	0	18	1.0	—	.08	.09	13.1	—
Heart, beef, raw, 3 ounces	78	90	14	3	1	8	3.9	30	.50	.75	6.6	5
Kidneys, beef, raw, 3 ounces	75	120	13	7	1	8	6.7	980	.32	2.16	5.5	11
Lamb, leg roast, cooked, 3 ounces	56	230	20	16	0	9	2.6	0	.12	.21	4.4	0
Lamb, canned, strained (infant food), 1 ounce	79	30	4	1	0	5	.7	0	.01	.07	1.1	0
Liver, beef, fried, 2 ounces	57	120	13	4	5	5	4.4	30,330	.15	2.25	8.4	18
Liver, canned, strained (infant food), 1 ounce	78	30	5	1	Tr.	7	2.0	5,440	.01	.61	1.8	—
Mackerel, canned, solids and liquid, 3 ounces	66	155	16	9	0	157	1.8	370	.05	.18	4.9	—
Oysters, meat only, raw, 1 cup (13-19 medium size oysters, selects)	80	200	24	5	13	226	13.4	770	.35	.48	2.8	—
Oyster stew, 1 cup with 6 to 8 oysters	80	245	17	13	14	262	7.0	820	.21	.46	1.6	—
Pork loin or chops, cooked 3 ounces without bone	50	285	20	22	0	9	2.6	0	.71	.20	4.3	0
Pork, cured ham, cooked, 3 ounces without bone	39	340	20	28	Tr.	9	2.5	0	.46	.18	3.5	0
Pork luncheon meat, canned, spiced, 2 ounces	55	165	8	14	1	5	1.2	0	.18	.12	1.6	0
Salmon, canned, pink, 3 ounces	70	120	17	5	0	159	.7	60	.03	.16	6.8	0
Sardines, canned in oil, drained solids, 3 ounces	57	180	22	9	1	328	2.3	190	.01	.15	4.1	0

2496 FACTS ABOUT FOOD

Food and approximate measure or common weight	Water	Food energy	Protein	Fat	Total carbohydrate	Calcium	Iron	Vitamin A value	Thiamine	Riboflavin	Niacin value	Ascorbic acid
	Pct.	Cal.	Gm.	Gm.	Gm.	Mg.	Mg.	I.U.	Mg.	Mg.	Mg.	Mg.
MEAT, POULTRY, FISH—Continued												
Sausage:												
Bologna, 1 piece (1 by 1-½ in diam.)	62	465	31	34	8	19	4.6	0	0.37	0.40	5.7	0
Frankfurter, 1 cooked	62	125	7	10	1	3	.6	0	.08	.09	1.3	0
Pork, bulk, canned, 4 ounces	55	340	17	29	0	10	2.6	0	.23	.27	3.4	0
Scallops, raw, 4 ounces	80	90	17	Tr.	4	29	2.0	0	.05	.11	1.6	—
Shad, raw, 4 ounces	70	190	21	11	0	—	.6	—	.17	.27	9.6	—
Shrimp, canned, meat only, 3 ounces	66	110	23	1	—	98	2.6	50	.01	.03	1.9	0
Soups, canned, ready-to-serve:												
Beef, 1 cup	91	100	6	4	11	15	.5	—	—	—	—	—
Chicken, 1 cup	94	75	4	2	10	20	.5	—	.02	.12	1.5	—
Chicken, strained (infant food), 1 ounce	87	15	1	1	2	11	.1	70	Tr.	.03	.1	Tr.
Clam chowder, 1 cup	91	85	5	2	12	36	3.6	—	—	—	—	—
Tongue, beef, raw, 4 ounces	68	235	19	17	Tr.	10	3.2	0	.14	.33	5.7	0
Tuna fish, drained solids, 3 ounces	60	170	25	7	0	7	1.2	70	.04	.10	10.9	0
Veal cutlet, cooked, 3 ounces without bone	60	185	24	9	0	10	3.0	0	.07	.24	5.2	0
MATURE BEANS AND PEAS; NUTS:												
Almonds, shelled, unblanched, 1 cup	5	850	26	77	28	361	6.2	0	.35	.95	6.5	Tr.
Beans, canned or cooked, 1 cup:												
Red kidney	76	230	15	1	42	102	4.9	0	.12	.12	2.0	0
Navy or other varieties with:												
Pork and tomato sauce	72	295	15	5	48	107	4.7	220	.13	.09	1.2	7
Pork and molasses	70	325	15	8	50	146	5.5	90	.13	.09	1.2	7
Beans, lima, dry, 1 cup	13	610	38	2	113	124	13.7	0	.88	.32	3.6	3
Brazil nuts, shelled, 1 cup	5	905	20	92	15	260	4.8	Tr.	1.21	—	—	—
Coconut, dried, shredded (sweetened), 1 cup	3	345	2	24	33	27	2.2	0	Tr.	Tr.	Tr.	0
Cowpeas, dry, 1 cup	11	685	46	3	123	154	13.0	60	1.84	.32	4.5	3
Peanuts, roasted, shelled, 1 cup	3	805	39	64	34	107	2.7	0	.42	.19	23.3	0
Peanut butter, 1 tablespoon	2	90	4	8	3	12	.3	0	.02	.02	2.6	0
Peas, split, dry, 1 cup	10	600	40	2	108	66	10.2	140	.75	.25	6.2	—

FACTS ABOUT FOOD

Food and approximate measure or common weight	Water	Food energy	Protein	Fat	Total carbohydrate	Calcium	Iron	Vitamin A value	Thiamine	Riboflavin	Niacin value	Ascorbic acid
	Pct.	Cal.	Gm.	Gm.	Gm.	Mg.	Mg.	I.U.	Mg.	Mg.	Mg.	Mg.
Pecans, 1 cup halves	3	750	10	79	14	80	2.6	50	.77	.12	1.0	2
Soybeans, dry, 1 cup	7	695	73	38	73	477	16.8	230	2.25	.65	4.9	Tr.
Walnuts, English, 1 cup halves	3	655	15	64	16	83	2.1	30	.48	.13	1.2	3
VEGETABLES:												
Asparagus:												
Cooked, 1 cup cut spears	92	35	4	Tr.	6	33	1.8	1,820	.23	.30	2.1	40
Canned green, 6 spears, medium size	92	20	2	Tr.	3	18	1.8	770	.06	.08	.9	17
Canned bleached, 6 spears, medium size	92	20	2	Tr.	3	15	1.0	70	.05	.07	.8	17
Beans, lima, immature, cooked, 1 cup	75	150	8	1	29	46	2.7	460	.22	.14	1.8	24
Beans, snap, green, cooked, 1 cup	92	25	2	Tr.	6	45	.9	830	.09	.12	.6	18
Beets, cooked, diced, 1 cup	88	70	2	Tr.	16	35	1.2	30	.03	.07	.5	11
Broccoli, cooked, flower stalks, 1 cup	90	45	5	Tr.	8	195	2.0	5,100	.10	.22	1.2	111
Brussels sprouts, cooked, 1 cup	85	60	6	1	12	44	1.7	520	.05	.16	.6	61
Cabbage, 1 cup:												
Raw, shredded	92	25	1	Tr.	5	46	.5	80	.06	.05	.3	50
Cooked	92	40	2	Tr.	9	78	.8	150	.08	.08	.5	55
Carrots:												
Raw, grated, 1 cup	88	45	1	Tr.	10	43	.9	13,200	.06	.06	.7	7
Cooked, diced, 1 cup	91	45	1	1	9	38	.9	18,130	.07	.07	.7	6
Canned, strained (infant food), 1 ounce	92	10	Tr.	0	2	7	.2	2,530	.01	.01	.1	1
Cauliflower, cooked, flower buds, 1 cup	92	30	3	Tr.	6	26	1.3	110	.07	.10	.6	34
Celery, 1 cup:												
Raw, diced	94	20	1	Tr.	4	50	.5	0	.05	.04	.4	7
Cooked, diced	94	25	2	Tr.	5	65	.6	0	.05	.04	.4	6
Collards, cooked, 1 cup	87	75	7	1	14	473	3.0	14,500	.15	.46	3.2	84
Corn, sweet:												
Cooked, 1 ear (5 in. long)	75	85	3	1	20	5	.6	390	.11	.10	1.4	8
Canned, solids and liquid, 1 cup	80	170	5	1	41	10	1.3	520	.07	.13	2.4	14
Cowpeas, immature seed, cooked, 1 cup	75	150	11	1	25	59	4.0	620	.46	.13	1.3	32
Cucumbers, raw, 6 slices (⅛ in. thick, center section)	96	5	Tr.	0	1	.5	.2	0	.02	.02	.1	4
Dandelion greens, cooked, 1 cup	86	80	5	1	16	337	5.6	27,310	.23	.22	1.3	29

2498 FACTS ABOUT FOOD

Food and approximate measure or common weight	Water	Food energy	Protein	Fat	Total carbohydrate	Calcium	Iron	Vitamin A value	Thiamine	Riboflavin	Niacin value	Ascorbic acid
	Pct.	Cal.	Gm.	Gm.	Gm.	Mg.	Mg.	I.U.	Mg.	Mg.	Mg.	Mg.
VEGETABLES—Continued												
Endive, raw, 1 pound	93	90	7	1	18	359	7.7	13,600	0.30	0.53	1.8	49
Kale, cooked, 1 cup	87	45	4	1	8	248	2.4	9,220	.08	.25	1.9	56
Lettuce, headed, raw, 2 large or 4 small leaves	95	5	1	Tr.	1	11	.2	270	.02	.04	.1	4
Mushrooms, canned, solids and liquid, 1 cup	93	30	3	Tr.	9	17	2.0	0	.04	.60	4.8	—
Mustard greens, cooked, 1 cup	92	30	3	Tr.	6	308	4.1	10,050	.08	.25	1.0	63
Okra, cooked, 8 pods (3 in. long, ⅝ in. diam.)	90	30	2	Tr.	6	70	.6	630	.05	.05	.7	17
Onions, raw:												
Mature, 1 onion (2-½ in. diam.)	88	50	2	Tr.	11	35	.6	60	.04	.04	.2	10
Young green, 6 small onions without tops	88	25	Tr.	Tr.	5	68	.4	30	.02	.02	.1	12
Parsnips, cooked, 1 cup	84	95	2	1	22	88	1.1	0	.09	.16	.3	19
Peas, green:												
Cooked, 1 cup	82	110	8	1	19	35	3.0	1,150	.40	.22	3.7	24
Canned, strained (infant food), 1 ounce	87	15	1	Tr.	2	5	.4	180	.03	.02	.3	2
Peppers, green, raw, 1 medium	92	15	1	Tr.	4	7	.3	400	.02	.04	.2	77
Potatoes:												
Baked, 1 medium (2-½ in. diam.)	74	95	2	Tr.	22	13	.8	20	.11	.05	1.4	17
Boiled in skin, 1 medium (2-½ in. diam.)	78	120	3	Tr.	27	16	1.0	30	.14	.06	1.6	22
Boiled after peeling, 1 medium (2-½ in. diam.)	78	105	3	Tr.	24	14	.9	20	.12	.04	1.3	17
French-fried, 8 pieces (2 by ½ by ½ in.)	20	155	2	8	21	12	.8	20	.07	.04	1.3	11
Potato chips, 10 medium (2 in. diam.)	3	110	1	7	10	6	.4	10	.04	.02	.6	2
Pumpkin, canned, 1 cup	90	75	2	1	18	46	1.6	7,750	.04	.14	1.2	—
Radishes, raw, 4 small	94	5	Tr.	0	1	7	.2	10	.01	Tr.	.1	5
Rutabagas, cooked, cubed or sliced, 1 cup	91	50	1	Tr.	12	85	.6	540	.08	.11	1.1	33

FACTS ABOUT FOOD

Food and approximate measure or common weight	Water	Food energy	Protein	Fat	Total carbohydrate	Calcium	Iron	Vitamin A value	Thiamine	Riboflavin	Niacin value	Ascorbic acid
	Pct.	Cal.	Gm.	Gm.	Gm.	Mg.	Mg.	I.U.	Mg.	Mg.	Mg.	Mg.
Sauerkraut, canned, drained solids, 1 cup	91	30	2	Tr.	7	54	.8	60	.05	.10	.2	24
Soybean sprouts, raw, 1 cup	86	50	7	1	6	51	1.1	190	.24	.21	.9	14
Spinach:												
Cooked, 1 cup	91	45	6	1	6	223	3.6	21,200	.14	.36	1.1	54
Canned, strained (infant food), 1 ounce	94	5	1	Tr.	1	22	.4	1,190	.01	.03	.1	2
Squash:												
Summer, cooked, diced, 1 cup	95	35	1	Tr.	8	32	.8	550	.08	.15	1.3	23
Winter, baked, mashed, 1 cup	86	95	4	1	23	49	1.6	12,690	.10	.31	1.2	14
Winter, canned, strained (infant food), 1 ounce	91	10	Tr.	Tr.	2	9	.1	560	.01	.02	.1	1
Sweetpotatoes, peeled, 1 sweetpotato:												
Baked (5 by 2-in.)	61	185	3	1	41	44	1.1	11,410	.12	.08	.9	28
Boiled (5 by 2-1/2 in.)	69	250	4	1	57	62	1.4	15,780	.18	.11	1.3	41
Tomatoes:												
Raw, 1 medium (2 by 2-1/2 in)	94	30	2	Tr.	6	16	.9	1,640	.08	.06	.8	35
Canned or cooked, 1 cup	94	45	2	Tr.	9	27	1.5	2,540	.14	.08	1.7	40
Tomato juice, canned, 1 cup	94	50	2	Tr.	10	17	1.0	2,540	.12	.07	1.8	38
Turnips, cooked, diced, 1 cup	92	40	1	Tr.	9	62	.8	Tr.	.06	.09	.6	28
Turnip greens, cooked, 1 cup	90	45	4	1	8	376	3.5	15,370	.09	.59	1.0	87
Vegetables, mixed, canned, strained (infant food), 1 ounce	90	10	Tr.	0	2	9	.3		.01	.01	.1	1
FRUITS:												
Apples, raw, 1 medium (2-1/2 in. diam.)	84	75	Tr.	1	20	8	.4	120	.05	.04	.2	6
Apple juice, fresh or canned, 1 cup	86	125	Tr.	0	34	15	1.2	90	.05	.07	Tr.	2
Apple betty, 1 cup	64	345	4	7	70	34	.2	370	.13	.09	1.1	3
Applesauce, canned, sweetened, 1 cup	80	185	1	Tr.	50	10	1.0	80	.05	.03	.1	3
Apricots:												
Raw, 3 apricots	85	95	1	Tr.	14	17	.5	2,990	.03	.05	.9	7
Canned in sirup, 4 medium halves and 2 tablespoons sirup	77	95	1	Tr.	26	12	.4	1,650	.02	.03	.4	5

2500 FACTS ABOUT FOOD

Food and approximate measure or common weight	Water	Food energy	Protein	Fat	Total carbohydrate	Calcium	Iron	Vitamin A value	Thiamine	Riboflavin	Niacin value	Ascorbic acid
	Pct.	Cal.	Gm.	Gm.	Gm.	Mg.	Mg.	I.U.	Mg.	Mg.	Mg.	Mg.
FRUITS—Continued												
Apricots—Continued												
Canned, strained (infant food), 1 ounce	83	15	Tr.	Tr.	4	6	0.3	480	0.01	0.01	0.1	1
Dried, cooked, unsweetened, fruit and liquid, 1 cup	75	240	5	Tr.	62	80	4.6	6,900	.01	.14	2.8	9
Avocados, raw, ½ peeled fruit (3-½ by 3-¼ in.)	65	280	2	30	6	11	.7	330	.07	.15	1.3	18
Bananas, raw, 1 medium (6 by 1-½ in.)	75	90	1	Tr.	23	8	.6	430	.04	.05	.7	10
Blackberries, raw, 1 cup	85	80	2	1	18	46	1.3	280	.05	.06	.5	30
Blueberries, raw, 1 cup	83	85	1	1	21	22	1.1	400	.04	.03	.4	23
Cantaloups, raw, ½ melon (5 in. diam)	94	35	1	Tr.	8	31	.7	6,190	.09	.07	.9	59
Cherries, 1 cup pitted:												
Raw	83	65	1	1	16	19	.4	710	.05	.06	.4	9
Canned red sour	87	120	2	1	30	28	.8	1,840	.07	.04	.4	14
Cranberry sauce, sweetened, 1 cup	48	550	Tr.	1	142	22	.8	80	.06	.06	.3	5
Dates, "fresh" and dried, pitted and cut, 1 cup	20	505	4	1	134	128	3.7	100	.16	.17	3.9	0
Figs, raw, 3 small (1-½ in. diam)	78	90	2	Tr.	22	62	.7	90	.06	.06	.6	2
Figs, dried, 1 large (2 by 1 in.)	24	55	1	Tr.	14	39	.6	20	.03	.02	.4	0
Fruit cocktail, canned, solids and liquid, 1 cup	81	180	1	1	48	23	1.0	410	.03	.03	.9	5
Grapefruit, raw, 1 cup sections	89	75	1	Tr.	20	43	.4	20	.07	.04	.4	78
Grapefruit juice:												
Canned, unsweetened, 1 cup	89	90	1	Tr.	24	20	.7	20	.07	.04	.4	85
Frozen concentrate, 6-ounce can	58	295	4	1	77	63	2.4	60	.24	.13	1.4	272
Grapes, 1 cup:												
American type (slip skin)	82	85	2	2	18	20	.7	90	.07	.05	.3	5
European type (adherent skin)	82	100	1	1	26	26	.9	120	.09	.06	.4	6
Grape juice, bottled, 1 cup	81	170	1	0	46	25	.8	—	.09	.12	.6	Tr.
Lemon juice, fresh, 1 cup	91	60	1	Tr.	19	34	.2	0	.11	.01	.3	122
Lime juice, fresh, 1 cup	91	60	1	0	20	34	.2	0	.11	.01	.3	65

FACTS ABOUT FOOD

Food and approximate measure or common weight	Water	Food energy	Protein	Fat	Total carbohydrate	Calcium	Iron	Vitamin A value	Thiamine	Riboflavin	Niacin value	Ascorbic acid
	Pct.	Cal.	Gm.	Gm.	Gm.	Mg.	Mg.	I.U.	Mg.	Mg.	Mg.	Mg.
Orange juice:												
Fresh, 1 cup	88	110	2	Tr.	27	47	.5	460	.19	.06	.6	122
Canned, unsweetened, 1 cup	88	110	2	Tr.	27	25	.7	240	.17	.04	.6	103
Frozen concentrate, 6-ounce can	58	300	5	1	75	69	2.0	670	.48	.11	1.5	285
Papayas, raw, cubed, 1 cup	89	70	1	Tr.	18	36	.5	3,190	.06	.07	.5	102
Peaches:												
Raw, 1 medium (2-½ by 2-in. diam.)	87	45	1	Tr.	12	8	.6	880	.02	.05	.9	8
Canned in sirup, solids and liquid, 1 cup	81	175	1	Tr.	47	13	1.0	1,160	.02	.05	1.8	11
Canned, strained (infant food), 1 ounce	83	15	Tr.	Tr.	4	2	.3	180	.01	.01	.2	1
Dried, cooked, unsweetened, 1 cup (10-12 halves and 6 tablespoons liquid)	76	225	2	1	59	38	5.9	2,750	.01	.16	4.3	11
Pears:												
Raw, 1 pear (3 by 2-½ in. diam.)	83	95	1	1	24	20	.5	30	.03	.06	.2	6
Canned in sirup, 2 medium size halves and 2 tablespoons sirup	81	80	Tr.	Tr.	22	9	.2	Tr.	.01	.02	.2	2
Canned, strained (infant food), 1 ounce	86	15	Tr.	Tr.	4	3	.1	10	Tr.	.01	.1	Tr.
Persimmons, Japanese, raw, seedless kind. 1 persimmon (2-¼ in. diam.)	78	95	1	Tr.	24	7	.4	3,270	.06	.05	Tr.	13
Pineapple: Raw, diced, 1 cup	85	75	1	Tr.	19	22	.4	180	.12	.04	.3	33
Canned in sirup, 2 small or 1 large slice and 2 tablespoons juice	78	95	Tr.	Tr.	26	35	.7	100	.09	.02	.2	11
Pineapple juice, canned, 1 cup	86	120	1	Tr.	32	37	1.2	200	.13	.04	.4	22
Plums, raw, 1 plum (2-in. diam.)	86	30	Tr.	Tr.	7	10	.3	200	.04	.02	.3	3
Prunes, cooked, unsweetened, 1 cup (16-18 prunes and ½ cup liquid)	65	310	3	1	82	62	4.5	2,210	.07	.20	2.0	2
Prune juice, canned, 1 cup	80	170	1	0	46	60	4.3	—	.07	.19	1.0	2
Raisins, dried, 1 cup	24	430	4	1	114	125	5.3	80	.24	.13	.8	Tr.
Raspberries, red, raw, 1 cup	84	70	1	Tr.	17	49	1.1	160	.03	.08	.4	29
Rhubarb, cooked with sugar, 1 cup	63	385	1	Tr.	98	112	1.1	70	.02	—	.2	17
Strawberries:												
Raw, 1 cup	90	55	1	1	12	42	1.2	90	.04	.10	.4	89
Frozen, 3 ounces	72	90	1	Tr.	23	19	.5	30	.02	.04	.2	35

FACTS ABOUT FOOD

Food and approximate measure or common weight	Water	Food energy	Protein	Fat	Total carbohydrate	Calcium	Iron	Vitamin A value	Thiamine	Riboflavin	Niacin value	Ascorbic acid
	Pct.	Cal.	Gm.	Gm.	Gm.	Mg.	Mg.	I.U.	Mg.	Mg.	Mg.	Mg.
FRUITS—Continued												
Tangerines, 1 medium (2-½ in. diam.)	87	35	1	Tr.	9	27	0.3	340	0.06	0.02	0.2	25
Tangerine juice, canned, 1 cup	89	95	2	1	23	47	.5	1,040	.15	.06	.6	64
Watermelon, ½ slice (¾ by 10 in.)	92	45	1	Tr.	11	11	.3	950	.08	.08	.3	10
GRAIN PRODUCTS:												
Barley, pearled, light, dry, 1 cup	11	710	17	2	160	32	4.1	0	.25	.17	6.3	0
Biscuits, baking powder, enriched flour 1 biscuit (2-½ in. diam.)	27	130	3	4	20	83	.7	0	.09	.08	.7	0
Bran flakes, 1 cup	4	115	4	1	32	24	2.0	0	.19	.09	3.5	0
Breads, 1 slice:												
Boston brown, unenriched	44	105	2	1	22	89	1.2	70	.04	.06	.7	0
Rye	35	55	2	Tr.	12	17	.4	0	.04	.02	.4	0
White, unenriched, 4 percent nonfat milk solids	35	65	2	1	12	18	.1	0	.01	.02	.2	0
White, enriched, 4 percent nonfat milk solids	35	65	2	1	12	18	.4	0	.06	.04	.5	0
White, enriched, 6 percent nonfat milk solids	34	65	2	1	12	21	.4	0	.06	.04	.5	0
Whole wheat	37	55	2	1	11	22	.5	0	.07	.03	.7	0
Cakes:												
Angel food, 2-inch sector (1/12 of cake, 8 in. diam.)	32	110	3	Tr.	23	2	.1	0	Tr.	.05	.1	0
Doughnuts, cake-type, 1 doughnut	19	135	2	7	17	23	.2	40	.05	.04	.4	0
Foundation, 1 square (3 by 2 by 1-¾ in.)	25	230	4	8	36	82	.3	100	.02	.05	.2	0
Foundation, plain icing, 2-inch sector, layer cake (1/16 of cake, 10 in. diam.)	24	410	6	11	72	121	.5	150	.03	.08	.2	0
Fruit cake, dark, 1 piece (2 by 2 by ½ in.)	23	105	2	4	17	29	.8	50	.04	.04	.3	0
Gingerbread, 1 piece (2 by 2 by 2 in.)	30	180	2	7	28	63	1.4	50	.02	.05	.6	0

FACTS ABOUT FOOD

Food and approximate measure or common weight	Water	Food energy	Pro-tein	Fat	Total carbo-hydrate	Cal-cium	Iron	Vitamin A value	Thia-mine	Ribo-flavin	Nia-cin value	Ascor-bic acid
	Pct.	Cal.	Gm.	Gm.	Gm.	Mg.	Mg.	I.U.	Mg.	Mg.	Mg.	Mg.
Plain cake and cupcakes, 1 cupcake (2-¾ in. diam.)	27	130	3	3	23	62	.2	50	.01	.03	.1	0
Sponge, 2-inch sector (1/12 of cake, 8 in. diam.)	32	115	3	2	22	11	.6	210	.02	.06	.1	0
Cereal foods, dry, precooked (infant food), 1 ounce	6	105	4	1	21	185	9.6	0	.34	.13	1.4	0
Cookies, plain and assorted, 1 3-inch cooky	5	110	2	3	19	6	.2	0	.01	.01	.1	0
Corn bread or muffins made with enriched, degermed corn meal, 1 muffin (2-¾ in. diam.)	49	105	3	2	18	67	.9	60	.08	.11	.6	0
Corn flakes, 1 cup	4	95	2	Tr.	21	3	.3	0	.01	.02	.4	0
Corn grits, degermed, cooked, 1 cup:												
Unenriched	87	120	3	Tr.	27	2	.2	100	.04	.01	.4	0
Enriched	87	120	3	Tr.	27	2	.7	100	.11	.08	1.0	0
Crackers:												
Graham, 4 small or 2 medium	6	55	1	1	10	3	.3	0	.04	.02	.2	0
Soda, plain, 2 crackers (2-½ in. diam.)	6	45	1	1	8	2	.1	0	.01	.01	.1	0
Farina, enriched, cooked, 1 cup	89	105	3	Tr.	22	7	.5	0	.10	.07	.4	0
Macaroni, cooked, 1 cup:												
Unenriched	61	210	7	1	42	13	.8	0	.03	.02	.7	0
Enriched	61	210	7	1	42	13	1.5	0	.24	.15	2.0	0
Muffins, made with enriched flour 1 muffin (2-¾ in. diam.)	37	135	4	4	20	99	.8	50	.09	.10	.7	0
Noodles, containing egg, unenriched, cooked, 1 cup	84	105	4	1	20	6	0.6	60	0.05	0.03	0.6	0
Oatmeal or rolled oats:												
Cooked, 1 cup	85	150	5	3	26	21	1.7	0	.22	.05	.4	0
Precooked (infant food), dry, 1 ounce	7	105	4	1	19	225	8.9	0	.36	.10	.7	0
Pancakes, baked, wheat, with enriched flour, 1 cake (4-in. diam.)	55	60	2	2	7	43	.4	50	.05	.06	.3	Tr.

2504 FACTS ABOUT FOOD

Food and approximate measure or common weight	Water	Food energy	Protein	Fat	Total carbohydrate	Calcium	Iron	Vitamin A value	Thiamine	Riboflavin	Niacin value	Ascorbic acid
	Pct.	Cal.	Gm.	Gm.	Gm.	Mg.	Mg.	I.U.	Mg.	Mg.	Mg.	Mg.
GRAIN PRODUCTS—Continued												
Pies, 4-inch sector (9 in. diam.):												
Apple	48	330	3	13	53	9	.5	220	.04	.02	.3	1
Custard	59	265	7	11	34	162	1.6	290	.07	.21	.4	0
Lemon meringue	47	300	4	12	45	24	.6	210	.04	.10	.2	1
Mince	43	340	3	9	62	22	3.0	10	.09	.05	.5	1
Pumpkin	59	265	5	12	34	70	1.0	2,480	.04	.15	.4	0
Pretzels, 5 small sticks	8	20	Tr.	Tr.	4	1	0	0	Tr.	Tr.	Tr.	0
Rice, cooked, 1 cup:												
Converted	72	205	4	Tr.	45	14	.5	0	.10	.02	1.9	0
White or milled	71	200	4	Tr.	44	13	.5	0	.02	.01	.7	0
Rice, puffed, 1 cup	4	55	1	Tr.	12	3	.3	0	.01	.01	.1	0
Rolls, plain, enriched, 1 roll (12 per pound)	29	120	3	2	21	21	.7	0	.09	.06	.8	0
Spaghetti, unenriched, cooked, 1 cup	61	220	7	1	44	13	.9	0	.03	.02	.7	0
Waffles, baked, with enriched flour, 1 waffle (4-1/2 by 5-5/8 by 1/2 in.).	40	215	7	8	28	144	1.4	270	.14	.20	1.0	0
Wheat flours:												
Whole, 1 cup stirred	12	400	16	2	85	49	4.0	0	.66	.14	5.2	0
All purpose or family flour:												
Unenriched, 1 cup sifted	12	400	12	1	84	18	.9	0	.07	.05	1.0	0
Enriched, 1 cup sifted	12	400	12	1	84	18	3.2	0	.48	.29	3.8	0
Wheat germ, 1 cup stirred	11	245	17	7	34	57	5.5	0	1.39	.54	3.1	0
Wheat, shredded, 1 large biscuit, 1 ounce	6	100	3	1	23	13	1.0	0	.06	.03	1.3	0
SUGARS, SWEETS:												
Candy, 1 ounce:												
Caramels	7	120	1	3	22	36	.7	50	.01	.04	Tr.	Tr.
Chocolate, sweetened, milk	1	145	2	9	16	61	.6	40	.03	.11	.2	0
Fudge, plain	5	115	Tr.	3	23	14	.1	60	Tr.	.02	Tr.	Tr.
Hard	1	110	0	0	28	0	0	0	0	0	0	0
Marshmallows	15	90	1	0	23	0	0	0	0	0	0	0
Chocolate sirup, 1 tablespoon	39	40	Tr.	Tr.	11	3	.3	—	—	—	—	—

FACTS ABOUT FOOD

Food and approximate measure or common weight	Water	Food energy	Protein	Fat	Total carbohydrate	Calcium	Iron	Vitamin A value	Thiamine	Riboflavin	Niacin value	Ascorbic acid
	Pct.	Cal.	Gm.	Gm.	Gm.	Mg.	Mg.	I.U.	Mg.	Mg.	Mg.	Mg.
SUGARS, SWEETS—Continued												
Honey, strained or extracted, 1 tablespoon	20	60	Tr.	0	17	1	.2	0	Tr.	.01	Tr.	1
Jams, marmalades, preserves, 1 tablespoon	28	55	Tr.	Tr.	14	2	.1	Tr.	Tr.	Tr.	Tr.	1
Molasses, cane, 1 tablespoon:												
Light	24	50	—	—	13	33	.9	—	.01	.01	Tr.	—
Blackstrap	24	45	—	—	11	116	2.3	—	.02	.04	.3	—
Sirup, table blends, 1 tablespoon	25	55	0	0	15	9	.8	0	0	Tr.	Tr.	0
Sugar, 1 tablespoon:												
Granulated, cane or beet	Tr.	50	0	0	12	—	—	0	0	0	0	0
Brown	3	50	0	0	13	10	.4	0	0	0	0	0
MISCELLANEOUS:												
Beverages, carbonated, kola type, 1 cup	88	105	—	—	28	—	—	—	—	—	—	—
Bouillon cubes, 1 cube	5	2	Tr.	Tr.	0	—	—	—	—	.07	1.0	0
Chocolate, unsweetened, 1 ounce	2	140	2	15	8	28	1.2	20	.01	.06	.3	0
Gelatin dessert, plain, ready-to-serve, 1 cup	83	155	4	0	36	0	0	0	0	0	0	0
Olives, pickled "mammoth" size, 10 olives:												
Green	75	70	1	7	2	48	.9	160	Tr.	—	—	—
Ripe, Mission variety	72	105	1	12	1	48	.9	40	Tr.	Tr.	—	—
Pickles:												
Dill, cucumber, 1 large (4 in. long)	93	15	1	Tr.	3	34	1.6	420	Tr.	.09	.1	8
Sweet, cucumber or mixed, 1 pickle (2-3/4 in. long)	70	20	Tr.	Tr.	5	3	.3	20	0	Tr.	Tr.	1
Sherbet, 1/2 cup	68	120	1	0	29	48	0	0	.02	.07	0	0
Vinegar, 1 tablespoon	—	2	0	—	1	1	.1	—	—	—	—	—
White sauce, medium, 1 cup	73	430	11	33	23	305	.3	1,350	.09	.41	.3	1
Yeast:												
Compressed, baker's, 1 ounce	71	25	3	Tr.	3	7	1.4	0	.13	.59	8.0	0
Dried brewer's, 1 tablespoon	7	20	3	Tr.	3	8	1.5	0	.78	.44	2.9	0

2505

RECOMMENDED DAILY DIETARY ALLOWANCES

These recommendations were worked out by a group of scientists of the Food and Nutrition Board of the National Research Council. They can be followed by eating a good variety of common foods, as suggested in Nutrition and Meal Planning.

Family Members	Food Energy Cal.	Protein Gms.	Calcium Gms.	Iron Mg.	Vitamin A I.U.	Thiamine Mg.	Riboflavin Mg.	Niacin Mg.	Vitamin C Mg.
CHILDREN UP TO 12 YEARS:									
Under 1 year	50/lb.	1.6/lb.	1.0	6	1500	0.4	0.6	4	30
1-3 years (27 pounds)	1,200	40	1.0	7	2000	0.6	0.9	6	35
4-6 years (42 pounds)	1,600	50	1.0	8	2500	0.8	1.2	8	50
7-9 years (58 pounds)	2,000	60	1.0	10	3500	1.0	1.5	10	60
10-12 years (78 pounds)	2,500	70	1.2	12	4500	1.2	1.8	12	75
GIRLS:									
13-15 years (108 pounds)	2,600	80	1.3	15	5000	1.3	2.0	13	80
16-20 years (122 pounds)	2,400	75	1.0	15	5000	1.2	1.8	12	80
BOYS:									
13-15 years (108 pounds)	3,200	85	1.4	15	5000	1.5	2.0	15	90
16-20 years (144 pounds)	3,800	100	1.4	15	6000	1.7	2.5	17	100
WOMEN: (123 pounds):									
Sedentary	2,000	60	1.0	12	5000	1.0	1.5	10	70
Moderately active	2,400	60	1.0	12	5000	1.2	1.5	12	70
Very active	3,000	60	1.0	12	5000	1.5	1.5	15	70
Pregnancy (latter half)	2,400	85	1.5	15	6000	1.5	2.5	15	100
Lactation	3,000	100	2.0	15	8000	1.5	3.0	15	150
MEN: (154 pounds):									
Sedentary	2,400	70	1.0	12	5000	1.2	1.8	12	75
Physically active	3,000	70	1.0	12	5000	1.5	1.8	15	75
With heavy work	4,500	70	1.0	12	5000	1.8	1.8	18	75